WHO'S WHO ON TELEVISION

Editorial and
Art Direction by
Colin Shelbourn

Sub-editing by
Liz Jones and Frances Jary

Published by
Independent Television Books Ltd.
247 Tottenham Court Road,
London W1P 0AU

In association with
Michael Joseph Ltd.

First published 1985
©Independent Television Books Ltd. 1985

ISBN: 0 907965 31 8

Typeset by CCC,
printed and bound
in Great Britain by
William Clowes Limited,
Beccles and London
a member of the McCorquodale Group

WHO'S WHO ON TELEVISION

3RD EDITION

EDITED BY
EDDIE PEDDER

IN ASSOCIATION WITH
MICHAEL JOSEPH

Foreword to the 3rd Edition

Welcome to this new edition of *Who's Who On Television*. As you'll see, it features a revised style of presentation which we hope will make the book easier to use and more enjoyable to read.

Sadly, some personalities are missing from this edition, but we will always remember them. Not everyone we would have wished is in the book: some did not want to be included, others—despite considerable effort—we were unable to contact.

To those who are included, to the press officers of the various TV companies, the agents and the publicity agents in England and America, to Flavia Potenza and Lois Linden in the *TV Times* Hollywood office, to Liz Jones and Frances Jary, who have helped check all the facts, we extend our thanks. A special thank-you must also go to Beverley Dunne, Kim Lloyd and Sue Lapwood, without whose help this edition would not have been completed.

Naturally, we hope the book is error-free, but mistakes do, regrettably, occur in publications like this. If you spot one, please bring it to our attention so that it can be corrected for the future. There's a note about submitting information for inclusion in *Who's Who On Television* on p. 263.

Eddie Pedder

Favourite Places

For this new *Who's Who On Television*, we've
continued the tradition established in previous
editions and asked each respondent to share
something personal with readers of the book.

This time it's a 'Favourite Place', which could
be anywhere from a particularly beautiful
geographical spot to a fondly remembered
childhood memory. Not everyone wanted to take
part in this, so not every entry includes it. Where
possible, we have used people's words verbatim,
and have tried not to edit them too brutally.

Incidentally, if you're puzzled by that back
cover quote about 'Our hot tub overlooking The
Pacific', you'll find out whose favourite place it is
on p. 108.

How to use this book

Entries are listed alphabetically by surname.

We have tried to include the same standard information on every entry, though for various reasons this has not been possible in every case.

Details of education have not been included in this edition unless considered particularly significant or unusual.

Our listings of work credits are not intended to be comprehensive (and couldn't possibly be, given the space available!) but aim to highlight important or well-known examples.

Agents' names and locations are included as appropriate in the entries, and there is a list of full addresses at the end of the book on p. 268.

Some other useful addresses appear on p. 264.

ABBOT, Russ
Comedian/entertainer/actor, b. 18 Sept Chester. Started showbiz career 1965 playing drums with The Black Abbots. Next 15 years worked in panto, summer season, cabaret and TV. 1980 set out on solo career. Toured British theatres with *Russ Abbot's Madhouse Show*. 1984 West End debut in *Little Me*. TV incl: *Who Do You Do?*; *The Comedians*; many guest appearances; own series *Russ Abbot's Madhouse* (five series), TV specials *Russ Abbot's Christmas Madhouse, Russ Abbot's Scottish Madhouse, Russ Abbot's Madhouse Annual*. Record: *Atmosphere*. Many awards incl: *TV Times* Award Funniest Man On TV 1982–84. m. Tricia; 3 s. Gary, Richard, Christopher, 1 d. Erika. Address: c/o Mike Hughes Entertainments, Liver House, 96 Bolt St, Liverpool. Birthsign: Virgo. **Favourite Place:** 'Out in the countryside away from the hustle and bustle of showbusiness.'

ACKLAND, Joss
Actor, b. 29 Feb 1928 London. Trained at Central School of Speech and Drama. Numerous stage appearances include seasons at London's Old Vic and Mermaid theatres, and at the Barbican as Falstaff in *Henry IV Parts I* and *II* and Captain Hook in *Peter Pan*. London musicals include: *Lock Up Your Daughters*; *A Little Night Music*; *Evita*; *Jean Seberg*. Films incl: *Great Expectations*; *Royal Flash*; *Operation Daybreak*; *Silver Bears*; *Lady Jane*. Has appeared in over 300 TV plays and shows, incl: *Kipling*; *The Crezz*; *Shadowlands*; *Coriolanus*; *The Barretts Of Wimpole Street*. m. Rosemary Kirkcaldy; 5 d. Melanie, Antonia, Penelope, Samantha, Kirsty, 2 s. Paul (dec.), Toby. Hobby: writing. Address: c/o ICM, London. Birthsign: Pisces. **Favourite Place:** 'Covent Garden, where I live, and the next place I visit.'

ADAMS, Tony
Actor, b. 11 Dec 1940. He started his career aged 10 in *The Magic Box*. Theatre incl: *West Side Story*; *The Rose And The Ring*; *Five Past Eight*; *The Boy Friend*; *Mame*. Films incl: *Reluctant Bride*; *Touch And Go*; *Villain*; *Lizard In Woman's Skin*. Radio incl: *Lord Of The Flies*; *Day Of The Triffids*; *The Silver King*. TV incl: *Kiss Me Kate*; *Court Martial*; *One Pair Of Eyes*; *The Two Ronnies*; *Crown Court*; *Doctor Who*; *General Hospital*. In 1978 he joined *Crossroads* as Adam Chance. Hobby: sailing. Address: c/o Michael Ladkin, London. Birthsign: Sagittarius. **Favourite Place:** at sea.

AGUTTER, Jenny
Actress, b. 20 Dec 1952 Taunton, Somerset. Trained at the Elmhurst Ballet School, Surrey. Started career in films aged 11 in *East Of Sudan*, followed by *Ballerina, Gates Of Paradise, I Start Counting* (1969), *Walkabout* and *The Railway Children* (1970). Theatre incl: *The Tempest* at the National Theatre; *Hedda Gabler*; *Betrayal*; with The Royal Shakespeare Company 1982 and 1983. Other films incl: *Logan's Run*; *The Eagle Has Landed*; *Equus* (BAFTA Best Supporting Actress Award); *Sweet William*; *An American Werewolf In London*. Most recent TV incl: Frederick Raphael's *School Play*; *A Dream Of Alice*; *Love's Labours Lost*; *This Office Life*; *Silas Marner*. Book: *Snap*. Hobby: photography. Address: c/o Cowan Bellew Assocs, London. Birthsign: Sagittarius. **Favourite Place:** the view of Dovers Hill from Chipping Campden, Glos.

AIRD, Holly
Actress, b. 18 May 1969
Aldershot, Hants. Trained at the
Bush Davies Ballet School and at
the age of 10 played Miss Polly in
The History Of Mr Polly,
followed by *The Flame Trees Of
Thika*, both for TV. Other TV
incl: *The Muse Secrets*; *Spider's
Webb*; *Seal Morning*; *TVTimes
Star Family Challenge*; *Affairs Of
The Heart*. Hobbies: dancing,
music. Address: c/o Hutton
Management, London. Birthsign:
Taurus. **Favourite Place:** 'My
bedroom—it's got all my homely
things in it and it's very cosy.'

ALDRIDGE, Michael
Actor, b. 9 Sept 1920
Glastonbury, Somerset. Trained
in rep at Nottingham and
Birmingham and made his first
professional appearance in *French
Without Tears* at Watford Palace
Theatre in 1937, then in *This
Way To The Tomb* at London
Garrick Theatre after the war.
TV incl: *Bleak House*; *Sense And
Sensibility*; *Fall Of Eagles*; *Tinker,
Tailor, Soldier, Spy*; *A Voyage
Round My Father*; *Last Of The
Summer Wine*. m. scenic designer
Kirsten Rowntree; 3 d. Charlotte,
Harriet, Emma. Hobbies: sailing,
carpentry. Address: c/o Plunket
Green, London. Birthsign: Virgo.

ALEXANDER, Maev
Actress, b. 3 Feb 1948 Glasgow.
Trained at the Royal Scottish
Academy of Music and Drama.
Joined the Royal Shakespeare
Company from 1970–71 playing
Perdita in *The Winter's Tale*.
Most recently Cleopatra in
Antony and Cleopatra at
Coventry. Also fringe work. Lots
of radio drama incl: *Emma*. TV
incl: *Sutherland's Law*; *The Gentle
Touch*; *Holding The Fort*; *Angels*;
A Leap In The Dark; *Kids*; *Take
The Stage*; *The Main Chance*;
This Man Craig; *The Kit Curran
Radio Show*; *By The Sword
Divided*; presents newsdesk on
That's Life! m. Simon Dunmore;
1 d. Alix. Hobbies: house
renovation, textile design,
dressmaking, knitting, crafts.
Address: c/o Fraser & Dunlop,
London. Birthsign: Aquarius.
Favourite Place: 'In the car—
no telephone, no letters, just
singing and thinking.'

ALEXANDER, Terence
Actor, b. 11 March 1923
London. Started with the White
Rose Players, Harrogate, at 16,
then wide rep experience before
working in London. Theatre incl:
Move Over Mrs Markham; *Two
And Two Make Sex*; *There Goes
The Bride*; *Fringe Benefits*. Films
incl: *League Of Gentlemen*; *Magic
Christian*; *Waterloo*; *Run A
Crooked Mile*; *The Day Of The
Jackal*; *Internecine Affair*. Radio
incl: *Law And Disorder*; *The Toff*.
TV incl: *Codename*; *The Forsyte
Saga*; *The Pallisers*; *Les Dawson*;
Dick Emery; *Devenish*; *Unity*; *Just
Liz*; *Terry And June*; *Bergerac*;
Crown Court. m. (1st) Juno, (2nd)
actress Jane Downs; 2 s. Nicholas,
Marcus (both from 1st m.).
Hobby: wine. Address: c/o ICM,
London. Birthsign: Pisces.
Favourite Place: 'My
bathroom, Edwardian style with
fireplace. In Summer Jane and I
lie in the bath with champagne
and look out over gardens.'

ALICIA, Ana

Actress, b. 10 Dec Mexico City. BA in Drama from University of Texas. Film: *Halloween II.* TV incl: *Ryan's Hope*; *Buck Rogers*; *Quincy*; *Falcon Crest*; and the TV films, *The Sacketts*; *Coward Of The County*; *Happy Endings*; *The Ordeal Of Bill Carney.* Hobbies: riding, tennis, cycling, rafting, skiing. Address: c/o Century Artists, 9744 Wilshire Blvd, Suite 206, Beverly Hills, CA 90212. Birthsign: Sagittarius. **Favourite**

Place: Ruy Doso, New Mexico. Spends every Christmas there with her family and they ski there.

ALKIN, John

Actor, b. 17 Jan 1947 Rugby, Warwickshire. Trained as an ASM. Theatre seasons at Cheltenham; Richmond; Bromley; Roundhouse, London; Redgrave Theatre, Farnham; Oxford Playhouse. Films incl: *Battle Of Britain*; *The Games*; *Sweeney*; *Sweeney 2*; *No Longer Alone*; *A Lady Vanishes*; *A Man Called Intrepid.* TV incl: *Z Cars*; *Happy Ever After*; *General Hospital*; *Space 1999*; *Family At War*; *Crown Court*; *The Misfit*; *Love Story*; *The Liver Birds*; *Yes, Honestly*; *The Sweeney*; *Secret Army*; *Law Centre*; *All Creatures Great And Small*; *Sandbaggers*; *To Serve Them All My Days*; *Minder.* m. Lee Everett; 2 s. Luke, Thomas. Hobby: boats. Address: c/o The House Of Spirits, Reading. Birthsign: Capricorn. **Favourite Place:** 'On board our boat, summer sunset over water and a glass of scotch.'

ALLEN, Linda Lou

Actress, b. 15 Feb Kansas. Trained at Stephens' College Columbia, Missouri, and at the Actors' Institute, London. Films incl: *Ain't That America?*; *The Martian Chronicles*; *Licensed To Kill*; *Down In The Valley.* TV incl: *What's On Next?*; *3-2-1*; *Game For A Laugh*; *Country Style*; *The Picnic*; *The Professionals*; *Square One*; *The Cracker Factory*; *Him And His Magic*; *Variety Madhouse*; *The Lenny Henry Show*; *CATS Eyes.* Address: c/o Byron Godfrey, Million Dollar Music, London. Birthsign: Aquarius. **Favourite Place:** 'Spent a working season in Somerset and used my spare time visiting the surrounding villages—one of the happiest times of my life.'

ALLEN, Patrick

Actor, b. 17 March 1927 Malawi. Evacuated to Canada during the war where he began his career in local radio. Returned to England in 1953. Has worked with the Royal Shakespeare Company. Films incl: *Dial M For Murder*; *High Tide At Noon*; *I Was Monty's Double*; *Dunkirk*; *The Troubleshooters*; *Codename*; *Murder Is Easy*; *Winds Of War*; *Who Dares Wins.* TV incl: *Crane*; *Hard Times*; *Kidnapped*; *The Trial Of Lady Chatterley*; *A Spy At Evening*; *The Brack Report.* m. actress Sarah Lawson; 2 s. Stephen, Stuart. Hobby: fishing. Address: c/o ICM, London. Birthsign: Pisces. **Favourite Place:** 'River Kennet for the peaceful pursuit of fishing for trout and contemplation.'

ALLEN, Ward
Ventriloquist, b. 29 April 1940 Pittington. A former coalminer and deliveryman, became a ventriloquist, magician and balloon sculptor and found fame in the northern clubs. Partnered by Roger the Dog and other pals, has presented TV series of *Roger & Co* and *The Roger The Dog Show*. TV appearances incl: *Children's Royal Variety Show*; *The Saturday Show*; *Saturday Superstore*. m. Mary; 2 d. Susan, Helen, 1 s. David. Hobby: watching TV, particularly comedy films. Address: c/o Beverley Artistes, South Shields. Birthsign: Taurus. **Favourite Place:** 'The view of Cape Town from the harbour with the majestic Table Mountain making this the most beautiful sight I've ever seen.'

ALTMAN, John
Actor, b. 2 March 1952 Reading, Berks. Graduated in photography but took up acting. Trained at York Academy of Speech and Drama. Theatre incl: *The Balcony*; *Dream Of A Ridiculous Man*; *Dracula*; *Masque Of The Red Death*; *Woyzeck*; *Down By The Greenwood Side*. Films incl: *The Revenge Of The Jedi*; *An American Werewolf In London*; *Memoirs Of A Survivor*; *The Birth Of The Beatles*; *Quadrophenia*; *The First Great Train Robbery*; *The John Lennon Story*. TV incl: *Going To Work*; *Take Two*; *Life After Death*; *Remembrance*; *Lucky Jim*; *The Scarlet Pimpernel*; *Bouncing Back*; *Minder*; *EastEnders*. Hobbies: running, swimming, photography, music, girls. Address: c/o Annette Stone Assocs, Harrow. Birthsign: Pisces. **Favourite Place:** 'Manhattan. It's the centre of the world, and the liveliest city I've ever visited.'

ALVAREZ, Tony
Actor/singer, b. 19 Dec 1956 Spain. Musicals incl: *Roberta*; *Evita*. Films incl: *Oliver*; *Nicholas And Alexandra*. TV incl: *Young Doctors*; *Skyways*; *Prisoner*; *Carson's Law*; guest appearances on *Don Lane Show*; *Mike Walsh Show*; *Ronnie Corbett Specials*. Hobbies: swimming, squash, travelling. Address: c/o Chadwick Kent Management, 206 Glenmore Rd, Paddington 2021, Australia. Birthsign: Sagittarius. **Favourite Place:** 'Byron Bay, my place for unwinding and relaxing. One of many beautiful places in Australia that give me freedom to be myself.'

ANDERSON, Jean
Actress, b. 1907 Eastbourne. Trained at RADA. Numerous theatre credits incl: with the National Theatre in *Martine* and *For Services Rendered*; *Lent*; *The Dame Of Sark*; *Hedda Gabler*. Films Incl: *The Lady Vanishes*; *Half A Sixpence*; *A Town Like Alice*; *The Kidnappers*. TV incl: *This Is Your Life*; *Little Women*; *Scoop*; *Dr Finlay's Casebook*; *The Railway Children*; *The Brothers*; *Tenko*. m. Peter Powell (dis.); 1 s. Aude, 2 grandchildren Emma, Mark. Hobbies: gardening, walking. Address: c/o Leading Artists, London. Birthsign: Sagittarius. **Favourite Place:** 'Howtown near Ullswater near my country retreat. Wonderful hills and lake.'

ANDREWS, Anthony

Actor, b. 12 Jan 1948 London. Started stage career at Chichester Festival Theatre. Recent stage appearance in *The Dragon Variation*. Films incl: *War Of The Children*; *Operation Daybreak*; *Under The Volcano*; *The Holcroft Covenant*. Numerous TV incl: *A Beast With Two Backs*; *Doomwatch*; *Follyfoot*; *The Pallisers*; *Upstairs, Downstairs*; *The Duchess Of Duke Street*; *Romeo And Juliet*; *Danger UXB*; *Brideshead Revisited* (BAFTA Award for Best TV Actor 1981); *The Love Boat*; *The Black Bayu*; *La Ronde*; *Ivanhoe*; *The Scarlet Pimpernel*; *Z For Zacariah*; *Sparkling Cyanide*; *AD*. m. former actress Georgina; 1 d. Jessica, 1 s. Joshua. Hobby: riding. Address: c/o Duncan Heath Assocs, London. Birthsign: Capricorn. **Favourite Place:** 'The view from the top of the Kriegerhorn in Lech, Austria.'

ANDREWS, Carl

Actor, b. 16 Nov 1946 Georgetown, Guyana. Trained as a dancer and has since worked in cabaret all over Europe. Has worked in various repertory companies. West End musicals incl: *Catch My Soul*; *Black Mikado*; *Rock Nativity*. TV incl: *Minder*; *Some Mothers Do 'Ave 'Em*; *Late Starter*; *Crossroads*; *Law Centre*. Hobbies: reading, travel, tennis, relaxing. Address: c/o Oriental Casting Agency, London. Birthsign: Scorpio. **Favourite Place:** Lamu in Kenya, 'It's just so peaceful and quiet, no cars or extraneous noise, plus the ocean. Paradise.'

ANDREWS, Eamonn CBE

Commentator/interviewer/presenter, b. 19 Dec 1922 Dublin. Started as a boxing commentator on radio 1939, Radio Eirann 1941–50, BBC radio 1950, BBC TV 1951. TV incl: *What's My Line?*; *Crackerjack*; *World Of Sport*; *This Is Your Life*; *Today*; *Time For Business*; *The Eamonn Andrews Show*; *Top Of The World*. Extensive business interests. Former All-Ireland Amateur Boxing Champion. Books: *This Is My Life*; *Surprise Of Your Life*. m. Grainne; 2 d. Emma, Niamh, 1 s. Fergal. Hobbies: walking and talking. Address: c/o Thames TV, London. Birthsign: Sagittarius. **Favourite Place:** 'It's on top of a hill. You can see it from a lighthouse, gulls wheeling, two islands and, on a clear day, three.'

ANNIS, Francesca

Actress, b. 14 May 1944 London. Trained for ballet at the Corona Academy but switched to drama after appearing in an *Armchair Theatre* play. Since worked in rep and with the Royal Shakespeare Company. Theatre incl: *The Sun And The Wind*; *Hamlet*; *A Month In The Country* (National Theatre). Films incl: *Cleopatra*; *Run With The Wind*; *The Walking Stick*; *Macbeth*; *Coming Out Of The Ice*; *Krull*; *Dune*. TV incl: *The Human Jungle*; *Heritage*; *Danger Man*; *Dr Finlay's Casebook*; *Great Expectations*; *View From The Bridge*; *The Family Is A Vicious Circle*; *Edward The Seventh*; *Lillie* (*TV Times* Best Actress on TV 1978–79); *Why Didn't They Ask Evans?*; *Partners In Crime*; *Magnum PI*. Hobby: travel. Address: c/o ICM, London. Birthsign: Taurus.

ANTHONY, Lysette

Actress, b. 26 Sept 1963 London. Spent four years acting with the National Youth Theatre and has since appeared on stage in

Reproductions, Ghosts and The Lady's Not For Burning. A successful film career, incl: Oliver Twist; Krull; Ivanhoe; Tug Of Love; Clock In The Ocean. TV incl: Frost In May; Dombey & Son; Auf Weidersehen Pet; The Gentle Touch; Crown Court; The House On Kirov Street; Princess Daisy; Three Up, Two Down; Oliver Twist. Address: c/o Jeremy Conway, London. Birthsign: Libra. **Favourite Place:** 'Anywhere near water.'

ARCHER, Anne

Actress, b. 25 Aug Los Angeles, California. Trained with acting coach Milton Katselas. Films incl: Lifeguard; Hero At Large; Waltz Across Texas; Paradise Alley; Good Guys Wear Black. TV incl:

The Family Tree; Seventh Avenue (TV movie); Falcon Crest. Anne and her husband now have their own production company. m. (1st) William Davis (dis.), (2nd) actor Terry Jastrow; 1 s. Tommy (from 1st m.). Hobbies: collecting antiques and Italian art, skiing. Address: c/o ICM, 8899 Beverly Blvd, Los Angeles, California. Birthsign: Virgo. **Favourite Place:** Aspen, Colorado, 'We have a house there and adore skiing.'

ARCHER, Geoffrey

ITN defence and diplomatic correspondent, b. 21 May 1944 London. Formerly a solicitor's articled clerk. Worked as a researcher, reporter and producer

for Southern TV 1964, Anglia TV 1965 and Tyne Tees TV before joining ITN in 1970, for which he has reported widely in Europe, Africa, the Middle East and Britain. m. Eva; 1 d. Alison, 1 s. James. Hobbies: gardening, sailing. Address: c/o ITN, London. Birthsign: Taurus/Gemini. **Favourite Place:** 'The Golden Horn in Istanbul. The colour and bustle round the Galata Bridge—a remarkable blend of beauty and decay.'

ARMSTRONG, Pamela

Journalist, b. 25 Aug 1951 Borneo. Trained in media and communications at Central London Polytechnic. Has worked as a presenter on Capital Radio in London and on TV presenting London Today, Well Being and as newscaster for ITN. Hobbies: running and swimming. Address: c/o ITN, London. Birthsign: Virgo.

17

ARTHUR, Toni

Presenter/author/playwright, b. 27 Dec Oxford. Trained at the Royal Academy of Music, Stanislavsky Institute of Drama. Toured the world with her husband as a folk music duo in the early 1960s. Her own stage show, *Toni Arthur's Music Box*. TV incl: *Playschool*; *Play Away*; *Take A Ticket To . . .*; *Seeing And Doing*; *What Do You Watch?*; *Watch This Space*; *Monkey Business*. Records incl: *Play Away*; *Bang On A Drum*; *Sing A Story*; songs from *Seeing And Doing*. Book: *All The Year Round*. m. Dave Arthur; 2 s. Jonathan Elliott, Timothy Gwion. Hobbies: music, folklore, yoga, studying alternative medicine. Address: c/o Blackbird Productions, Boar's Head, Crowborough. Birthsign: Capricorn. **Favourite Place:** 'The highest point on top of the Sun God pyramid in Mexico, because it is so peaceful.'

ASHCROFT, Dame Peggy

Actress, b. 22 Dec 1907 Croydon. Trained at Central School of Dramatic Art under Elsie Fogerty. Theatre debut Birmingham 1926; London debut 1927. Has played all great Shakespearian heroines; leading roles at Old Vic; Sadlers Wells; John Gielgud's Company. 1962 Ashcroft Theatre, Croydon opened, named in her honour. 1975 joined National Theatre at Old Vic. Film: *A Passage To India* (Oscar). TV debut 1956 in *Shadow Of Heroes*. TV incl: *Caught On A Train*; *Cream In My Coffee*; *The Jewel In The Crown*. CBE 1951; DBE 1956. m. (1st) Rupert Hart-Davis (dis.), (2nd) Theodore Komsarjevsky (dis.), (3rd) Jeremy Nicholas Hutchinson (dis.); 1 d. Eliza, 1 s. Nicholas. Address: c/o ICM, London. Birthsign: Capricorn.

ASHER, Jane

Actress, b. 5 April 1946 London. First professional appearance aged five in film *Mandy*. West End debut 1960 *Will You Walk A Little Faster*. 1961 Wendy in *Peter Pan*. Joined Bristol Old Vic 1965. New York debut as Juliet in *Romeo And Juliet*. 1969 *Look Back In Anger* at Royal Court Theatre, London. 1976 joined National Theatre. West End also incl: *Whose Life Is It Anyway?*; *Before The Party*. Films incl: *Greengage Summer*; *Alfie*; *Runners*; *Dream Child*. TV incl: *Brideshead Revisited*; *A Voyage Round My Father*; *East Lynne*; *The Mistress*; *Bright Smiles*. Books: *Jane Asher's Party Cakes*; *Jane Asher's Fancy Dress*; *Silent Night For You And Your Baby*. m. Gerald Scarfe; 1 d. Katie, 2 s. Alexander, Rory. Hobbies: cookery, music. Address: c/o Chatto & Linnit, London. Birthsign: Aries. **Favourite Place:** 'At home with my family.'

ASKWITH, Robin

Actor/writer, b. 12 Oct 1950 Southport, Lancs. Has appeared in the West End in *I Love My Wife* and *Run For Your Wife* and wrote and directed world tours of *Casanova's Last Stand* and *Confessions From A Health Farm*. Films incl: *If . . .*; *Canterbury Tales*; *Bless This House*; *Carry On Girls*; *Confessions Of A Window Cleaner*; *Stand Up Virgin Soldiers*; *Let's Get Laid*; *Britannia Hospital*. TV incl: *Menace*; *The Misfit*; *On The House*; *Please Sir!*; *Fenn Street Gang*; *Bless This House*; *Father Dear Father*; *Dixon Of Dock Green*; *Beryl's Lot*; *Star Games*; *Give Us A Clue*; *Play Of The Month*; *Bottle Boys*. Hobbies: ocean sailing, sub aqua diving. Address: c/o ICM, London. Birthsign: Libra. **Favourite Place:** Victoria Falls: 'You wouldn't ask why if you'd been there.'

ASNER, Edward

Actor, b. 19 Nov 1926 Kansas City. Started his acting career in school productions but it was not until 1960, after several off-Broadway productions, that his career took off. This was after playing opposite Jack Lemmon in *Face Of A Hero.* Films incl: *Peter Gunn*; *The Slender Thread*; *The Satan Bug*; *Kid Galahad*; *Fort Apache, The Bronx*; *O'Hara's Wife.* TV incl: *Naked City*; *The Mary Tyler Moore Show*; *Lou Grant.* m. Nancy; 1 s. Matthew, 2 d. Lisa, Kate. Hobbies: reading, animals, current events. Address: c/o Mike Mamakos, 4348 Van Nuys Blvd, Suite 207, Sherman Oaks, CA 91403. Birthsign: Scorpio. **Favourite Place:** the Bahamas, he loves to snorkel.

ASPEL, Michael

Broadcaster/writer, b. 12 Jan 1933 London. After a brief business career became a radio actor with BBC rep company in Cardiff in 1954. BBC TV announcer and newsreader in London 1957–68 when he switched to freelancing, both on radio and TV. Radio incl: *Today*; *Family Favourites*; daily programme on Capital Radio. TV incl: *Ask Aspel*; *Crackerjack*; *Aspel And Company*; *Give Us A Clue*; *Child's Play*; *The 6 O'Clock Show.* Books: *Polly Wants A Zebra*; *Hang On!* m. actress Elizabeth Power. Hobbies: cinema, travel, letter-writing. Address: c/o Bagenal Harvey, London. Birthsign: Capricorn. **Favourite Place:** 'The square of a medieval village overlooking a certain Italian lake.'

ATKINS, Eileen

Actress, b. 16 June 1934 Clapton, London. Trained at Guildhall School of Music and Drama. Theatre incl: *The Killing Of Sister George*; *The Cocktail Party*; *Vivat Vivat Regina*; *Suzanna Andler*; *Sergeant Musgrave's Dance*; *As You Like It*; *Heartbreak House.* Films incl: *Equus*; *The Dresser.* TV Incl: *The Duchess Of Malfi*; *The Jean Rhys Woman*; *Elektra*; *The Three Sisters*; *Sons And Lovers*; *Smiley's People*; *The Burston Rebellion*; *Titus Andronicus*; *Eden End*; *Nellie's Version*; *Too Young To Fight Too Old To Forget.* m. Bill Shepherd. Hobbies: walking, tap dancing. Address: c/o Duncan Heath, London. Birthsign: Gemini. **Favourite Place:** 'My house, because it's on the Thames and I find it peaceful watching the boats, birds and water.'

ATKINSON, Rowan

Actor/writer, b. 6 Jan 1955 Newcastle-upon-Tyne. Trained as an electrical engineer, but decided on a show business career while at Queen's College, Oxford. First came to viewers' notice in *Canned Laughter* in 1979, then with *Not The Nine O'clock News* (1979–82) and *The Black Adder* (1983–85). Numerous guest appearances include *The Innes Book Of Records*, *The Lena Zavaroni Show* and *The Secret Policeman's Ball.* Variety Club Award BBC Personality of the Year 1980. Hobbies: all good music, electronics, truck driving, cars. Address: c/o Noel Gay, London. Birthsign: Capricorn.

AYERS-ALLEN, Phylicia
Actress, b. 19 June Houston,
Texas. Trained at the Negro
Ensemble Company. Stage incl:
The Wiz; *Dream Girls*; *Ain't
Supposed To Die A Natural Death*;
Duplex. TV incl: *One Life To
Live*; *The Crosby Show*. Winner
of the Delco Award for her
performance in the title role of
Zora. m. (dis.); 1 s. William.
Hobbies: Siddha meditation,
music, riding, cooking. Address:
c/o Bret Adams Ltd, 448 West

44th St, New York, NY 10036.
Birthsign: Gemini. **Favourite
Place:** India, 'I love its ancient
traditions and cultures.'

AYRES, Rosalind
Actress, b. 7 Dec 1946
Birmingham. Many theatre
appearances incl: Windsor,
Nottingham, Guildford,
Brighton, Birmingham and West
End in *I, Claudius* and *Dracula*.
Films incl: *That'll Be The Day*;
Stardust; *The Lovers*; *The Slipper
And The Rose*; *Cry Wolf*. Many
radio plays. Numerous TV
appearances incl: *Two's
Company*; *Rings On Their
Fingers*; *Agony*; *The Gentle*

Touch; *Only When I Laugh*; *The
Bounder*; *The Weather In The
Streets*; *Father's Day*; *Juliet Bravo*.
m. actor Martin Jarvis. Hobby:
interior decorating. Address: c/o
London Management, London.
Birthsign: Sagittarius. **Favourite
Place:** 'Our home.'

AZIZ, Khalid
Broadcaster, b. 9 Aug 1953
Lahore, Pakistan. At 16 he
worked for BBC Plymouth, then
for *Spotlight South West*. Spent a
year with BBC Radio 4. Moved
to East Midlands as freelance
reporter and became producer at
Radio Leicester. Went to Leeds in
1977 as reporter on *Look North*
and became presenter after two
years. In 1981 moved to TVS as
presenter of *Coast To Coast*, then
of *The Number One Show*. 1984

Enterprise South. In August 1984
moved to Thames to present
Daytime. Other TV incl: *What
Am I Bid?*; *The Object In
Question*; *Mainstream*. m.
Barbara; 2 d. Nadira, Fleur.
Hobbies: riding, flying, shooting,
fishing. Address: c/o PVA
Management, London. Birthsign:
Leo. **Favourite Place:** 'Shangri
La—it really exists! High in the
Himalayas with breathtaking
views. I visited the place 10 years
ago and would love to return.'

BAILEY, Robin
Actor, b. 5 Oct 1919 Hucknall,
Nottingham. Worked in the Post
Office then War Office and
became interested in amateur
dramatics. Joined Nottingham
Theatre Royal 1938. Rep at
Newcastle-upon-Tyne,
Birmingham, Worthing. Films
incl: *Private Angelo*; *Catch Us If
You Can*; *Blind Terror*. TV incl:
The 64,000 Challenge as compère;
The Pallisers; *Upstairs,
Downstairs*; *North And South*; *A*

Legacy; *I Didn't Know You Cared*;
For Services Rendered; *If You Go
Down In The Woods*; *Cupid's
Darts*; *Sorry, I'm A Stranger Here
Myself*; *Janet*; *Potter*; *Sharing
Time*; *Tales From A Long Room*;
Charters And Caldicott; *Bleak
House*. m. Patricia; 3 s. Nicholas,
Simon, Justin. Hobbies:
gardening, cricket. Address: c/o
Derek Glynne, London.
Birthsign: Libra. **Favourite
Place:** Sissinghurst Castle
garden.

BAKER, Cheryl

Singer/presenter, b. 8 March 1955 Bethnal Green, London. Started singing as a member of the group CoCo, and then joined Bucks Fizz. They came to fame in 1981 on winning the *Eurovision Song Contest* with *Making Your Mind Up*. They have since had many hit records and appeared on TV incl: *Top Of The Pops*, *Razzmatazz* and *Tiswas*. She is now also working as a TV presenter for *The Saturday 6 O'Clock Show* and *How Dare You*. Hobbies: crosswords, reading. Address: c/o London Weekend TV, London. Birthsign: Pisces.

BAKER, Colin

Actor, b. 8 June 1943 London. Trained at LAMDA. First performed at the Arts Theatre Cambridge, 1969. Appeared in rep and in the West End in *The Other House* and *The Price Of Justice*. Films incl: *Clockwork Orange*; *Dangerous Davies*; *No Longer Alone*. TV incl: *The Edwardians—Daisy*; *War And Peace*; *Harriet's Back In Town*; *For Maddy With Love*; *Swallows And Amazons Forever*. Best known in *The Brothers* and as the sixth Doctor in *Doctor Who*. m. Marion Wyatt Baker; 1 s. Jack (dec.), 1 d. Lucy. Hobbies: tennis, games, most sport (as a spectator), collecting cats, walking the red setter and whippet. Address: c/o Barry Burnett, London. Birthsign: Gemini. **Favourite Place:** 'Sitting in my study at my father's old giant roll-top desk, looking out of the window at the birds feeding from the bird table.'

BAKER, Danny

Presenter, b. 22 June 1957 Deptford, London. First worked as a shop assistant, receptionist and rock journalist. Regular presenter on LWT's *The 6 O'Clock Show*. m. Wendy Janet; 1 d. Bonnie Rae Alice. Hobbies: football, videotaping. Address: c/o LWT, London. Birthsign: Cancer/Gemini cusp. **Favourite Place:** 'Home and Millwall Football Club, which is an almost unnatural obsession.'

BAKER, George

Actor/writer, b. 1 April 1931 Varna, Bulgaria. First film was *The Dambusters*. Other films incl: *The Ship That Died of Shame*; *The Feminine Touch*; *Hill In Korea*; *The Moonraker*; *Goodbye, Mr Chips*; *On Her Majesty's Secret Service*; *The Thirty-Nine Steps*; *Hopscotch*; *North Sea Hijack*. TV incl: *Bowler* (his own series); *I, Claudius*; *Died In The Wool*; *Minder*; *Triangle*; *Chinese Detective*; *The Secret Adversary*; *Hart To Hart*; *Goodbye, Mr Chips*; *Robin Of Sherwood*; *The Bird Fancier*; *Marjorie And Men*; *Dead Head*. Author of many radio and TV plays, incl award-winning TV play *The Fatal Spring*. m. actress Sally Home; 1 d. Sarah. Hobbies: reading, riding, cooking. Address: c/o ICM, London. Birthsign: Aries.

BAKER, Richard, OBE, RD

Presenter, b. 15 June 1925 Willesden, London. While at Peterhouse, Cambridge joined Cambridge ADC and Footlights. Actor 1948–49. Joined BBC 1950; radio announcer 1951–54. BBC TV newsreader 1954–82. Presenter *Omnibus* 1983. Presenter of numerous music programmes incl: *The Proms*; panellist on *Face The Music*; *New Year's Day Concert From Vienna*. m. Margaret Martin; 2 s. Andrew, James. Hobbies: music, theatre, the sea. Address: c/o Bagenal Harvey, London. Birthsign: Gemini. **Favourite Place:** 'Kyle of Lochalsh in western Scotland, from which there is a glorious view of the Isle of Skye.'

BALL, Bobby

Comedian, b. 28 Jan 1944 Shaw. Half of the comedy partnership Cannon and Ball. Former welders in a Lancashire factory by day and a singing duo, The Harper Brothers, at night. Changed names to Cannon and Ball for *Opportunity Knocks* appearance. Voted clubland's top comedy duo, they have also won The Variety Club Showbusiness Personalities of the Year and topped various magazine and newspaper popularity polls. Starred in their own LWT series, *The Cannon And Ball Show*, since 1979. Subjects of *This Is Your Life*. They have also made a film, *The Boys In Blue*. m. Yvonne; 1 d. Joanne, 2 s. Darren, Robert. Hobbies: writing songs and poetry, music, especially rock 'n' roll. Address: c/o Stuart Littlewood Assocs, Oldham. Birthsign: Aquarius. **Favourite Place:** 'In the arms of my wife Yvonne.'

BALL, Johhny

Writer/presenter, b. 23 May 1938 Bristol. Trained as a Butlins Redcoat and as a comedian in northern clubs and cabaret. As writer/presenter TV incl: *Playschool*; *Play Away*; *Star Turn*; *Great Egg Race*; *Secrets Out*; *Cabbages And Kings*; *Think of A Number* (BAFTA award 1979); *Think Again* (Prix Jeunesse, Munich 1982); *You Are What You Eat* (video, ITVA Merit Award 1985). Books incl: *Think Of A Number: Think Box*; *Plays For Laughs*. m. Dianne; 1 d. Zoe, 2 s. Nicholas, Daniel. Hobbies: recreational maths, social history, Liverpool FC. Address: c/o Arlington Enterprises, London. Birthsign: Gemini. **Favourite Place:** 'Any new, totally deserted holiday spot with my wife and kids.'

BARBER, Glynis

Actress, b. October South Africa. Theatre incl: *Hamlet*; *Some Of My Best Friends Are Husbands*; *Ring Around The Moon*; *Rebecca*; *Black Comedy*; *My Cousin Rachel*. Films incl: *The Wicked Lady*; *Greed*; *The Haunted Mirror*; *Yesterday's Hero*; *Terror*. TV incl: *Jane At War*; *Lucky Jim*; *Blake's Seven*; *A Fine Romance*; *Bognor*; *History Of Mr Polly*; *Behind The Bike Sheds*; *Sandbaggers*; *The Voysey Inheritance*; *Dempsey And Makepeace*. m. Paul Anthony Barber (dis.). Hobbies: jogging, swimming, keeping fit. Address: c/o Rolf Kruger, London. Birthsign: Scorpio.

BARBER, Neville
Actor, b. 1 March 1931
Manchester. Trained at RADA.
Acted in many rep companies
including Perth and Nottingham.
Theatre incl: *The Bed Sitting
Room*; *The Mousetrap*. Over 150
parts on TV incl: *Doctor Who*;
The Onedin Line; *Upstairs,
Downstairs*; *Z Cars*; *The Duchess
Of Duke Street*; *Secret Army*; *The
Fall And Rise Of Reginald Perrin*;
Grange Hill; *Butterflies*; *Nanny*; *A
Fine Romance*; *The Gentle Touch*;
We'll Meet Again; *Whoops
Apocalypse*; *No. 10*; *Shine On
Harvey Moon*; *Potter*; *Bergerac*;
Roll Over Beethoven; *Brookside*;
Magnox; *Paradise Postponed*.
Hobbies: cats, reading, DIY.
Address: c/o Jimmy Garrod,
Walton-on-Thames. Birthsign:
Pisces. **Favourite Place:** 'In my
own sitting room surrounded by
my cats—here is perfect
relaxation.'

BARKER, Judith
Actress, b. 22 June 1943 Oldham.
Trained at the Coliseum,
Oldham. Theatre incl: *Billy Liar*;
Andy Capp; *Crime And
Punishment*; *Harvey*; *Love On The
Dole*; *Chamber Music*; *St Joan*;
The Taming Of The Shrew; *All
Things Bright And Beautiful*; *Love
For Love*; *Total Eclipse*; *The
Devil's Disciple*; *Zack*. Numerous
roles in plays on Radio 4. TV
incl: *Scully*; *Coronation Street*;
Turn Out The Lights; *Crossroads*;
Strangers; *Pardon The Expression*;
Vinegar Trip; *All For Love*; *Dixon
Of Dock Green*; *Seeing A Beauty
Queen Home*; *Persuasion*;
Inheritance. m. Kenneth Alan
Taylor, director Nottingham
Playhouse; 1 s. Jason, 1 d. Jessica.
Hobbies: horse riding, cooking,
tap dancing. Birthsign: Cancer.
Favourite Place: Tommyfield
Market, Oldham. A warm,
friendly place that epitomises my
background—down to earth like
me.'

BARKER, Ronnie, OBE
Actor/comedian, b. 25 Sept 1929
Bedford. Started as an amateur;
Aylesbury Rep 1948, then
Manchester and Oxford. Films
incl: *Futtocks End*; *Home Of Your
Own*; *Robin And Marian*;
Porridge. Radio incl: *Floggitts*; *The
Navy Lark*. TV incl: *I'm Not
Bothered*, *Frost Report*; *Foreign
Affairs*; *The Ronnie Barker
Playhouse*, *Frost On Sunday*; *Hark
At Barker*; *His Lordship Entertains*;
A Midsummer Night's Dream;
Seven Of One; *The Picnic*; *The
Two Ronnies*; *Porridge*; *Open All
Hours*; *Going Straight*. m. Joy
Tubb; 1 d. Charlotte, 2 s. Larry,
Adam. Hobby: collecting
Victoriana (postcards, books and
prints). Birthsign: Libra.
Favourite Place: 'The family
dinner table on Christmas Day.'

BARKWORTH, Peter
Actor, b. 14 Jan 1929 Margate.
Trained at RADA and, after rep
at Folkestone, was called up for
the army. West End incl: *Roar
Like A Dove*; *Crown Matrimonial*
(and on TV); *Donkey's Years*;
Can You Hear Me At The Back?;
A Coat Of Varnish. Directed
Sisterly Feelings (tour). TV incl:
The Power Game; *Manhunt*;
Melissa; *The Country Party*; *The
Saturday Party*; *Professional Foul*;
Secret Army; *Telford's Change*;
*Winston Churchill—The
Wilderness Years*; *The Price*; *Late
Starter*. Books: *About Acting*; *First
Houses*; *More About Acting*.
Hobbies: the countryside and
paintings, music, walking,
gardening, entertaining. Address:
c/o London Management,
London W1. Birthsign:
Capricorn. **Favourite Place:**
'The balcony of my penthouse flat
in Folkestone from which I can
see France (on a clear day).'

BARLOW, Thelma

Actress, b. 19 June Middlesbrough, Yorks. Secretary in Huddersfield before joining Joan Littlewood's Theatre Workshop in East London. Then appeared in London's West End and classical repertory productions before joining Granada TV's *Coronation Street* as Mavis in 1974. 2 s. Clive, James. Hobbies: yoga, cookery, gardening. Address: c/o Granada TV, Manchester. Birthsign: Gemini. **Favourite Place:** 'My cottage in the beautiful Yorkshire Dales.'

BARNES, Carol

TV journalist, b. 13 Sept 1944 Norwich, Norfolk. Was a public relations officer at London's Royal Court Theatre. Before joining ITN was in radio (BBC and LBC) as reporter; production manager *Time Out* magazine. m. Nigel Thomson; 1 d. Clare, 1 s. James. Hobbies: tennis, skiing. Address: c/o ITN, London. Birthsign: Virgo. **Favourite Place:** 'Top of the Alps on a clear day: the views are stunning.'

BARNETT, Jeni

Actress/writer/presenter, b. 24 March 1949 East London. Trained at New College of Speech and Drama. Started alternative theatre work with Pip Simmons Theatre Group then worked with Ken Campbell's Roadshow Co and formed Belt and Braces Roadshow Co. Performed everywhere from streets in Corby to prisons in Cumbria. Appeared in *Accidental Death Of An Anarchist* in West End and then went into situation comedy on TV in *Cabbage Patch*, as presenter on BBC's *Grapevine* and then TV-am, where she writes three spots a week including Postbag and Pick Of The Week. TV also incl: *Revolting Women*; *You And Me*; *Crying Out Loud*. m. James Bywater. Hobbies: music, eating, dieting, reading, TV, exercise. Address: c/o MPC Assocs, London. Birthsign: Aries. **Favourite Place:** home.

BARON, Lynda

Actress, b. 24 March Manchester. Trained in ballet at the Royal Academy of Dancing. Appeared in cabaret, principal boy in panto, films, West End plays and on TV. Theatre incl: *Living For Pleasure*; *The Bedwinner*; *The Real Inspector Hound*; *One Over The Eight*; *Bedful Of Foreigners*; *After Magritte*; *Talk Of The Town*; *Move Over Mrs Markham*; *Not Now, Darling*; *Goodbye Charlie*; *Butterflies Are Free*; *Abigail's Party*; *Little Me*. TV incl: *That Was The Week That Was*; *Play Of The Month*; *Don't Forget To Write*; *Heartlands*; *Grundy*; *Open All Hours*. m. John M Lee; 1 d. Sarah, 1 s. Morgan. Hobbies: writing, wine-making, squash. Address: c/o Peter Charlesworth, London. Birthsign: Aries. **Favourite Place:** 'Bed, especially on a Sunday morning, drinking tea and reading the Sunday papers.'

BARRACLOUGH, Roy
Actor, b. 12 July 1935 Preston, Lancs. With no formal training he entered acting after working in an engineering works when he was 28. Has since appeared in many TV comedy shows and is probably best known for his partnership with Les Dawson. Starred in his own children's TV series, *Pardon My Genie*, and claims the record, with George Waring, for appearing as the most characters in *Coronation Street*. Hobbies: good food and music. Address: c/o Peter Graham Assocs, London. Birthsign: Cancer. **Favourite Place:** 'Jeffrey Hill, overlooking Chipping village in Lancashire. A wonderful view which inspires feelings of peace.'

BARRON, John
Actor, b. 24 Dec 1920 Marylebone, London. Trained at RADA, then rep at Croydon, Leicester and Brighton. Films incl: *To Catch A King*; *13 For Dinner*; *Jigsaw*; *The Great Question*. TV incl: *Fly Away Peter*; *Emergency Ward 10*; *Softly, Softly*; *All Gas And Gaiters*; *Doomwatch*; *Crown Court*; *Timeslip*; *Ace Of Wands*; *The Fall And Rise of Reginald Perrin*; *The Foundation*; *Potter*; *Bernie*; *Spooner's Patch*; *Shelley*; *The Glums*; *The Wizard Of Crumm*; *Yes, Minister*; *To The Manor Born*; *The Gentle Touch*; *The Taming Of The Shrew*; *Othello*; *Cowboys*; *Whoops Apocalypse*; *No Place Like Home*; *Me And My Girl*. m. actress Joan Peart; 1 step-d. Hobby: collecting wine. Address: c/o Green & Underwood, London. Birthsign: Capricorn. **Favourite Place:** the Coffee Room at the Garrick Club.

BARRON, Keith
Actor, b. 8 Aug 1936 Mexborough, Yorks. Started acting career with Sheffield Rep. Small parts on TV and appearances with the Bristol Old Vic led to the series *The Odd Man* and *Lucky Jim*. Other TV incl: *My Good Woman*; *A Family At War*; *Let's Get Away From It All*; *Nigel Barton, Telford's Change*; *Watching Me, Watching You*; *West Country Tales*; *Duty Free*; *Leaving*. m. stage designer Mary Pickard; 1 s. Jamie. Hobby: walking his beagle George. Address: c/o Duncan Heath Assocs, London. Birthsign: Leo. **Favourite Place:** Calábria, Southern Italy, 'Sun, sand, sea, wonderful food and lovely people.'

BATEY, Derek
Compère/presenter, b. 8 Aug 1928 Brampton, Carlisle. Trained as an accountant before going into broadcasting. Director of Programme Policy at Border Television. Producer and host of *Mr & Mrs* and *Look Who's Talking*. Introduced several series of Yorkshire TV's *Your Hundred Best Hymns* and guest appearances on *3-2-1*; *Family Fortunes*; *This Is Your Life*; *Celebrity Squares*; *Sale Of The Century*; *It'll Be Alright On The Night*. Executive producer and presenter on New Year's Eve show *A Century of Stars* which traced the history of the Grand Order of Water Rats, of which he is a member. m. Edith; 1 d. Diane. Hobbies: golf, tennis, family, travel. Address: c/o Border Television, Carlisle. Birthsign: Leo. **Favourite Place:** his home county of Cumbria. 'It has the most beautiful scenery in the world.'

BAXTER, Anne

Actress, b. 7 May Michigan City, Indiana. Studied acting with Maria Ouspenskaya. Films incl: *The Magnificent Ambersons*; *The Pied Piper*; *Five Graves To Cairo*; *The Razor's Edge* (Oscar for Best Supporting Actress in 1946); *All About Eve*; *The Luck Of The Irish*; *O Henry's Full House*; *The Ten Commandments*; *Cimarron*; *Fool's Parade*. TV films incl: *Masks Of Death*; *Little Mo*. TV series incl: *East Of Eden*; *The Money Changers*. TV incl: *Hotel*; *The Love Boat*. Book: *Intermission: A True Story*. m. (1st) John Hodiak (dis.), (2nd) Randolph Galt (dis.), (3rd) David Klee (dec.); 2 d. Katrina, Melissa, 1 s. Maginel. Hobbies: writing, gardening. Address: c/o Joyce Wagner, PMK, 8642 Melrose Avenue, Los Angeles, California 90069. Birthsign: Taurus. **Favourite Place:** 'The world, because I am a travelling nut!'

BAXTER, Stanley

Actor, b. 24 May 1928 Glasgow. Revues and pantomimes in Scotland after three and a half years with Glasgow Citizens' Theatre. Moved to London in 1959. TV revues for BBC then LWT. West End shows incl: *The Amorous Prawn*; *On The Brighter Side*; *What The Butler Saw*; *Phil The Fluter*. TV incl: *The Stanley Baxter Picture Show (Parts I–III)*; *Stanley Baxter's Christmas Box* (1976); *Merrie Old Christmas* (1977); *Stanley Baxter On Television* (1979); *The Stanley Baxter Series* (1981). m. Moira. Hobbies: swimming, cycling, reading. Address: c/o David White Assocs, London. Birthsign: Gemini. **Favourite Place:** 'My living room in Highgate. It's simple and has the few things I need—warmth, decent light for reading, a gramophone and a TV if I wish to view.'

BAYLDON, Geoffrey

Actor, b. 7 Jan Leeds. Amateur theatricals before training at Old Vic Theatre School. First professional appearance in Cochrane's *Tough At The Top*. Films incl: *Casino Royale*; *A Night To Remember*; *To Sir With Love*; *The Pink Panther Strikes Again*; *Porridge*; *Bullshot*. TV incl: *An Age of Kings*; *Nicholas Nickleby*; *Under Western Eyes*; *Platonov*; *The Wood Demon*; *Catweazle* (title role); *The Avengers*; *The Saint*; *Devenish*; *Alice Through The Looking Glass*; *Abide With Me*; *Edward The Seventh*; *The Venlo Incident*; *Worzel Gummidge*; *All Creatures Great And Small*; *Bergerac*; *Juliet Bravo*; *Hallelujah!*; *There Comes A Time*; *This Office Life*; *Blott On The Landscape*. Hobbies: gardening, walking, painting. Address: c/o Joy Jameson, London. Birthsign: Capricorn. **Favourite Place:** 'A friend's villa in Corfu.'

BEACH, Ann

Actress/singer, b. 7 June 1938 Wolverhampton. Trained at RADA but aged 12 sang opera in *Hansel And Gretel*. After RADA went into West End in *Beth*. Joined Joan Littlewood's Theatre Workshop and appeared in *The Hostage*; *'Fings 'Aint Wot They Used To Be*; *Oh! What A Lovely War*; *The Dutch Courtesan*. Royal Court London *Inadmissible Evidence*; *Under Plain Cover*. Original Barbara in *Billy Liar*; *The Boy Friend*; *Mame*; *On The Twentieth Century*. Films incl: *Under Milk Wood*; *Oliver Twist*. TV incl: *The Government Inspector*; *Bouquet Of Barbed Wire*; *The Winslow Boy*; *The Vanishing Army*; *Fresh Fields*. m. TV producer Francis Coleman; 2 d. Charlotte, Lisa. Hobbies: music, painting. Address: c/o Joyce Edwards Agency, London. Birthsign: Gemini. **Favourite Place:** 'Hampstead Heath, near the ponds.'

BEADLE, Jeremy
Writer/broadcaster/curator of oddities/professional hoaxer, b. 12 April Hackney, London. Hosted radio shows incl: *Beadlebum Phone-In*; *Nightcap*; *The Odditarium*; *Animal, Vegetable, Mineral*. Hosted TV shows incl: *The Deceivers*; *Eureka*; *Definition*; *Fun Factory*; *Today's The Day*; *Game For A Laugh*. As writer/consultant incl: *Celeberity Squares*; *Under*

Manning; *You Must Be Joking*; *Lucky Numbers*; *Ultra Quiz*. Publications incl: *Today's The Day*; cartoon strip, *Today's The Day*; *Outlawed Inventions* (with Chris Winn); *Book Of Lists*; *The People's Almanac*; *Book Of Predictions*; co-editor *Time Out*. Chief consultant to Action Time, game show company. Hobby: work. Address: c/o MPC Artists, London. Birthsign: Aries.
Favourite Place: 'In the arms of the woman I love.'

BEAUMONT, Bill, OBE
Sports commentator, b. 9 March 1952 Preston. TV incl: *A Question Of Sport*; *Grandstand*. m. Hilary; 1 s. Daniel. Hobbies: water-skiing, eating out, sport. Address: c/o John Hockey, London. Birthsign: Pisces.
Favourite Place: 'The Lake District for its water sports and beautiful scenery.'

BECHER, Michael
Actor, b. 20 Nov 1939 Sydney, Australia. Trained as an actor at

the Independent Theatre School, Sydney. Theatre credits incl: *King Richard*. TV credits incl. *Possession*; *Grundy Organisation*. Hobbies: gardening, playing bridge, flirting, camping. Address: c/o Holt Williams, PO Box 75, Milson's Point, New South Wales 2061, Australia. Birthsign: Scorpio. **Favourite Place:** 'My garden, because it is full of birds and magic nooks and crannies and serrendipitous happenings.'

BEENY, Christopher
Actor, b. 7 July 1941 London. Wanted to be a dancer and joined Ballet Rambert 1949 while at stage school. First acting role in *Peter Pan* 1951. First TV series *The Grove Family*, aged 12; *Dixon Of Dock Green*; *Emergency Ward 10*; *The Plane Makers*; *Armchair Theatre*. Went to RADA but gave up acting due to lack of work. An episode of *Softly, Softly* brought him back to acting, followed by *Upstairs*,

Downstairs; *Miss Jones And Son*; *The Rag Trade*; *In Loving Memory*. m. (1st) (dis.), (2nd) singer Diana Kirkwood; 1 d. Joanne, 1 s. Richard. Hobbies: photography, swimming, relaxing in the sun, water-skiing. Address: c/o Felix de Wolfe, London. Birthsign: Cancer.
Favourite Place: 'A good restaurant in Hong Kong, because I love Chinese food and Hong Kong is the most exciting place I've visited.'

BEGLEY, Ed Jr
Actor, b. 16 Sept Hollywood, California. Son of the late character actor Ed Begley, Sr. Films incl: *Stay Hungry*; *Cat People*; *Buddy-Buddy*; *Private Lessons*; *Goin' South*; *Streets of Fire*. TV incl: *Happy Days*; *Room 222*; *Quincy*; *MASH*: *Mary Hartman, Mary Hartman*; *Laverne And Shirley*. Received two Emmy nominations for role as Dr Victor Ehrlich in *St Elsewhere*. m. Ingrid; 1 s. Nicholas, 1 d. Amanda. Hobbies: woodwork, gardening. Address: c/o Belson and Klass Assocs, 211 South Beverly Drive, Beverly Hills, California 90212. Birthsign: Virgo. **Favourite Place:** 'Far from Los Angeles in Ojai, California.'

BELAFONTE-HARPER, Shari
Actress, b. 22 Sept New York City. Films incl: *If You Could See What I Hear*; *The Time Walker*. TV films incl: *The Night The City Screamed*; *Velvet*. TV incl: *Hotel*; *The Love Boat*; *Hart To Hart*; *Sheriff Lobo*; *Trapper John, MD*; *Diff'rent Stokes*; *Today's FBI*; *Code Red*. m. Robert Harper. Hobbies: fencing, racquetball, water-skiing, riding. Address: c/o Pam Prince, The William Morris Agency, 151 El Camino Drive, Beverly Hills, California 90212. Birthsign: Virgo. **Favourite Place:** 'The mountains—where my husband and I have a weekend retreat to escape the rat race of the city.'

BELL, Ann
Actress, b. 29 April 1940 Wallasey, Merseyside. Trained at RADA then rep at Nottingham. She then joined the Old Vic. Many stage appearances in London and America. Films incl: *To Sir With Love*; *The Reckoning*; *The Statue*; *Champions*. TV incl: *Jane Eyre*; *Company Of Five*; *Uncle Vanya*; *The Lost Boys*; *Very Like A Whale*; *Three Sisters*; *Ghost Sonata*; *Macbeth*; *Way Of The World*; *War And Peace*; *For Whom The Bell Tolls*; *Resurrection*; *Tenko*. m. Robert Lang; 1 d. Rebecca, 1 s. John. Hobbies: reading, swimming. Address: c/o Leading Artists, London. Birthsign: Taurus. **Favourite Place:** 'Anywhere warm and sunny and preferably near the sea.'

BELL, Tom
Actor, b. 1932 Liverpool. Local rep aged 15; trained at Bradford Civic Theatre School. After a spell in the army, rep and tours before London debut. Theatre incl: *Progress In The Park*; *The Ring Of Truth*; with the Royal Shakespeare Company; *Bent*; *Hedda Gabler*. Many films, the most recent incl: *Quest*; *The Sailor's Return*; *The Innocent*. Numerous TV roles, the most recent incl: *Out*; *Love Story–Sweet Nothings*; *Sons And Lovers*; *King's Royal*; *Reilly Ace Of Spies*; *Desert Of Lies*; *Summer Lightning*; *The Detective*. m. Lois Daine (dis.); 1 s. Aran. Hobby: growing sunflowers. Address: c/o Chatto & Linnit, London.

BELLAMY, David
Botanist/writer/broadcaster, b. 18 Jan 1933 London. No idea what he wanted to do until became a lab assistant. Within five years a lecturer then senior lecturer in botany at Durham University. Entered TV/radio with his opinions on the Torrey Canyon oil disaster 1967. TV programmes incl: *Bellamy On Botany*; *Bellamy's Europe*; *Don't Ask Me*; *Botanic Man*; *Up A Gum Tree*; *Backyard Safari*; *Discovery*; *The End Of The Rainbow Show*; *Turning The Tide* (due 86). Written 15 books, latest: *The Queen's Hidden Garden*. Also written a ballet, *Heritage*. m. marine biologist Rosemary; 3 d. Henrietta, Brighid, Iseabal, 2 s. Rufus, Eoghain (all adopted). Hobbies: children, ballet. Address: c/o Tyne Tees TV, Newcastle. Birthsign: Capricorn. **Favourite Place:** 'Home in the Pennines or in any open space with my family.'

BELLI, Anjela
Actress, b. 11 Nov 1958 Bolton. Trained at RADA. Theatre experience incl: *Play It Again Sam*; *Bad Language*; *The Fosdyke Saga*. TV credits incl: *Company*, a drama documentary for C4; *Let's Murder Vivaldi* for the BBC Director Course; Christina Scott in Thames series *Gems*. Hobbies: weight training, playing tennis. Address: c/o Morgan & Goodman, London. Birthsign: Scorpio. **Favourite Place:** 'Taking the dogs to the woods near my parents' home very early in the morning.'

BELLINGHAM, Lynda
Actress, b. 31 May 1948 Montreal, Canada. Trained at Central School of Speech and Drama then rep at Coventry, Crewe and Oxford. Theatre incl: *Bordello*; *Norman Is That You?*; *Noises Off*; *Salad Days*; *Norman Conquests* Oxford Playhouse tour. Films incl: *Sweeney*; *Waterloo Bridge Handicap*; *Stand Up Virgin Soldiers*. TV incl: *General Hospital*; *Angels*; *The Sweeney*; *Z Cars*; *Hazell*; *Funny Man* with Jimmy Jewel; *Mackenzie*. Also appeared on numerous panel games incl: *Punchlines*; *Tell The Truth*. m. Nunzio Peluso; 1 s. Michael. Hobbies: reading, cooking. Address: c/o Saraband Assocs, London. Birthsign: Gemini. **Favourite Place:** 'Naples, because my husband comes from Naples and I spent my wedding weekend there.'

BELLWOOD, Pamela
Actress, b. 26 June Scarsdale, New York. Trained at RADA in London. Films incl: *Airport 77*; *Serial*; *The Incredible Shrinking Woman*; *Two Minute Warning*. TV films incl: *Cocaine: One Man's Seduction*; *Emily, Emily*; *War Widow*; *Baby Sister*; *Sparkling Cynaide*. TV series include *Web* and *Dynasty*; guest TV appearances incl: *Mannix*; *Police Story*; *Baretta*. m. photo journalist Nik Wheeler. Hobbies: travelling and writing travel articles, playing the piano, photography, gardening. Address: c/o Sue Cameron, Leading Artists, 445 North Bedford Drive, Beverly Hills, California 90210. Birthsign: Cancer. **Favourite Place:** Kenya.

BENEDICT, Dirk

Actor, b. 1 March Helena, Montana. Trained at the John Fernald Academy of Dramatic Arts in Rochester, Michigan. Theatre incl: *Abelard And Heloise*; *Butterflies Are Free*. Films incl: *Georgia, Georgia*; *ssssSnake*; *W*. TV incl: *Chopper One*; *Battlestar Galactica*; as Face in *The A-Team*. Hobby: flying. Address: c/o 7083 Hollywood Blvd, California 90028. Birthsign: Pisces. **Favourite Place:** 'At my ranch in Montana. That is my home and where I feel most comfortable. There is a lot of open land, beautiful scenery and clean air.'

BENJAMIN, Christopher

Actor, b. 27 Dec 1934 Trowbridge, Wilts. Trained at RADA and rep seasons at Salisbury and Bristol Old Vic. West End theatre incl: *A Severed Head*; *Maigret And The Lady*; *Artuo Ui*; *John Bull's Other Island*; *Nicholas Nickleby*; since 1982 with Royal Shakespeare Company. Films incl: *Brief Encounter*. TV incl: *The Forsyte Saga*; *Poldark*; *Doctor Who*; *Dick Turpin*; *Donkey's Years*; *Thérèse Raquin*; *We The Accused*; *It Takes A Worried Man*; *Holding The Fort*; *Nicholas Nickleby*; *Blott On The Landscape*. m. actress Anna Fox; 2 d. Kate, Emilia, 1 s. Sebastian. Hobbies: music, cricket, gardening. Address: c/o Scott Marshall, London. Birthsign: Capricorn. **Favourite Place:** 'The Quantock Hills. I dream of them when I'm in New York and other far away places.'

BENJAMIN, Floella

Actress, b. 23 Sept Trinidad. Began working in a bank but soon left to start show business career. West End shows incl: *Hair*; *Jesus Christ Superstar*; *The Black Mikado*; *The Husband In Law*. Film: *Black Joy*. TV appearances incl: *The Gentle Touch*; *Mixed Blessings*; *Within These Walls*; *Waterloo Sunset*; *Hole In Babylon*; *Bergerac*; *Strangers*. As presenter incl: *Playschool*; *Play Away*; *How Dare You*; *Fast Forward*; *Switch On To English*; *Lay On Five*. Numerous game shows incl: *Give Us A Clue*; *Blankety Blank*; *Monkey Business*. Books incl: *Floella's Fun Book*; *Why The Agouti Has No Tail*; *Fall About With Flo*. m. Keith Taylor; 1 s. Aston. Hobbies: photography, good food. Address: c/o Benjamin-Taylor Assocs, London. Birthsign: Libra. **Favourite Place:** 'Venice—the most beautiful city on earth.'

BENNETT, Alan

Dramatist, b. 9 May 1934 Leeds. On stage he has appeared in two of his own works, *Beyond The Fringe* and *Forty Years On* (which won London's *Evening Standard* Award). Co-author of *Sing A Rude Song*. Author of *Habeas Corpus*; *The Old Country*; *Enjoy*. Screenplays incl: *Parson's Pleasure*; *Handful Of Dust*; *Prick Up Your Ears*; *A Private Function*. TV appearances incl: *Sunday Night*: *Plato—The Drinking Party*; *Famous Gossips*; *Alice In Wonderland*; *Merry Wives Of Windsor*. Writing for TV incl: *A Day Out*; *Sunset Across The Bay*; *A Little Outing*; *Me—I'm Afraid Of Virginia Woolf*; *Afternoon Off*; *All Day On The Sands*; *A Woman Of No Importance*; *Rolling Home*; *An Englishman Abroad*. Address: c/o Chatto & Linnit, London. Birthsign: Taurus.

BENNETT, Hywell

Actor, b. 8 April 1944 Garnant, S Wales. Family moved to London when he was five. Joined National Youth Theatre at 14 to play Ophelia. Went to RADA. Appeared in West End in London, Edinburgh Festival and on TV before big break in film *The Family Way* with Hayley Mills. Most recent theatre incl: *Fly Away Home* (also as producer). Most recent film: *Murder Elite*. Now best known on TV as *Shelley*. Other TV incl: *The Sweeney*; *Pennies From Heaven*; *Strangers*; *Malice Aforethought*; *Tinker, Tailor, Soldier, Spy*; *Artemis 81*; *The Critic*; *The Consultant*; *Absent Friends*; *Frankie And Johnny*. m. Cathy McGowan (dis.); 1 d. Emma. Address: c/o James Sharkey, London. Birthsign: Aries.

BENNETT, Lennie

Comedian, b. 26 Sept 1938 Blackpool. A former journalist with the West Lancs *Evening Gazette*, he became a professional entertainer in 1965. First TV was in *The Good Old Days* in 1966, and now is best associated with *Punchlines*. Other TV incl: *International Cabaret*; *Lennie And Jerry Show*; *London Night Out*; *Rising Stars*; *Starburst*; *The Railway Carriage Game*; *All Star Secrets*; *The Kenny Everett Show*. m. Margaret; 1s. Tony. Hobbies: running, squash. Address: c/o MPC, London. Birthsign: Libra. **Favourite Place:** 'The finishing line in the London Marathon! Have now completed 10 marathons in aid of Leukaemia Research.'

BENTINE, Michael James

Writer/actor/comedian/parapsychologist, b. 26 Jan 1922 Watford, Herts. Started in Cardiff 1940 in *Sweet Lavender*. Volunteered for the RAF. Founder member of the Goons. Radio incl: *Round The Bend*; *Best Of Bentine*. Films incl: *The Sandwich Man*; *Bachelor Of Arts*. TV incl: *Quick On The Draw*; *The Bumblies*; *It's A Square World*, *Arts Bazaar*; *Potty Time*; *Mad About*; *Village Action*. Books incl: *The Long Banana Skin*; *The Door Marked Summer* (autobiographies); *Doors Of The Mind*; *The Shy Person's Guide To Life*. m. (1st) (dis.), (2nd) ex-ballet dancer Clementina Stuart; 3 d. Elaine (from 1st m.) (dec.), Fusty, Suki (from 2nd m.), 2s. Gus (dec.), Richard. Hobbies: fencing, sailing, archery, guns, Egyptology, astronomy, restoring paintings. Birthsign: Aquarius. **Favourite Place:** 'My home, wherever my heart is.'

BERTISH, Suzanne

Actress, b. 7 Aug 1954 London. TV incl: *The Limbo Connection (Armchair Thriller)*; *Are You Watching The Mummy?*; *Wings Of A Dove*; *The Three Sisters*; *Maybury*; *The RSC On Tour (Southbank Show)*; *The Making Of Nicholas Nickleby*; *The Life And Times Of Nicholas Nickleby*; *To The Lighthouse*; *Freud*; *A Comedy Of Errors*; *Rainy Day Women*; *Shine On Harvey Moon*. Hobby: tennis. Address: c/o Duncan Heath, London. Birthsign: Leo. **Favourite Place:** New York City, 'As a realistic, as opposed to a romantic or aesthetic choice, I do feel myself there.'

BEVAN, Gillian
Actress, b. Stockport, Cheshire. Trained at the Manchester Youth Theatre and at the Central School of Speech and Drama. Worked in rep at Perth, Dundee, Stratford East, Harrogate and Farnham, and for three seasons at the Theatre in the Round, Scarborough. Stage appearances incl: *Tapster*; *Out Front*; *Me, Myself And I*; *Way Upstream*; *A Trip To Scarborough*; *Incidental Music*; *Making Tracks*; *Absent Friends*; *The Merry Gentleman*; *A Doll's House*; *Hamlet*. TV incl: *Never The Twain*; *Sharon And Elsie*; *Lost Empires*. Hobbies: gardening, tennis. Address: c/o Barry Brown, London. Birthsign: Aquarius. **Favourite Place:** 'North Bay, Scarborough; Formentor, Majorca; my bed, London.'

BEWES, Rodney
Actor, b. 27 Nov 1938 Bingley, Yorks. Interested in acting at 12 when BBC advertised for a Billy Bunter. He didn't get the part but was cast in two other plays. Went to RADA then rep. First break in 1960s in Harold Pinter's *A Night Out*. Decided to concentrate on TV, which led to *The Likely Lads*; *Whatever Happened To The Likely Lads?* and the series he wrote and produced, *Dear Mother . . . Love Albert*. Films incl: *Billy Liar*; *Decline And Fall*; *Spring And Port Wine*; *Dance To Your Daddy*; *Whatever Happened To The Likely Lads?* TV incl: *Love Story*; *Z Cars*; *Albert*; *Jonah And The Whale*; *Just Liz*. m. fashion designer Daphne Black; 1 d. Daisy, 3 s. Joe, Tom, Billy (triplets). Hobbies: antiques, children. Address: c/o ICM, London. Birthsign: Sagittarius. **Favourite Place:** Cadgwith Cove, The Lizard, Cornwall.

BICKNELL, Andrew
Actor, b. 28 April 1957 Colchester, Essex. Trained at the Webber Douglas Academy and first job was at Bristol Old Vic. Theatre incl: appearances at Exeter, Dundee, Perth, Guildford; in *Betrayal*. Films incl: *Lady Jane Grey*; *The Meaning Of Life*; *Fords On Water*. TV Incl: *To Serve Them All My Days*; *The Crime Of Captain Cathurst*; *By The Sword Divided*; *Jane Eyre*; *Miss Marple*; *Winston Churchill—The Wilderness Years*; *Mr Palfrey Of Westminster*; *Agatha Christie Hour*; *Sorrell And Son*; *The Optimist*; *Tales Of The Unexpected*; *Paradise Postponed*. Hobbies: horses, tennis, rugby, music, fencing. Address: c/o Barry Burnett, London. Birthsign: Taurus. **Favourite Place:** 'The Hermitage, Dunkel, Perthshire. It is the most emotive garden in Britain.'

BIGGINS, Christopher
Actor, b. 16 Dec 1948 Oldham, Lancs. Trained at the Bristol Old Vic Theatre School, then rep at Salisbury, Derby, Royal Shakespeare Company. Other theatre incl: *Winnie The Pooh*; *Beyond The Fringe*; *Touch Of Spring*; *Side By Side By Sondheim*. Films incl: *The Rocky Horror Picture Show*; *The Tempest*; *Masada*. TV incl: *Paul Temple*; *The Likely Lads*; *Porridge*; *Man of Straw*; *Upstairs, Downstairs*; *Some Mothers Do 'Ave 'Em*; *Kidnapped*; *Brontë Connection*; *Dancing Princess*; *Brendan Chase*; *Shoestring*; *I, Claudius*; *Poldark*; *On Safari*; *Surprise Surprise*. Hobbies: eating, going to the cinema and theatre, travel, staying in luxury hotels, cooking, badminton, swimming. Address: c/o Marina Martin, London. Birthsign: Sagittarius. **Favourite Place:** 'New York and Shrublands Health Farm.'

BIRD, John

Writer/actor/director, b. 22 Nov 1936 Nottingham. After acting and directing while at Cambridge University, joined Royal Court Theatre, London as assistant to the director and later associate artistic director. In *Habeas Corpus* in West End 1973. Films incl: *Take A Girl Like You*; *The Seven Per Cent Solution*; *Yellow Pages*. TV incl: *BBC3*; *Last Laugh*; *The Late Show*; *My Father Knew Lloyd George*; *A Series Of Birds*; *With Bird Will Travel*; *John Bird/John Wells*; *Blue Remembered Hills*; Graham Greene series; *Timon Of Athens*; *King Lear*; *The Falklands Factor*; *Marmalade*; *Blue Money*; *Oxbridge Blues*; *Travelling Man*. Hobbies: music, reading, walking, animals. Address: c/o Chatto & Linnit, London. Birthsign: Scorpio. **Favourite Place:** 'Clare Bridge, Cambridge. Nice view with romantic memories.'

BLACK, Isobel

Actress. No formal training but started career with rep companies in Manchester and Edinburgh. She has also appeared on stage in Manchester and Birmingham and at the Regent's Park Open Air Theatre, London. TV incl: *The Troubleshooters*; *The Likely Lads*; *The White Bird Passes*; *Reid The Sheepstealer*; *Boswell For The Defence*; *Three Sisters*; *The Brief*; *Scotland's Story*; *The Tempest*; *The Hostage*. m. James Gatward; 3 d, Annabel, Celia, Eloise. Hobbies: cooking, music, gardening, riding. Address: c/o Eileen Williams, LWA, London. Birthsign: Sagittarius. **Favourite Place:** 'Apart from our home—Italy, because it is warm, beautiful and temperamental.'

BLACKMAN, Honor

Actress, b. 22 Aug London. West End theatre incl: *The Gleam*; *Blind Goddess*; *Wait Until Dark*; *Who Killed Santa Claus?*; *Exorcism*; *The Sound Of Music*; *On Your Toes*. Films incl: *Quartet*; *Diamond City*; *Goldfinger*; *Life At The Top*; *Shalako*; *Something Big*; *The Virgin And The Gypsy*. Best known for her TV role of Cathy Gale in *The Avengers* from 1962–64. 1 d. Lottie, 1 s. Barnaby. Hobbies: travelling, reading. Address: c/o London Management, London. Birthsign: Leo. **Favourite Place:** 'Chiswick Park, for happy childhood memories reinforced by similar memories of my own children there.'

BLACKNELL, Steve

TV Presenter, b. 6 Sept 1952 Lambeth, London. First trained as a nurse then had 32 different jobs. TV incl: *Riverside*; *Sight And Sound*; *Breakfast Time* pop music slots; *Life Games*; *Whistle Test*; *Off The Record*; *London Plus*; *Punchlines*; *Pop The Question*; co-hosted UK's first cable music show which led to own *London Calling* cable show, shown in various UK regions and on US MTV. Winner of award for cable TV excellence in US 1984. Book: *Top Of The Pops*. Hobbies: TV, film and music trivia, The Duke of Edinburgh Award scheme, cooking dinner for friends, acupuncture. Address: c/o Hamper-Neafsey Assocs, London. Birthsign: Virgo. **Favourite Place:** 'To be with my family at Christmas—it's the one time each year we all get together.'

BLACQUE, Taurean (born Herbert Middleton)
Actor, b. 10 May. Trained at the Arts High School, American Musical and Dramatic Academy, New York. Joined the Negro Ensemble Company, New York; New Federal Theater. Appeared on Broadway in *River Niger* and *We Interrupt This Program*. TV appearances incl: *The Bob Newhart Show*; *The Tony Randall Show*; *Paris*; *The White Shadow*; *The Last Resort*; *Snip*; *What's Happening?* Nominated for an Emmy for his role as Detective Neal Washington in *Hill Street Blues*. m. (dis.); 2 s. Rodney, Shelby. Hobbies: refurbishing houses, acting in plays. Address: c/o Jack Fields and Assocs, 9255 Sunset Blvd, Suite 1105, Los Angeles, California 90069. Birthsign: Taurus. **Favourite Place:** 'New York!'

BLAIR, Isla
Actress, b. South India. Trained at RADA, went straight into the West End in *A Funny Thing Happened On The Way To The Forum*. Theatre incl: *The Rivals*; *King Lear*; *What The Butler Saw*; *Othello*; *Jumpers*; *Hobson's Choice*; *The Cherry Orchard*; *Hay Fever*; *Design For Living*; *Private Lives*; *The Browning Version*; *Black Comedy*. Films incl: *The Blood Of Dracula*; *The Battle Of Britain*. TV incl: *The Doctors*; *The Regiment*; *The Crezz*; *When The Boat Comes In*; *Forgotten Love Songs*; *Wilde Alliance*; *The History Man*; *Alexa*; *The Bounder*; *Six Centuries Of Verse*; *Off Peak*; *Poppyland*; *The Tennis Court*. m. Julian Glover; 1 s. Jamie Blair. Hobbies: tennis, writing. Address: c/o William Morris, London. Birthsign: Libra. **Favourite Place:** 'My kitchen, where I talk long into the night with my two best friends—my husband and son.'

BLAIR, Lionel
Actor/TV personality, b. 12 Dec 1934 Montreal, Canada. Started as a child actor. First stage appearance in *Wizard Of Oz*, Croydon in 1942. With no professional training and with sheer hard work has acted, danced, sung, choreographed and directed numerous plays, musicals, revues and appeared in several *Royal Variety Performances*. Many TV appearances in variety shows. Men's team captain in TV's *Give Us A Clue* and host on *Name That Tune*. Autobiography: *Stage Struck*. m. Susan; 2 s. Daniel, Matthew, 1 d. Lucy. Hobbies: watching TV, film buff. Address: c/o Peter Charlesworth, London. Birthsign: Sagittarius. **Favourite Place:** 'Hong Kong—it's like a giant cut-price supermarket.'

BLAKE, Christopher
Actor, b. 23 Aug 1949 London. Trained at Central School of Speech and Drama. Theatre incl: *The Trials of Oscar Wilde*. Film: *Aces High*. TV incl: *Anne Of Avonlea*; *Death Or Glory Boy*; *Love For Lydia*; *The Lost Boys*; *Mill On The Floss*; *Mixed Blessings*; *Alexa*; *That's My Boy*; *Love's Labours Lost*. m. Wendy; 2 d. Charlotte, Louise, 1 s. Sean. Hobbies: cricket, photography. Address: c/o ICM, London. Birthsign: Leo/Virgo. **Favourite Place:** 'Highbury North Bank. Good company, good atmosphere.'

BLAKELY, Colin
Actor, b. 23 Sept 1930 Bangor, Wales. Extensive theatre experience including with the Royal Shakespeare Company, National Theatre, Old Vic and West End. Films incl: *Young Winston*; *Murder On The Orient Express*; *Evil Under The Sun*; *Red Monarch*. Numerous TV credits incl: *King Lear*; *Churchill's People*; *Donkey's Years*; *Operation Julie*; *The Dumb Waiter*. m. Margaret Whiting; 3 s. Drummond, Cameron, Hamish. Address: c/o Leading Artists, London. Birthsign: Virgo. **Favourite Place:** 'Home in Ireland and Italy.'

BLAKISTON, Caroline
Actress, b. 13 Feb London. Trained at RADA where she won a bronze medal and a contract with Liverpool Playhouse. Theatre incl: *A Midsummer Night's Dream*; *Look Back In Anger*; *King Lear*; *The Cocktail Party*; founder member of the *Actors Company* and appeared in *Knots*, *Way Of The World*. West End incl: *Everything In The Garden*; *The Real Inspector Hound*; *Murderer*. Films incl: *Sunday, Bloody Sunday*; *Yanks*; *Return Of The Jedi*. TV incl: *The Avengers*; *The Saint*; *The Forsyte Saga*; *Crown Court*; *Private Schultz*; *Shoestring*; *Nanny*; *Brass*; *Charters And Caldicott*; *Mr Palfrey Of Westminster*. m. Russell Hunter (dis.); 1 s. Adam, 1 d. Charlotte. Hobbies: sun, opera. Address: c/o Chatto & Linnit, London. Birthsign: Aquarius. **Favourite Place:** 'A thirteen-and-a-half mile beach, northern Cyprus.'

BLANCH, Dennis
Actor, b. 4 Feb 1947 Barnet, Herts. Rep experience at Exeter, Billingham and Newcastle. Films incl: *Permission To Kill*; *International Velvet*. TV incl: *The XYY Man*; *Strangers*; *Thriller*; *Villains*; *New Scotland Yard*; *Warship*; *The Sweeney*; *No, Honestly*; *General Hospital*; *Give Us A Break*; *Grange Hill*; *Bulman*. m. Carol Wilks, 1 s. David. Hobbies: football, cricket, snooker. Address: c/o Michelle Braidman Assocs, London. Birthsign: Aquarius. **Favourite Place:** 'Mytholmroyd Cricket Club, where I can sit and dream that I might score 50 one day.'

BLETHYN, Brenda
Actress, b. 20 Feb 1946 Ramsgate, Kent. Trained at Guildford School of Drama and joined Bubble Theatre Company, London. Joined National Theatre 1976 and appeared in *Tamburlaine The Great*; *Strife*; *Force of Habit*; *The Double Dealer*; *The Fruits Of Enlightenment*; *The Nativity*; *The Passion*; *Doomsday*; *Bedroom Farce*; *A Midsummer Night's Dream*; *The Guardsman*; *The Provoked Wife*. West End incl: *Steaming*; *Benefactors*. TV incl: *King Lear*; *Henry VI*; *The Imitation Game*; *Tales Of The Unexpected*; *Floating Off*; *Grown Ups*; *Sheppey*; *Alas Smith And Jones*; *Death Of An Expert Witness*; *Chance In A Million*. Hobbies: needlework, crossword puzzles. Address: c/o Ken McReddie, London. Birthsign: Pisces. **Favourite Place:** 'A bracing walk along the East Cliff at Ramsgate on a winter's day.'

BLOOM, Claire

Actress, b. 15 Feb 1931 London. Trained at Guildhall School of Music and Drama and Central School of Speech and Drama. Oxford Rep in 1946; West End 1947; Stratford-upon-Avon, 1948; Old Vic 1952–54. Theatre incl: *A Streetcar Named Desire*; *The Innocents*. Films incl: *The Blind Goddess*; *Look Back In Anger*; *Richard III*; *The Spy Who Came In From The Cold*; *Limelight*. TV incl: *Romeo And Juliet*; *Anna Karenina*; *The Legacy*; *Wessex Tales*; *In Praise Of Love*; *Henry VIII*; *Hamlet*; *Brideshead Revisited*; *Cymbeline*; *King John*; *Anne And Debbie*; *Ellis Island*; *Time And The Conways*; *Shadowlands*. Autobiography: *Limelight And After*. m. actor Rod Steiger (dis.), 1 d. Anna. Hobby: yoga. Address: c/o Chatto & Linnit, London. Birthsign: Aquarius. **Favourite Place:** Palasca, Corsica.

BLUMENAU, Colin

Actor, b. 7 Aug 1956 London. Took a degree in drama at Hull University. Theatre incl: *Altogether Now*; rep at Basingstoke, Salisbury, Exeter and Milford Haven. Also appeared at New End and Tricycle theatres in London. TV incl: *Jockey School*; *Andy Robson*; *Woodentop And The Bill*. m. Deborah O'Brien; 1 s. Dan. Hobbies: horse riding, the countryside, collie dogs, brass music. Address: c/o Green & Underwood, London. Birthsign: Leo. **Favourite Place:** 'Hound Tor, Dartmoor. A place where you can see for miles and where I spent a great deal of my youth.'

BLUNT, Gabrielle

Actress, b. 8 Jan 1919 Herne Bay, Kent. Trained at Central School of Speech and Drama. Theatre incl: *Quiet Weekend*; *Pink String And Sealing Wax*; *Dark Of The Moon*; *Hedda Gabler*; *Just Between Ourselves*; *The Importance Of Being Earnest*; *Heartbreak House*; *Deathtrap*; *The Duchess Of Malfi*. Films incl: *Whisky Galore*; *Tony Draws A Horse*; *The Rossiters*; *The Love Lottery*; *The Godsend*. TV incl: *Woman Of Today*; *Life At Stake*; *Within These Walls*; *Crown Court*; *Last Wishes*; *Love In A Cold Climate*; *Goodbye Darling*; *Emmerdale Farm*; *Metal Mickey*; *The Secret Adversary*; *Roll Over Beethoven*; *Eh Brian, It's A Whopper*; *Shine On Harvey Moon*. Hobby: archaeology. Address: c/o Bill Horne, London. Birthsign: Capricorn. **Favourite Place:** 'Bed, for all the obvious reasons.'

BLYTHE, Benedick

Actor, b. June London. Trained at Bristol Old Vic Theatre School. Started career in rep at Nottingham, York, Bristol Old Vic, Coventry. Appeared with the Royal Shakespeare Company in *Good* in London's West End. Film: *The Keep*. TV incl: *Hammer House Of Horror—The Corvini Inheritance*; *Murder Of A Moderate Man*; *The Winning Streak*. Hobbies: running, cricket, theatre, sport, cooking. Address: c/o London Management, London. Birthsign: Gemini. **Favourite Place:** 'Home, where I can relax with the people I most want to be with.'

BOARDMAN, Stan
Comedian, b. 7 Dec Liverpool.
Ran his own haulage business
before winning a holiday camp
competition which set him onto a
show business career. Summer
season 1982 Lowestoft; Aladdin
panto 1982; panto Liverpool
Empire, 1985. TV incl:
*Opportunity Knocks; Celebrity
Squares; Seaside Special;
Runaround; The Comedians; The
Video Entertainers; Success; The
Railway Carriage Game; The
Fame Game.* m. Vivien; 1 d.
Andrea, 1 s. Paul. Hobbies:
football, all sport. Address: c/o
Bernard Lee Management,
Warlingham, Surrey. Birthsign:
Sagittarius. **Favourite Place:** 'In
the middle of The Kop at
Liverpool football ground.'

BOHAY, Heidi
Actress, b. 15 Dec New Jersey.
Studied acting with Roy London,
Laura Rose, Herbert Berghof and
at Wynn Handman's Studio.
Film: *Superstititon.* TV films incl:
*The Grace Kelly Story; Thursday's
Child.* TV incl: *Hotel; The Love
Boat; Two Marriages; Buck
Rogers; Happy Days; CHiPs;
Quincy; The Devlin Connection;
Here's Boomer; Teachers Only.*
Hobbies: classical piano,
swimming, cooking, tennis,
aerobic exercise. Address: c/o
Martin Gage, The Gage Group,
9229 Sunset Boulevard, Suite
306, Los Angeles, California
90069. Birthsign: Sagittarius.
Favourite Place: 'At home
with my family because I love
them so much.'

BOLAM, James
Actor, b. 16 June 1938
Sunderland. Stage debut in 1959
in *The Kitchen* at Royal Court
Theatre, London. Numerous
theatre appearances incl: *Butley;
Time and Time Again; Macbeth;
Treats; King Lear; A Night In Old
Peking; Run For Your Wife.* Films
incl: *A Kind Of Loving; Half A
Sixpence.* TV incl: *The Likely
Lads* (1965–69); *Whatever
Happened To The Likely Lads?*
(1973); *When The Boat Comes In;
Only When I Laugh; The
Beiderbecke Affair.* m. actress Sue
Jameson, 1 d. Lucy. Hobby:
horses. Address: c/o Barry
Burnett, London. Birthsign:
Gemini.

BORGNINE, Ernest
Actor, b. 24 Jan 1917 Hamden,
Connecticut. Trained at the
Randall School of Dramatic Art
and then with the Barter Theater.
Has appeared in over 40 films
incl: *The Wild Bunch; The
Poseidon Adventure; From Here To
Eternity; Bad Day at Black Rock;
Marty* (Best Actor Academy
Award, Cannes Film Festival Best
Actor Award, New York Film
Critics' Award, National Board
of Review Award, 1961). TV
incl: *McHale's Navy; Airwolf.* m.
Tovah; 1 d. Nancy. Hobby:
stamp collecting. Address: c/o
CC Oscard Agency, 19 West
44nd St, New York City, NY
10036. Birthsign: Aquarius.

BOSSON, Barbara
Actress, b. 1 Nov Bellvernon,
Pennsylvania. Attended drama
school at Carnegie-Mellon
University. Trained at the
Pittsburgh Playhouse, with The
Committee in San Francisco and
with Herbert Berghoff. Was
nominated four times for the
Emmy for her role as Fay Furillo
in *Hill Street Blues*. Films incl:
Bullitt; *Capricorn One*; *The Last
Starfighter*. TV films incl: *The
Impatient Heart*; *Calendar Girl
Murders*. TV appearances incl:
Richie Brockelman; *Sunshine*;
McMillan And Wife; *Owen
Marshall*. m. Steven Bocho,
executive producer of *Hill Street
Blues*; 1 s. Jesse John, 1 d. Melissa.
Hobbies: writing, has sold three
TV scripts, but family is most
important. Address: c/o Writers
and Artists Agency, 11726 San
Vicente Blvd, Suite 300, Los
Angeles, California 90049.
Birthsign: Scorpio. **Favourite
Place:** 'We love our home.'

BOUGH, Frank
Sports commentator/presenter, b.
15 Jan 1933 Fenton, Stoke-on-
Trent. After Oxford University,
started with ICI. Then started TV
career with BBC Newcastle
1962 on *Look North* news
magazine; BBC London 1964 in
Sportsview. Presenter BBC's
Grandstand since 1970; also
Olympic Games, World Cups,
Commonwealth Games.
Presenter *Nationwide* from 1972
until he left to co-present
Breakfast Time at its launch in
1983. Richard Dimbleby
(BAFTA) Award 1977. m.
Nesta; 3 s. David, Stephen,
Andrew. Hobbies: music,
gardening, the river. Address: c/o
BBC TV, London. Birthsign:
Capricorn.

BOULAYE, Patti
Singer/actress, b. 3 May Nigeria.
Trained at the London School of
Dramatic Art. Numerous theatre,
film, cabaret and TV appearances
and recordings. m. Stephen
Komlosy; 1 d. Emma, 1 s.
Sebastian. Hobbies: drawing,
dress designing, cooking.
Address: c/o Dorland House,
London. Birthsign: Taurus.
Favourite Place: 'Home—
security provided by my husband
and children.'

BOVELL, Brian
Actor, b. 26 Oct 1959 London.
Started with the Royal Court
Youth Theatre Group. Theatre
incl: *Romeo And Juliet*; *One Fine
Day*; *Sink Or Swim*; *Strange
Fruit*; at the National Theatre
Measure For Measure, *The
Caretaker*, *Bit Of Business* and *Up
For None*; *Macbeth*. Awarded
Best Supporting Actor for *Where
There Is Darkness* by British
Theatre Assoc. Films incl:
Babylon; *Burning An Illusion*; *Up
High*; *Real Life*. TV incl: *Best Of
British*; *The Gentle Touch*;
Strangers; *Bulman*; *The Hard
Word*; *Driving Ambition*; *Miracles
Take Longer*. Hobbies:
swimming, reading, films, old
comics, fencing. Address: c/o
Hope & Lyne, London.
Birthsign: Scorpio. **Favourite
Place:** 'The countryside, because
it makes me feel at one with
nature.'

BOWEN, Jim
Comedian/entertainer, b. 20 Aug 1937 Heswall, Cheshire. Originally a teacher in Lancs and a deputy head. An entertainer in his spare time, discovered by *The Comedians*, and chose to turn professional, working in clubs and cabaret. TV incl: *Starburst*; *Up For The Cup*; *Take Two*; presenter of *Bullseye* since 1981; *Muck And Brass*. m. Phyllis; 1 d. Susan, 1 s. Peter. Hobbies: horses, boating, tennis, running a pub. Address: c/o George Bartram Enterprises, Birmingham. Birthsign: Leo. **Favourite Place:** 'My home is a converted railway station and my favourite view is from the platform as the Flying Scotsman goes past.'

BOWLES, Peter
Actor, b. 16 Oct 1936 London. Trained at RADA and professional actor at 18. At Old Vic for a year then rep. Break in *Happy Haven* at Bristol Old Vic, repeated London 1960. Theatre incl: *Absent Friends*; *Dirty Linen*; *Born In the Gardens*. Films incl: *The Informer*; *Live Now, Pay Later*; *The Yellow Rolls Royce*; *Blow Up*. TV incl: *The Avengers*; *The Saint*; *The Prisoner*; *Isadora*; *A Thinking Man As Hero*; *Napoleon And Love*; *The Survivors*; *Churchill's People*; *Only On Sunday*; *The Crezz*; *Vice Versa*; *Rumpole Of The Bailey*; *To the Manor Born*; *Only When I Laugh*; *The Bounder*; *Experiences Of An Irish RM*; creator and star of *Lytton's Diary*. m. Susan; 1 d. Sasha, 2 s. Guy, Adam. Hobby: modern British art. Address: c/o Leading Arists, London. Birthsign: Libra. **Favourite Place:** 'A breakfast table—any time, any place.'

BOXLEITNER, Bruce
Actor, b. 12 May 1950 Elgin, Illinois. Films incl: *Tron*; *The Baltimore Bullet*. TV incl: *The Mary Tyler Moore Show*; *Gunsmoke*; *How The West Was Won*; *Police Woman*; *Baretta*; *Bring 'Em Back Alive*; *Scarecrow And Mrs King*; *The Gambler*; *East Of Eden*; *The Last Convertible*. m. Kathryn Holcomb; 1 s. Sam. Hobbies: tennis, jogging, keeping fit. Address: c/o Rogers & Cowan, 9665 Wilshire Blvd, Suite 200, Beverly Hills, Los Angeles, California 90212. Birthsign: Taurus. **Favourite Place:** 'Walking in the mountains.'

BOYD, Tommy
Broadcaster/journalist/ entertainer, b. 14 Dec 1952 London. Joined BBC Radio Brighton as producer/presenter 1971–73 and was also a stand-up comic from 1972–73 at Butlins Bognor Regis. Dolphin trainer at Brighton Dolphinarium 1974–75. Joined LBC in London as producer of *AM* show 1975–76. Independent Radio Personality of the Year 1981. TV incl: *Magpie*, presenter 1977–80; *Jigsaw*; *Puzzle Trail*; *What's Happening* as presenter/writer; *The Saturday Show*; *Starship*; *Wide Awake Club*. Hobbies: playing football, vegetarian food, studying whales and dolphins. Address: c/o John Mahoney, London. Birthsign: Sagittarius. **Favourite Place:** 'Swimming with wild dolphins and whales—in any ocean.'

39

BOYLE, Katie
TV and radio presenter and panellist/*TV Times* 'Dear Katie' columnist, b. 29 May 1926 Florence, Italy. Live TV and radio during the Fifties. Introduced four Eurovision Song Contests between 1961 and 1974. m. Sir Peter Saunders. Hobbies: animal welfare, particularly dogs, driving and road safety, embroidery, jigsaw puzzles, swimming, walking, talking, and listening. Address: c/o *TV Times* Magazine, London. Birthsign: Gemini. **Favourite Place:** 'Any unspoilt beach on a tropical island. Can't name one in particular as I'm always moving on to avoid the "fashionable set".'

BRADY, Terence
Playwright/actor, b. 13 March 1939. Probably best known as a writer with his wife. On stage in *Beyond The Fringe*, *In The Picture* and *Present From The Corporation*. Films incl: *Baby Love*; *Foreign Exchange*. Scripts for TV incl: *Upstairs, Downstairs*; *No, Honestly*; *Yes, Honestly*; *Thomas And Sarah*; *Plays Of Marriage*; *Take Three Girls*; *Pig In The Middle*; *Nanny*. He played Barty in *Pig In The Middle* and also in *First Impressions*; *Broad And Narrow*; *Boy Meets Girl*; *Love Story*; *Three Resounding Tinkles*. m. Charlotte Bingham; 1 d. Candida, 1 s. Matthew. Hobbies: music (piano), painting, riding and breeding horses, racing, gardening , playing the drums, avoiding parties. Address: c/o AD Peters, London. Birthsign: Pisces. **Favourite Place:** 'On top of my horse coming over the last fence cross country clear.'

BRAGG, Melvyn
Writer/presenter/editor, b. 6 Oct 1939 Carlisle, Cumbria. Went to Oxford; Fellow of the Royal Society of Literature. BBC Radio/TV producer; *Monitor* 1962–65; presenter *2nd House* 1973–77; *Read All About It* 1976–77; editor of *The South Bank Show* since 1978. Plays written incl: *Mardi Gras*; *The Hired Man*; *Orion*. Film scripts incl: *Isadora*; *Jesus Christ Superstar* (with Ken Russell); *Clouds Of Glory*. Books incl: *A Place In England*; *The Nerve*; *Josh Lawton*; *The Silken Net*; *Speak For England*; *A Christmas Child*; *Autumn Manoeuvres*; *Kingdom Come*; *Laurence Olivier*. m. (1st) Marie-Elisabeth (dec.), (2nd) Catherine; 2 d. Marie Elsa (from 1st m.), Alice Mary, 1 s. Tom (both from 2nd m.). Hobbies: walking, books. Address: c/o LWT, London. Birthsign: Libra. **Favourite Place:** Central Lake District.

BRANDRETH, Gyles
Writer/presenter, b. 8 March 1948 Wuppertal, W Germany. While at Oxford presented *Child Of The Sixties*. Is the scriptwriter for *Dear Ladies* with Hinge and Bracket. TV incl: *Opportunity Knocks*; *Call My Bluff*; *Puzzle Party*; *Chatterbox*; *Memories*; *The Time Of Your Life*; *Connections*; *Babble*; *Tell The Truth*; *Countdown*; *All Star Secrets*; *The Railway Carriage Game*; *Good Morning Britain*. Author of the world's shortest poem and over 50 children's books. Has written biographies of Sir John Gielgud, Dan Leno and Harry Houdini; *The Complete Husband*; *The Complete Home Entertainer*; *Great Theatrical Disasters*; *Great Sexual Disasters*. m. Michele Brown; 1 s. Benet, 2 d. Saethryd, Aphra. Hobby: former European Monopoly champion. Address: c/o International Artistes, London. Birthsign: Pisces. **Favourite Place:** home.

BRETT, Jeremy

Actor, b. 3 Nov 1938 Berkswell, nr Coventry. Trained at Central School of Speech and Drama and began acting career at the Library Theatre, Manchester. Joined Old Vic in London 1956. Has appeared in London, America and Canada and was with the National Theatre at the Old Vic 1967. Played Hamlet at Royal Court Theatre in London 1961.

Other theatre incl: *Hedda Gabler*; *A Voyage Round My Father*; *Traveller Without Baggage*; *Rosmersholm*; *Design For Living*; *The Way Of The World*. TV incl: *Rebecca*; *The Good Soldier*; *The Last Visitor*; *William Pitt The Younger*; *Sherlock Homes*. Hobbies: archery, riding. Address: c/o William Morris Agency, London. Birthsign: Scorpio. **Favourite Place:** Alice's Restaurant, Malibu, California.

BRIERLEY, Tim

Actor, b. 29 July 1951 Cheshire. Trained in the drama department at university. Joined the Royal

Shakespeare Company 1976. Rep at Watford, Birmingham, Leeds and Derby. TV incl: *By The Sword Divided*; *Ladykillers*; *Young Sherlock*; *Disraeli*; *The Dancing Years*; *Keats*; *Mayhury*; *The Gentle Touch*; *Partners In Crime*; *Crown Court*; *A Comedy Of Errors*; *All The World's A Stage*; *The Practice*. m. Carole Hancock; 1 d. Charlotte, 1 s. Adam. Hobbies: music, children, Oxford United. Address: c/o Hope & Lyne, London. Birthsign: Leo.

BRIERS, Richard

Actor, b. 14 Jan 1934 Merton, Surrey. Started as a clerk then went to RADA 1954–56. Rep at Liverpool, Leatherhead, Coventry. London debut 1959. Theatre incl: *Present Laughter*; *Arsenic And Old Lace*; *Cat Among The Pigeons*; *Butley*; *Absurd Person Singular*; *Absent Friends*; *The Wild Duck*; *Middle-Age Spread*; *Arms And The Man*; *Run For Your Wife*; *Why Me?* Films

incl: *Fathom*; *All The Way Up*. Radio incl: *Doctor In The House*. TV incl: *Brothers In Law*; *Marriage Lines*; Ben Travers farces; *Norman Conquests*; *The Good Life*; *The Other One*; *Goodbye Mr Kent*; *PQ17*; *Ever Decreasing Circles*. m. actress Ann Davies, 2 d. Katy, Lucy. Hobby: theatre history. Address: c/o International Famous Agency, London. Birthsign: Capricorn. **Favourite Place:** 'The Atlantic Ocean from Botallack, Cornwall.'

BRIGGS, Johnny

Actor, b. 5 Sept 1935 London. Was a pupil at Italia Conti Stage School 1947–53. Films incl: *Cosh Boy*; *Hue And Cry*; *Perfect Friday*; *Best Pair Of Legs In The Business*; *HMS Defiant*; *Sink The Bismarck*; *The Last Escape*. TV incl: *No Hiding Place*; *The Young Generation*; *The Saint*; *The*

Avengers; *Crime Of Passion*; *Danger Man*; *The Persuaders*; *Softly, Softly*; Mike Baldwin in *Coronation Street* and many more TV appearances too numerous to mention. Male TV Personality of the Year 1983. m. (1st) Carole, (2nd) Christine; 1 s. Mark, 1 d. Karen (from 1st m.), 2 d. Jennylou, Stephanie, 1 s. Michael (from 2nd m.). Hobbies: golf, squash, snooker. Address: c/o Marina Martin Management, London. Birthsign: Virgo.

BRISTOW, Eric
Professional dart player, b. 25 April 1957 Stoke Newington, London. Says he trained on 'the streets'. Five times World Master 1977, 79, 81, 83, 84. Four times World Champion 1980, 81, 84, 85. Ranked No 1 in the world since 1979. Hobbies: playing snooker and watching TV sport. Address: c/o Dick Allix, MHE Ltd, PO Box 3, Hessle, North Humberside HU13 9LF. Birthsign: Taurus. **Favourite** **Place:** 'Running my own pub, The Crafty Cockney, in Burslem, Stoke-on-Trent.'

BRITTON, Tony
Actor/company director, b. 9 June 1924 Birmingham. After war service in army, rep in Manchester, two seasons at Stratford-upon-Avon, Old Vic, toured 1964–66 in *My Fair Lady*. Theatre incl: *Move Over Mrs Markham*; *No, No, Nanette*; *The Dame Of Sark*; *My Fair Lady* (London and tour), 1978–82. Films incl: *Sunday, Bloody Sunday*; *There's A Girl In My Soup*; *The Day Of The Jackal*. TV Incl: *Romeo And Juliet*; *The Six Proud Walkers*; *Melissa*; *The Nearly Man*; *Father, Dear Father*; *Robin's Nest*; *Strangers And Brothers*; *Don't Wait Up*. m. (1st) Ruth (dis.), (2nd) Danish sculptress Eve Birkefeldt; 2 d. Cherry, Fern (from 1st m.), 1 s. Jasper (from 2nd m.). Hobbies: golf, cricket, gardening, photography, wine, food, flying. Address: c/o ICM, London. Birthsign: Gemini. **Favourite Place:** Helford River, Cornwall.

BROLIN, James
Actor. Made film debut in *Take Her She's Mine*, then *Goodbye Charlie*. Other films incl: *Pickup On South Street*; *Dear Brigitte*; *Von Ryan's Express*; *Morituri*; *Our Man Flint*; *Fantastic Voyage*; *Skyjacked*; *Westworld*; *The Amityville Horror*; *High Risk*; *Capricorn One*; *The Car*; *The Night Of The Juggler*; *Gable And Lombard*. TV incl: *Bus Stop*; *The Monroes*; *Twelve O'Clock High*; *Marcus Welby, MD*; *A Short* *Walk To Daylight*; *Trapped*; *White Water Rebels*; *Cowboy*; *Hotel*. Emmy award in 1970 for his portrayal of Dr Steve Kiley in *Marcus Welby, MD*. m. (sep.); 1 s. Josh, 1 d. Jess. Hobbies: designing homes and offices, flying, motor sports, sailing, water-skiing, hiking and fishing, restaurant development, horses, reading, jazz. Address: c/o Jeff Wald, 23844 Malibu Road, Malibu, California 90265.

BROOKE-TAYLOR, Tim
Actor/writer, b. 17 July 1940 Buxton, Derbyshire. Has a law degree but started career in Cambridge Footlights Revue. Then came the radio show *I'm Sorry I'll Read That Again*. Theatre incl: *The Unvarnished Truth*. Films incl: *Twelve Plus One*; *The Statue*. Radio incl: *I'm Sorry I Haven't A Clue*. TV incl: *At Last The 1948 Show*; *Marty*; *Broaden Your Mind*; *The Goodies*; *Hello Cheeky* (and radio); *The* *Rough With The Smooth*; *Me And My Girl*; *Assaulted Nuts*; as presenter in *Does The Team Think?*, *Loose Ends* and *The Fame Game*. Records incl: *Funky Gibbon*; *The New Goodies* LP. m. Christine; 2 s. Ben, Edward. Hobbies: travel, skiing, golf, watching sport, films and TV. Address: c/o Jill Foster Ltd, London. Birthsign: Cancer. **Favourite Place:** 'The baseball ground when Derby County have won a cup match.'

BROOKS, Ray
Actor, b. 20 April 1939 Brighton, Sussex. Started in rep incl Nottingham in 1957. Theatre incl: *Backbone*. Films incl: *HMS Defiant*; *Play It Cool*; *Some People*; *The Knack*; *The Last Grenade*. TV incl: *Taxi*; *Cathy Come Home*; *The Raging Moon*; *That Woman Is Wrecking Our Marriage*; *Death Of An Expert Witness*; *Office Romances*; *Pennywise* (TVS); *Big Deal*. m. Sadie; 1 d. Emma, 2 s. William, Tom. Hobbies: supporting Fulham FC, writing songs. Address: c/o Marmont Management, London. Birthsign: Aries.

BROWN, Duggie
Actor/comedian, b. 7 Aug 1940 Rotherham, Yorks. One of the highest paid club and cabaret performers. Played guitar with The Four Imps for 12 years and appeared on the *Six-Five Special*. Chosen for *The Good Old Days* and *The Comedians*. Theatre incl: *The Price Of Coal*. Light entertainment on TV incl: *The Wheeltappers And Shunters Social Club*; *3-2-1*; *Square One*; *Pro-Celebrity Snooker*. Part in film *Kes* led to acting roles on TV incl: *The House That Jack Built*; *Days Of Hope*; *The Price Of Coal*; *Leeds United*; *Say Goodnight To Grandma*; *Crown Court*; *The Combination*, *The Enigma Files*, *The Mersey Pirates*; *Take My Wife*; *The Glamour Girls*; *The Cuckoo Waltz*; *The Zodiac Game*. m. Jacqueline. Hobbies: golf, darts, snooker. Address: c/o Richard Stone, London. Birthsign: Leo. **Favourite Place:** 'The patio in my garden.'

BROWN, Faith
Singer/impressionist, b. 28 May 1944 Liverpool. Entered show business through local talent shows and started singing with a Liverpool-based band at 16, before forming a group with three of her four brothers. Went solo and has toured world-wide. TV incl: *Who Do You Do?*; *For My Next Trick*; *Celebrity Squares*; *The Faith Brown Awards*; *Blankety Blank*; *The Faith Brown Chat Show*; *Golden Gala*; *Starburst*; many guest appearances. Speciality Act of the Year 1980, *TVTimes* Award for Funniest Woman on TV 1980; COPS (Californian Organisation of Police and Sheriffs) Award 1981 for services to charities in America. m. Len Wady; 1 d. Danielle. Hobbies: fishing, cooking. Address: c/o Tony Lewis Entertainments, London. Birthsign: Gemini. **Favourite Place:** 'The Seychelles, peace and quiet, lots of sun and sea food.'

BROWN, Janet
Comedienne, b. Glasgow. Began doing impressions while still a teenager. After serving with the ATS during the war, went to London and worked on a radio show in Scarborough, in which she met her husband. More radio and TV, followed by a stage play with Alastair Sim, *Mr Gillie*. TV incl: *Rainbow Room*; *Where Shall We Go?*; *Friends And Neighbours*; *Who Do You Do?*; *Mike Yarwood In Persons*; *Janet And Co* (1981 and 1982). m. comedian Peter Butterworth (dec.); 1 d. Emma, 1 s. Tyler. Hobbies: collecting antiques, cooking, sitting in the sun by the sea. Address: c/o Bernard Lee Management, Caterham, Surrey. **Favourite Place:** 'In my own cottage in the country.'

BROWN, Joe

Entertainer/musician, b. 13 May 1941 Swarby, Lincs. Brought up in London and a self-taught guitarist, he was spotted by Jack Good to appear in *Boy Meets Girls* on TV. Has since made hit records, toured, appeared in cabaret and stage shows such as *Charley Girl*; *Sleuth*; *Pump Boys And Dinettes*; and pantomimes. TV incl: *Set 'Em Up, Joe*; the revival of *Oh Boy!*; *Square One*; and many guest appearances. His hit records incl: *A Picture Of You*; *It Only Took A Minute*; *That's What Love Will Do*; *All Things Bright And Beautiful* (with his wife). m. Vicki; 1 d. Samantha, 1 s. Peter. Hobbies: snooker, skin-diving, wind-skiing, windsurfing. Address: c/o Derek Block, London. Birthsign: Taurus. **Favourite Place:** 'I'm in love with the view from my house at the moment—it's in the Hambleden Valley and all I can see is fields!'

BRUCE SCOTT, Jean

Actress, b. 25 Feb Monterrey. Started as a model and has appeared on TV in *Days Of Our Lives*; *Magnum PI*; *St Elsewhere*; *Airwolf*. Hobbies: flute, piano, needlepoint, embroidery, jogging. Address: c/o Freeman & Sutton, San Fernando Valley. Birthsign: Pisces. **Favourite Place:** London.

BRUNSON, Michael

Journalist, b. 12 Aug 1940 Norwich, Norfolk. After Queen's College, Oxford worked for BBC Radio and TV; joined ITN 1968. US Correspondent 1973–77 covering Watergate, US Presidential election. Has since been reporter/newscaster and has covered both of Mrs Thatcher's election campaigns and has watched her at almost every summit since. m. Susan; 2 s. Jonathan, Robin. Hobby: 'Being in England (after so much travelling) and a little gardening.' Address: c/o ITN, London. Birthsign: Leo. **Favourite Place:** 'My cottage in north Norfolk, where it is as near heaven as you'll get on this earth!'

BRYAN, Dora

Actress, b. 7 Feb 1924 Southport. Stage debut as a child in pantomime 1935. Numerous theatre appearances, the most recent incl: *The Merry Wives Of Windsor*; *She Stoops To Conquer*. Films incl: *The Blue Lamp*; *A Taste Of Honey*; *The Great St Trinian's Train Robbery*. Most recent TV incl: *Both Ends Meet*; *Triangles*; *Foxy Lady*; *Dora*; *Rookery Nook*. m. Bill Lawton; 1 d. Georgina, 2 s. Daniel, William (both adopted). Address: c/o James Sharkey Assocs, London. Birthsign: Aquarius.

BUCKLEY, Bill
TV presenter/reporter/
songwriter/musician, b. 8 Jan
1959 Burton-on-Trent. Trained
as a journalist and former pub/
club singer/pianist. Three years as
presenter/reporter on *That's Life!*
Topical songwriter/performer;
reporter and regional presenter
on BBC's *Breakfast Time*. Former
film reporter on BBC's *South East
At Six*. Theatre incl: *Joseph And
The Amazing Technicolour
Dreamcoat*. TV incl: *Children In
Need Telethon*; *Call My Bluff*.
Hobbies: food, theatre- and
cinema-going, listening to and
creating music. Address: c/o
Jimmy Daisley Assocs, London.
Birthsign: Capricorn. **Favourite
Place:** 'The main high street in
Woodstock, Oxfordshire because
it's so beautiful, unspoilt and
"English".'

BULLOCH, Jeremy
Actor, b. 16 Feb 1945 Market
Harborough, Leics. Trained at the
Corona Academy stage school
1957–62. Films incl: *The Virgin
And The Gypsy*; *For Your Eyes
Only*; *Octopussy*; *Summer
Holiday*; *The Spy Who Loved Me*;
Mary Queen Of Scots. Many TV
plays and series incl: three years in
soap opera *The Newcomers*; *Billy
Bunter*; *The Professionals*; *George
And Mildred*; *Agony*. m. Maureen
Patricia; 3 s. Christian, Jamie,
Robbie. Hobbies: football,
cricket. Address: c/o Barry
Brown, London. Birthsign:
Aquarius. **Favourite Place:**
'The Far East, the most exotic
place to visit, with its culture and
glorious food.'

BURDIS, Ray
Actor, b. 23 Aug 1958 London.
Trained at the Anna Scher
Theatre and has been a member
of that theatre since July 1970.
TV incl: most recently, *Three Up,
Two Down*. Other TV incl:
Dream Stuffing; *Now And Then*;
Minder; *The Professionals*; *West*;
The Gentle Touch; *Going Out*;
Triangle; *Ain't Many Angels*;
Mary's Wife. m. Jackie. Hobby:
music. Address: c/o Anna Scher
Theatre Management, London.
Birthsign: Leo/Virgo. **Favourite
Place:** Mojácar, Southern Spain,
'It's a nice place to be.'

BURKE, Alfred
Actor, b. 28 Jan 1918 Peckham,
London. Trained at RADA and
started career at the Barn Theatre,
Shere, Surrey 1939. Rep at
Birmingham, Leeds and
Manchester. First West End
appearance in *Desire Caught By
The Tail*; also in *Sailor Beware*.
Films incl: *The Angry Silence*;
Yangste Incident; *Interpol*; *Bitter
Victory*; *The House In Garibaldi
Street*; *One Day In The Life of
Ivan Denisovich*; *John Paul II*;
Kim. Was Frank Marker in TV's
Public Eye. Also in *The Exiles*;
The Brontës; *The Tip*; *Treasure
Island*; *Enemy At The Door*; *Mary
Blandy*; *The Rod Of Iron*; *No 10*;
The Glory Boys. m. Barbara,
former stage manager; two sets of
twins, Jacob and Harriet, Kelly
and Louisa. Hobbies: football,
music, historic houses. Address:
c/o Joy Jameson, London.
Birthsign: Pisces. **Favourite
Place:** Munich Opera House.

BURKE, James

Writer/broadcaster, b. 22 Dec 1936 Londonderry, Northern Ireland. Has been involved in television documentary work since 1965. TV incl: *World In Action*; *Tomorrow's World*; chief commentator for the Apollo launches, 1967–72; *The Burke Special*; (RTS Gold and Silver Medals); *Connections*; *The Real Thing*; *The Day The Universe Changed*. Books: *Connections*; *The Day The Universe Changed*. m. Madeline. Hobby: classical guitar. Address: c/o Jonathan Clowes, London. Birthsign: Sagittarius.

BURNET, Sir Alastair

Newscaster, b. 12 July 1928 Sheffield. Worked on *The Glasgow Herald* and *The Economist* before joining ITN in 1963 as political editor. TV incl: *News At Ten*; *News At 5.45*; *TV Eye*; and with the BBC from 1972–74, *Panorama*. Anchorman for major programmes incl: Apollo space missions, general elections, budgets, the Royal wedding, the visit of Pope John Paul II to Britain. Three-times winner of the Richard Dimbleby Award; Royal Television Society Judges Prize, 1982; Political Broadcaster of the Year, 1970. Editor of *The Economist*, 1965–74; and of the *Daily Express*, 1974–76. ITN board member and independent national director of *The Times*. m. Maureen Sinclair. Address: c/o ITN, London. Birthsign: Cancer.

BURNS, Gordon

TV producer/presenter (freelance), b. 10 June 1942 Belfast. Trained in newspaper journalism and radio on *East Antrim Times*, *Belfast Telegraph* and BBC London. TV incl: reporter, *World In Action*; commentator on political party conferences; reporter/presenter *Reports Politics*; presenter *Granada 500*; *The Gordon Burns Hour*; presenter *UTV Reports* (1969–73); sports editor UTV (1967–73); *Granada Reports* presenter; presenter *The Krypton Factor*. m. Sheelagh; 1 s. Tristrun, 1 d. Anna. Hobbies: Liverpool Football Club, Irish politics. Address: c/o David Anthony Promotions, Warrington. Birthsign: Gemini. **Favourite Place:** 'A window seat upstairs on a British Airways jumbo jet en route to Sydney, Australia.'

BURTON, Amanda

Actress, b. 10 Oct 1956 Derry. Studied acting at the School of Theatre, Manchester Polytechnic. Theatre incl: *Mother Goose*; *She Stoops To Conquer*; *Good Morning Bill*; *Joking Apart*; *Henry V*; *King Lear*; *Much Ado About Nothing*; *Jack And The Beanstalk*. Plays Heather Haversham in C4's *Brookside*. Other TV incl: *Mersey Pirate*; *My Father's House*; *Thomas De Quincy*; *The Effective Manager* (BBC Open University). Hobbies: riding, collecting watches, avoiding housework, everything 'out of doors'. Address: c/o Brookside Productions, Liverpool. Birthsign: Libra. **Favourite Place:** 'I love Donegal in Ireland for its beautiful beaches, with no one on them and those great wild seas.'

BURTON, Humphrey

Presenter/producer/executive, b. 25 March 1931 Trowbridge, Wilts. Began as radio effects boy with BBC Radio, then studio manager and music producer BBC TV 1958–67. Joined LWT as founder member. Edited and introduced *Aquarius* 1970–75 then BBC Head of Music and Arts and introduced *Omnibus*. Other TV incl: *In Performance*; *Opera Month*; *Young Musician Of The Year*. 1983 Guest Director Hollywood Bowl, Los Angeles. Since 1976 Chairman TV Music Group of European Broadcasting Union. m. (1st) Gretel (dis.), (2nd) Christina, photographer; 2 d. Clare (from 1st m.), Helena (from 2nd m.), 2 s. Matthew (from 1st m.), Lukas (from 2nd m.). Hobbies: tennis, ping pong, playing duets, travel. Address: c/o BBC TV, London. Birthsign: Aries. **Favourite Place:** Venice.

BYGRAVES, Max, OBE

Entertainer, b. 16 Oct 1922 Rotherhithe, London. Won a talent contest at 13. West End debut at London Palladium 1949 after service in RAF. Films incl: *Charlie Moon*; *A Cry From The Streets*; *Spare The Rod*. Radio incl: *Educating Archie*. TV incl: *Max Bygraves*; *Max*; *Singalongamax*; *Max Rolls On*; *Side By Side*. Has made more Royal Variety Performances than any other artist. Has three platinum, 29 gold and 15 silver discs, all from his *Singalong* LPs. Books: *I Wanna Tell You A Story* (autobiog); *The Milkman's On His Way* (novel). m. Gladys (Blossom); 2 d. Christine, Maxine, 1 s. Anthony. Hobbies: golf, vintage cars, reading, travel. Address: c/o Jennifer Maffini, London. Birthsign: Libra. **Favourite Place:** 'My home in Bournemouth—it's what I worked for—this is it.'

BYRNE, Peter

Actor/director, b. 29 Jan 1928 London. Trained at Italia Conti Stage School. Director Productions Bournemouth Theatre Co 1965–66. Theatre incl: *There's A Girl In My Soup*; *Underground*; *There's A Small Hotel*; *Move Over Mrs Markham* (Toronto); *Run For Your Wife*; *Sleuth*; *The Ghost Train*; *The Unexpected Guest* and *Murder Is Announced* (Canada); *Murder Among Friends* (tour). Films incl: *Large Rope*; *Reach For The Sky*; *Carry On Cabby*. TV incl: *Dixon Of Dock Green*; *Mutiny At Spithead*; *The New Canadians*; *Whodunnit?*; *Friday Live*; *What's Ahead*; *Looks Familiar*; *Blake's Seven*. m. Renée Helen. Hobbies: squash, swimming, riding, golf, travel. Address: c/o Bill McLean, London. Birthsign: Aquarius. **Favourite Place:** 'Papua New Guinea. Swam with dolphins, witnessed turtles hatching, found peace.'

BYRON, Kathleen

Actress, b. 11 Jan 1923 London. Trained at the Old Vic Theatre School. After the war came her acclaimed part of a mad nun in the film *Black Narcissus*. Other films incl: *Small Back Room*; *Prelude To Fame*; *Madness Of The Heart*; *The Elephant Man*; *From A Far Country*. TV incl: *Emergency Ward 10*; *The Avengers*; *Who Is Sylvia?*; *Countercrime*; *That Woman Is Wrecking Our Marriage*; *Emmerdale Farm*; *The Golden Bowl*; *Portrait Of A Lady*; *Moonstone*; *Heidi*; *Tales Of The Supernatural*; *The Professionals*; *Minder*; *General Hospital*; *Hedda Gabler*; *Together*; *Unity*; *Nancy Astor*; *Angels*; *Dearly Beloved*. m. writer Alaric Jacob; 1 d. Harriet, 1 s. Jasper. Hobbies: pottery, gardening. Address: c/o Rolf Kruger, London. Birthsign: Capricorn. **Favourite Place:** 'My Mexican dining room mural painted by Harriet.'

CADELL, Simon

Actor, b. 19 July 1950 London. Trained at Bristol Old Vic Theatre School, then joined the company itself and has since appeared in many productions. TV incl: *Hadleigh*; *Hine*; *Love Story*; *A Man From Haven*; *Love School*; *Glittering Prizes*; *Wings*; *She Fell Among Thieves*; *Enemy At The Door*; *Edward And Mrs Simpson*; *Hi-De-Hi!*; *Blott On The Landscape*. Hobby: travel. Address: c/o MLR, London.

Birthsign: Cancer. **Favourite Place:** Southern France, 'Because of the weather, the people, and the food and wine.'

CAINE, Marti

Singer/actress/entertainer/ comedienne, b. 26 Jan Sheffield. A former model, she entered showbusiness at the age of 19 as a singer and then compère. Since appearing on and winning TV's *New Faces*, she has worked extensively in cabaret, concerts and theatre seasons throughout Britain and in Australia, New Zealand and America. Stage incl: *Funny Girl*. Films incl: *Birds Of Paradise*. TV incl: *This Is Your Life*; *Des O'Connor Tonight*; *Parkinson*; *The Marti Caine Show*; *Marti Caine*; *Hilary*. m. (1st) Malcolm Stringer (dis.); (2nd) Ken Ives; 2 s. Lee, Max (both from 1st m.). Hobby: running her Sherbets health, fitness and dance centres. Address: c/o Johnnie Peller, Broomhill, Sheffield. Birthsign: Aquarius.

CALDICOT, Richard

Actor, b. 7 Oct 1908 London. Trained at RADA and made his first professional appearance in Huddersfield in 1928. Stage incl: *No Sex Please, We're British*; *My Fair Lady*; *Me And My Girl*. Films incl: *The Spy Who Came In From The Cold*. On TV he has made numerous appearances, including plays and series. Recent TV incl: *Let There Be Love*; *The Other Side Of Me*; *Crown Court*; *Fawlty Towers*; *Coronation Street*; *Minder*; *The Pickwick Papers*; *Bulman*. m. Judith; 1 s. Jonathan. Hobbies: golf, stamps. Address: c/o Essanay, London. Birthsign: Libra. **Favourite Place:** 'In the garden of my cottage in Sussex. It's quiet and peaceful.'

CALLOW, Simon

Actor, b. 15 June 1949 London. Trained at The Drama Centre before rep. West End performances incl: *Total Eclipse*; *Beastly Beatitudes Of Balthazar B*; *The Relapse*; *On The Spot*. At the National Theatre he has been in *As You Like It*; *Galileo*; *Amadeus*; *Sisterly Feelings*. He went on to appear in the film of *Amadeus*. TV incl. *Wings Of Song*; *Instant Enlightenment Plus VAT*; *Man Of Destiny*; *Deadhead*; *Chance In A Million*. Hobby: spending money pointlessly. Address: c/o Marina Martin Management, London. Birthsign: Gemini. **Favourite Place:** 'Two thousand feet above Albuquerque, in a balloon, motionless. A taste of serenity.'

CAMERON, Robin
Actor, b. 29 July 1960 Stewarton, Ayrshire. After obtaining an MA at Glasgow University, he decided to become an actor, and entered the theatre with roles in *Jack And The Beanstalk*; *Romeo And Juliet*. TV incl: *Maggie*; *A Woman Calling*; *Take The High Road*. Hobbies: theatre, watching Kilmarnock Football Club. Address: c/o Freddie Young, Glasgow. Birthsign: Leo. **Favourite Place:** 'Islay—an island of breathtaking variety: sweeping sandy beaches, rugged coastline and tree-lined lochs.'

CAMPBELL, Gavin
Actor/presenter/journalist/ broadcaster, b. 17 March 1946 Letchworth, Herts. Trained as an actor at Central School of Speech and Drama in London then worked with Joan Littlewood Theatre Workshop. In British première *When One Is Somebody* (York). Season with the Royal Shakespeare Company. Acted on TV incl: *Play For Tomorrow*; *Department S*; *Vendetta*; *Armchair Theatre*. With BBC Radio as newsreader/announcer, then producer until joined BBC TV's *That's Life!* as reporter/presenter. Also reported for *Breakfast Time*; *Nationwide*; *London Plus*; *South-East At Six*. m. Liz Hendry. Hobbies: scuba-diving, mountaineering, golf, tennis, cricket, music, travel. Address: c/o Noel Gay, London. Birthsign: Pisces. **Favourite Place:** 'Rannoch Moor, Highlands of Scotland–it's one of the last wild places in Britain.'

CAMPBELL, Joanne
Actress, b. 8 Feb 1964 Northampton. TV work has included BBC's *Parents And Teenagers* for Open University; *Night Kids*, on ITV includes *All Electric Amusement Arcade*; *Dramarama*; *Me And My Girl*. Hobbies: playing tennis, reading, jazz dance. Address: c/o Evans & Reiss, London. Birthsign: Aquarius. **Favourite Place:** 'The Serpentine, in London's Hyde Park, in a rowing boat, because it's so peaceful, especially on a warm summer's evening.'

CANNON, Tommy
Comedian, b. 27 June 1938 Oldham. Half of the comedy partnership Cannon and Ball. Former welders in a Lancashire factory by day and a singing duo, The Harper Brothers, at night. Changed names to Cannon and Ball for *Opportunity Knocks* appearance. Voted clubland's top comedy duo, they have also won The Variety Club Showbusiness Personalities of the Year and topped various magazine and newspaper popularity polls. Starred in their own LWT series, *The Cannon And Ball Show*, since 1979. Subjects of *This Is Your Life*. They have also made a film, *The Boys In Blue*. m. Margaret; 2 d. Janette, Julie. Hobbies: golf, keep-fit and most sports. Address: c/o Stuart Littlewood Assocs, Oldham. Birthsign: Cancer. **Favourite Place:** 'The view from the plane window as we land in my favourite island, Tenerife.'

CAPRON, Brian
Actor, b. 11 Feb 1949 Woodbridge, Suffolk. Trained at LAMDA, followed by over three years at Northcott Theatre, Exeter. Has also spent time at other theatres countrywide incl: Welsh National; Gardner Centre; Bush; King's Head. His many TV appearances incl: *General Hospital*; *A Place To Hide*; *The Sweeney*; *Coronation Street*; *Bergerac*; *Grange Hill*; *The Gentle Touch*; *Minder*; *Up The Elephant...*; *Full House*. m. Janette Legge; 2 d. Lucy-Jane, Ellen Louise. Hobbies: reading, writing, riding. Address: c/o Plant & Froggatt, London. Birthsign: Aquarius. **Favourite Place:** Pedn Vounder Beach, Cornwall, 'For the sheer beauty of its staggering craggy cliffs and secluded shell beach.'

CARBY, Fanny
Actress, b. 2 Feb Sutton Coldfield, Warwicks. Spent eight years at Joan Littlewood's Theatre Workshop where she was in such productions as *Ned Kelly*; *Oh! What A Lovely War*. Also in rep at Watford and Sheffield. Other stage incl: *Look After Lulu*; *The Threepenny Opera*; *Billy*; and plays at Hampstead Theatre Club and Manchester's Royal Exchange. Films incl: *The Elephant Man*; *Loophole*; *The Nightingale Saga*; *The Silent Scream*. Extensive TV incl: *The Good Companions*; *Forgive Our Foolish Ways*; *Angels*; *The Cost Of Loving*; three series with Spike Milligan; *Cockles*; *Juliet Bravo*. Hobbies: gardening, antiques. Address: c/o Brian Wheeler, London. Birthsign: Aquarius. **Favourite Place:** 'Under the oak tree at the end of my garden, looking at the spectacular view of the Chilterns.'

CAROLGEES, Bob
Comedy entertainer/puppeteer, b. 12 May 1948 Birmingham. Considerable experience in cabaret and theatre, including four Royal Gala Performances and two entertainment trips to the Falkland Islands. TV appearances incl: *Tiswas*; *3-2-1*; *Russel Harty*; *OTT*; *Saturday Stayback*; *Aspel & Co*; *Wogan*; *Blankety Blank*; *Surprise Surprise*. m. Alison; 1 child. Hobbies: windsurfing, swimming. Address: c/o Tony West Entertainments, Liverpool. Birthsign: Taurus. **Favourite Place:** 'My patio—on summer days off I spend hours relaxing there with a long drink.'

CARPENTER, Harry
Sports commentator, b. 17 Oct 1925 London. Former Fleet Street sports journalist. Presenter of BBC's weekly *Sportsnight* programme and former *Grandstand* linkman. Commentator at world heavyweight title fights since 1955 and every Olympic Games since 1956. Joined BBC full-time in 1962. Also presenter of Wimbledon Lawn Tennis; Open Golf Championships; greyhound racing; Oxford-Cambridge boat race. Author of three books on boxing. m. Phyllis; 1 s. Clive. Hobbies: golf, classical music. Address: c/o BBC TV, London. Birthsign: Libra. **Favourite Place:** 'The house in Sandwich where I look out on to the graveyard of St Clement's, which has an 11th-century Norman tower. Peace, perfect peace.'

CARROLL, Diahann

Actress/singer, b. 17 July 1935 New York. She began singing at the age of six with a church choir, and at 15 became a model. She then went on to study drama at New York's High School of Music and Art on a Metropolitan Opera Scholarship. Stage appearances incl: *House Of Flowers*; *No Strings*, for which she won a Tony Award; *Agnes Of God*. Films: *Carmen Jones*; *Paris Blues*; *Porgy And Bess*; *The Split*; *Hurry Sundown*; *Claudine*. TV: *Chance Of A Lifetime* (talent programme—won three weeks running); *Julia*; *Sister, Sister*; *Dynasty*. m. (1st) Monte Kay, (2nd) Fredde Glusman, (3rd) Robert DeLeon (dis.); 1 d. Suzanne. Hobbies: experimenting in the kitchen, designing clothes, entertaining friends. Address: c/o Agency for the Performing Arts, 9000 Sunset Blvd, Los Angeles, CA 90069. Birthsign: Cancer.

CARROTT, Jasper

Comedian, b. 14 March 1945 Birmingham. Started his career in 1969 in a club where he was host and compère. Became an all-round entertainer in clubs, universities and in concerts. Had own show, *Folk Club*, in 1972. TV debut in *The Golden Game*. Other TV Incl: *An Audience With Jasper Carrott*; *Half Hour With Jasper Carrott*; *The Unrecorded Jasper Carrott*; *Carrott Gets Rowdy*; *Carrott De Sol*; and *Carrott's Lib* which was awarded the BAFTA Award For Best TV Comic Show in 1984. His records have earned him three gold and three silver discs. m. Hazel; 3 d. Lucy, Jennifer, Hannah, 1 s. Jake. Hobbies: golf, squash. Address: c/o John and Sandra Starkey, Coventry. Birthsign: Pisces. **Favourite Place:** home.

CARSON, Frank

Comedian, b. 6 Nov 1926 Belfast. Was a TV favourite in Ireland before coming to England to try his luck in clubland. After *The Good Old Days*, *Opportunity Knocks* and *The Comedians*, he has become one of the country's leading performers and is much in demand and much televised. Other TV incl: *The Melting Pot*; *Celebrity Squares*; *The Ballyskillen Opera House*; a regular on *Tiswas*; subject of *This Is Your Life*. m. Ruth; 1 d. Majella, 2 s. Tony, Aidan. Hobbies: golf, collecting money. Address: c/o Diane Carson, Blackpool. Birthsign: Scorpio. **Favourite Place:** 'Belfast—it's home to me.'

CARTER, Lynda

Actress/singer/dancer, b. 24 July Phoenix, Arizona. Former Miss USA is best known for her portrayal of Diana Prince, *Wonder Woman*. TV film *Rita Hayworth: The Love Goddess*. Other TV: *Partners In Crime*; *Body And Soul*; *Born To Be Sold*; *The Last Song*; *The Lynda Carter Special*; *Muppets*. Besides her acting career, she is also a Fashion Consultant, Beauty and Fashion Director for Maybelline Cosmetics. m. (1st) Ron Samuels (dis.), (2nd) Robert Altman. Hobbies: tennis, riding, swimming, music, ballet, Renaissance art. Address: c/o William Morris, 151 El Camino Drive, Beverly Hills, CA 90212. Birthsign: Leo.

CARTERET, Anna

Actress, b. 11 Dec 1942 Bangalore, India. After rep, she played many leading parts at the Old Vic incl: *Oedipus*; *Love's Labours Lost*; *The Merchant Of Venice*; *Twelfth Night*; and *Saturday, Sunday, Monday* (Clarence Derwent Award). After a two-year break from the Old Vic when she did seasons at St George's Theatre and Greenwich, she returned to play in the opening production at the new National Theatre, and followed it with plays such as *As You Like It*, *Richard III*, and *Man And Superman*. TV incl: *Glittering Prizes*; *Send In The Girls*; *Juliet Bravo*. m. Christopher Thomas Morahan; 2 d. Rebecca, Harriet. Hobbies: running, gardening, music. Address: c/o Fraser & Dunlop, London. Birthsign: Sagittarius. **Favourite Place:** 'A stunning view from a clearing on the edge of the Devil's Punch Bowl called Gibbets Hill.'

CARTHEW, Anthony

ITN reporter specialising in coverage of the Royal Family, b. 2 April 1927 London. Started in journalism as a graduate trainee reporter on the *Sheffield Telegraph*. Worked on the *Daily Herald* and the *Sun* before joining the *Daily Mail* as a foreign reporter. Also wrote for the *New York Times*. Reporter of the Year 1965, 1968. Moved to ITN in 1971. BAFTA Award for coverage of the Iranian Embassy siege, 1981; RTS Award for Canberra homecoming from the Falklands, 1982; *TVTimes* Special Award for coverage of Royal Tours, 1984. m. Olwen; 2 d. Rachel, Henrietta. Hobbies: cooking, cricket. Address: c/o ITN, London. Birthsign: Aries. **Favourite Place:** 'The terrace of a fifth-floor room, Hotel Danieli, Venice, for the world's greatest waterscape.'

CASHMAN, Michael

Actor/writer, b. 17 Dec 1950 London. Started as a child actor. Theatre incl: *Oliver*; *Peter Pan*; *Passion Flower Hotel*; *Zigger Zagger*; *Before Your Very Eyes*; *Bricks 'N' Mortar*. Films incl: *The Virgin Soldiers*. TV incl: *Angels*; *Waste*; *The Sandbaggers*; *Nobody's Perfect*; *The Gentle Touch*; *The Brief*; *A Cut In The Rates*; *Seven Deadly Virtues*; *Game For A Laugh*; *Bird Of Prey*; *Dempsey And Makepeace*; *The Winning Streak*. Hobbies: walking, gardening, music, travel, photography. Address: c/o Equity, London. Birthsign: Sagittarius. **Favourite Place:** 'Victoria Park, London. Forever changing, but forever attractive.'

CASTLE, Roy

Entertainer/actor, b. 31 August 1932 Scholes, near Huddersfield. Started in amateur concert party. Turned pro in 1953. Stooge for Jimmy James and Jimmy Clitheroe. Stage incl: *Pickwick* (in America); *Singing In The Rain*. Films incl: *Doctor Who And The Daleks*; *Carry On Up The Khyber*. Radio incl: *Castle's On The Air*. TV incl: *The Roy Castle Show*; *Roy Castle Beats Time*; *Show Castle*; and 11 series as presenter of *The Record Breakers*. m. Fiona; 2 d. Julia, Antonia, 2 s. Daniel, Benjamin. Hobbies: gardening, squash, golf, charity cricket, sleep. Address: c/o London Management, London. Birthsign: Virgo. **Favourite Place:** 'A litter-free pavement.'

CAZENOVE, Christopher

Actor, b. 17 Dec 1945 Winchester. Trained at Bristol Old Vic Theatre School and rep in Leicester, Leatherhead, Windsor and Pitlochry before arriving in London's West End. Stage incl: *Darling Daisy*; *The Lionel Touch*; *The Winslow Boy*; *Joking Apart*. Films incl: *East Of Elephant Rock*; *The Girl In Blue Velvet*; *Zulu Dawn*; *The Eye Of The Needle*; *From A Far Country*; *The Letter*; *Heat And Dust*; *Mata Hari*. TV Incl: *The Regiment*; *Affairs Of The Heart*; *Jennie*; *Lady Randolph Churchill*; *The Duchess Of Duke Street*; *Jenny's War*; *Lace II*; *Cain And Abel*. m. actress Angharad Rees; 2 s. Linford, Rhys William. Address: c/o Chatto & Linnit, London. Birthsign: Sagittarius. **Favourite Place:** 'In front of a camera.'

CHADBON, Tom

Actor, b. 27 Feb 1946 Luton. Trained for the stage at RADA and followed this with work in rep. He has worked extensively in films and TV. Recent theatre includes *It's My Party*. Films incl: *Dance With A Stranger* with Rupert Everett and Miranda Richardson. TV incl. *Love Song*; *Paradise Postponed*. m. Jane; 2 d. Milly, Felicity, 2 s. Dominic, Nicholas. Hobbies: ornithology, gardening. Address: c/o Michael Ladkin, London. Birthsign: Pisces. **Favourite Place:** 'Alone on a stage when the show is going well.'

CHALMERS, Judith

Broadcaster, b. 10 Oct Manchester. Auditioned for BBC Manchester at the age of 13 and started broadcasting with her own radio programme on *Northern Children's Hour* when she was 17. Now works regularly for BBC Radio 4's *Tuesday Call*. TV incl: *Wish You Were Here ...?*; commentator for ITV's major outside broadcasts including the Derby and Royal and State Occasions. Travel Editor *Woman's Realm* magazine. In 1984 appointed to the National Consumer Council, and is Chairman of the Appeals Committee for the Women's National Cancer Control Campaign. m. Neil Durden-Smith; 1 d. Emma, 1 s. Mark. Address: c/o International Management, London. Birthsign: Libra. **Favourite Place:** 'Many, including France, Corsica, Kenya, the Nile, the Algarve, Italy, Ischia, USA.'

CHASE, Lorraine

Actress, b. 16 July 1951 South London. Former model. TV incl: *The Max Bygraves Show*; *Blankety Blank*; *Pygmalion*; *The Other 'Arf* (series); *Lame Ducks* (series). Address: c/o Peter Charlesworth, London. Birthsign: Cancer.

CHATER, David
TV reporter, b. 5 March 1953
Meopham, Kent. Initially worked
for the *Kent Messenger* and then
joined ITN as a graduate trainee.
Hobby: reading in bed. Address:
c/o ITN, London. Birthsign:
Pisces. **Favourite Place:** 'The
bedroom because I don't see
nearly enough of it.'

CHEGWIN, Keith
TV presenter, b. 17 Jan 1957
Liverpool. Attended a London
stage school for six years. Stage
shows incl: *The Good Old Bad Old
Days*; *Tom Brown's Schooldays*.
Films incl: Polanski's *Macbeth*;
and, for the Children's Film
Foundation, *Eggheads Robot*;
Robin Hood Junior. Radio: regular
Sunday morning show on Radio
Liverpool; contributes to Radio
1; Radio 4's *The Wally! Scott!*
TV incl: *Swap Shop*; *Cheggers
Plays Pop*; *Wackers*; *Armchair
Theatre*; *Anything Goes*. m.
Maggie Philbin of BBC's
Tomorrow's World. Hobbies:
horse riding, music. Address: c/o
Dave Winslett, Purley, Surrey.
Birthsign: Capricorn. **Favourite
Place:** 'Watership Down on
Hampshire/Berkshire borders for
peace and quiet on my day off.'

CHERITON, Shirley
Actress, b. 28 June 1955 London.
Trained at the Italia Conti Stage
School. Stage shows: *Goldilocks
And The Three Bears*; *Pyjama
Tops*; *Dick Whittington*. TV
work has incl: *Crown Court*;
Within These Walls; *The Cuckoo
Waltz*; *Z Cars*; *Bless This House*;
General Hospital; *Angels*; *Hazell*;
Secombe With Music; *The Final
Frontier*; *EastEnders*. m. Howard
Grant; 2 s. Mark, Adam.
Hobbies: jogging, keep-fit, gym
training. Address: c/o St James's
Management, London. Birthsign:
Cancer. **Favourite Place:** 'A
sunny roof top in Jersey listening
to *Steve Wright In The Afternoon*.'

CHILD, Jeremy
Actor, b. 20 Sept 1944 Woking,
Surrey. Attended the Bristol Old
Vic Theatre School. Theatre incl:
Conduct Unbecoming; *Twelfth
Night*; *Donkey's Years*; *Hay Fever*.
Films incl: *The Stud*; *Winston
Churchill*; *Oh! What A Lovely
War*; *Send My Regards To Broad
Street*. Extensive TV incl: *Father,
Dear Father*; *Robin's Nest*; *Edward
And Mrs Simpson*; *When The
Boat Comes In*; *Bird Of Prey*;
Minder; *Bergerac*; *The Jewel In
The Crown*; *Sleeps Six* (*Oxbridge
Blues* series). m. (1st) Deborah
Grant (dis.), (2nd) Jan Todd; 2 d.
Melissa, Leonora, 1 s. Alexander.
Hobbies: flying, gardening,
cooking, laughing. Address: c/o
Duncan Heath Assocs, London.
Birthsign: Virgo. **Favourite
Place:** 'Sahara Desert. A place
that makes you realise how
insignificant man and his ego are.'

CHILDS, Peter

Actor, b. 1 Sept 1939 Eastbourne. Trained at Birmingham Theatre School. Appeared with the Manchester 59 Company in *ERB* which transferred to London's West End. Numerous appearances at Stratford East, and appearances at the Royal Court include *The Changing Room*, which also had a West End run. Films incl: *Sweeney*; *Trial By Combat*; *O Lucky Man*. TV incl: *Public Eye*; *The Sweeney*; *Blake's Seven*; *Rumpole Of The Bailey*; *Cuckoo Waltz*; *Coronation Street*; *Mitch*; *Foxy Lady*; *Give Us A Break*; *Doctor Who*; *Juliet Bravo*; *Minder*. m. Jacqueline McMullan; 1 step-s. Simon, 3 step-d. Amanda, Vanessa, Sarah. Hobbies: horse-racing, piano playing, reading, cooking. Address: c/o Felix de Wolfe, London. Birthsign: Virgo. **Favourite Place:** 'I don't have favourite places any more—they've always changed when you go back to them.'

CHRISTIAN, Glynn

Food broadcaster and author, b. 1 Jan 1942 Auckland, New Zealand. Came to England in 1965 to break into TV and do research on his ancestor Fletcher Christian of Mutiny On The Bounty fame. This resulted in the biography *Fragile Paradise*, and a cookery series on *Pebble Mill At One*. In 1983 became Food Reporter and Chef on BBC's *Breakfast Time*. Regular contributor to Gloria Hunniford's Radio 2 programme. Books incl: *The No-cook Cook Book*; *Get Fresh With Glynn Christian*; *The Delicatessen Cookbook*. Hobbies: cooking, campaigning to save Pitcairn Island. Address: c/o Joe Gurnett, London. Birthsign: Capricorn. **Favourite Place:** 'The ledge outside Fletcher Christian's cave, high on Pitcairn Island, because I can see history, my family's past, and adventure spread before me.'

CHURCHILL, Donald

Writer/actor, b. 6 Nov 1930 Southall, Middx. Both as an actor and playwright his output has been impressive, including 40 plays for TV. Stage incl: *Under My Skin*; *Fringe Benefits* (with Peter Yeldham). Films incl: *My Family And Other Animals*. TV incl: *The Cherry On The Top*; *Feeling The Pinch*; *You Don't Know Me, But*; *Hearts And Flowers*; *Moody And Peg* (with Julia Jones); *Feeling His Way*; *Spooner's Patch*; *Good Night—God Bless* (with Joe McGrath). Latest work includes the adaptation for TV of Mervyn Peake's *Mr Pye*. m. Pauline Yates; 2 d. Jemma, Polly. Hobby: trying to learn French. Address: c/o Fraser & Dunlop, London, and Marina Martin Management, London. Birthsign: Scorpio. **Favourite Place:** 'In bed because you can say you're not available without hurting anyone's feelings.'

CLARKE, Jacqueline

Character actress, b. 13 Feb 1942 Bucks. Trained at RADA and rep experience at York, Harrogate and Bournemouth. Theatre incl: *The Boy Friend*. Radio incl: Roy Castle's radio show *Castles On The Air* from 1976. Light entertainment shows for TV incl: *Dave Allen At Large* (for seven years); and with Mike Yarwood, Mike Reid, Les Dawson, Kelly Monteith, Terry Scott; *Sharp Intake Of Breath*; Sheridan's Restoration comedy *The Critic*; a new series *Eureka*. 1 d. Catherine Anne. Hobbies: walking, pastel painting and gardening. Address: c/o Barry Burnett, London. Birthsign: Aquarius. **Favourite Place:** Butterton in the Derby Dales. 'A majestic, off-the-beaten-track corner of England for a serene and contented escape.'

CLEESE, John

Writer/actor, b. 27 Oct 1939 Weston-Super-Mare. Started in the Cambridge Footlights Revue. Travelled to America with the Revue and stayed on to play in *Half A Sixpence*. Returned to make *Frost Report*; *I'm Sorry I'll Read That Again*; *At Last The 1948 Show*; *Monty Python's Flying Circus*; *Fawlty Towers*, for which he won *TV Times* Award for Funniest Man on TV (1978–79). m. (1st) actress Connie Booth (dis.), (2nd) film director Barbara Trentham; 2 d. Cynthia, Camilla. Hobby: filling in questionnaires. Address: c/o Roger Hancock, London. Birthsign: Scorpio. **Favourite Place:** 'La Gavroche.'

CLIVE, John

Actor/author/screenwriter, b. 6 Jan 1938 London. Started as child actor, working at the Shakespeare Theatre in Liverpool and in *Casey's Court*. After RAF stage incl: *Absurd Person Singular*; *The Real Inspector Hound*; *The Mating Game*; *The Happy Apple*. Films incl: *The Italian Job*; *Clockwork Orange*; *Great Expectations*. TV incl: *Valley*; *The History Of Mr Polly*; *The Government Inspector*; *The Nesbitts Are Coming*; *A Dream Of Alice*. Produced *Some Of Our Airmen Are No Longer Missing* (documentary). Books: *KG 200*; *The Last Liberator*; *Barossa*; *Broken Wings*; *ARK*. m. Carole; 1 d. Hannah, 1 s. Alexander. Hobbies: cinema, TV, football. Address: c/o London Management, London. Birthsign: Capricorn. **Favourite Place:** Delgany, Co Wicklow, Ireland. 'I spent three happy years there working on *Broken Wings*.'

CLUTE, Sidney

Actor, b. 21 April 1916 Brooklyn, New York. His considerable number of stage appearances incl: *Storm In The Sun*; *All The King's Men*; *The Big Knife*; *The Laughmakers*; *Merrily We Roll Along*; *The Milky Way*. Films incl: *The Russians Are Coming*; *Alice B Toklas*. TV incl: co-starring in the award winning *Cagney And Lacy* and *Lou Grant*; *Hallmark Hall Of Fame*. Hobbies: tennis, swimming, backpacking, literature. Address: c/o 2902 Grand Canal, Venice, California 90291. Birthsign: Taurus. **Favourite Place:** 'Rome, Italy—lived there in a prior life—ancient Rome.'

COCKERELL, Michael

TV reporter, BBC's *Panorama*, b. 26 Aug 1940 London. Trained in magazine journalism, radio and television production. Emmy award for Investigative Journalism, 1980; Royal Television Society Award for Best Current Affairs Programme, 1983. In 1984 he wrote *Sources Close To The Prime Minister*. m. Bridget; 1 d. Sophia, 1 s. William. Hobbies: tennis, cricket, collecting political cartoons. Address: c/o BBC TV, London. Birthsign: Virgo. **Favourite Place:** 'In bed.'

COLE, George
Actor, b. 22 April 1925 London. Discovered in 1940 by Alastair Sim to play a Cockney evacuee in *Cottage To Let* and became a star overnight. Stage incl: *Flare Path*; *Mr Bolfy*; *Too True To Be Good*; *The Philanthropist*; *Brimstone And Treacle*; *The Pirates Of Penzance*. Films incl: *Cottage To Let*; *My Brother's Keeper*; *Laughter In Paradise*; *Top Secret*; *The Belles Of St Trinians*; *Blue Murder At St Trinians*; *One Way Pendulum*. On radio he was a household name for 15 years in *A Life Of Bliss*. TV incl: *Sex Game*; *Murder*; *Don't Forget To Write*; *Minder* (five series); *The Bounder*; *Blott On The Landscape*; *Comrade Dad*. m. (2nd) Penny Morrell; 1 d. Tara, 1 s. Toby; and from 1st m, 1 d. Harriet, 1 s. Crispin. Hobby: gardening. Address: c/o Joy Jameson, London. Birthsign: Taurus. **Favourite Place:** 'My home. I live in a wood and the view is lovely.'

COLEMAN, Charlotte
Actress, b. 3 April 1968 London. Trained at Anna Scher Children's Theatre, London. Best known as Marmalade Atkins on TV. Theatre incl: *Cavalcade*. TV incl: *Two People*; *Worzel Gummidge*; *Marmalade Atkins In Space*; *Educating Marmalade*; *Danger Marmalade At Work*. Hobbies: parties, riding her moped. Address: c/o Wendy Fletcher, London. Birthsign: Aries. **Favourite Place:** 'Orangerie, Les Tuileries Gardens in Paris, because of the Monet paintings of water lillies.'

COLEMAN, David
Reporter/interviewer, b. 26 April 1926 Alderley Edge, Cheshire. Started as newspaper journalist, Editor of *Cheshire County Express* at 23. Freelance radio contributor before joining BBC in Birmingham and later in London. Many years of TV experience incl: *Match Of The Day*; *Grandstand*; *Sportsnight With Coleman*; *A Question Of Sport*. m. Barbara; 3 d. Anne, Mandy, Samantha, 3 s. David, Dean (twins), Michael. Hobby: golf. Address: c/o Bagenal Harvey, London. Birthsign: Taurus.

COLEMAN, Jack
Actor, b. 21 Feb Philadelphia, USA. Studied drama at Duke University, North Carolina, and then attended the National Theatre Institute, Waterford, Connecticut. Stage appearances have incl: *Grease*; *Othello*. TV soap operas: *Days Of Our Lives*; Steven Carrington in *Dynasty*. Hobbies: basketball, music, singing, skiing, sailing. Address: c/o Abrams, Harris and Goldberg, 9220 Sunset Blvd, Los Angeles, CA 90069. Birthsign: Pisces. **Favourite Place:** Massachusetts.

COLLINS, Joan

Actress, b. 23 May 1936 London. Studied at RADA. Stage incl: *The Last Of Mrs Cheyney*. Made her film debut in *Lady Godiva Rides Again*. Other films incl: *The Girl On The Red Velvet Swing*; *Island In The Sun*; *Rally Round The Flag, Boys*; *The Road To Hong Kong*; *The Big Sleep*; *The Day Of The Fox*; *The Stud*; *The Bitch*. TV incl: *Tales Of The Unexpected*; *The Money Changers*; *Dynasty*. Books: *Past Imperfect*; *Joan Collins' Beauty Book*; *Katy—A Fight For Life*. m. (1st) actor Maxwell Reed (dis.), (2nd) actor Anthony Newley (dis.), (3rd) film producer Ron Kass (dis.); 3 d. Tara, Sacha (from 2nd m.), Katyana (from 3rd m.). Hobbies: photography, collecting antiques, designing clothes. Birthsign: Gemini. Address: c/o Rogers & Cowan, London. **Favourite Place:** 'London because it's simply the most civilised city in the world.'

COLLINS, John D

Actor, b. 2 Dec 1942 London. Trained at RADA. Stage experience has included Noel Coward's *Tonight at 8.30*, and *Time And Time Again* in Vienna and Sweden respectively. TV incl: *Chance In A Million*; *Hammer House Of Horror*; *Only Fools And Horses*; *Yes, Minister*; *'Allo 'Allo!* m. Caryll Newnham; 1 d. Philippa, 1 s. Christopher. Hobbies: computers, golf, music. Address: c/o Evans & Reiss, London. Birthsign: Sagittarius. **Favourite Place:** 'On any stage just after the curtain has come down.'

COLLINS, Lewis

Actor, b. 26 May Birkenhead. A number of jobs incl a hairdresser and playing in pop groups before deciding to become an actor. Trained at the London Academy of Music and Drama then rep; tour with the Prospect Theatre Company. Theatre incl: *City Sugar*; *The Threepenny Opera*; *Tamburlaine The Great*; *Babes In The Wood*; *Cinderella*. Films incl: *Who Dares Wins*; *Codename Wild Geese*; *Commando Leopard*. TV incl: *Warship*; *The New Avengers*; *The Cuckoo Waltz*; *The Professionals*; *Must Wear Tights*; *A Night On The Town*. Hobbies: running, tennis, weight training, swimming, target shooting, ju-jitsu, writing stories, film-making. Address: c/o Tricliff Ltd, London. Birthsign: Gemini. **Favourite Place:** 'Home—I so rarely see it these days.'

COLVILL, Robin

Comedian/drummer/impressionist, b. 8 Aug 1944 Leeds. Started his career in working men's clubs, then night club and theatre appearances. Since joining the Grumbleweeds, he has made various appearances incl: TV-am; Granada's *Weekend*; *Children's Royal Variety Performance*; and several series of *The Grumbleweeds Radio Show*. m. Avril; 1 s. Richard, 1 d. Janine-Louise. Hobbies: rebuilding cars, hypnotism. Address: c/o Time Artists, Manchester. Birthsign: Leo. **Favourite Place:** 'Home, old theatres, and Florida for its sun and way of life.'

CONNERY, Jason

Actor, b. 11 Jan 1963 London. Started career with rep companies in plays incl: *West Side Story*; *Man From Thermopolye*; *Night And Day*. Films incl: *Lords Of Discipline*; *Dream One*; *The Boy Who Had Everything*. TV incl: *The First Modern Olympics*; *Doctor Who*; Robin Hood in *Robin Of Sherwood*. Hobbies: sport, rugby, tennis, swimming. Address: c/o Joy Jameson, London. Birthsign: Capricorn. **Favourite Place:** 'Australia, far north Queensland, because of the heat, beauty and the all-round atmosphere.'

CONTI, Tom

Actor/director, b. 22 Nov 1941 Paisley, Scotland. Stage incl: *Savages* (debut); *Other People*; *The Black And White Minstrels*; *Don Juan*; *The Devil's Disciple*; *Whose Life Is It Anyway?* (played the lead, both in the West End and on Broadway, and received a Tony Award for his performance); *They're Playing Our Song*; *Romantic Comedy*. Films incl: *Flame*; *Full Circle*; *Eclipse*; *Gallileo*; *Merry Christmas Mr Lawrence*; *American Dreamer*; *Saving Grace*; *Miracles*. TV incl: *Madame Bovary*; *Treats*; *The Norman Conquests*; *Blade On The Feather*; *Glittering Prizes*. Work as a director incl: *Before The Party*; *The Housekeeper*; *Last Licks*. m. Kara Wilson; 1 d. Nina. Address: c/o Chatto & Linnit, London. Birthsign: Scorpio.

COOK, Nathan

Actor, b. 9 April Philadelphia. Stage: *Leander Stillwell*; *Estonia You Fall*. Films: *The Number*; *Abby*; *National Lampoon's Vacation*. Films for TV: *The Ambush Murders*; *Scared Straight (Another Story)*; *Dawn: Portrait Of A Centrefold*. TV: *Hotel*, *Hill Street Blues*; *Family*; *The Odd Couple*; *Games*; *Lest We Forget*, *Popular Neurotics*. m. Kara Grannum. Hobbies: playing blues harmonica and flute, tennis. Address: c/o Blake/Glenn Agency, 409 N Camden, Suite 202, Beverly Hills, CA 90210. Birthsign: Aries. **Favourite Place:** 'Home because I enjoy being with my family.'

COOK, Sue

Presenter, b. 30 March 1949 Ruislip, Middx. Spent ten years in radio and TV journalism— Capital Radio, BBC Radios 1 and 4, BBC TV and Thames TV. From 1979 to 1983 was presenter of BBC's *Nationwide*; in 1984 presented BBC 2's *Out Of Court* and BBC 1's *Crimewatch UK*. m. John Williams; 1 s. Charlie. Hobbies: music—listening to it and making it, learning the piano, driving. Address: c/o BBC TV Documentary Features, London. Birthsign: Aries. **Favourite Place:** 'My bathroom, soaking up to my neck in hot fragrant water—a haven of peace.'

COOMBS, Pat

Actress, b. 27 Aug London. After a scholarship to LAMDA, she was in rep with companies all over England. First came to the fore in *Hello Playmates*, with Irene Handl. More recently, films incl: *Oooh . . . You Are Awful*; *Adolf Hitler—My Part In His Downfall*. TV appearances incl: *Beggar My Neighbour*; *Celebrity Squares*; *Blankety Blank*; *3-2-1*; *This Is Your Life* (as a subject); two series of *The Lady Is A Tramp*; four series of *You're Only Young Twice*; and for children's TV *Ragdolly Anna*. Hobbies: writing letters, driving, reading, 'puss-cats!'. Address: c/o Richard Stone, London. Birthsign: Virgo. **Favourite Place:** 'A tiny spot in Hampshire where my caravan has rested—literally!'

COOPER, Henry, OBE, KSG

Ex-boxer, b. 3 May 1934 London. After a highly successful boxing career (ex-British, European, Commonwealth Heavyweight Champion), has become a popular TV personality in programmes such as *A Question Of Sport*; *Be Your Own Boss*; *Henry Cooper's Golden Belt*. He has also written four books: *Henry Cooper's Book Of Boxing*; *H For Henry*; *The Big Punchers*; *Henry Cooper— An Autobiography*. m. Albina; 2 s. Henry Marco, John Pietro. Hobby: golf. Address: c/o Johnny Risco, London. Birthsign: Taurus. **Favourite Place:** 'Home, golf course and a good restaurant—they all give me a lot of pleasure.'

COOPER, Jilly

Writer, b. 21 Feb 1937 Hornchurch, Essex. Trained as a journalist and has written 27 books so far. Well known for her columns in *The Sunday Times* and *The Mail On Sunday*. TV series: *It's Awfully Bad For Your Eyes Darling*. Frequent appearances on *What's My Line?* Many quiz shows, magazine programmes, TV commercials. m. Leo Cooper; 1 s. Felix, 1 d. Emily. Hobby: home. Address: c/o Desmond Elliott, London. Birthsign: Pisces. **Favourite Place:** 'Being at home.'

COPLEY, Paul

Actor/writer, b. 25 Nov 1944 Denby Dale, Yorkshire. Trained as an English and drama teacher. Later joined Leeds Playhouse Theatre as actor/teacher. Stage appearances incl: *For King And Country*; *Sisters*; *Whose Life Is It Anyway?*; *Working Class Hero*. Films incl: *Alfie Darling*; *A Bridge Too Far*. Radio incl: *Famous Last Words*; *King Street Junior*. TV incl: *Treasure Island*; *Cries From A Watchtower*; *Death Of A Princess*; *A Room For The Winter*; *The Bright Side*; *Bird Fancier*; *Silas Marner*. Work as a writer has included five full length plays, the most recent of which is *Fire-Eaters*. m. Natasha Pyne. Hobbies: swimming, motorcycling. Address: c/o Kate Feast Management, London. Birthsign: Sagittarius. **Favourite Place:** 'Behind the wheel of my ageing, much-loved Peugeot on mountain roads; Pyrenees preferred, Pennines'll do!'

CORBETT, Matthew
Entertainer, b. 28 March 1948 Yorkshire. Trained as an actor at Central School of Speech and Drama, and in rep at Bristol, York, Chelmsford, Dundee and Richmond. TV incl: *Magpie*; *Rainbow*; *Matt And Gerry Ltd*; *The Sooty Show*, which he took over after his father's (Harry)

heart attack. m. Sallie; 1 d. Tamsin, 2 s. Benjamin, Joe. Hobbies: music (writing and recording), travel. Address: c/o Vincent Shaw Assocs, London. Birthsign: Aries. **Favourite Place:** 'There is a place to the west of Katmandu where my wife and I found peace, tranquillity, humility and a 22-year-old Sherpa who had never heard of Elvis Presley or the Beatles! I shall never forget Nepal.'

CORBETT, Ronnie, OBE
Actor/comedian, b. 4 Dec 1930 Edinburgh. Started amateur dramatics at 16. Many TV shows incl: *Crackerjack*; *Dickie Henderson Show*; *Frost Report*, after being spotted by David

Frost in Danny La Rue's nightclub; *No—That's Me Over Here*; *Frost On Sunday*; *The Corbett Follies*; *The Two Ronnies*; *Sorry!* m. Anne Hart; 2 d. Emma, Sophie. Hobbies: football, golf, horse-racing. Address: c/o Sonny Zahl Associates, London. Birthsign: Sagittarius. **Favourite Place:** 'Three views: over Edinburgh from the Braid Hills; from the 7th hole at Gullane down the Forth; 12th hole at the Addington.'

CORBIN, Jane
TV/investigative reporter, b. 16 July 1954 Exeter, Devon. Foreign and home reporter for *C4 News*. Won the Topical Feature category award from the Royal TV Society 1984/5. Hobbies: swimming, keep-fit, tennis. Address: c/o ITN, London. Birthsign: Cancer. **Favourite Place:** Taj Mahal, India—'Embodies the spirit and culture of a fascinating and diverse nation.'

CORD, Alex
Actor, b. 3 May Long Island, New York. After university he was accepted for the American Shakespeare Festival at Stratford, Connecticut. Stage incl: *Play With A Tiger*; *The Umbrella*. Films incl: *Synanon*; *Stagecoach*; *The Brotherhood*; *Stiletto*; *The Last Grenade*; *Sidewinder I*. TV incl: *The Rose Tattoo*; *Airwolf*; *The*

Joker; *Fire!*; *Beggarman Thief*; *Goliath Awaits*. m. Joanna Pettet (sep.); 2 s. Wayne, Damian Zackery, 1 d. Toni. Hobbies: writing novels (two published: *Sandsong*; *The Harbinger*) and screenplays, horse riding. Address: c/o Milton Kahn Assocs, 9229 Sunset Blvd, Los Angeles, CA 90069. Birthsign: Taurus. **Favourite Place:** 'Africa—most enchanting place on earth, points out the insignificance of man and purity which is disappearing.'

CORNWELL, Judy
Actress, b. 22 Feb London.
Trained as a dancer and singer.
London debut in *Oh! What A
Lovely War*. Stage also incl: *Mr
Whatnot; Don't Let Summer
Come; Old Flames*; a season at
Stratford with RSC in 1972;
*Mecca; Bed Before Yesterday;
Who's Who*. Films incl: *Every
Home Should Have One;
Wuthering Heights; Devil's
Lieutenant; Santa Claus*. TV incl:
Younger Generation; Call Me

Daddy (Emmy Award, 1967);
*Relatively Speaking; Man Of
Straw; The Chinese Prime
Minister; Moody And Peg; Good
Companions; Cakes And Ale;
There Comes A Time*. m. John
Parry; 1 s. Edward. Hobbies:
writing, cooking, psychology,
gardening. Address: c/o Michael
Ladkin, London. Birthsign:
Pisces. **Favourite Place:** 'By the
sea at sunset; anywhere I can see
the stars clearly; by my fireside,
reading.'

COSBY, Bill
Comedian/actor, b. 12 July 1937
Philadelphia. Started out in
Philadelphia night club. Has
made many successful comedy
records. Films incl: *Hickey and
Buggs; Uptown Saturday Night;
Let's Do It Again; A Piece Of The
Action; California Suite*. Became
well known in England when he
starred with Robert Culp in *I
Spy*; now has his own television
series *The Cosby Show*. m.
Camille; 1 s Ennis, 4 d. Erika,

Erinn, Ensa, Evin. Hobby: tennis.
Address: c/o William Morris,
151 El Camino Drv, Beverly
Hills, CA 90212. Birthsign:
Cancer. **Favourite Place:** home
with his family.

COSSINS, James
Actor, b. 4 Dec 1933 Beckenham,
Kent. Trained for the stage at
RADA where he was awarded
the Silver Medal in 1952. After
serving in the Royal Air Force,
spent several years in rep. West
End appearances incl: *Bonne
Soupe; Celebration; She Stoops To
Conquer; The Beggar's Opera; The
Anniversary; Man And Superman;
Stage Struck*. Films incl: *How I
Won The War; Otley; The Rise
And Rise Of Michael Rimmer;*

SWALK; Gandhi. TV incl: *Mad
Jack; The Breaking Of Colonel
Keyser; A Day Out; Dombey &
Son; The Pickwick Papers;
Marjorie And Men*. Hobbies:
gardening, cooking, avoiding the
telephone. Address: c/o Leading
Artists, London. Birthsign:
Sagittarius. **Favourite Place:**
'Shrubland Hall Health Clinic,
Coddenham, Suffolk. Lovely
food, peace and quiet, sweet and
helpful staff.'

COURTENAY, Margaret
Actress, b. 14 Nov 1923 Cardiff.
Trained at LAMDA and rep,
incl: Stratford, Bristol Old Vic,
Oxford, Regent's Park, Welsh
National Theatre, Chichester, and
many foreign tours. Stage incl:
*Ring Round The Moon; Alfie; The
Killing Of Sister George; 13 Rue
de l'Amour* (Society of West End
Managers Award for Best
Supporting Performance, 1976);
*The Rivals; The Importance Of
Being Earnest; 42nd Street*. Films

incl: *Isadora; Under Milk Wood;
The Mirror Crack'd*. TV incl: *Billy
Liar; It Ain't Half Hot Mum; Best
Of Friends; A Sharp Intake Of
Breath; Good Companions; Never
The Twain; Fresh Fields; Tom,
Dick And Harriet*. m. (dis.); 1 s.
Julian. Hobbies: painting,
gardening, mini-exploring,
talking. Address: c/o London
Management, London. Birthsign:
Scorpio. **Favourite Place:** San
Francisco—'Memories.'

COX, Doc
Presenter/singer, b. 1 July 1946 Sheffield, Yorks. TV incl: *Back* Room Boy; *Nationwide*; *Look Stranger*; *Grapevine*; research and origination of *Forty Minute's Skiffle*; *Children In Need*; presenter/film director of *That's Life!* Hobbies: blues, rhythm and blues, rock and roll, DIY, cycling, playing in the band Ivors Jivers, collecting vintage records. Address: c/o Arlington Agency, London. Birthsign: Cancer. **Favourite Place:** Ysclosky, Louisiana, 'Because "the road kinda runs out on you".'

COX, Frances
Actress, b. 16 April 1913 Halifax, West Yorks. Trained at LAMDA, followed by rep. More recent TV has incl: *Open All Hours*; *Last Of The Summer Wine*; *How's Your Father*; five episodes of *Coronation Street*; *South Riding*; *One By One*; *Morgan's Boy*; *Stay With Me Till Morning*; *Airline*; *Victoria Wood As Seen On TV*; *Dear Ladies*; *The Practice*. m. Austin Cox. Hobbies: writing—short stories, especially for children, and plays—music, piano and organ. Address: c/o ATS Casting, Leeds. Birthsign: Aries. **Favourite Place:** Great Budworth in Cheshire—'Happy working days there with Hinge and Bracket on *Dear Ladies*.'

CRAIG, Michael
Actor, b. 27 Jan 1929 Poona, India. Started acting at the Castle Theatre, Farnham. Rep at York, Windsor, Oxford. From 1954–61, film contract with the Rank Organisation. Stage incl: season at Stratford, 1963–64; *A Whistle In The Dark*; *Funny Girl*. Films incl: *Passage Home*; *Yield To The* Night; *The Angry Silence* (also the writer); *Doctor In Love*; *The Killing In Angel Street*. Over 40 TV appearances incl: *Tiger Trap* (also the writer); *Husbands And Lovers*; *Second Time Around*; *The Foundation*; *Triangle*. m. Susan; 1 d. Jessica, 2 s. Stephen, Michael. Hobbies: sport, golf, snooker, reading. Address: c/o ICM, London. Birthsign: Aquarius. **Favourite Place:** 'Venice because it is unique and has many good memories.'

CRAIG, Wendy
Actress, b. 20 June 1934 Sacriston, Co Durham. Won first acting award at the age of three. Trained at London's Central School of Dramatic Art before going to Ipswich Rep. Leading theatre appearances incl: *Mr Kettle And Mrs Moon*; *Ride A Cock Horse*; *Peter Pan*; *Taming of The Shrew*; *The Constant Wife*. Films incl: *Room At The Top*; *I'll Never Forget What's His Name*. TV incl: *Not In Front Of The* Children; *And Mother Makes Three*; *Butterflies*; *Nanny*. *TV Times* readers' Funniest Woman on TV, 1972/73/74. Woman of the Year, BBC, 1984. m. musician/writer Jack Bentley; 2 s. Alaster, Ross. Hobbies: music, horticulture. Address: c/o Hatton-Baker Agency, London. Birthsign: Gemini. **Favourite Place:** 'A stone seat at the top of Hedser Hill, Bourne End with a glorious view of the Bucks-Berks countryside.'

CRANHAM, Kenneth
Actor, b. 12 Dec 1944
Dunfermline, Scotland. Trained
at RADA and with the National
Youth Theatre. Wide TV
appearances incl: *Coronation
Street*; *Danger UXB*; *Thérèse
Raquin*; *Sound Of The Guns*;
Sergeant Cribb; *Butterflies Don't
Count*; *The Caretaker*; *'Tis A Pity
She's A Whore*; *The Bell*; *The
Merchant Of Venice*; *La Ronde*;
Shine On Harvey Moon; *Reilly
Ace Of Spies*; *The Dumb Waiter*.

m. Charlotte Cornwell (sep.); 1 d.
Nancy Grace. Hobbies:
photography, music, walking.
Address: c/o Plant & Froggatt,
London. Birthsign: Sagittarius.
Favourite Place: 'Sean's Bar,
Athlone, Ireland. Perfect bar,
perfect Guinness.'

CRAVEN, Gemma
Actress/singer, b. 1 June 1950
Dublin. Trained at the Bush
Davies School in Romford, Essex.
Stage incl: *Let's Get Divorced*
(debut); *Fiddler On The Roof*;
Trelawny; *Dandy Dick*; *Black
Comedy*; *Songbook*; *They're
Playing Our Song*; *Song And
Dance*; *Loot*. Also appeared at
Bristol Old Vic and Chichester.
Films incl: *The Slipper And The
Rose* (Royal Film Performance,
1976); *Why Not Stay For
Breakfast?*; *Wagner*. TV incl: *So
You Think You Know About
Love?*; *Call My Bluff*; *The Royal
Variety Performance* (1979 and
1983); *Pennies From Heaven*; *This
Is Your Life* (as subject); *East
Lynne*; *Child's Play*; *Robin Of
Sherwood*; *Gemma, Girls And
Gershwin*. Hobbies: crochet,
eating out. Address: c/o Stella
Richards Management, London.
Birthsign: Gemini. **Favourite
Place:** 'My new house. It's a
perfect haven, after a busy day.'

CRAVEN, John
TV and radio journalist, b. 16
Aug Leeds. Began as a junior
reporter on weekly papers in
Yorkshire, later worked for
regional and national newspapers
before joining the BBC. TV incl:
Look North; *Points West*; *Search*;
John Craven's Newsround; *Swap
Shop*; *Saturday Superstore*; *The
Show Me Show*; and
documentary series *Breakthrough*;
Story Behind The Story; and
Newsround Extra. Author of
several books incl: *And Finally—
Funny Stories From John Craven's
Newsround*. Also writes weekly
column for the *Radio Times*. m.
Marilyn; 2 d. Emma, Victoria.
Hobbies: aviation, wildlife.
Address: c/o BBC TV, London.
Birthsign: Leo. **Favourite
Place:** 'The view across
Wharfedale from the top of Otley
Chevin.'

CRIBBINS, Bernard
Actor, b. 29 Dec 1928 Oldham,
Lancs. First appeared on stage at
Oldham Rep in 1942. Other rep
work in Manchester and
Hornchurch before coming to
London where his more recent
stage work incl: *Not Now,
Darling*; *The Love Game*; *There
Goes The Bride*; *Run For Your
Wife*; *Guys And Dolls*. Films incl:
Casino Royale; *The Railway
Children*; *The Water Babies*. Vast
amount of TV incl: two series of
his own show, *Cribbins*; *Comedy
Playhouse*; *Get The Drift*;
Jackanory; *Call My Bluff*; *The
Good Old Days*; *The Wombles*;
You Must Be Joking; *Fawlty
Towers*; *Star Turn* (presenter);
Shillingbury Tales. m. Gillian
McBarnet. Hobbies: golf, fly
tying, bird watching. Address:
c/o Crouch Assocs, London.
Birthsign: Capricorn. **Favourite
Place:** Dingle, West of Ireland,
'Great fishing—wild,
a lonely place.'

CRICKET, Jimmy
Comedian, b. 17 Oct 1945
Belfast. Started as camp
entertainer for Butlins and
Pontins and then spent some time
on the club circuit. TV incl:
Children's Royal Variety Show;
The Royal Variety Show; his own
TV series, *And There's More*; plus
pantomime, cabaret, concert
tours and guest appearances. m.
May; 3 s. Dale, Frank, Jamie, 1 d.
Katy. Hobbies: jogging, reading,
listening to romantic music,
watching old Hollywood
musicals, playing football and
chess with the children. Address:
c/o International Artistes
Representation, London.
Birthsign: Libra. **Favourite
Place:** 'The view of Ireland from
the boat crossing from England—
the sense of going home.'

CROSBIE, Annette
Actress, b. 12 Feb Edinburgh.
Trained at Bristol Old Vic
Theatre School and has worked
extensively in the theatre, the
most recent incl: *Tramway Road*.
TV incl: *Edward The Seventh*
(TV Times Best Actress Award,
also BAFTA Actress of the Year
1975); *The Six Wives Of Henry
VIII*; *Lillie*; *Family Dance* (and
theatre); *Northern Lights*; *The
Disappearance Of Harry*; *Off Peak*,
Paradise Postponed. m. Michael
Griffith; 1 s. Owen, 1 d. Selina.
Address: c/o James Sharkey
Assocs, London. Birthsign:
Aquarius.

CROWTHER, Leslie
Actor/comedian, b. 6 Feb 1933
Nottingham. Originally intended
for a musical career. While
studying drama he appeared in
school broadcasts for the BBC,
then rep at Regent's Park Open
Air Theatre. Stage appearances
incl: *High Spirits*; *Let Sleeping
Wives Lie*; *Underneath The
Arches*; *Royal Variety Performance*.
TV incl: *Crackerjack*; *The
Saturday Crowd*; *Crowther's In
Town*; *Leslie Crowther's Scrap
Book*; *The Crowther Collection*;
Whose Baby?; *The Price Is Right*;
Time Of Your Life (as subject);
Spotlight On Leslie Crowther. m.
Jean, 4 d. Lindsay and Elizabeth
(twins), Caroline, Charlotte, 1 s.
Nicholas. Hobbies: cricket,
collecting pot lids. Address: c/o
London Management, London.
Birthsign: Aquarius. **Favourite
Place:** 'The view from our
gazebo which overlooks the
Avon Valley. It changes
constantly and is quite magical.'

CRYER, Barry
Writer, b. 23 March 1934 Leeds,
Yorks. Has been writing and
performing since 1957. Work for
TV incl: *The Two Ronnies*;
Morecambe And Wise; Les
Dawson; Kenny Everett; David
Frost. Awards incl: BAFTA;
Writers' Guild; Press; Royal
Society. m. Terry; 3 s. Anthony,
David, Robert, 1 d. Jacqueline.
Hobbies: walking, study of
public transport. Address: c/o
Brian Codd, London. Birthsign:
Aries. **Favourite Place:**
'Home—the atmosphere, the
views, the people.'

CULLEN, Sarah
TV journalist, b. 6 Oct 1949
Newcastle-upon-Tyne. Joined
ITN as graduate trainee in 1972
and has since worked extensively,
both home and abroad, as TV
reporter. Appointed ITN Home
Affairs Correspondent in 1983
specialising in social policy and
local government. Book: *In
Praise Of Panic*. Hobbies:
cooking, books. Address: c/o
ITN, London. Birthsign: Libra.
Favourite Place: home.

CULVER, Michael
Actor, b. 16 June 1938 London.
Trained for the stage at LAMDA.
Films incl: *Goodbye, Mr Chips*;
Conduct Unbecoming; *A Passage
To India*. Extensive TV work
incl: *Philby, Burgess And Maclean*;
The Adventures Of Black Beauty;
both series of *Secret Army*;
Diamonds; *Fanny By Gaslight*;
Squadron; *Chessgames*. m. Lucinda
Curtis; 2 s. Roderic, Justin.
Hobby: golf. Address: c/o John
Redway & Assocs, London.
Birthsign: Gemini. **Favourite
Place:** 'First tee at most good
golf courses, and just occasionally
the last green!'

CUTHBERTSON, Iain
Actor, b. 4 Jan 1930 Glasgow.
Began as radio actor while
studying at Aberdeen University,
then became radio journalist with
the BBC in Glasgow. Started
acting at Glasgow Citizens'
Theatre, of which he became
General Manager and Director of
Productions in 1962. In 1965
became Associate Director of
London's Royal Court. Films
incl: *The Railway Children*; *Up
The Chastity Belt*. TV incl: *The
Borderers*; *The Onedin Line*; *Scotch
On The Rocks*; *Black Beauty*; *The
Ghosts Of Motley Hall*; *Charlie
Endell*; *Vice Versa*; *The Assam
Garden*; *Supergran*. m. actress
Anne Kirsten. Hobbies: sailing,
fishing. Address: c/o French's,
London. Birthsign: Capricorn.
Favourite Place: 'The west
coast of Scotland for its endless
islands which I love visiting.'

DALLAS, Lorna
Singer/actress, b. 4 March Illinois,
USA. Bachelor of Music from
Indiana University. New York
debut in *The Marriage Of Figaro*
before coming to London in
Show Boat, 1971. Theatre incl:
Hello Dolly; *Don Giovanni*; *The
Merry Widow*; *La Bohème*; *Der
Rosenkavalier*; *Kismet*; *Sammy
Kahn's Songbook*; *Side By Side By
Sondheim*. Film: *Inside Out*. TV
incl: *The Royal Variety Show*;
The Many Wives Of Patrick; *Look
Who's Talking*; *Highway*; *Super
Troupers*; own show *The Sound
Of Lorna Dallas*. m. Garry
Brown. Hobbies: music, tennis,
swimming, avid reader of current
events. Address: c/o Garry
Brown Assocs, Cheam, Surrey.
Birthsign: Aries. **Favourite
Place:** 'The beautiful island of
Maui in Hawaii, where Garry
and I spent our honeymoon.'

DALTON, Abby

Actress, b. 15 Aug Las Vegas, Nevada. Studied for her acting career with Jeff Corey. Films incl: *Plainsman*; *Rock All Night*; *Cole Younger, Gunfighter*. TV incl: *Hennesey*; *The Jonathan Winters Show*; *The New Joey Bishop Show*; *Belle Starr*; *Falcon Crest*. m. Jack Smith; 2 s. Matthew, John, 1 d. Kathleen. Hobbies: cooking, skiing, tennis. Address: c/o David Shipera & Assocs, 15301 Ventura Blvd, Suite 345, Sherman Oaks, CA 91403. Birthsign: Leo. **Favourite Place:** 'Our family's second home in the mountains near Los Angeles.'

DALY, Tyne

Actress, b. 21 Feb Madison, Wisconsin. Daughter of actor James Daly. Appeared in many student productions. Attended American Musical and Dramatic Academy. Films incl: *The Enforcer*; *John And Mary*; *Telefon*; *Zoot Suit*; *The Aviator*; *Movers And Shakers*. Numerous guest TV roles incl: *The Virginian*; *General Hospital*; *Quincy*; *Lou Grant*; *Magnum PI*. TV films incl: *Intimate Strangers*; *The Women's Room*; *Cagney & Lacey*, which led to the successful TV series. Her role as Mary Beth Lacey has won her two Emmys. Other TV incl: *The Entertainer*; *Larry, The Man Who Could Talk To Kids*. m. Georg Stanford Brown; 2 d. Elisabeth, Kathryne. Hobbies: reading, knitting. Address: c/o CBS, Los Angeles, CA 90036. Birthsign: Pisces. **Favourite Place:** 'Anywhere my husband and daughters are.'

DANA

Singer/entertainer, b. Rosemary Brown, 30 Aug Londonderry, Ireland. Started her singing career at local concerts and music festivals. In 1970, representing Ireland, she won the Eurovision Song Contest with *All Kinds Of Everything*. Other singles incl: *Who Put The Lights Out*; *It's Gonna Be A Cold, Cold Christmas*; *Never Gonna Fall in Love Again*; *You Never Gave Me Your Love*. Extensive concert, cabaret and theatre seasons, incl. London Palladium; Royal Festival Hall. Films incl: *The Flight Of Doves*. TV incl: *3-2-1*; *Summertime Special*; *Night Music*; *Highway*; *Ladybirds*; *Dana*; *A Day With Dana*; *Wake Up Sunday*. m. Damien Scallon; 2 d. Grace, Susanna, 1 s. John. Address: c/o Tony Cartwright, Southwood, Christchurch Rd, Virginia Water, Surrey. Birthsign: Virgo.

DANCE, Charles

Actor, b. 10 Oct 1946 Rednal, Worcs. Theatre incl: *The Beggars' Opera*; *The Taming Of The Shrew*; *Saint Joan*; *Sleeping Beauty*; *The Three Sisters*; *Toad Of Toad Hall*; *Travesties*. Joined Royal Shakespeare Company 1975 and appeared in many productions incl: title role in *Henry V* New York tour 1975; title role *Coriolanus* tour to Paris 1979. Other theatre incl: *Irma La Douce*; *The Heiress*; *Turning Over*. Films incl: *For Your Eyes Only*; *Plenty*. TV incl: *Edward The Seventh*; *Father Brown*; *Raffles*; *Dreams Of Leaving*; *Nancy Astor*; *Saigon—The Last Day*; *The Jewel In The Crown*; *Rainy Day Women*; *The Secret Servant*. m. Joanna; 1 s. Oliver, 1 d. Rebecca. Hobbies: music, tennis, photography. Address: c/o Caroline Dawson, London. Birthsign: Libra. **Favourite Place:** a deserted beach in South Devon.

DANDO, Suzanne

TV presenter/actress, b. 3 July 1961 Tooting, London. British Gymnastics Champion; Champion of Champions; Captain World Games and Olympic gymnastics teams 1980; all major titles 1979–80. Retired from competitive gymnastics after 1980 Olympics and entered TV by presenting/demonstrating gymnastics and other sports. Theatre incl: *Cheers Mrs Worthington*; *Cinderella*. Film: *Octopussy*. TV incl: *Anything Goes*; *Blankety Blank*; *Game For A Laugh*; *Give Us A Clue*; *Punchlines*. Hobbies: riding, water-skiing, sunbathing. Address: c/o International Artists, London. Birthsign: Cancer. **Favourite Place:** 'The stage–it's the place I want to be most.'

DANEMAN, Paul

Actor, b. 26 Oct 1925 London. Trained at RADA, then rep and joined Old Vic. First stage appearance as front legs of a horse in *Alice In Wonderland*. Original Vladimir in *Waiting For Godot* at the Arts Theatre, London. Theatre incl: *Camelot*; *Hadrian VII*; *Don't Start Without Me*; *Who Do They Think They Are?* (one-man show); *Double Edge*; *Pygmalion*; *Shut Your Eyes And Think Of England*; *The Jeweller's Shop*. TV incl: *Our Mutual Friend*; *Emma*; *Persuasion*; *An Age Of Kings*; *Not In Front Of The Children*; *Spy Trap*; *Waste*; *Arnold*; *Partners*; *Stay With Me Till Morning*; *Tishoo*; *Two Gentlemen Of Verona*; *Antigone*. m. (1st) Susan (dis.), (2nd) Meredith; 2 d. Sophie, Flora. Hobby: painting. Address: c/o Chatto & Linnit, London. Birthsign: Scorpio. **Favourite Place:** 'The view from my studio over the Thames.'

DANIELLE, Suzanne

Actress, b. 14 Jan 1957 London. Trained at the Bush Davies Stage School. Stage debut at 12 with season at Hornchurch Repertory Theatre. West End debut in *Billy* at Drury Lane. Theatre incl: *Sweet Charity*. Films incl: *Boys In Blue*; *Escape From D'Ablo*; *Trouble With Spies*. Famous for impersonation of Princess Diana opposite Mike Yarwood on TV. Other TV incl: *Hammer House Of Thriller*; *Tales Of The Unexpected*; *Jane*; *Just Amazing*. Hobbies: golf, swimming, dancing. Address: c/o ICM, London. Birthsign: Capricorn.

DANIELS, Martin

Comedian, b. 19 Aug 1963 South Bank, nr Middlesbrough. Trained on the club and cabaret circuit. Summer seasons in Newquay, Guernsey, Margate, Blackpool. TV appearances incl: *Junior Royal Variety Show*; *Saturday Superstore*; *Swap Shop*; *Little And Large Show*; *3-2-1*; *Sooty*; *Paul Daniels Magic Show*; *Russell Harty Show*; *Freetime*; *The Generation Game*; *Game For A Laugh*. Hobbies: tap dancing, playing guitar, dating women. Address: c/o Artist Management, Doncaster, South Yorks. Birthsign: Leo. **Favourite Place:** 'Bed. Reason, I like to play the guitar in bed!'

DANIELS, Paul

Comedian/magician, b. 6 April 1938 Middlesbrough. Became interested in magic aged 11. First job was junior clerk, and after a spell in the army returned to office work but did part-time entertaining. Ran a grocer's shop before becoming an entertainer full-time. His father makes his apparatus. TV debut on *Opportunity Knocks*. TV incl: *Be My Guest*; *Wheeltappers And Shunters Social Club*; *The Paul Daniels Show*; *Fall In The Stars*; *Blackpool Bonanza*; *Paul Daniels Magic Show*; won Montreux Golden Rose 1985; *Odd One Out*. m. (dis.); 3 s. Paul, Martin, Gary. Hobby: photography. Address: c/o BBC TV, London. Birthsign: Aries. **Favourite Place:** 'Florida—there is so much to see and do there.'

DANIELS, William

Actor, b. 31 March 1927 Brooklyn, New York. Studied acting with Lee Strasberg in New York. Films incl: *Family Honeymoon*; *Ladybug, Ladybug*; *Marlowe*; *The Graduate*; *Black Sunday*; *The One And Only*; *Oh, God*; *The Blue Lagoon*; *Sunburn*. TV films incl: *A Case Of Rape*; *Blind Ambition*; *The Adams Chronicles*. TV series incl: *Captain Nice*; *The Nancy Walker Show*; *Freebee And The Bean*; *Knightrider*. Emmy nomination for his role as Dr Mark Craig in *St Elsewhere*. m. actress Bonnie Bartlett; 2 s. Hobbies: classical guitar, chess, tennis, reading, cooking. Address: c/o Studio City, California. Birthsign: Aries.

DANSON, Ted

Actor, b. 29 Dec San Diego, California. Graduated from Carnegie-Mellon University with a drama degree. Films incl: *The Onion Field*; *Body Heat*; *Creepshow*. Best known on TV starring in *Cheers*, for which he was nominated for an Emmy. Other TV incl: *The Doctors*; *Somerset*; *Laverne And Shirley*; *Family*; *Magnum PI*; *The Women's Room*; *Something About Amelia*, for which he won Golden Globe Best Actor Award 1984. m. Casey; 2 d. Kate, Alexis. Hobbies: American Indian artifacts, racquetball, charity work. Address: c/o Bauman Hiller Agency, 9220 Sunset Blvd, Suite 202, Los Angeles, CA 90069. Birthsign: Capricorn. **Favourite Place:** 'Where I spent my childhood—Flagstaff, Arizona.'

DAVENPORT, Nigel

Actor, b. 23 May 1928 Shelford, Cambridge. Was a member of the Oxford University Dramatic Society while a student there. After military service worked as a disc jockey. Extensive theatre work more recently incl: *Three Sisters*; *Murder Among Friends*; *Cowardice*. Recent films incl: *Zulu Dawn*; *The London Affair*; *Hawks*; *Chariots Of Fire*; *Greystoke*. TV incl: *South Riding*; *The Applecart*; *Oil Strike North*; *Romance*; *Much Ado About Nothing*; *Goodbye Darling*; *His Name Was Mudd*; *The Inspector Calls*; *Bird Of Prey*; *Don't Rock The Boat*; *The Biko Inquest*. m. (1st) Helena (dis.), (2nd) actress Maria Aitken; 1 d. Laura, 1 s. Hugo (from 1st m.), 1 s. Jack (from 2nd m.). Address: c/o Leading Artists, London. Birthsign: Gemini.

DAVIDSON, Linda
Actress, b. 18 June 1964 Toronto, Canada. Trained at the Italia Conti Academy in London. Appeared in *A Midsummer Night's Dream* and in cabaret with Freddie Starr. TV incl: *Bulman*; *Who Dares Wins*; *EastEnders*. Hobbies: reading, ballet, swimming. Address: c/o Essanay, London. Birthsign: Gemini. **Favourite Place:** 'The family house in Southport holds the key to all my happiest memories.'

DAVIDSON, Ross
Actor, b. 25 Aug 1949 Airdrie, Scotland. Theatre incl: *Rosencrantz And Guildenstern Are Dead*; *The Importance Of Being Earnest*; *Royal Hunt Of The Sun*; *Animal Farm*; *Joseph*; *Godspell*; *Piaf*; *Robin Hood*. London theatre incl: *Guys And Dolls* at the National Theatre; *The Merchant Of Venice* and *Robin Hood* at Young Vic; *Layers* at ICA. Films incl: *The Pirates Of Penzance*; *The Meaning Of Life*; *Paracelsus*. TV incl: *Stanley Baxter*; *Marco Baccer*; *Songs Of Britain*; *Thingumyjig*; *EastEnders*. Hobbies: all sport—swimming (ex water polo international), tennis, squash, football. Address: c/o Nina Quick, London. Birthsign: Virgo. **Favourite Place:** 'Being with my parents and brother and little niece.'

DAVIES, Ann
Actress, b. London. Trained with Liverpool rep as a student. Stage appearances at Liverpool, Windsor, Leatherhead, Guildford, Coventry; London appearances at Arts Theatre, Stratford East, Cafe Theatre, Elephant Theatre, King's Head. TV incl: *Doctor Who*; *Poldark*; *Equal Terms*; *The Nation's Health*; *Happy*; *A Voyage Round My Father*; *Widows*; *Shine On Harvey Moon*; *Paradise Postponed*. m. Richard Briers; 2 d. Kate, Lucy. Hobbies: swimming, reading, music. Address: c/o Margery Armstrong, 10 Greycoat Gdns, Greycoat Place, London SW1P 1QA. Birthsign: Sagittarius. **Favourite Place:** 'Julie's Restaurant, Notting Hill Gate in London. Sunday lunch at Julie's is a wonderful treat.'

DAVIES, Deddie
Actress, b. 2 March 1938 Bridgend, S Wales. Trained at RADA. TV incl: *You're Only Young Twice*; *The Gentle Touch*; *Father Charlie*; *Wentworth BA*; Agatha Christie's *Partners In Crime*; *Grange Hill*; *Metal Mickey*; *Pickwick Papers*; *Solo*; *That's My Boy*; *Titus Andronicus*; *Chance In A Million*. m. actor Paddy Ward. Hobbies: reading, classical music, the Victorian era, having adventures. Address: Kingston-on-Thames, Surrey. Birthsign: Pisces. **Favourite Place:** 'My sitting room, because in my imagination I can go anywhere and do anything!'

DAVIES, Dickie
TV presenter, b. 30 April 1933 Cheshire. Started career as entertainments purser on Queen Mary and Queen Elizabeth before joining Southern TV as announcer/newscaster. Joined *World Of Sport* as presenter in 1968. Presented major sporting events including Olympic Games. m. Liz; 2 s. Daniel, Peter (twins). Hobbies: riding horses, playing golf. Address: c/o LWT, South Bank, London. Birthsign: Taurus. **Favourite Place:** 'South of France—the perfect blend of sun, ambiance, food and wine.'

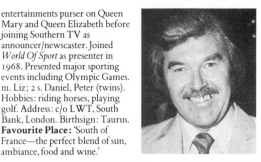

DAVIES, Gary
Presenter, b. 13 Dec 1957 Manchester. Started his radio career with a local commercial station. Now has own daily radio show on BBC Radio 1. TV appearances incl: *Top Of The Pops*; *Super Dance 1984*; *Saturday Picture Show*; *Hold Tight*; *Cheggars Plays Pop*; *The Oxford Road Show*; *World Disco Dance Championships*. Hobbies: water-skiing, squash, tennis, fashion, music, girls. Address: c/o John Noel Personal Management, Manchester. Birthsign: Sagittarius. **Favourite Place:** 'Marbella, it's just great fun all the time.'

DAVIES, Lynn, MBE
Athlete/athletics commentator, b. 20 May 1942 Nantymoel, Wales Teacher and lecturer in physical education. Competed in three Olympic Games (Tokyo 1964, Mexico 1968, Munich 1972). Winner Olympic Gold Medal Long Jump, Tokyo; European Gold Medal Budapest 1966; Commonwealth Gold Medals Jamaica 1966 and Edinburgh 1970. First British athlete to hold Olympic, European and Commonwealth titles. GB team manager LA Olympics 1984. Competed in British, European and World *Superstars* on TV. Appointed 1985 as ITV commentator on athletics. m. Meriel; 1 d. Kathryn Sian. Hobbies: photography, keeping fit, gardening, reading. Address: c/o MSW, London. Birthsign: Taurus. **Favourite Place:** 'A golf course near my house with superb views where I can run early in the morning.'

DAVIES, Sharron
Sports personality, b. 1 Nov 1962 Plymouth. Britain's most successful woman swimmer, she started swimming at the age of six. Swam for England at 11, youngest member of 1976 Montreal Olympic team. Winner of numerous medals, including Olympic silver for 400 m individual medley, Moscow 1980. Voted Sportswoman of the Year 1978; 80. Broke and re-broke over 200 British records. Retired from competition swimming 1981, but recently took up power boat racing. Has worked as a model and designer; lectured on the QEII; a guest on TV and radio and presented her own series. Autobiography: *Against The Tide*. Hobbies: most sports, reading, music, power boat racing. Address: Croydon. Birthsign: Scorpio. **Favourite Place:** 'On the beach in Plymouth on a crisp sunny day in winter.'

DAVIES, Windsor

Actor, b. 28 Aug 1930 Canning Town, London. Worked as a miner, in National Service, in a factory and as a teacher. Theatre incl: *Run For Your Wife*; *Roll On Four O'Clock*; *Baron Hardup*. TV incl: *It Ain't Half Hot Mum*; *Never The Twain*; *Sporting Chance*. m. Lynne; 4 d. Jane, Sarah, Nancy, Beth, 1 s. Daniel. Hobbies: rugby football, reading, walking, bird watching. Address: c/o Peter Prichard, London. Birthsign: Virgo. **Favourite Place:** 'Home. Next to home, the Gower Peninsula—it's beautiful and it's Welsh.'

DAVIS, Steve

Professional snooker player, b. 22 Aug 1957 Plumstead, London. Embassy World Professional Snooker Champion 1981, 83, 84. He led the England State Express world team to victory and first player to score a maximum break of 147 on TV (in the Lada Cars Classic Final which he lost to Terry Griffiths). Numerous other championships incl: Coral UK Open Champion 1984; Tolly Cobbold Champion 1985. Hobbies: jazz and soul music. Address: c/o Barry Hearn, Romford, Essex. Birthsign: Leo. **Favourite Place:** 'Matchroom Club, because that's where winning began.'

DAVISON, Peter

Actor, b. 13 April Streatham, London. After school plays and amateur dramatics, trained at Central School of Speech and Drama. Season at Nottingham Playhouse and then Edinburgh Festival before TV in *The Tomorrow People*. Big TV break was in *Love For Lydia*, then *All Creatures Great And Small*. TV incl: *Print-Out*; *Once Upon A Time*; *Holding The Fort*; *Sink Or Swim*; *Doctor Who*; *Anna Of The Five Towns*. Writes songs, incl theme TV's *Mixed Blessings*. Singing debut on *Pebble Mill At One*. m. actress Sandra Dickinson; 1 d. Georgia. Hobbies: driving, reading, cricket. Address: c/o John Mahoney Management, London. Birthsign: Aries.

DAVRO, Bobby

Comedian/impressionist, b. 13 Sept 1959 Ashford, Middx. Started in amateur music hall, talent contests, then working men's clubs. Appeared in clubs and theatres throughout Britain. Many TV appearances incl: *Up For The Cup*; *Starburst*; *Crackerjack*; *Live From Her Majesty's*; *Go For It*; *Night Of 100 Stars*; *Punchlines*; *Blankety Blank*; *Bobby Davro On The Box*; *Copy Cats*. Hobbies: golf, fishing, photography. Address: c/o Yellow Balloon Productions, Surrey. Birthsign: Virgo. **Favourite Place:** 'Virginia Water Lake—escape from hectic showbiz scene.'

DAWN, Elizabeth
Actress, b. Leeds. Best known for her role as Vera Duckworth in *Coronation Street* since 1976. Other TV incl: *Play For Today*; *Kisses At Fifty*; *Speech Day*; *Daft As A Brush*; *Sunset Across The Bay*; *Z Cars*; *Leeds United*; *Larry Grayson Special*; *All Day On The Sands*; *Crown Court*; *Sam*; *Raging Calm*. m. Donald Ibbetson; 1 s. Graham, 3 d. Dawn, Ann, Julie. Hobbies: embroidery, decorating, collecting china. Address: c/o Granada TV, Manchester. Birthsign: Scorpio. **Favourite Place:** 'Granada TV studios—it's home from home. Spain and Blackpool for holidays.'

DAWSON, Anna
Comedienne, b. 27 July 1937 Bolton, Lancs. Trained at Elmhurst Ballet School and Central School of Speech and Drama. Theatre incl: Brian Rix Company; Theatre of Laughter revue. TV incl: *The Benny Hill Show*; appeared with Morecambe and Wise; *Life Begins At Forty*; with Bob Monkhouse; *3-2-1*; many panel games. Hobbies: cooking, gardening, the Loch Ness monster. Address: c/o Barrucchi Leisure, London. Birthsign: Leo. **Favourite Place:** 'Sorrento, the happiest place I have been to. Birds singing all the time.'

DAWSON, Les
Comedian, b. 2 Feb 1934 Manchester. Began as jazz pianist with Manchester band, Cotton City Slickers. Worked in pubs and clubs as solo comic before success on *Opportunity Knocks* 1967. TV appearances in *Big Night Out*, *Sunday Night At The London Palladium* before own series, *Sez Les*. Other TV incl: *This Is Your Life*; *Holiday With Strings*; *The Loner*, also own series; host of *Blankety Blank*. Writer of *A Card For The Clubs*; *The Spy Who Came*; *Smallpiece Guide To Male Liberation*; *British Book Of Humour*. m. Margaret; 2 d. Julie, Pamela, 1 s. Stuart. Hobbies: golf, writing, gardening. Address: c/o London Management, London. Birthsign: Aquarius. **Favourite Place:** 'My garden, which has cost a veritable fortune in plants, shrubs and backache lotions—it's peaceful and my corner of a heavily mortgaged heaven.'

DAY, Sir Robin
Interviewer/presenter, b. 24 Oct 1923 London. Started as a barrister 1952. With British Information Services, Washington 1953–54. Freelance journalist 1954–55 and BBC Radio talks producer before becoming ITN newscaster and parliamentary correspondent 1955–59. Joined *Panorama* 1959 and introduced the programme 1967–72. TV incl: *Roving Report*; *Tell The People*; *The Parliamentarians*; *Question Time*. Radio: *The World At One*. Books: *Television: A Personal Report*; *The Case Of Televising Parliament*; *Day By Day*; *A Dose Of My Own Hemlock*. BAFTA Richard Dimbleby Award 1974; Royal TV Society Judges' Award for 30 years outstanding contribution to TV journalism. m. Katherine; 2 s. Alexander, Daniel. Hobbies: reading, talking, skiing. Address: c/o BBC TV, London, Birthsign: Scorpio.

DEACON, Brian

Actor, b. 13 Feb 1949 Oxford. Member of Oxford Youth Theatre then trained at Webber Douglas School in London. Rep seasons at Bristol, Coventry, Leicester, Soho Poly, Leeds, Edinburgh, Exeter, Ludlow Festival. Other theatre incl: *Curse Of The Starving Class*; *Antony And Cleopatra*; *Great And Small*; *As I Lay Dying*. Films incl: *Triple Echo*; *Il Bacio*; *Vampyres*; *Jesus*. TV incl: *First Sight*; *The Guardians*; *Public Eye*; *Love And Mr Lewisham*; *Ghosts*; *The Emigrants*; *Lillie*; *Watching Me, Watching You*; *Henry VI Parts I, II, III*; *Richard III*; *Bleak House*; *Separate Tables*; *Mr Palfrey Of Westminster*. 1 d. Lara. Hobbies: tennis, squash, football, bridge, reading, cinema, gardening, entertaining friends. Address: c/o Leading Artists, London. Birthsign: Aquarius. **Favourite Place:** 'Any airport departure lounge.'

DEAN, Bill

Actor, b. 3 Sept Liverpool. Worked in local government before becoming a comedian in clubs and pubs in Lancs. First role as an actor in the film *Gumshoe* (1972). Theatre incl: *Runway* and *Touched* at the Royal Court Theatre, London. Films incl: *Family Life*; *Nightwatcher*. TV incl: *Oh No It's Selwyn Froggitt*; *Emmerdale Farm*; *Good Companions*; *When The Boat Comes In*; as Harry Cross in C4's *Brookside*. m. (dec.); 1 s. 1 d. Hobbies: lifelong supporter of Everton FC, snooker, reading. Address: c/o Crouch Assocs, London. Birthsign: Virgo.

DeCOURCEY, Roger

Ventriloquist, b. 10 Dec 1944 London. Best known for partnership with Nookie Bear. Entered Stock Exchange on leaving school but studied opera in the evenings. After a season as holiday camp sports organiser, he turned professional. With the Fol-de-Rols at Worthing before going into *Sweet Charity* in London. TV's *New Faces* turned him into overnight success after 10 years in showbusiness. Two visits to Las Vegas to star with Dean Martin; *Royal Variety Show*; own TV series *Now For Nookie*. m. Cheryl; 1 s. Jamie. Hobbies: golf, squash. Address: c/o International Artistes, London. Birthsign: Sagittarius. **Favourite Place:** 'Any golf course! The scenery makes the walk worthwhile.'

DELANEY, Delvene

Actress, b. 26 Aug 1951 Mackay, Australia. Trained with the National Theatre of Australia. Started on TV as a weather girl for Channel O in Brisbane 1970. Won Photographic Model of the Year 1974. Acting debut in *The Box* on TV. Theatre: *The Anyhow Show* with Paul Hogan. TV incl: *The Paul Hogan Show*; original cast member *The Young Doctors*; *The Love Boat*; *You Asked For It*; *Sale Of The Century*. Book: *The Nine Month Calendar* guide to pregnancy. m. John Cornell; 1 d. Allira. Hobbies: photography, dress making, collage. Address: c/o 22 Bendigo St, Richmond, Victoria 3121, Australia. Birthsign: Virgo. **Favourite Place:** 'The view from our verandah on the coast of Australia—Pacific blue sea, misty mauve mountains, hills green enough for England.'

DELANEY, Pauline
Actress, b. 8 June Dublin. Trained at the Brendan Smith Academy of Acting, Dublin, and then rep. 1962 O'Casey season at London's Mermaid Theatre and West End in *The Poker Session* and *The Hostage*. Other theatre incl: *Richard III*; *A Lovely Day Tomorrow*. Films incl: *Nothing But The Best*; *The Young Cassidy*; *Percy*; *Brannigan*; *Rooney*; *Trenchcoat*. TV incl: *The Seagull*; *The Playboy Of The Western World*; *The Expert*; *The Avengers*; *Z Cars*; *Fallen Hero*; *Mixed Blessings*; *Maybury*; *Touch Of Evil*; *Shoestring*; *Dangerous Davies*; *The Mourning Thief*; *Late Starter*; *Travellers By Night*; *Bergerac*. m. Gerry Simpson; 1 d. Sarah. Hobbies: reading, classical music, gardening. Address: c/o Green & Underwood, London. Birthsign: Gemini. **Favourite Place**: 'Parts of Dublin, with echoes of Joyce, O'Casey, Wilde.'

DE LA TOUR, Frances
Actress, b. 30 July 1944 Bovingdon, Herts. Trained at the Drama Centre. With the Royal Shakespeare Company 1965–71, roles incl: Hoyden in *The Relapse*; Helena in Peter Brook's production *A Midsummer Night's Dream*. Other theatre incl: *Duet For One*, for which she won SWET Award for Best Actress 1981, also *Evening Standard* Award and Critics Award for Best Actress; *A Moon For The Misbegotten*, for which she won SWET Award for Best Actress 1983; *St Joan*. Film: *Rising Damp* (*Standard* film award for Best Actress). TV incl: various *Plays For Today*; Miss Jones in *Rising Damp*; *Skirmishes*; *Duet For One*. 1 d. Tamasin, 1 s. Josh. Address: c/o Saraband Assocs, London. Birthsign: Leo. **Favourite Place:** 'Opening the door of my children's bedroom and seeing them asleep spread-eagled across their beds.'

DENCH, Judi, OBE
Actress, b. 9 Dec 1934 York. Attended art school before training at Central School of Speech and Drama. Debut as Ophelia in *Hamlet* at Liverpool 1957 with Old Vic. Four seasons at the Old Vic, several seasons with the Royal Shakespeare Company, rep at Oxford. Also *Cabaret*, *The Good Companions*. TV incl: *The Teachers*; *Z Cars*; *Love Story*; *Talking To A Stranger*; *The Morecambe And Wise Show*; *Love In A Cold Climate*; *Going Gently*; *The Cherry Orchard*; *A Fine Romance* (co-starring with her husband); *Saigon—The Year Of The Cat*. Won BAFTA Award for Best Actress in a Comedy Series 1985. Voted Funniest Female on TV 1981–82 by *TV Times* readers. m. actor Michael Williams; 1 d. Tara. Hobbies: sewing, painting, tapestry. Address: c/o Leading Artists, London. Birthsign: Sagittarius.

DENISON, Michael, CBE
Actor, b. 1 Nov 1915 Doncaster. Trained at Webber Douglas School, London. Acting debut in *Charley's Aunt*, Frinton-on-Sea 1938. London same year in *Troilus And Cressida*. Shakespeare Memorial Theatre Company 1955. Theatre incl: *Robert And Elizabeth*; *The Cabinet Minister*; *Twelfth Night*; *The Lady's Not For Burning*; *Bedroom Farce*; *A Coat Of Varnish*; *The School For Scandal*; *See How They Run*. Films incl: *The Importance Of Being Earnest*; *There Was A Young Lady*; *The Truth About Women*; *Faces In The Dark*. Numerous TV appearances incl: as Boyd QC 1957–63; *Private Schultz*; *Bedroom Farce*; *Good Behaviour*; *Rumpole*; *Cold Warrior*. m. actress and novelist Dulcie Gray. Hobbies: golf, gardening, painting, motoring. Address: c/o ICM, London. Birthsign: Scorpio.

DENNIS, Les

Comedy and impressions double act with Dustin Gee, b. 12 Oct 1954 Liverpool. Started showbiz career at 14 in Merseyside clubs. TV debut on *New Faces* then *The Golden Shot, Blackpool Bonanza, The Comedians, Who Do You Do?, Live At Her Majesty's.* Summer seasons and cabaret in Britain. m. Lynne; 1 s. Philip James. Hobbies: running, cinema, theatre. Address: c/o Mike Hughes Entertainments, Liver House, Bold St, Liverpool. Birthsign: Libra. **Favourite Place:** 'Home . . . because I see it too rarely.'

DERBYSHIRE, Eileen

Actress, b. 6 Oct Manchester. Trained at the Northern School of Music (now Royal Northern College), LRAM. Speech and drama teaching before rep and radio work. Has played Emily in *Coronation Street* since 1961. m. Thomas W Holt; 1 s. Oliver. Hobbies: the Arts, the countryside, the home. Address: c/o Granada TV, Manchester. Birthsign: Libra. **Favourite Place:** 'Italian Chapel, Orkney. Happy family memories and represents the triumph of creativity over destructiveness.'

DIAMOND, Anne

TV presenter/journalist, b. 8 Sept 1954 Birmingham. 1975 joined the *Bridgwater Mercury* in Somerset and was art and music correspondent. 1977 joined the Bournemouth *Evening Echo*; 1979 joined ATV as reporter and presenter of *ATV Today*. When succeeded by Central became presenter *Central News.* 1982 became presenter BBC's *Nationwide* and lunchtime newsreader. In May 1983 joined TV-am as presenter. Hobby: music. Address: c/o TV-am, London. Birthsign: Virgo. **Favourite Place:** 'Sunday lunch at home with my family in Birmingham.'

DICKINSON, Sandra

Actress, b. 20 Oct Washington DC. After studying at University of Wisconsin and Boston University, trained at Central School of Speech and Drama in London. First became known in TV commercials but has done much theatre work, including *Legend*, in which she played Marilyn Monroe, and *Barefoot In The Park.* TV incl: *The Tomorrow People; What's On Next?; Cover; Hitch-Hiker's Guide To The Galaxy; Triangle; The Clairvoyant.* m. actor Peter Davison; 1 d. Georgia. Address: c/o Howes and Prior, London. Birthsign: Libra.

DIMBLEBY, David

Interviewer/presenter, b. 28 Oct 1938 London. After Paris Sorbonne and Universities of Perugia and Oxford, joined BBC in Bristol as a reporter 1961, reporting for *Enquiry* 1964. Left TV in 1965 to concentrate on family newspapers when father Richard Dimbleby died. Managing Director Dimbleby Newspaper Group from 1966. After six months in America for CBS, joined *Panorama* 1967 as a freelance, then *24 Hours* (1969). Other TV incl: *Yesterday's Men*; *Reporter At Large*; *Dimbleby Talk-In*; *Panorama* 1974–77; *General Election Results*; *The White Tribe Of Africa*; *Person To Person*; *This Week Next Week*. m. Josceline; 2 d. Liza, Kate, 1 s. Henry. Hobby: sailing. Address: c/o BBC TV, London. Birthsign: Scorpio.

DIMBLEBY, Jonathan

Broadcaster/journalist/writer, b. 31 July 1944 London. Son of the late Richard Dimbleby and brother of David. Joined BBC Bristol 1969 as television/radio reporter. *The World At One* 1970–71. Thames TV's *This Week* 1972–78 and *TV Eye* until 1979, when he produced and presented *Jonathan Dimbleby In South America*. Since 1979 TV incl: *The Bomb*; *The Eagle and The Bear*; *The Cold War Game*. 1983 presenter/interviewer *First Tuesday*; 1984 *Jonathan Dimbleby In Search of The American Dream* and *Four Years On: The Bomb*. 1985 joined TV-am to present *Good Morning Britain*. 1974 Richard Dimbleby Award for factual TV. Books: *Richard Dimbleby*; *The Palestinians*. m. journalist Bel Mooney; 1 s. Daniel, 1 d. Kitty. Hobbies: music, sailing, tennis, walking. Address: c/o David Higham Assocs, London. Birthsign: Leo.

DINENAGE, Fred

Presenter, b. 8 June 1942 Birmingham. A journalist with the *Evening Mail*, Birmingham and *Evening Argus*, Brighton, joined Southern TV 1964 to introduce *Three Go Round*. TV incl: *Day By Day*; *Afloat*; *Calendar Sport*; *Sunday Sport*; *World Of Sport*; *Bank Holiday Sport*; *Southsport*; *Gambit*; *How?*; *Miss Great Britain*; *Pro-Celebrity Snooker*; *Pro-Celebrity Darts*; *Cuckoo In The Nest*; Munich and Moscow Olympics. Joined TVS 1982. Presented *Friday Sports Show* and *Sunday Sports Show*. Host *Coast To Coast*; presenter *Vintage Quiz*, *Starkids*. m. Beryl; 1 d. Caroline, twins Sarah, Christopher. Hobbies: sport, family, reading, running a badge-making business with his wife. Address: c/o TVS, Southampton. Birthsign: Gemini. **Favourite Place:** 'The village where I live—Hambledon, Hants.'

DOBSON, Anita

Actress, b. 29 April 1949 London. Trained at the Webber Douglas Academy. Stage appearances incl: *Ardele*; *A Night In Old Peking*; *Dick Whittington* (title role); *Charley's Aunt*. TV incl: *What's Your Poison?*; *Play Away*; *Nanny*; *Partners In Crime*; *Up The Elephant And Round The Castle*; *EastEnders*. Hobbies: reading, watching old black and white movies. Address: c/o London Management, London. Birthsign: Taurus. **Favourite Place:** 'Venice because it's so very beautiful!'

77

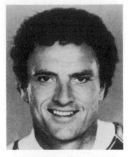

DOBSON, Kevin

Actor, b. 18 March Queens, New York. Started in commercials and first acting part in the stage play *The Impossible Years* starring Tom Ewell. He then studied at the Neighborhood Playhouse, New York, and appeared in off-off Broadway plays. Films incl: *Love Story*; *Midway*; *Klute*; *The French Connection*. TV films incl: *Transplant*; *Orphan Train*; *Hard Hat And Legs*; *Reunion*; *Mark, I Love You*. TV incl: *The Mod Squad*; the part of Det Crocker in *Kojak* for five years; *Shannon*; *Tales Of The Unexpected*; *Knots Landing*. m. Susan; 1 d. Miriah, 2 s. Patrick, Shawn Kevin. Hobbies: sports—golf, baseball, swimming, football. Address: c/o Freeman & Sutton, 8961 Sunset Blvd, Los Angeles, CA 90069. Birthsign: Pisces. **Favourite Place:** 'My home with my family. They mean everything to me in the world!'

DODD, Ken, OBE

Comedian/singer/actor, b. 8 Nov 1927 Liverpool. Professional comedian since 1954. Inventor of 'The Diddymen'. Many summer and variety shows and own TV and radio programmes. Theatre incl: Malvolio in *Twelfth Night*; *Ha Ha—A Celebration Of Laughter*; *Ken Dodd's Laughter Show* at London Palladium and provinces. TV incl: *Ken Dodd Show*; *Doddy's Music Box*; *The Good Old Days*; *Super Troupers*; *Funny You Should Say That*; *Look Who's Talking*; *Ken Dodd's World Of Laughter*; *Stars On Sunday*; *Ken Dodd's Showbiz*; *The Railway Carriage Game*. Records incl: *Love Is Like A Violin*; *Tears*; *Happiness*. Hobbies: watching racing, reading science fiction and psychology. Address: Knotty Ash, Liverpool. Birthsign: Scorpio. **Favourite Place:** 'The Liverpool pier-head and skyline from the Mersey as I return home.'

DOONICAN, Val

Singer, b. 3 Feb 1929 Waterford, Ireland. Worked in a steel foundry and orange box factory before first professional engagement in 1946. Radio in Ireland, joined The Four Ramblers 1951 in *Riders Of The Range*. First radio *Your Date With Val* 1959. Famous chair and sweaters arrived with TV show 1964. TV incl: *The Val Doonican Show*; *The Val Doonican Music Show*; *Sunday Night At The London Palladium*; *Stars On Sunday*. Records incl: *Walk Tall*; *Paddy McGinty's Goat*; *No Charge*; *Rafferty's Motor Car*; *Morning*; *If The Whole World Stopped Lovin'*; *What Would I Be?* m. former cabaret and revue star Lynette Rae; 2 d. Sarah, Fiona. Hobbies: golf, oil painting, archery. Address: c/o Bernard Lee Management, Caterham. Birthsign: Aquarius. **Favourite Place:** 'On the golf course.'

DOUGLAS, Alton

Comedian, b. 22 Jan 1940 Birmingham. Began as leader of own jazz band and progressed to comedy. Sophisticated cabaret, hotel and theatre comedian and writes comedy material and scripts. TV incl: *Crossroads*; *A Soft Touch*; *The Golden Shot*; own BBC Show *The Original Alton Douglas*; *Nights At The Swan*; *Seconds Out*; *Know Your Place*; *Muck And Brass*; *Operation Democrat*; *Cautionary Tales*; *Angels*; *Property Rites*. Also own Beacon Radio series *Beacon Swing With Alton Douglas*. m. Jo. Hobbies: pet dog Groucho Marx (old English Sheepdog), jazz records, books on theatre and comedy, paintings, models, information on clowns, keep fit. Address: c/o George Bartram Enterprises, Birmingham. Birthsign: Aquarius. **Favourite Place:** 'The village of Hay-on-Wye which must rate as the book capital of the country.'

DOUGLAS, Angela
Actress/writer, b. 29 Oct 1940
Gerrards Cross, Bucks. Started
acting as a teenager then rep in
Worthing until West End break
in *Anniversary Waltz*. Theatre
incl: *The Birthday Party*; *The First
Mrs Frazer*; *The Scenario*;
Something's Afoot. Films incl: *Feet
of Clay*; *Cleopatra*; *Some People*;
It's All Happening; *The Comedy
Man*; *John Goldfarb, Please Come
Home*; *Carry On Cowboy*; *Digby,
The Biggest Dog In The World*.

TV incl: *The Hard Knock*; *A
Smashing Day*; *The Slaughter
Men*; *Wuthering Heights*;
Rosemary; *The Dragon's
Opponent*; *The Gentle Touch*.
Autobiography: *Swings And
Roundabouts*. Regular contributor
to newspapers and magazines. m.
actor Kenneth More (dec.).
Hobbies: design, music, cooking.
Address: c/o ICM, London.
Birthsign: Scorpio. **Favourite
Place:** 'My home—pleasure,
peace and privacy.'

DOUGLAS, Jack
Comedian/actor/writer, b. 26
April 1927 Newcastle-upon-
Tyne. Acting debut at 21 in *Dick
Whittington*. Partnered Joe Baker
for nine years then solo. With Des
O'Connor five years on stage, TV
and *Royal Variety Show*. Theatre
incl: *Sting In The Tail*; *Make A
Break*; *Habeas Corpus*; *Oliver!*;
Treasure Island; *Love At A Pinch*.
Well known as member of 'Carry
On' team in films. TV incl: *The*

Reluctant Juggler; own cookery/
chat show for Channel TV; *Red
Saturday*; *The Shillingbury
Blowers*; *Shillingbury Tales*; *Cuffy*.
Writer of cook books. m. Susan;
2 d. Deborah, Sarah, 1 s. Craig.
Hobbies: painting, antiques,
photography, cooking, shooting,
driving. Address: c/o Richard
Stone, London. Birthsign:
Taurus. **Favourite Place:** 'On
stage of any theatre that's sold
out; a feeling that cannot be
described or replaced.'

DOUGLAS, Sarah
Actress, b. 12 Dec 1952 Straford-
upon-Avon. Trained with the
English National Youth Theatre
and at the Rose Bruford Drama
School. Films incl. *The Final
Programme*; *The People That Time*

Forgot; *Superman I, II*; *Conan
The Destroyer*. TV incl:
Thundercloud; *Harlequinade*;
Secrets; *Justice*; *The Inheritors*;
*The Ghost Girl And Esther
Waters*; *Warship And Black Ale*;
Falcon Crest. m. writer Richard
LeParmentier. Hobbies:
swimming, gardening, aerobics.
Address: c/o Paul Kohner
Agency, 9169 Sunset Blvd, Los
Angeles, CA 90069. Birthsign:
Sagittarius. **Favourite Place:**
the Orient, Hawaii, Mexico.

DOUGLAS, Su
Actress, b. 8 Nov 1942
Nottingham. Attended Aida
Foster School and the Pauline
Grant Ballet School. Stage incl: *A
Dead Secret*; *Houseguest*; *Don't
Just Lie There, Say Something*;
Sleeping Beauty; *A Sting In The
Tale*. Films incl: *Ghost Train*

Murder; *Those Nice Americans*;
Funny Money; *Boys In Blue*. TV
incl: *Within These Walls*;
Triangle; *Spotlight*; *A Chance In
A Million*; *Prospects*. m. Jack
Douglas; 1 d. Sarah, 1 step-s.
Craig, 1 step-d. Debbie. Hobbies:
keep-fit, squash, tennis, cooking.
Address: c/o Thomas & Benda
Assocs, London. Birthsign:
Scorpio. **Favourite Place:**
'Under the walnut tree in my
garden reading a wonderful script
that includes a part for me.'

DRABBLE, Phil

Countryman, b. 14 May 1914 Staffs. First radio broadcast 1947 and first TV 1953. Best known as presenter of sheep dog series *One Man And His Dog* and *In The Country*. Also for contributing to radio's *Living World*. Has written 16 books about the countryside, natural history and dogs. m. Hobbies: natural history and working dogs. Address: Abbots Bromley, Rugeley, Staffs. Birthsign: Taurus. **Favourite Place:** 'My own 90 acre woodland nature reserve. This is a bird sanctuary for birds, not birdwatchers, and deer and badgers also thrive there because they have complete seclusion.'

DRAKE, Gabrielle

Actress, b. Lahore, Pakistan. Trained for the stage at RADA. Stage appearances incl: seasons at Manchester's Royal Exchange, Bristol Old Vic, New Shakespeare Company, and the Young Vic; *Tea Party*; *Noises Off*; *Jeeves*. TV incl: *The Brothers*; *The Kelly Monteith Show*; *Crossroads*; and the TV plays, *The Importance Of Being Earnest* and *No 10: Wellington*. m. Louis de Wet. Hobbies: 'My husband, his work and his life.' Address: c/o Fraser & Dunlop, London. Birthsign: Aries. **Favourite Place:** 'My home, which is a medieval priory, in which I can regain sanity and a sense of perspective.'

DRINKWATER, Carol

Actress, b. 22 April 1948 London. Trained at Central School of Speech and Drama, London, then rep, incl: Birmingham and Leeds; National Theatre; Dublin, Edinburgh and Malvern festivals. Toured South East Asia 1981. *Black Ball Game*, Lyric Theatre, London. Films incl: *Clockwork Orange*; *The Dawn Breakers*; *Mondo Candido*; *Queen Kong*; *Joseph Andrews*; *The Shout*. TV incl: *Public Eye*; *Bill Brand*; *The Sweeney*; *Raffles*; *Sam*; *Bouquet Of Barbed Wire*; *All Creatures Great And Small* (shared 1979 Variety Club Award BBC TV Personality); *The Lady Killers*; *Tales Of The Unexpected*; *Take The Stage*; *Chocky*; *Golden Pennies*. Hobbies: scuba-diving, swimming, writing, music, travel, riding, skiing. Address: c/o London Management, London. Birthsign: Taurus. **Favourite Place:** Lizard Island, Great Barrier Reef, Australia.

DRIVER, Betty

Actress, b. 20 May 1920 Leicester. Trained in variety and rep before moving into films and television. Joined *Coronation Street* in 1968 as Betty Turpin. Hobbies: gardening, collecting antiques. Address: c/o Granada TV, Manchester. Birthsign: Taurus. **Favourite Place:** 'My own home and garden, because it's heaven.'

DRYER, Fred
Actor, b. 6 June 1946 Los
Angeles, California. Trained for
his acting career with coach Nina
Foch. Films incl: *Cannonball Run
II*. TV incl: commentary for
CBS Sport; *Cheers*; *Lou Grant*;
Laverene And Shirley; *Hunter* and
the TV films, *The Kid From
Nowhere*; *Starmaker*; *Girl's Life*;
The Marshal Of Slade Town; *Force
Seven*. m. actress Tracy Vaccaro;
1 d. Caitlin. Hobbies: managing
his Californian real estate
investments, weightlifting,
spending time with his family.
Address: c/o William Morris
Agency, 151 El Camino Drive,
Beverly Hills, CA 90212.
Birthsign: Gemini. **Favourite
Place:** good Mexican
restaurants; going to the parks
with his family.

DU SAUTOY, Carmen
Actress, b. 26 Feb 1952 London.
Has worked in rep at
Nottingham, Crewe and Oxford.
From 1976–80 was a leading
player with the Royal
Shakespeare Company, where
plays incl: *Love's Labours Lost*; *A
Midsummer Night's Dream*; *War
Of The World*; *Children Of The
Sun*; *Once In A Lifetime* (1980
London Critics' Award). Other
stage incl: *Antony And Cleopatra*;
Macbeth; and a tour of America
with the Old Vic. Films incl: *The
Man With The Golden Gun*;
Dracula's Daughter. TV incl: *The
Citadel*; *Strangers And Brothers*;
The Barretts Of Wimpole Street;
Chessgame; *Praying Mantis*. m.
Charles Savage. Hobbies: reading,
tennis, skiing, computers.
Address: c/o Duncan Heath
Assocs, London. Birthsign: Pisces.
Favourite Place: 'Sitting in my
garden with a good book.'

DUCE, Sharon
Actress, b. 17 Jan 1950 Sheffield.
Trained at drama school and rep
at York, Scarborough and Bristol
Old Vic. Theatre incl: *The
Foursome*; with the Actors
Company 1974–76; *Touched*;
Tibetan Inroads; *The Changeling*.
Numerous TV appearances incl:
Renoir My Father; *Helen, Woman
Of Today*; *Girl On The M1*; *Play
For Today*; *Minder*; *The House
That Jack Built*; *Funny Man*; *The
Hard Word*; *Big Deal*. m.
Dominic Guard; 1 s. William.
Hobbies: football, photography.
Address: c/o Susan Angel,
London. Birthsign: Capricorn.
Favourite Place: 'Fulham
Football Ground because I love
the Club passionately.'

DUNCAN, Peter
Actor, b. 3 May 1954 London.
First major role as Jim Hawkins
in *Treasure Island* at the Mermaid
Theatre, London, then two years
with National Theatre. Films
incl: *Stardust*; *The Lifetaker*;
Quilp; *Flash Gordon*. TV incl:
Oranges And Lemons; *Play For
Today*; *John Halifax Gentlemen*;
Sam; *Fathers And Families*; *Renoir
My Father*; *King Cinder*; *Flockton
Flyer*; *Space 1999*; *Fallen Hero*;
Family Affair; *Sons And Lovers*;
presenter *Blue Peter* 1980–84;
own series *Duncan Dares*. His
exploits for TV have incl:
cleaning the face of Big Ben; four
London marathons; fought a
Sumo wrestler. Also a
songwriter. m. Annie. Hobbies:
DIY, football, singing. Birthsign:
Taurus. **Favourite Place:**
'Centre stage, home, Italy, bed,
out of cities, skiing!'

DUNN, Kevin
Journalist, b. 20 Jan 1953
Liverpool. After Clare College,
Cambridge entered journalism in
1975 with Reuters News Agency.
Correspondent in Spain 1976–80.
Correspondent in Peru 1980–82.
Joined ITN 1984. m. Cheryl; 2 d.
Elena, Cristina. Address: c/o ITN,
London. **Favourite Place:**
'Goodison Park—home of
Everton Football Club.'

DURDEN-SMITH, Neil
Commentator/presenter, b. 18
Aug 1933 Richmond, Surrey.
Served in the Royal Navy 1952–
62. BBC producer 1963–66.
Film: *The Games*. Radio incl:
Test Match; World Cup; County
Championship; Gillette Cup;
panellist *Treble Chance, Forces
Chance, Sporting Chance*;
presenter *Champion's Choice,
Sports Special, Review Of The
Sporting Press*; reporter for *Today,
World At One, Outlook, Movie-*
*Go-Round, The World Today,
Trooping the Colour*. TV incl:
reporter for ITN; *World Of
Sport; Grandstand*; chairman
Tournament and *Money Matters*.
m. TV presenter Judith
Chalmers; 1 d. Emma. Hobbies:
theatre, playing sport,
newspapers. Address: c/o 344
Kensington High St, London.
Birthsign: Leo. **Favourite
Place:** 'A bath, because I can
dream, think, sing and listen to
the radio.'

DUTTINE, John
Actor, b. 15 April 1949 Barnsley,
Yorks. Trained at Drama Centre,
London, then rep at Glasgow
Citizens' Theatre, Watford and
Nottingham. Films incl: *Who
Dares Wins*. TV incl: *Armchair
Theatre; Z Cars; Holding On;
Warship; Lord Peter Wimsey;
Rooms; Coronation Street; Spend,
Spend, Spend; Jesus Of Nazareth;
Beryl's Lot; Angels; Law Centre;
Saturday, Sunday, Monday;
Devil's Crown; People Like Us;*
*Wuthering Heights; Strangers; The
Mallens; To Serve Them All My
Days; PS7-Warriors; The Day Of
The Triffids; The Outsider; Tales
Of The Unexpected; Family Man;
Woman Of Substance; Lame
Ducks*. 1 s. Oscar. Hobbies:
making wine/beer and drinking
it, gardening, walking. Address:
c/o Peter Browne Management,
London. Birthsign: Pisces.
Favourite Place: 'Pass of the
Cattle—a long hairpin road over
the mountains in Scotland.'

EDDINGTON, Paul
Actor, b. 18 June 1927 London.
First stage appearance with ENSA
1944. Rep at Birmingham and
Sheffield before RADA, 1951.
Then Ipswich rep and TV (incl:
The Adventures Of Robin Hood);
London stage debut 1961. Joined
Bristol Old Vic following year,
leaving 1963 to appear in *A
Severed Head* in US. Bristol Old
Vic 1965 and has been in many
plays there and West End incl:
Absurd Person Singular; Donkey's
*Years; Ten Times Table; Middle-
Age Spread; Who's Afraid Of
Virginia Woolf?; Noises Off;
Lovers Dancing; Forty Years On;
Jumpers*. TV incl: *Special Branch;
The Good Life; Yes, Minister; Let
There Be Love*. A governor of Old
Vic Theatre Trust. m. actress
Patricia Scott; 1 d. Gemma, 3 s.
Toby, Hugo, Dominic. Hobbies:
music, reading, art. Address: c/o
ICM, London. Birthsign:
Gemini. **Favourite Place:**
'Renato's Trattoria, Bristol.'

EDMONDS, Noel
TV worker, b. 22 Dec 1948 London. Started his broadcasting career with Radio Luxembourg before moving to Radio 1, where he presented early morning show. TV shows incl: *Swap Shop*; *Late Late Breakfast Show*; *Time Of Your Life*. Also *Foul Ups, Bleeps And Blunders*, for ABC in America. Hobbies: gardening, photography, helicopters. Address: c/o BBC TV, London. Birthsign: Capricorn. **Favourite Place:** 'The Lake District—peace, tranquillity, serenity and privacy.'

EDNEY, Beatie
Actress, b. 23 Oct 1962 London. Theatre experience incl: *In Nomine Patris* (Edinburgh Fringe 1984); *The Glass Menagerie*. Films incl: *A Day At The Beach*; *Highlander*. TV incl: *Mr Clay Mr Clay*; *Time For Murder*; most recently as Nancy in Granada's *Lost Empires*. Hobby: collecting pigs of any shape or size. Address: c/o Ken McReddie, London. Birthsign: Scorpio/Libra. **Favourite Place:** 'A field just outside Denby Dale in West Yorkshire, because there were plenty of pigs in it.'

EDWARDS, Glynn
Actor, b. 2 Feb 1931 Malaya. Trained at Central School and Joan Littlewood's Theatre Workshop. Stage incl: *Good Soldier Schweik*; *Quare Fellow*; *Macbeth*; *The Glass Menagerie*; *Have You Any Dirty Washing Mother Dear?* Films incl: *Zulu*; *The Ipcress File*; *Under Milk Wood*; *Shaft In Africa*; *Get Carter*; *Minder*. TV incl: *Madame Bovary*; *For Whom The Bell Tolls*, *Softly Softly*; *Steptoe And Son*; *The Main Chance*; *Man About The House*; *You're Only Young Twice*; *Sweet Sixteen*; and five series of *Minder*. m. (1st) actress Yootha Joyce (dis.), (2nd) Christine Pilgrim (dis.), (3rd) Valerie; 1 s Tom (from 2nd m.). Hobbies: messing about in boats. Address: c/o Green & Underwood, London. Birthsign: Aquarius. **Favourite Place:** 'Winchester Barge (his houseboat), because we can cast off and get lost.'

EGAN, Peter
Actor, b. 28 Sept 1946 London. Studied for the stage at RADA. Joined the Chichester Festival Theatre Company, followed by the Royal Shakespeare Company and National Theatre. Stage incl: *The Rivals*; *Journey's End*; *What Every Woman Knows*; *Rolls Hyphen Royce*; *Arms And The Man*. Also directed *Battle Of A Simple Man*, *Landmarks* and *A Midsummer Night's Dream*. Films incl: *The Hireling* (BAFTA Award for Best Actor, 1972); *Chariots Of Fire*. TV incl: *Lillie Langtry*; *Reilly Ace Of Spies*; *The Dark Side Of The Sun*; *Ever Decreasing Circles*; *Woman Of Substance*; *Paradise Postponed*. m. actress Myra Frances; 1 d. Rebecca. Hobbies: travel, swimming, poker, good wine. Address: c/o James Sharkey Assocs, London. Birthsign: Libra. **Favourite Place:** 'San Francisco because it's beautiful and looks wonderful at night.'

ELDER, Michael
Actor/writer, b. 30 April 1931 London. Trained at RADA, followed by work at Byre Theatre, Citizens' Theatre, Edinburgh Gateway Company, Pitlochry Festival Theatre, Lyceum Company, and the Scottish Theatre Company. TV appearances have incl: *Sam*; *Edward The Seventh*; *Five Red Herrings*; *The Prime Of Miss Jean Brodie*; *Take The High Road.* Author of over 150 radio scripts and 24 novels. TV scripts incl: *The Walls Of Jericho*; *King's Royal*; *Murder Not Proven*; *Take The High Road.* m. Sheila Donald; 2 s. Simon, David. Hobbies: cricket, reading, Scottish history. Address: c/o Young Cas'ing Agency, Glasgow. Birthsign: Taurus. **Favourite Place:** Blackwater Foot, Isle of Arran. 'The clock there moves at only half the normal speed.'

ELÈS, Sandor
Actor, b. 15 June Hungary. Trained at Bristol Old Vic Theatre School. Appeared at the National Theatre in *Watch On The Rye.* Is well known for his role as Paul Ross in TV's *Crossroads*, a part he has played since 1982. Other TV incl: *Treachery Game*; *Aubrey*; *The Seven Dials Mystery.* Hobbies: writing, making things. Address: c/o Brian Wheeler Personal Management, London. Birthsign: Gemini. **Favourite Place:** 'Casares, Costa Del Sol, Spain. It suits me one hundred per cent.'

ELLIOTT, Denholm
Actor, b. 31 May 1922 London. Although he spent one term at RADA his acting career really began in a POW camp after being shot down in 1942. First stage appearance was at the Amersham Playhouse, followed by *The Guinea Pig* in the West End. Many plays followed in London, Manchester, Stratford and with the Royal Shakespeare Company, plus many tours. Films incl: *The Cruel Sea*; *Alfie*; *The Seagull*; *A Bridge Too Far*; *Zulu Dawn*; *Trading Places*; *A Private Function*; *Razor's Edge.* TV incl: *Gentle Folk*; *Donkey's Years*; *Sextet*; *Bleak House.* BAFTA Award for Best Actor of the Year, 1980. m. Susan Robinson; 1 d. Jennifer, 1 s. Mark. Hobby: gardening. Address: c/o London Management, London. Birthsign: Gemini.

ELLIOTT, Su
Actress, b. 18 Dec 1950 Newcastle-on-Tyne. Trained at the Guildhall School of Music and Drama. Many appearances in fringe and rep in Newcastle, Clwyd and Hornchurch. West End plays incl: *Can't Pay, Won't Pay*; *The Secret Diary Of Adrian Mole.* Also own three woman show *Wandsworth Warmers.* TV incl: *Home Sweet Home* (*Play For Today*); *Auf Wiedersehen Pet*; *Tales Out Of School*; *When The Boat Comes In*; *Minder.* Hobbies: drinking, talking, visiting friends, helping the Labour Party. Address: c/o Barry Brown, London. Birthsign: Sagittarius. **Favourite Place:** 'Druidstone Hotel, Pembrokeshire, because of Rod and Jane who run it, wonderful food, views, walks, staff, bar. The best.'

ELLIS, Janet
TV presenter/actress, b. 16 Sept 1955 Kent. Trained at the Central School of Speech and Drama. Now the presenter of the children's programme *Blue Peter*, she started her career in *Princess Griselda*, a BBC *Jackanory* playhouse, followed by rep at Harrogate, Leeds and Manchester's Royal Exchange. After various TV plays, she appeared in four series of *Jigsaw*. m. TV director Robin Ellis-Bextor; 1 d. Sophie. Hobbies: collecting small teddy bears, changing her mind. Address: c/o Arlington Enterprises, London. Birthsign: Virgo. **Favourite Place:** 'Bed on Sunday morning with all the newspapers and a cup of tea—combines indolence, recreation and thought.'

ELLIS, Peter
Actor, b. 30 May 1936 Bristol. After training at the Central School, he entered rep in Leeds, Sheffield, Nottingham and Birmingham. He spent three years with the Old Vic Company and a further three years with the Royal Shakespeare Company. Also worked at Chichester and with Theatre Workshop and Belt and Braces Co. Theatre incl: *The Beggar's Opera*; *Trafford Tanzi*; *The Tulip Tree*. Films incl: *An American Werewolf In London*; *Agatha*; *Remembrance*. TV incl: *The Bill*; *Lytton's Diary*; *Knock Back*; *The Victoria Wood Show*; *Coronation Street*; *Edward And Mrs Simpson*; *In Two Minds*; *How We Used To Live*; *The Outsider*. m. (dis.); 3 s. Christopher, Hugh, Charlie. Hobby: gliding. Address: c/o Lou Coulson, London. Birthsign: Gemini. **Favourite Place:** Orford, Suffolk.

ELPHICK, Michael
Actor, b. 19 Sept 1946 Chichester. Worked as an electrician at Chichester Theatre before training at Central School of Speech and Drama. Worked extensively in rep, toured in *Hamlet* and was in *The Winter's Tale* at Ludlow Festival. Other theatre incl: *Measure For Measure*; *Ticket Of Leave Man* (National Theatre). Films incl: *Quadrophenia*; *The Elephant Man*; *The Curse Of The Pink Panther*; *Privates On Parade*. TV incl: *Holding On*, *The Nearly Man*; *Blue Remembered Hills*; *The Sweeney*; *The Knowledge*, *Wobble To Death*; *Private Schultz*; *Pocketful Of Dreams*; *Don't Write To Mother*; *Chains*; *Bloomfield*; *Andy Robson*; *All The World's A Stage*; *Crown Court*; *Supergran*; *Three Up, Two Down*; *Box 13*. m. Julia; 1 d. Kate. Address: c/o Crouch Assocs, London. Birthsign: Virgo.

EMBERG, Bella
Character actress/comedienne, b. 16 Sept 1937 Brighton, Sussex. Started in rep and recent stage work incl: *Macbeth*; *The Mating Game*; *All Laughter Showtime*; *Cinderella*; summer season and tours with Russ Abbot. TV incl: *Take Three Girls*; *Softly, Softly*; *Pennies From Heaven*; *Testament Of Youth*. Many TV Comedy roles incl: *And Mother Makes Three*; *Man About The House*; *Robin's Nest*; the *Russ Abbot's Madhouse* series. Stooged for Benny Hill, Frankie Howerd, Stanley Baxter, Les Dawson. Hobbies: opera, driving, old films, reading biographies. Address: c/o Mike Hughes Entertainments, London. Birthsign: Virgo. **Favourite Place:** 'Paris. I spent my fortieth birthday there and yes, life does begin at forty!!'

ENGLISH, Arthur

Actor, b. 9 May 1919 Aldershot. Became famous by parodying the Spiv, but went 'straight' 20 years later. Stage incl: *Royal Variety* (twice); revues; pantomimes; Chichester Festival; summer season; *On The Rocks*; *Die Fledermaus*. TV incl: *Follyfoot*; *Copper's End*; *How's Your Father*; *Dixon Of Dock Green*; *Crown Court*; *Doctor In The House*; *The Ghosts Of Motley Hall*; *Are You Being Served?*; *Funny Man*; *Pygmalion*. m. (1st) Ivy (dec.), (2nd) dancer Teresa Mann; 1 d. Ann, 1 s. Anthony (both from 1st m.), 1 d. Clare (from 2nd m.). Hobbies: DIY, oil painting. Address: c/o Patrick Freeman, 4 Cromwell Gr, London W6 7RG. Birthsign: Taurus. **Favourite Place:** 'Tintagel—with a name like Arthur I must be at peace with the world.'

ENRIQUEZ, Rene

Actor, b. 24 Nov San Francisco, USA. Attended the American Academy of Dramatic Arts, followed by Lincoln Center Repertory Company. Films incl: *Harry And Tonto*; *Under Fire*; *The Evil That Men Do*. TV appearances incl: *Police Story*; *Charlie's Angels*; *Quincy*; *Benson*; *Hill Street Blues*; and a film for TV, *Choices Of The Heart*. Awarded the Golden Eagle Award for Consistent Outstanding Achievement. Hobbies: soccer, teaching theatre workshops. Address: c/o SGA Representation, 12750 Ventura Blvd, Studio City, CA 91604. Birthsign: Sagittarius. **Favourite Place:** Mazatlán, Mexico.

ESHLEY, Norman

Actor, b. 30 May 1945 Bristol. Trained at the Bristol Old Vic Theatre School. Stage incl: *Measure For Measure*; *Hamlet*; *Arms And The Man*; *The Importance Of Being Earnest*; *Lady Chatterley's Lover*; *Way Upstream*; *The Exorcism*. His first professional appearance was in Orson Welles' film *The Immortal Story*. Other films incl: *Blind Terror*; *The Disappearance*; *Yanks*. Has appeared in many TV plays and series incl: *Randall And Hopkirk (Deceased)*; *The Onedin Line*; *I, Claudius*; *Secret Army*; *Return Of The Saint*; *The Sweeney*; *The Professionals*; *Maybury*. m. (1st) actress/singer Millicent Martin (dis.), (2nd) Lynette Braid. Hobbies: football, cricket, horse racing, sailing. Address: c/o Michael Ladkin, London. Birthsign: Gemini. **Favourite Place:** Carlisle Bay, Barbados—'Where I landed after sailing the Atlantic in 1984.'

EVANS, Barry

Actor/director, b. 18 June 1943 Guildford, Surrey. Trained for the stage at the Central School of Speech and Drama. TV incl: *Doctor In The House*, which made him a household name; *Crossroads*; *Armchair Theatre*; *Love Story*; *Mind Your Language*; *Emery—A Legacy Of Murder*. Hobbies: photography, gardening, animals, ecology. Address: c/o Hazel Malone Management, London. Birthsign: Gemini. **Favourite Place:** 'Home, and in the garden for peace and quiet and pottering about.'

EVANS, Clifford
Actor/writer, b. 17 Feb 1912 Senghennydd, South Wales. Studied for the stage at RADA, receiving Northcliffe and Academy scholarships. First appearance in London's West End was in 1933. Has since played in and directed many plays. Was appointed Director of Productions for the Festival of Britain 1952, and in 1957 founded the St David's Theatre Trust to establish a National Theatre for Wales. Films incl: *Love On The Dole*; *A Run For Your Money* (which he wrote). TV incl: *The Power Game*; *Kilverts' Diary*; *Dylan Thomas*; *Ten Years On*; *The Extremist*. Author of TV's *Where There's A Will*. m. Hermione Hannen. Hobbies: chess, reading Welsh literature. Address: c/o London Management, London. Birthsign: Aquarius. **Favourite Place:** 'Venice—a happy holiday spent there with my wife.'

EVANS, Linda
Actress, b. 18 Nov 1944 Hartford, Connecticut. Studied drama at Hollywood High School. Films incl: *Tom Horn*; *Avalanche Express*; *The Klansman*; *Mitchell*; *Twilight Of Honor*. TV incl: *The Big Valley*; *The Love Boat*; *Those Calloways*; *Bachelor Father*; *Bare Essence*; *Gambler II*; *Dynasty*. Awards incl: two Golden Globe Awards for Best Actress in a Dramatic Series; People's Choice Award for Best Actress in a New Dramatic Series. Book: *The Linda Evans Beauty Book*. m. (1st) John Derek (dis.), (2nd) Stan Herman (dis.). Hobbies: tennis, cooking, horse riding, metaphysics. Address: c/o Lippin & Grant Public Relations, 8124 West 3rd St, Los Angeles, CA 90048. Birthsign: Scorpio.

EVANS, Tenniel
Actor, b. 17 May 1926 Nairobi. Trained at RADA. Extensive theatre incl: *Unexpected Guest*; *The Kitchen*; *The Keep*; *Portrait Of Murder*; *Hamlet*; *Ten Times Table*; plus seasons acting and directing with the Actors' Company and Oxford, Birmingham and Swindon reps. Films incl: *Exodus*; *HMS Valiant*; *Only Two Can Play*; *Walk A Crooked Path*; *Sakharov*. TV incl: *The Avengers*; *Empty Bottles*; *Take Three Girls*; *My Brother's Keeper*; *The Citadel*; *The All Electric Amusement Arcade*; *Driving Ambition*; *Dream Stuffing*; *Lytton's Diary*; *Shine On Harvey Moon*. m. Evangeline Banks; 1 s. Matthew, 1 d. Serena. Hobbies: gardening, writing. Address: c/o Caroline Dawson Assocs, London. Birthsign: Taurus. **Favourite Place:** 'Bird Rock Valley in Mid-Wales. You have to be there to see why.'

EVERAGE, Dame Edna
Actress, b. Wagga Wagga, Australia. From household duties and invalid management has become a megastar. Monologues with Barry Humphries were so successful she was engaged as supporting artist in his shows. Films incl: *Adventures of Barry McKenzie*; *Barry McKenzie Holds His Own*. She achieved British stardom in *Housewife Superstar*, followed by *A Night With Dame Edna*; *Last Night Of The Poms*; *An Evening's Intercourse*. TV incl: *Barry Humphries's Scandals*; two *Audiences With Dame Edna*; and several BBC Specials. m. Norman Stoddart Everage; 1 d. Valmai, 2 s. Bruce, Kenneth Montgomery. Address: c/o Dennis Smith Promotions, Victoria, Australia. **Favourite Place:** 'Most spooky Aboriginal sacred sites.' (see also Humphries, Barry).

EVERETT, Kenny

Disc jockey/presenter, b. 25 Dec 1944 Seaforth, Liverpool. Originally wanted to become a priest and had various jobs before making a name as DJ with Radio London. Subsequently with Capital Radio and BBC Radio. TV incl: *Nice Time*; *The Kenny Everett Explosion*; *Making Whoopee*; *Ev*; *The Kenny Everett Video Show*; *The Kenny Everett Television Show*. Created the fabulous Capt Kremmen and many other comical characters. Hobby: squash. Address: c/o BBC TV, London. Birthsign: Capricorn.

EYRE, Charmian

Actress, b. 22 Feb 1927 Birmingham. Trained at the Birmingham Repertory Theatre, followed by the Young Vic, the Old Vic and various rep incl: Guildford, Salisbury, Coventry, Birmingham and Oxford. Stage incl: *The Indifferent Shepherd*; *As You Like It*. TV incl: *Shooting Star*; *Emergency Ward 10*; *Crossroads*. Hobbies: indoor plants, knitting, crochet, cooking. Address: c/o Ellison Combe Assocs, Richmond, Surrey. Birthsign: Pisces. **Favourite Place:** 'A place in a dream I had years ago—a sort of stepping stone or launch pad to nirvana.'

FARRELL, Shea

Actor/producer, b. 21 Oct Cornwall, New York. Took part in a number of college theatrical productions, from Shakespeare to Tennessee Williams. Film: *Ordinary People*. TV: *Hotel*; *Capitol*; *The Love Boat*; *Fantasy Island*. m. Ronda Pierson. Hobbies: writing, tennis, golf, sailing, water-skiing, snow-skiing. Address: c/o Howard Goldberg, Abrams, Harris & Goldberg, 9220 Sunset Blvd, Los Angeles, CA 90069. Birthsign: Libra. **Favourite Place:** 'Cape Cod because I can totally relax.'

FENTON, Leonard

Actor, b. 29 April 1926 London. Trained at the Webber Douglas Academy after the Second World War and began acting career in 1955. After being with various repertory companies, he toured India with the Bristol Old Vic. Stage appearances incl: Samuel Beckett's *Happy Days*; *The Seagull*; *The Bed Before Yesterday*; *The Square*; *The Irish Hebrew Lesson*. His radio work has included two spells with the BBC Drama Company. Recent films incl: *Give My Regards To Broad Street*; *Morons From Outer Space*. TV incl: *Z Cars*; *Colditz*; *The Secret Army*; *The Fourth Arm*; *Shine On Harvey Moon*. m. cellist Madeline Thorner; 3 s. Daniel, Sam, Toby, 1 d. Nina. Hobbies: painting, singing, Address: c/o Howes & Prior, London. Birthsign: Taurus. **Favourite Place:** 'Rural and coastal Suffolk—peaceful and a good place to paint.'

FIELDING, Fenella
Actress, b. 17 Nov 1934 London.
Numerous stage appearances incl:
Cockles And Champagne (West
End debut); *See You Later*; *Five
Plus One*; *The Rivals*; *The
Establishment*; *Let's Get A
Divorce*; *The High Bid*; *Hedda
Gabler*; *Colette*; *Fielding
Convertible* (one-woman show);
Chapter Seventeen; *Once A
Catholic*; *The Ghost Train*. Films
incl: *Carry On Screaming*; the
Doctor series; *No Love For*
Johnnie. Radio incl: *Something To
Shout About*; *Taming Of The
Shrew*; *Man And Superman*; *The
Rivals*. TV incl: *Ooh La La!*; *Ides
Of March*; *Rhyme And Reason*;
Nobody's Perfect; plus game and
chat shows. Also cabaret, and
several albums incl: *Pieces Of
Eight*; *Façade*. Hobbies: reading,
diarising. Address: c/o Hamper
Neafsey Assocs, London.
Birthsign: Scorpio. **Favourite
Place:** Greece, 'The climate, the
reality, the continuity.'

FISH, Michael
Weatherman, b. 27 April 1944
Eastbourne, East Sussex. Has been
with the Meteorological Office
for 23 years and made
appearances as TV weatherman
for 12 years. He has written and
narrated several schools radio
programmes. Also various TV
appearances where a 'scientific
expert' has been needed. Scripted
and appeared with Patrick Moore
on *Sky At Night*. Other TV incl:
Basil Brush; *Val Doonican Show*;
Whose Baby?; *3-2-1*; *Return To
Waterloo*; *Blue Peter*. m. Susan; 2
d. Alison, Nicola. Hobbies:
philately, travel, gardening, DIY,
genealogy. Address: c/o BBC,
London. Birthsign: Taurus.
Favourite Place: France for the
food and wine.

FITZALAN, Marsha
Actress, b. Bonn, W Germany.
Trained at the Webber Douglas
Academy in London and theatre
incl: *84 Charing Cross Road*.
Films incl: *International Velvet*;
Anna Karenina. Many TV
appearances incl: *The Duchess Of
Duke Street*; *Angels*; *Upstairs,
Downstairs*; *Shelley*; *Diamonds*;
Pride And Prejudice; *Nancy Astor*;
The Wife's Revenge; *Pygmalion*;
By The Sword Divided; *A Comedy
Of Errors*; *Three Up, Two Down*;
Paradise Postponed. m. Patrick
Ryecart; 2 d. Mariella, Jemima.
Hobbies: riding, hunting.
Address: c/o Duncan Heath
Assocs, London. Birthsign: Pisces.

FLANDERS, Ed
Actor, b. 29 Dec Minneapolis,
Minnesota. Films incl:
Grasshopper; *MacArthur*; *Pursuit
Of D B Cooper*; *True Confessions*;
Killer Kane. TV incl: *Backstairs
At The White House*; *The
Amazing Howard Hughes*; *Blind
Ambition*; *Mary White*; *Things In
Their Season*; six episodes of
Hawaii Five-O. Emmy Award for
the TV film *Harry Truman: Plain
Speaking*, and for Outstanding
Lead Actor for his portrayal of
Dr Westphall. Also won Emmy
and a Tony for his role in *Moon
Of The Misbegotten*. 3 children.
Hobbies: fishing, listening to
music. Address: c/o The Artists
Agency, 10000 Santa Monica,
Los Angeles, CA 90067.
Birthsign: Capricorn.

FLAX, Fogwell

Comedy entertainer, b. 9 March 1951 Liverpool. No formal training, he held various jobs, then four years as physiological measurement technician (cardiology) at the Royal Liverpool Children's Hospital. Turned professional 1975 as half of Union Jack duo and won *New Faces*. Went solo 1979 and won TV's *Search For A Star* 1980. TV incl: *Punchlines*; *3-2-1*; *Live From Two*; *After All That, This*; *Clubland*; *Northern Life*; *Tiswas*; *Starburst*; *A Foggy Outlook*; *Entertainment Express*; *Saturday Starship*. m. Andrea (sep.); 1 d. Deborah, 2 s. Neil, Timothy. Hobbies: Roman archaeology in Britain, model railways, music. Address: c/o Kim Newman, Manchester. Birthsign: Pisces. **Favourite Place:** 'I spend so long waiting for my agent's cheque, the porch is my second home!'

FLEMYNG, Robert, OBE, MC

Actor, b. 3 Jan 1912 Liverpool. First appeared on stage in Truro in 1931. His first London part was in 1935 after three seasons at the Liverpool Playhouse. After serving with the RAMC and being awarded the Military Cross and other decorations, returned to the stage in 1945. Stage incl: *French Without Tears*; *The Cocktail Party*; *The Guinea Pig* (also the film). Films incl: *The Blue Lamp*; *The Man Who Never Was*; *Medusa Trap*; *Four Feathers*; *The Thirty-Nine Steps*. TV incl: *Family Solicitor*; *Compact*; *Probation Officer*; *Spy Trap*; *Enemy At The Door*; *Rebecca*; *Edward And Mrs Simpson*; *The Lady Killers*; *Fame Is The Spur*; *Play For Today*. m. Carmen; 1 d. Caroline. Hobby: work. Address: c/o ICM, London. Birthsign: Capricorn. **Favourite Place:** New York.

FLETCHER, Cyril

Comedian, b. 25 June 1913 Watford. First made his name on radio and TV broadcasting his Odd Odes in 1936. Starred in West End revues and at the London Palladium during the Second Word War. Presented his own pantomimes and summer shows for 25 years. Had his own series on both radio and TV with his odes, the most famous being *Dreaming Of Thee*. TV incl: *What's My Line*; *That's Life!*; *Gardening Time*. President of the Pantomime Society, and author of 12 books. m. actress Betty Astell; 1 d. actress/comedienne Jill Fletcher. Hobbies: gardening and the countryside. Address: Fort George, St Peter Port, Guernsey. Birthsign: Cancer. **Favourite Place:** 'The balcony of my bedroom with its glorious maritime view which looks on to fabulous blue sea with Herm and Sark as the background.'

FORBES, Natalie

Actress, b. 1 Nov 1959 Doncaster, Yorks. She began her acting career in summer season and pantomimes. Her first West End appearance was in *Beyond The Rainbow*. Other stage incl: *Outside Edge*; *The Best Little Whorehouse In Texas*; *The Collector*. TV incl: *The Other 'Arf*; *Nanny*; *The Kelly Monteith Show*; *The Incredible Mr Tanner*; *Blood Money*; *The Gentle Touch*; *A Ferry Ride Away*; *Out On The Floor*; *Full House*. Hobbies: classical music, reading, Doncaster Rovers. Address: c/o Hamper-Neafsey Assocs, London. Birthsign: Scorpio. **Favourite Place:** Buckden Pike, Yorkshire Dales.

FORSYTH, Brigit
Actress, b. 28 July Edinburgh.
Trained at RADA, followed by
rep incl, Salisbury, Lincoln,
Cheltenham, Edinburgh,
Watford, Hornchurch. Stage incl:
My Fat Friend; *The Norman
Conquests*; *Dusa, Fish, Stas and
Vi*. Films incl: *The Road Builder*;
The Likely Lads. Radio work has
included many plays. TV incl:
Adam Smith; *Holly*; *Glamour*
Girls; *The Master Of Ballantrae*;
The Likely Lads; *Holding The
Fort*; *Tom, Dick And Harriet*;
Sharon And Elsie; *Bazaar And
Rummage (Play For Today)*; *The
Practice*. m. TV director Brian
Mills; 1 d. Zoe, 1 s. Ben. Hobbies:
walking, music, cello, guitar.
Address: c/o Jeremy Conway,
London. Birthsign: Leo.
Favourite Place: 'The
playroom in our house. I play the
cello there and with the children's
toys!'

FORSYTH, Bruce
Entertainer/comedian/singer, b.
22 Feb 1928 Edmonton, London.
Started as Boy Bruce, The
Mighty Atom, but not
discovered until 1958 when asked
to compère *Sunday Night At The
London Palladium*. Stage incl:
Windmill Theatre; *Little Me*;
The Bruce Forsyth Show; *Bruce
Forsyth On Broadway*. Films incl:
Bedknobs And Broomsticks; *Seven
Deadly Sins*; *Pavlova*. TV incl:
The Bruce Forsyth Show; *The
Mating Game*; *The Generation
Game*; *Bring On The Girls*;
Bruce's Big Night; *Play Your Cards
Right*; *Forsyth Follies*; *Hollywood
Or Bust*. m. (1st) Penny Calvert
(dis.), (2nd) Anthea Redfern (dis.),
(3rd) Wilnelia; 5 d. Deborah,
Julie, Laura (from 1st m.),
Charlotte, Louisa (from 2nd m.).
Hobbies: golf, tennis. Address:
c/o London Management,
London. Birthsign: Pisces.
Favourite Place: Puerto Rico:
'My wife lives there!'

FORSYTHE, John
Actor, b. 29 Jan 1918 New
Jersey. Began career as a sports
announcer, then went on to radio
acting. Studied at the New York
Actors Studio. Theatre incl:
Mister Roberts; *The Teahouse Of
The August Moon*. Films incl:
Destination Tokyo (film debut);
And Justice For All; *Goodbye And
Amen*; *Madame X*; *In Cold Blood*;
Topaz; *The Happy Ending*. TV
incl: host/narrator of *World Of
Survival*; *Bachelor Father* (1957–
62); *To Rome With Love*;
Charlie's Angels; *Dynasty*. Golden
Globe Award for Best
Performance in a TV Drama,
1983 and 1984 for *Dynasty*. m.
Julie Warren; 1 s. Dall, 2 d. Page,
Brooke. Hobbies: tennis,
racehorses. Address: c/o William
Morris Agency, Beverly Hills,
CA 90212. Birthsign: Aquarius.

FOSTER, Barry
Actor, b. 21 August Beeston,
Notts. After training at the
Central School of Speech and
Drama joined classical rep.
London debut in *Fairy Tales Of
New York*. Stage also incl: *My
Place*; *Let's Get A Divorce*; *Getting
Away With Murder*; *Next Time
I'll Sing To You*; *The Basement*;
Master Builder; *The Trojan War
Will Not Take Place*; *Passion Play*.
Films incl: *King And Country*;
Twisted Nerve; *A Woman Called
Golda*; *Heat And Dust*; *To Catch
A King*. TV incl: *Hamlet*; *Mogul*;
Ghosts; *Taste Of Honey*; *Van Der
Valk*; *Divorce His, Divorce Hers*;
Old Times; *Wingate*; *A Family
Affair*. m. singer Judith Shergold;
2 d. Joanna, Miranda, 1 s. Jason.
Hobbies: music, golf. Address:
c/o Al Parker, London.
Birthsign: Leo. **Favourite
Place:** Venice, 'A jewel-
encrusted treasure house built on
water.'

FOWLDS, Derek

Actor, b. 2 Sept 1937 London. Trained at RADA and has since worked mainly in TV. First became well known in *The Basil Brush Show* (1969–73). Other TV incl: *Francis Durbridge's The Doll*; *After That This*; *Miss Jones And Son*; *Clayhanger*; *Edward The Seventh*; *Robin's Nest*; *Cribb*; *Give Us A Clue*; *Strangers*; *Triangle*; three series of *Yes, Minister*. m. (dis.); 2 s. James, Jeremy. Hobby: sport. Address: c/o Barry Burnett, London. Birthsign: Virgo. **Favourite Place:** 'The first tee on any golf course in England. One always believes this could be *the* round!'

FOWLER, Harry, MBE

Actor, b. 10 Dec 1926 Lambeth Walk, London. After being interviewed on *In Town Tonight*, he was always being asked to play Cockney parts in British films. Has since been in more than 100 films, incl: *Hue And Cry*; *Went The Day Well*; *The Longest Day*; *Ladies Who Do*; *The Prince And The Pauper*. Entered TV as Corporal Flogger Hoskins in *The Army Game* in 1957. Recent TV incl: *Stalingrad*; *World's End*; *The Little World Of Don Camillo*; *Dead Ernest*; *Entertainment Express*; *Dramarama*; *Me And The Girls*; *Scarecrow And Mrs King*. Awarded MBE 1970 Birthday Honours. m. Catherine. Hobbies: tennis, model railways. Address: c/o Essanay, London. Birthsign: Sagittarius. **Favourite Place:** The Algarve, Portugal, 'For comparatively clean Atlantic, fairly unspoilt scenery, Clive Dunn's swimming pool and Roger Taylor's tennis ranch!'

FOXWORTH, Robert

Actor, b. Houston, Texas. Trained for the stage at the Stratford University Contemporary Theater Workshop. Stage incl: *The Crucible* for which he received the Theater World Award. Films incl: *Damien—Omen II*; *The Black Marble*; *Prophecy*. TV incl: *Sadbird*; *The Storefront Lawyers*; *Falcon Crest* and the TV films: *The Questor Tapes*; *The FBI Versus Alvin Karpis*; *Mrs Sundance*; *The Memory Of Eva Ryker*; *Act Of Love*; *The Acts Of Peter And Paul*; *Frankenstein*; *James Dean*. m. (dis.) actress Elizabeth Montgomery; 1 s. 1 d. Hobbies: carpentry, gardening. Address: c/o Triad Artists, 10100 Santa Monica Blvd, Los Angeles, California.

FRANCIS, Stu

Comedian, b. 30 Jan 1948 Bolton, Lancs. Began as holiday camp entertainer, then worked in pubs and clubs as singer and comedian. Has worked in summer seasons and pantomime. Has had own series and many guest spots on radio and TV. TV incl: host of *Crackerjack* since 1980; *Ultra Quiz*. m. Wendy; 1 d. Zoe, 1 s. Andrew. Hobby: running. Address: c/o Time Artists, Chadderton, Lancs. Birthsign: Aquarius. **Favourite Place:** 'Finishing line of a marathon. After 26 miles there is no better sight, believe me!'

FRANKAU, Nicholas

Actor, b. 16 July 1954 Stockport, Cheshire. Trained at the Webber Douglas Academy. Started his career at Southwold Summer Season in 1977. Played in *Peter Pan* at Shaftesbury Theatre. Recent film: *Plenty*. TV incl: *'Allo 'Allo!*; *The Last Term (Play For Today)*; *I Remember Nelson*; *CATS Eyes*. Hobbies: cycle touring, repairing things. Address: c/o Jim Thompson, London. Birthsign: Cancer. **Favourite Place:** East Sussex, 'Boyhood memories when my grandparents lived there.'

FRANKLIN, Gretchen

Actress, b. Covent Garden, London. Has been in the business for 50 years. Most recent TV series is BBC's *EastEnders*. m. Caswell Garth. Hobbies: gardening, needlepoint, animals. Address: 50 Boileau Rd, Barnes, London SW13. Birthsign: Cancer. **Favourite Place:** 'My home, I can bang the front door and keep all intruders out!'

FRANKLYN, Sabina

Actress, b. 15 Sept London. Began in weekly rep in Southwold and then for five years throughout the country. Tours incl: *Charley's Aunt; The Man Most Likely To ...; Move Over Mrs Markham;* and at the National Theatre, *The Moving Finger*. TV incl: *Pride And Prejudice; Fawlty Towers;* and with Kelly Monteith, Dave Allen, Mike Yarwood, and Jim Davidson; *Keep It In The Family; When The Boat Comes In; Happy Ever After; Return Of The Saint; Blake's Seven; Full House.* Hobbies: antiques, decorating, films, travelling, children. Address: c/o Leading Artists, London. Birthsign: Virgo. **Favourite Place:** 'The road leading down to Loch Maree in Scotland, and the Amalfi coast in Italy—both for their magnificent views.'

FRANKLYN, William

Actor, b. 22 Sept 1925 Kensington, London. At the age of 15 appeared in *My Sister Eileen* at the Savoy Theatre. After the war, *Arsenic And Old Lace* followed by rep at Ryde and Margate and *The Love Of Four Colonels*. Many West End plays and has directed in London and Rome. Has been in more than 50 films. Recent TV incl: *Paradise Island; Masterspy; The Purple Twilight; The Steam Video Company*. Nine years of Schweppes commercials. m. (1st) actress Margot Johns (dis.), (2nd) actress Susanna Carroll; 3 d. Sabina (from 1st m.), Francesca, Melissa. Hobbies: cricket, philately, photography, Italy. Address: c/o John Redway Assocs, London. Birthsign: Virgo. **Favourite Place:** 'Acquafredda di Maratea in Southern Italy. It is *eterno paradiso*. Sun, sea, mountains, olive and lemon groves, wine and wonderment.'

FRASER, Bill

Actor, b. 5 June 1918 Perth, Scotland. Started his career with a touring rep company. Has since played everything from a Dame in pantomime to Shakespeare, including performances with the National Theatre Company. Before the Second World War he ran the Connaught Theatre, Worthing. Most recent theatre incl: *Uncle Vanya*; *The Cherry Orchard*; *School For Scandal*. Has also toured the capitals of Europe for the British Council. Films incl: *Doctor At Large*; *Up Pompeii*; *Up The Front*; *The Corn is Green*. TV incl: *Foreign Affairs*; *That's Your Funeral*; *The Corn is Green*; *Cover Her Face*; *The Secret Diary of Adrian Mole*; *Flesh and Blood*; *K9 & Co*; *A Girl's Best Friend*. m. Pamela Cundell. Hobby: working. Address: c/o Peter Crouch Assocs, London. Birthsign: Gemini. **Favourite Place:** 'Palace Hotel, Corfu, it's heaven!'

FRASER, John

Actor/director/writer/designer, b. 18 March 1931 Glasgow. Worked at Pitlochry Festival Theatre, Glasgow's Citizens' Theatre. Stage incl: *Any Wednesday*; *Strike A Light*; *Sleuth*; *Crown Matrimonial*. Films incl: *The Good Companions*; *Times Of Glory*; *The Trials Of Oscar Wilde*. TV incl: *A Legacy*; *The Doll*; *The Lady Killers*; *The Practice*. Books incl: *Clap Hands If You Believe In Fairies*; *The Bard In The Bush*. Pop records: *Good Companions*; *Why Don't They Understand*. For the past 10 years has directed, designed and acted for The London Shakespeare Group, which is sponsored by the British Council. Hobbies: work, riding. Address: c/o Fraser & Dunlop, London. Birthsign: Pisces. **Favourite Place:** 'The Campo in Siena and the Klongs in Bangkok to look at; favourite places to be, home—London and Tuscany.'

FRASER, Liz

Actress, b. 14 August 1935 London. Trained at the London School of Dramatic Art, since when she has worked extensively. Stage incl: *Too True To Be Good*; *Next Time I'll Sing To You*; *Black Comedy*; *Bedful of Foreigners*; *Donkey's Years*; *Sweeney Todd*; *Annie*. Films incl: *I'm All Right, Jack*; *Two Way Stretch*; *Live Now, Pay Later*; and in many of the *Carry On* and *Confessions* films. TV incl: *Shroud For A Nightingale*; *Fairly Secret Army*; and numerous panel games. Hobby: bridge. Address: c/o Barry Burnett, London. Birthsign: Leo. **Favourite Place:** 'Anywhere in the country in any country.'

FRAZER, Dan

Actor, b. 20 Nov New York City. Trained at WPA Federal Theater Project and Piscator Dramatic Workshop, New York. Theatre incl: *Every Good Boy Does Fine*; *Saturday, Sunday, Monday*; *Diary Of Anne Frank*; *Death Of A Salesman*; *All My Sons*. Films incl: *Soldier In The Rain*; *Take The Money And Run*; *Cleopatra Jones*; *The Super Cops*; *Breakout*. TV incl: *Kojak*; *The Secret Storm*; *Love Of Life*; *Love Is A Many Splendored Thing*. m. Lee; 1 d. Susanna. Hobbies: piano, writing poetry, photography. Address: c/o Bauman-Hiller, New York. Birthsign: Scorpio. **Favourite Place:** New York, 'It has such a variety of living—ocean, theatre, family. I'm a city kid.'

FROST, David, OBE
Author/interviewer/presenter/
tycoon, b. 7 April 1939
Tenterden, Kent. Began TV as
reporter for *This Week*, but
achieved overnight success as host
of *That Was The Week That Was*.
Other TV incl: *A Degree Of
Frost*; *Not So Much A Programme,
More A Way Of Life*; *The Frost
Report*; *The Frost Programme*;
Frost Over England; *Frost Over
America*; *We British*; *The Wilson
Interviews*; *The Nixon Interviews*;
The Shah Speaks; *The Falklands:
Where Will It End?*; *The
Guinness Book Of Records Specials*.
Founder of LWT; founder and
director of TV-am. m. Lady
Carina Fitzalan-Howard; 1 s.
Miles. Hobbies: football, cricket.
Address: c/o David Paradine,
London. Birthsign: Aries.
Favourite Place: 'Home, a 747,
Lord's, a Caribbean beach, and
almost any TV studio.'

FULLERTON, Fiona
Actress, b. 10 Oct 1956 Kaduna,
Nigeria. Her first appearance was
in the film *Run Wild, Run Free* at
the age of 11. She has since
worked extensively. Stage
appearances incl: *Caught
Napping*; *I Am A Camera*;
Barnado; *The Beggar's Opera*;
Gypsy; *The Boy Friend*; *Camelot*;
Films incl: *Nicholas And
Alexandra*; *The Human Factor*;
The Ibiza Connection; *A View To
A Kill*. TV incl: *A Friend Indeed*;
Angels; *Dick Barton Special Agent*;
Gaugin—The Savage; *Lev
Tolstoy: A Question Of Faith*; *The
Sailing Barge*; *Shaka Zulu*.
Hobbies: collecting elephants,
travel, antiques. Address: c/o
Theo Cowan, London. Birthsign:
Libra. **Favourite Place:** Hong
Kong Harbour, 'From the top of
the Hilton looking across to
Kowloon. At night it's a
breathtaking sight.'

FURST, Stephen
Actor, b. 8 May Norfolk,
Virginia. Film appearances incl:
Scavenger Hunt; *Take Down*;
*National Lampoon's Animal
House*; *Midnight Madness*; *Silent
Rage*; *Up The Creek*; *Class
Reunion*. TV incl: *The Day After*;
The Bastard; *Delta House*; *St
Elsewhere*. m. Lorraine; 2 s.
Nathan, Griffith. Hobbies:
antiques, cooking Italian cuisine,
coaching a small league T-ball
team. Address: c/o Dade, Rosen,
Lichtman, 12345 Ventura Blvd,
Studio City, California 91604.
Birthsign: Taurus.

GALL, Sandy
TV journalist, b. 1 Oct 1927
Penang, Malaya. Started career on
Aberdeen Press and Journal.
Worked for Reuters 1953–63 and
has worked for ITN since 1963.
Has travelled virtually all over
the world and speaks fluent
French and German. Was Rector
of Aberdeen University 1977–81.
Documentaries for ITV incl:
Behind Russian Lines (1982);
Allah Against The Gunships
(1984); *The Cresta Run, 1885–
1985*. Books: *Gold Scoop*, a novel
about Africa; *Chasing The
Dragon*, a novel about the Far
East; *Don't Worry About The
Money Now*, his memoirs; *Behind
Russian Lines: An Afghan Journal*.
m. Eleanor; 3 d. Fiona, Carlotta,
Michaela; 1 s. Alexander.
Hobbies: golf, writing thrillers.
Address: c/o ITN, London.
Birthsign: Libra. **Favourite
Place:** 'Sheekey's Oyster Bar,
with a bottle of Sancerre.'

GARDEN, Graeme
Actor/writer, b. 18 Feb 1943
Aberdeen. Cambridge Footlights
while at university. Studied
medicine at King's College
Hospital, London but entered
showbusiness after writing for
radio, incl: *I'm Sorry, I'll Read
That Again.* With Bill Oddie
wrote some of the *Doctor* TV
series and *Astronauts.* Other TV
incl: *Broaden Your Mind; The
Goodies; Tell The Truth; A Sense
Of The Past.* Records incl: *Funky*
Gibbon; The In-Betweenies. m.
Emma; 1 d. Sally, 2 s. John, Tom.
Hobbies: fishing, drawing, music.
Address: c/o Roger Hancock,
London. Birthsign: Aquarius.
Favourite Place: home.

GARDNER, Ava
Actress, b. 24 Dec 1922
Grabpoint, North Carolina. Best
known for her numerous film
roles during the 40s and 50s, she
was once voted the world's most
beautiful woman. Films incl:
*Show Boat; Pandora And The
Flying Dutchman; Mogambo; The
Barefoot Contessa; Bhowani
Junction; The Little Hut; The Sun
Also Rises; The Night Of The
Iguana; Earthquake; Cassandra
Crossing; The Sentinel.* TV incl:
Knots Landing. Address: c/o
London Management, London.
Birthsign: Capricorn. **Favourite
Place:** 'London, especially Hyde
Park, near my friends.'

GARNER, James
Actor, b. 7 April 1928
Oklahoma. Had 50 jobs before
becoming an actor, when he was
offered a part in *The Caine
Mutiny Court Martial* by a
producer friend. Started in TV in
Cheyenne followed by the
successful *Maverick.* Films incl:
*Darby's Rangers; Marlowe;
Support Your Local Sheriff; Grand
Prix; Victor, Victoria.* TV incl:
*The Rockford Files; Bret Maverick;
Heart Sounds.* Served in US army
in Korea and was awarded the
Purple Heart. m. actress Lois
Clarke; 1 d. Greta, 1 step-d.
Kimberly. Address: c/o Bill
Robinson, Lutrell Robinson, Los
Angeles, California. Birthsign:
Aries.

GARRETT, Cornelius
Actor, b. 3 Nov 1947 Hamburg,
Germany. Theatre incl: Half
Moon, London; Citizens'
Theatre, Glasgow; Royal
Shakespeare Company; Bristol
Old Vic; Tyneside Theatre,
Newcastle; Young Vic, London.
Films incl: *Disappearance Of
Harry; For Your Eyes Only.* Radio
incl: *Lorna Doone;* many
Afternoon Theatre productions for
Radio 4. TV incl: *Heartlands;
Bognor;* BBC Shakespeare series;
*Artemis 81; Animal Behaviour;
Robin Of Sherwood; The Master
Of Ballantrae; Gems.* m. Sarah
Jane; 1 d. Amy, 2 s. Eugenie,
Henry. Hobbies: knocking down
walls and rebuilding them.
Address: c/o Carole James
Management, Richmond, Surrey.
Birthsign: Scorpio. **Favourite
Place:** 'Home. The view from
the back window over pear, cedar
and chestnut trees, Bristol and
Dundry Hill beyond.'

GARWOOD, Patricia
Actress, b. 28 Jan 1941 Paignton, Devon. Her first part was in the film *The Lavender Hill Mob* aged nine. Trained at RADA and then Bromley rep. Appeared in many plays incl: *Any Woman Can; Old Times; Letters Home.* Many TV plays incl: *Poor Baby; Clouds Of Glory; Space Station Milton Keynes; A Walk Under Ladders.* TV drama incl: *The Victorians; You Can't Win; Our Sister Dora; Accident; Blunt Instrument; The Brack Report.* Also TV comedy: *No Place Like Home.* m. playwright Jeremy Paul; 4 d. Amanda, Tara, Sasha, Sophie. Hobbies: novel writing, riding, knitting, tobogganing, sunbathing, reading. Address: c/o Dodo Watts, Teddington. Birthsign: Aquarius. **Favourite Place:** 'Top of hill, Heddington, Wiltshire. Wet, windy day. Panoramic view. Beneficial to body and soul.'

GASCOIGNE, Bamber
Much-travelled question master, b. 24 Jan 1935 London. Scholarship to Yale School of Drama. Educated at Cambridge. Wrote *Share My Lettuce*, 1957. Later drama critic *The Spectator* and *The Observer.* Chairman of TV's *University Challenge* since 1962. Also presenter of *Cinema* 1964. Devised *The Auction Game* and scripted *The Four Freedoms, The Trouble With Women*; wrote and presented *The Christians.* Books: *World Theatre; The Great Moghuls; Treasures And Dynasties Of China; Murgatreud's Empire; The Heyday; The Christians; Quest For The Golden Hare.* m. Christina Ditchburn. Address: c/o Granada TV, Manchester. Birthsign: Aquarius. **Favourite Place:** 'Udaipur in India—the best place to stroll and marvel at the fascinations of life and landscape.'

GASCOINE, Jill
Actress, b. 11 April 1937 Lambeth, London. Trained at the Italia Conti Stage School, then rep at Nottingham, Dundee, Glasgow, Worthing, Hornchurch and Leicester. TV incl: *Rooms; Plays For Britain; General Hospital; The Norman Wisdom Show; Three Kisses; Balzac; Z Cars; Softly, Softly; Dixon Of Dock Green; Within These Walls; Holding On; Six Days Of Justice; Raffles; Beryl's Lot; Peter Pan; Oranges And Lemons; The Onedin Line; The Gentle Touch; CATS Eyes.* Voted Best Actress by *TV Times* readers 1984. 2 s. Sean, Adam. Hobby: gardening. Address: c/o Marina Martin Management, London. Birthsign: Aries. **Favourite Place:** 'My garden—viewed from any window of our house that looks over the terrace. I love it.'

GAUNT, William
Actor, b. 3 April 1937 Yorkshire. Trained at RADA, but had already started as a child actor in the Otley Little Theatre. After RADA, worked in Dallas Theater Center, Texas, then rep in UK. Films incl: *The Revolutionary.* TV incl: over 100 plays; *The Foundation; Crown Court; Love And Marriage; No Place Like Home.* Was also artistic director Liverpool Playhouse 1979–81. m. Carolyn Lyster; 1 d. Matilda, 1 s. Albert. Hobbies: gardening, walking. Address: c/o Julia MacDermot, London. Birthsign: Aries. **Favourite Place:** 'The Yorkshire Dales. I walked the Pennine Way some years ago.'

GEAKE, Nicholas
Actor, b. 28 Sept 1957 Woking, Surrey. Trained at Bristol Old Vic Theatre School then rep seasons at Manchester, York, Coventry, Liverpool, Basingstoke, Plymouth, National Theatre. Radio incl: *Silvertrain Day*; *Four Tales Of A City*. TV incl: *Secret Army*; *London Belongs To Me*; *The Professionals*; *Enemy At The Door*; *The Further Adventures Of Oliver Twist*; *Sherlock Holmes*; *The Demon Lover*; *Snoop*. m. Judith Sidney; 1 d. Fiona. Hobbies: fishing, golf, gardening, beer. Address: c/o Bill Horne Personal Management, London. Birthsign: Libra. **Favourite Place:** 'Any trout stream within walking distance of an old country pub where I can meet my wife and daughter.'

GEE, Dustin
Comedy and impressions double act with Les Dennis, b. 24 June 1942 York. Went to art college in York but entered showbusiness as singer with rock 'n' roll group. Formed own group, Gerry B and the Rockafellas. Later became stand-up comedian and impressionist. TV incl: *Who Do You Do?*; *Wheeltappers And Shunters Social Club*; *Blackpool Bonanza*; *Rock Follies*. Hobbies: music, theatre, DIY. Address: c/o Mike Hughes Entertainments, Liver House, Bold St, Liverpool. Birthsign: Cancer. **Favourite Place:** 'My bed . . . because I see it too rarely.'

GHOSH, Shreela
Actress, b. 25 Sept 1962 Shillong, India. No formal acting training but has trained in Indian classical dance since aged four. Educated in India until coming to London at the age of 11. Theatre incl: Joint Stock Theatre Group's *Great Celestial Cow*; *Doolaly Days*; M6 Theatre Company; Borderline Workshops at Royal Court Theatre, London. TV incl: *The Garland*; *Angels*; *Living On The Edge*; *The Chinese Detective*; *The Jewel In The Crown*; *Pravina's Wedding*; *The Prince And The Demons*; *EastEnders*. Hobbies: Indian classical dance, playing pool, going to the theatre, squash, scrabble, reading, cooking. Address: c/o David Daly, London. Birthsign: Libra. **Favourite Place:** 'An oasis in the Algerian Sahara called Djanet—the nearest one to the magnificent Tassili N'Ajer, the valley of chasms. A true "oasis" for the soul.'

GIBSON, Richard
Actor, b. 1 Jan 1954 Kampala, Uganda. Trained at Central School of Speech and Drama, London. Began acting as Marcus in the film *The Go-Between*, then in *Tom Brown's Schooldays* on TV. After leaving drama school worked in rep at Windsor, Chichester, Bristol Old Vic, Birmingham and The King's Head, London in *The Browning Version*. Theatre incl: *In Praise Of Love*; *French Without Tears*; *Escapade*; *The Winslow Boy*. TV incl: *Secret Diaries*; *Hadleigh*; *The Children Of The New Forest*; *The Gate Of Eden*; *Poldark*; *My Father's House*; *The Coral Island*; *'Allo 'Allo!* Hobbies: picture-framing, song-writing, carpentry. Address: c/o Annette Stone Assocs, Hatch End. Birthsign: Capricorn. **Favourite Place:** 'The Roof Garden, Kensington. Beautiful gardens in the middle of London with a ravishing view.'

GIELGUD, Sir John, CH
Actor/director, b. 14 April 1904
London. A great-nephew of
Dame Ellen Terry, he trained at
Lady Benson's school and RADA.
First stage appearance at the Old
Vic in 1921. Theatre incl:
numerous Shakespearian roles;
one-man show, *Ages Of Man*;
The Importance Of Being Earnest;
No Man's Land. Films incl: *The
Good Companions*; *Gold*; *Chariots
Of Fire*; *Arthur* (for which he
won an Oscar); *Wagner*; *The
Wicked Lady*. TV incl: *A Day By
The Sea*; *The Cherry Orchard*;
Ivanov; *Edward The Seventh*;
Why Didn't They Ask Evans?;
Brideshead Revisited; *Parson's
Pleasure*. Books: *Early Stages*
(autobiog); *Stage Directions*;
Distinguished Company; *An Actor
And His Time*. Hobbies: reading,
walking, puzzles, travel. Address:
c/o ICM, London. Birthsign:
Aries. **Favourite Place:** Oxford
and Venice.

GILES, Bill
BBC TV senior weatherman, b.
18 Nov 1939 Dittisham, Devon.
Studied at Bristol College of
Science and Technology and
Meteorological Office College.
As well as presenting BBC TV
weather bulletins, has appeared
on TV in *The Val Doonican
Show*; *Blue Peter*; *Saturday
Superstore*. Presented *A Change In
The Weather* on BBC 1 and 2. m.
Eileen; 1 s. Philip, 1 d. Helen.
Hobbies: gardening, cricket.
Address: c/o BBC TV, London.
Birthsign: Scorpio. **Favourite
Place:** 'Malden Island in the
South Pacific. Peace, perfect peace
and no telephones.'

GILLESPIE, Robert
Actor, b. 9 Nov 1933 Lille,
France. Mother Hungarian, father
Canadian of Scottish descent.
Arrived Plymouth 1940 unable
to speak English. Joined an
amateur acting group and
appeared as a semi-professional in
1951. After RADA, spent two
years at the Old Vic and then rep.
Also a director, playwright and
contributor to BBC's *That Was
The Week That Was*. Films incl:
A Severed Head; *The National
Health*; *The Thirty-Nine Steps*;
The Prisoner Of Zenda. Radio
incl: *Whatever Happened To The
Likely Lads?*; *Lord Peter Wimsey*.
Numerous TV appearances incl:
The Good Life; *Couples*; *Rising
Damp*; *Agony*; five series of *Keep
It In The Family*; *I Woke Up One
Morning*. Hobbies: reading,
cinema, travel, archaeology.
Address: c/o William Morris
Agency, London. Birthsign:
Scorpio. **Favourite Place:**
'Where wild plants grow.'

GLOVER, Brian
Actor, b. 2 April 1934 Sheffield.
Was a teacher and professional
wrestler before becoming an
actor. Debut in 1968 in the film
Kes when he played a
schoolmaster. Theatre incl: *Much
Ado About Nothing*; *The Passion*
at the National Theatre. Films
incl: *Brannigan*; *O Lucky Man*;
Quilp; *Trial By Combat*; *The
Great Train Robbery*; *An
American Werewolf In London*.
TV incl: *Rank And File*; *The
Frighteners*; *A Day Out*; *Speech
Day*; *The Regiment*; *Porridge*; *The
Wild Bunch*; *Secret Army*; *Return
Of The Saint*; *Sounding Brass*;
Minder; the voice for the Tetley
Tea Folk commercials. Also a
playwright. m. (dis.); 1 d.
Maxine, 1 s. Gus. Hobby:
breathing gently. Address: c/o
Felix de Wolfe, London.
Birthsign: Aries. **Favourite
Place:** 'Bed.'

GLOVER, Julian
Actor, b. 27 March 1935 London. Trained at RADA and began career as a spear carrier for the Royal Shakespeare Company 1957—he played lead roles for the RSC 20 years later. Theatre incl: the National Theatre; Old Vic; Prospect; Bristol Old Vic; West End. Also, his own adaptation of *Beowulf*; one-man show on the life and works of Robert Graves. Films incl: *Kim*; *Heat And Dust*; *For Your Eyes Only*. TV incl: *An Age Of Kings*; *Dombey And Son*; *By The Sword Divided*; *Six Centuries Of Verse*; *Cover Her Face*. m. actress Isla Blair; 1 s. Jamie. Address: c/o Jeremy Conway, London. Birthsign: Aries. **Favourite Place:** 'A hillside outside Deyá, Mallorca, where was spent the happiest week of my life.'

GODDARD, Liza
Actress, b. 20 Jan 1950 Smethwick. Trained with the Arts Educational Trust. Started career in Australia on TV in *Point Of Departure*, *Antigone*, *Romeo And Juliet* and *Skippy*. Returned to UK in 1969 and theatre incl: *Signs Of The Times*; *One Fair Daughter*; *The Three Sisters*; *See How They Run*. Radio incl: *The Victoria Line*; *A Midsummer Night's Dream*. TV incl: *Take Three Girls*; *Yes, Honestly*; *Queen Of A Distant Country*; *The Brothers*; *The Upchat Line*; *The Greatest*; *Pig In The Middle*; *Murder At The Wedding*; *The Parlour Game*; *Roll Over Beethoven*; *Take Three Women*; *Minder*; *Doctor Who*; *Bergerac*. m. Alvin Stardust; 1 s. Thom, 1 d. Sophie. Hobbies: riding, reading, chicken breeding, mucking out. Address: c/o Barry Burnett, London. Birthsign: Aquarius. **Favourite Place:** 'Home. I'm never bored there.'

GODWIN, Christopher
Actor, b. 5 Aug 1943 Loughborough, Leics. Started career in stage management with no drama school training. Played the leading roles in Alan Ayckbourn's plays at Scarborough for seven years before coming to London to star in Ayckbourn's *Ten Times Table*. Other theatre incl: *School For Scandal*; *Noises Off*. Films incl: *Porridge*. TV incl: *Don't Be Silly*; *Nice Work*; *Holding The Fort*; *Astronauts*; *The Other 'Arf*; *Nearly A Happy Ending*; *A Foggy Outlook*; *Return To Waterloo*; *Roll Over Beethoven*. m. Christine; 2 s. Ben, Tom. Hobbies: cycling, cricket, roller-skating. Address: c/o ICM, London. Birthsign: Leo. **Favourite Place:** 'Prussia Cove in Cornwall, because it's like the seaside you remember as a child.'

GOLDING, Charles B
TV presenter/journalist, b. 29 Oct 1957 London. After studying government and law at university, trained at the National Broadcasting School, London. Film critic for TV-am since June 1984. Presenter of *Boxing Day Show*, *Disney Dog Show* and *Wide Awake Club* at TV-am. Presenter and producer of *The Computer Show* for cable TV. Hobbies: writing, cinema, swimming, collecting 78 records and playing them, collecting bow ties. Address: c/o TV-am, London. Birthsign: Scorpio with Leo rising. **Favourite Place:** 'Jerusalem, because I keep on saying I'll be there next year!'

GONSHAW, Francesca
Actress/comedienne, b. London.
Trained at the Academy of Live
and Recorded Arts and the
Actors' Centre. Theatre incl: *You*
Should See Us Now; *Sailors'*
Dreams; *Monty Cliff*; *Dear Janet*
Rosenberg, Dear Mr Kooning.
Films incl: *Biggles*. TV incl:
Shades; *The Cleopatras*; *Gesualdo*;
Crossroads; *Sidni*; *'Allo 'Allo!*;
Cold Warrior. Hobbies: dance,
painting, chess, music. Address:
c/o Powerscot, London.
Birthsign: Sagittarius. **Favourite**
Place: 'Morocco: mountains and
water, smells and ambience,
danger and dark mysteries,
beauty.'

GOODALL, Caroline
Actress, b. 13 Nov 1959 London.
First trained with the National
Youth Theatre and left school to
play the lead in a BBC TV series.
Studied drama and English at
Bristol University. Theatre incl:
rep at Manchester Royal
Exchange; Oxford Playhouse;
Plymouth Theatre Royal; British
tour with Eric Sykes and
Matthew Kelly in *Time And*
Time Again; *Romeo And Juliet*;
Twelfth Night; *Private Lives*;
Erpingham Camp; *While The Sun*
Shines; *Daisy Pulls It Off* (original
cast member); comedy revue;
founder member of Stiletto
Theatre Playwrights Company.
TV incl: *The Moon Stallion*;
Gems. Hobbies: writing, chewing
biros, collecting shoes, eating out.
Address: c/o Michael Ladkin,
London. Birthsign: Scorpio.
Favourite Place: 'Sunday
morning at home with all the
papers and nothing planned all
day.'

GOODWIN, Harold
Actor, b. 22 Oct 1917
Wombwell, Yorks. Trained at
RADA and was three years at
Liverpool rep. First stage
appearance in London's West End
in *Venus Observed*. Many stage
productions since and 150 films
incl: *The Dam Busters*; *Bridge On*
The River Kwai; *The Longest*
Day, *All Creatures Great And*
Small. Numerous TV
appearances, most recent incl:
Love Story; *The Crucible*; *That's*
My Boy; *The Gentle Touch*; *Juliet*
Bravo; *Never Too Late*; *Shoreline*;
Bulman. m. Beatrice. Hobbies:
reading, cricket. Address: c/o
Joan Gray, Sunbury-on-Thames.
Birthsign: Libra. **Favourite**
Place: 'Aysgarth Falls, because I
feel at home.'

GOODWIN, Ken
Comedian, b. 7 April 1933
Manchester. Idolised George
Formby and taught himself to
play the ukelele. Entertained in
local clubs playing the ukelele and
telling jokes while working in a
variety of jobs. Eventually he
won on *Opportunity Knocks* and
was spotted by producer Johnny
Hamp, who was planning TV
series *The Comedians*. Ken
became a regular member, also
on stage at the London Palladium.
Also tours, pantomimes and
summer seasons. m. Vicki; 2 d.
Hobby: football. Address: c/o
Richard Stone, London.
Birthsign: Aries. **Favourite**
Place: 'The view of the orange
grove from my villa in Alicante,
Spain.'

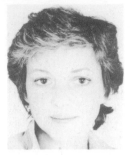

GOODWIN, Trudie
Actress, b. 13 Nov 1951 London. First professional work with the Theatre Centre, London, acting in two tours and directing another. Then rep at Nottingham, Worcester, Leicester Phoenix Theatre. Returned to London with the Young Vic. London theatre also incl: *The Beggars' Opera*; *Womberang*; *Godspell*. TV incl: *Fox*; *The Gentle Touch*; *The Law Machine*; *Woodentop*; *The Bill*. m. actor Kit Jackson; 1 d. Jessica. Hobbies: painting and drawing, gardening, bridge. Address: c/o Frenchs', London. Birthsign: Scorpio. **Favourite Place:** 'Tourrettes-sur-Loup, a village in the South of France where I spent a wonderful honeymoon!'

GOOSSENS, Jennie
Actress, b. 21 Aug 1936 Chelsea, London. Trained at Central School of Speech and Drama, London. First job at Eastbourne Rep then joined Old Vic for US tour 1958–59 and season in London. Theatre incl: *Twelfth Night*; *Much Ado About Nothing*; *Butley*; *Whose Life Is It Anyway?*; joined Royal Shakespeare Company 1982. Appeared in *Cyrano De Bergerac* in Los Angeles for Olympic Arts Festival 1984. TV incl: *Churchill's People*; *Shades Of Greene*; *Angels*; *Rooms*; *The Other One*; *Z Cars* as the "BD Girl"; *A Voyage Round My Father*; *Dodger, Bonzo And The Rest*; *The Secret Garden*; *Paradise Postponed*. m. Brian Spink; 1 s. Alexander, 2 d. Susannah, Léonie. Hobbies: 'My children and garden.' Address: c/o Spotlight, London. Birthsign: Leo. **Favourite Place:** 'A field in Sussex under the South Downs—my roots are there.'

GORDON, Hannah
Actress, b. 9 April 1941 Edinburgh. Trained at Glasgow College of Dramatic Art then rep. West End theatre incl: *Can You Hear Me At The Back?*; *The Killing Game*; *Baggage*; *The Jewellers Shop*; *The Country Girl*. Films incl: *Spring And Port Wine*; *The Elephant Man*. Radio incl: *Macbeth*; *Hedda Gabler*; *Candida*; *St Joan*; *A Winter's Tale*. TV incl: *What Every Woman Knows*; *Middlemarch*; *Abelard and Heloise*; *My Wife Next Door*; *Dear Octopus*; *Upstairs, Downstairs*; *Telford's Change*; *Waste*; *Miss Morison's Ghosts*; *Goodbye Mr Kent*; *Good Behaviour*. m. lighting cameraman Norman Warwick; 1 s. Ben. Address: c/o David White Assocs, London. Birthsign: Aries. **Favourite Place:** 'Overlooking Crail Harbour. I have a love of the sea, nurtured by a childhood spent on the east coast of Scotland.'

GOULD, John
Composer/musical comedian, b. 1 July 1940 Newquay. Revues at Oxford University while taking a degree in music led to stage debut at the Fortune Theatre, London in *Four Degrees Over*. Revues as writer/performer incl: *Three To One On*; *Postscripts*; *Down Upper Street*; *Just The Ticket*; *Think Of A Number*. One-man show: *John Gould*. Theatre scores incl: *Sweet Fanny*; *A Present From The Corporation*; *Who Was That Lady?*; *The Luck Of The Bodkins*; *The Frogs*; pantomimes. Radio series: *Bars of Gould* (adapted for the stage). TV incl: *Late Night Line-Up*; *Nationwide*; *Live From Tub*; *Scene 84*; *That's Life!* Address: c/o Jill Foster Ltd, London. Birthsign: Cancer. **Favourite Place:** 'The dining room of Lochalsh Hotel for the view of Skye across Kyle of Lochalsh.'

GRACE, Nickolas
Actor, b. 21 Nov 1949 West Kirby. Trained at Central School of Speech and Drama, London. Founded The Redgrave Society 1963 and directed British entries for Berlin Interdrama Festival 1965 and 1968. Appeared at the Old Vic and member Royal Shakespeare Company 1972–74; 1976–78. Played *Hamlet* at Derby Playhouse; played *Richard II* at the Young Vic. Also *Cabaret*, *Dracula*, *Amadeus*, *The Mikado*, *HMS Pinafore*. Films incl: *Heat And Dust*. TV incl: *The Love School*; *A Comedy Of Errors*; *Brideshead Revisited*; *Robin of Sherwood*; *The Master of Ballantrae*; *The Last Place On Earth*; *The Max Headroom Show*. Hobbies: cinema, swimming, running, riding, travel. Address: c/o Leading Artists, London. Birthsign: Scorpio. **Favourite Place:** 'Somewhere so special I daren't give it away.'

GRANT, Deborah
Actress, b. 22 Feb 1947 London. Trained at Joyce Butler School of Dancing and Central School of Speech and Drama. Theatre incl: *Barnum*; *Bedroom Farce*; *Watch On The Rhine* at the National Theatre. TV incl: *Bergerac*; *Bouquet Of Barbed Wire*; *Outside Edge*; *Mr Pulfrey Of Westminster*; *Victoria Wood As Seen On TV*. m. Gregory Floy; 2 d. Melissa, Miranda. Hobbies: 'Too busy helping children with theirs . . .' Address: c/o Larry Dalzell, London. Birthsign: Pisces. **Favourite Place:** 'At home with my family.'

GRANT, Russell
TV and radio astrologer, b. 5 Feb 1952 Hillingdon, Uxbridge, Middx. *TV Times* astrologer and largest syndicated astrology column in Europe. Resident astrologer for TVS, TSW and LWT and BBC's *Breakfast Time*. Own radio series for Radio Luxembourg and BBC Radio Wales. Other TV incl: *A Question Of Stars*; *Star Choice*; *The Zodiac Game*. Books incl: *Your Sun Signs*; *TV Times* special *Your Year Ahead* (published annually). Hobby: collecting maps and gazetteers of the British Isles. Address: c/o Jacque Evans, MAM (Agency), London. Birthsign: Sun and Moon Aquarius, Libra rising. **Favourite Place:** 'The British Isles—there's nothing like it on earth; home is where the heart is.'

GRAY, Linda
Actress, b. 12 Sept Santa Monica, California. Trained with Charles Conrad's Acting Class and as a model appeared in hundreds of TV and magazine advertisements. Made her acting debut as a guest on TV's *Marcus Welby, MD* and then starred in the series *All That Glitters*. Films incl: *Haywire*; *The Two Worlds of Jenny Logan*. As well as starring in CBS-TV's *Dallas* as Sue Ellen, has appeared in TV films incl: *Chimps*; *Not In Front Of The Children*. She has also hosted a TV special *The Body Human: The Loving Process*. TV guest appearances incl: *McCloud*; *Big Hawaii*; *Emergency*; *Switch*. m. director Ed Thrasher (dis.); 1 s. Jeff, 1 d. Kelly. Hobbies: skiing, exercising. Address: c/o Lippin & Grant Inc, 8124 West Third St, Suite 204, Los Angeles, California 90048. Birthsign: Virgo. **Favourite Place:** her home, secluded in the mountains.

103

GRAY, Muriel
Presenter, b. 30 Aug 1958
Glasgow. Attended Glasgow
School of Art and until recently
was assistant head of design at the
Museum of Antiquities in
Edinburgh, and was also an
illustrator for three years and
played in a band. TV incl:
presenter on C4's *The Tube*;
presenter on *Scotland Today*; *The
Works*; *Studio One*; *Case-Book
Scotland*; *Bliss*. Has also worked as
a journalist and on radio,
including her own show on
Radio Forth. Hobbies: hill
climbing, young bands, squash,
the Arts. Address: c/o
Schoolhouse Management,
Edinburgh. Birthsign: Virgo.
Favourite Place: 'The north-
west Highlands of Scotland. The
only remaining wilderness in
Europe, and possibly the most
beautiful place on earth.'

GRAYSON, Larry
Comedian, b. 31 Aug 1930
Banbury. Never anything but an
entertainer, he learned his trade in
summer shows and touring
revues. Unknown until an
appearance on *Saturday Variety*
1972. His *Shut That Door!!* series
followed and other TV incl: *The
Good Old Days*; *Celebrity Squares*;
his own shows; *The Generation
Game*. Address: c/o PVA
Management, London. Birthsign:
Virgo. **Favourite Place:**
'Torquay, where I am now very
fortunate enough to be able
to live.'

GREAVES, Jimmy
TV presenter, b. 20 Feb 1940 East
Ham, London. A professional
football player with Chelsea,
West Ham, Tottenham, AC
Milan, England. He retired from
football 1971. Joined TV-am as
presenter 1983. m. Irene; 2 d.
Lynn, Mitzi, 2 s. Daniel, Andrew.
Hobbies: TV, gardening.
Address: c/o TV-am, London.
Birthsign: Pisces. **Favourite
Place:** 'TV-am—it's nice to leave
after a show!'

GREEN, Michael
TV journalist, b. 8 Oct 1943
York. Started career as a
newspaper journalist, working
for local papers then the *Daily
Mail* and *Daily Telegraph*. One of
three-man industrial reporting
team for ITN since 1973.
Covered major national industrial
news stories incl the 1974 miners'
strike, the 'winter of discontent'
1979 and most recently the
miners' strike of 1984–85. m.
Pamela Judith; 1 d. Xanthe, 2 s.
Oliver, Freddie. Hobbies: sailing,
running, gardening. Address: c/o
ITN, London. Birthsign: Libra.
Favourite Place: 'The
Quantock Hills in Somerset
where I spent much of my
childhood and which hold many
tranquil memories.'

GREENE, Sarah

Actress/presenter, b. 24 Oct London. Started career in films and commercials as a child and after studying drama at Hull University worked in rep at Birmingham and Manchester. Played the lead role in *The Swish Of The Curtain* in London. This led to her career as a presenter on BBC TV's *Blue Peter* for three years. She left in 1983 to join *Eureka* and *Saturday Superstore*. She helped her father, Harry Greene, to build TV-am's 'Dream Home' in 1984 and is a presenter on *Friday People* for BBC TV as well as on *Superstore*. She has also appeared in pantomime including *Dick Whittington* and *Cinderella*. Hobbies: scuba diving, dancing, Trivial Pursuits, Scrabble, crosswords. Address: c/o Michael Ladkin, London. Birthsign: Scorpio. **Favourite Place:** 'At home, sitting by the fire with my best friend, Mike—because it's warm, safe and private!'

GREENWOOD, Paul

Actor, b. 2 Aug 1943 Stockton-on-Tees. Trained at Guildhall School of Music and Drama then rep at Chesterfield, Harrogate and Birmingham. Theatre incl: *Goose Pimples*; *Cinderella*; *A Comedy Of Errors*; *Henry VIII*; *Time Of Your Life*; *Piaf*; *Once In A Lifetime*. TV incl: *It's Lulu*; *No Trams To Lime Street*; *The Growing Pains Of PC Penrose*; *Rosie*; *Heartland*; *The Secret Diary Of Adrian Mole*. Wrote and sang the *Rosie* signature tune. Address: c/o Saraband Assocs, London. Birthsign: Leo. **Favourite Place:** 'Any wild place by the sea.'

GRIER, Sheila

Actress, b. 11 Feb 1959 Glasgow. Trained at the Royal Scottish Academy of Music and Drama. Theatre incl: *Pals*; *Foodstuff*; *Babes In The Wood*; *Cinderella*; *Dick Whittington*. TV incl. *Take The High Road*; *The Odd Job Man*; *The End Of The Line*; *Scotch And Wry*; *The Untied Shoelaces Show*; *Brookside*. Hobbies: designer knitwear business, dancing, skiing, singing. Address: c/o Ruth Tarko, Glasgow. Birthsign: Aquarius. **Favourite Place:** 'Being in my car—to go to the places I love most, when I most want to!'

GRIFFITHS, Terence Martin

Professional snooker player, b. 16 Oct 1947 Llanelli, Wales. Embassy World Championship 1979; Benson & Hedges Masters 1980; Irish Benson & Hedges 1980, 81, 82; Lada Classic 1982; World Team Championships 1979, 80. m. Annette; 2 s. Wayne, Darren. Hobbies: golf, riding his motor bike. Address: c/o Barry Hearn Ltd, Romford. Birthsign: Libra. **Favourite Place:** 'Home, because I love it.'

GROOM, Simon

TV presenter, b. 12 Aug 1950 Derby. After University of Birmingham and a post graduate teacher training course worked as a teacher and night club disc jockey before joining BBC TV's *Blue Peter* as presenter, a job which he has done for the past seven years. m. Ann. Hobbies: classic cars, football, music, farming, Tina Turner. Address: c/o Arlington Enterprises, London. Birthsign: Leo.

Favourite Place: 'The field by the house at my parents' farm in Derbyshire—it's very steep, the view is breathtaking; very peaceful. I sit and talk to the cows and I went sledging there as a child (still do!).'

GROTH, Michael

Presenter/musician, b. 28 Oct 1953 Ilkley, West Yorks. From 1972–82 was a solo guitarist/singer/songwriter and formed the group Valentino in 1977, went on a German tour and appeared on TV. Joined the group Trickster in 1979 and released an album, *Back To Zero*. Wrote a hit single released in Germany and which reached number 35 in the charts. Joined BBC TV's *That's Life!* in 1982 as a presenter.

Hobbies: singing, playing and writing music, tennis, squash, art, buying old cars. Address: c/o International Artists, London. Birthsign: Scorpio. **Favourite Place:** 'Ilkley Moor—it holds a lot of fond memories for me.'

GROUT, James

Actor, b. 22 Oct 1927 London. Trained at RADA and made his professional debut at the Old Vic 1950 in *Twelfth Night*. Theatre incl: three seasons at Stratford Memorial Theatre; *The Mousetrap*; *Ross*; *Half A Sixpence* (and on Broadway); *Flint*; *Straight Up*; *Lloyd George Knew My Father*; *13 Rue De L'Amour*; *Make And Break*; *Sweet Bird Of Youth*. Has also directed for reps. TV incl: *The First Lady*; *Turtle's Progress*; *Diary Of A Nobody*; *Born And Bred*; *All Creatures Great And Small*; *Z Cars*; *Sister Dora*; *The Marriage Counsellor*; *Hymn For Jim*; *Juliet Bravo*; *Stan's Last Game*; *A Fine Romance*; *Reith*; *Cockles*; *Box Of Delights*; *The Beiderbecke Affair*; *Yes, Minister*; *No Place Like Home*. m. Noreen. Hobby: music. Address: c/o Peter Crouch, London. Birthsign: Libra. **Favourite Place:** 'A garden in Malmesbury, Wiltshire.'

GUARD, Christopher

Actor/singer, b. 5 Dec 1953. No formal training but comes from a theatrical family. Theatre experience with the National Theatre, Royal Shakespeare Company and in *Filumena* in London's West End. Films incl: *A Little Night Music*; *Loophole*; *Memoirs Of A Survivor*; *Lord Of The Rings*. TV incl: *David Copperfield* (title role); *Tom Brown's Schooldays*; *Vienna 1900*; *Wilfred And Eileen*; *My Cousin Rachel*; *A Woman Of Substance*; *Return To Treasure Island*. m. actress Lesley Dunlop; 2 d. Daisy, Rosie. Hobbies: music, football, running, painting. Address: c/o Plant & Froggatt, London. Birthsign: Sagittarius. **Favourite Place:** 'Coverack in Cornwall. A changeless fishing village I have visited regularly since 1955!'

GUBBA, Tony
Sports commentator/broadcaster, b. 23 Sept 1943 Manchester. Started his career as a national newspaper journalist and then joined the BBC as correspondent in the north west. Has presented BBC sports programmes incl: *Grandstand*; *Sportsnight*. Commentator on *Match Of The Day* and at both summer and winter Olympic Games and World Cups since 1974. m. (dis.); 2 d. Claire, Libby. Hobbies: squash, golf, all sport, DIY. Address: c/o John Hockey Assocs, London. Birthsign: Libra/Virgo. **Favourite Place:** 'All open countryside for its majestic peace and beauty.'

GUILLAUME, Robert
Singer who acts, b. 30 Nov St Louis, Missouri. From choirboy at his local church he went on to study classical singing at Washington University. Sang in shows and festivals before appearing in *Porgy And Bess* and *Guys And Dolls* on Broadway. On TV played the wise-cracking butler in the comedy series *Soap* which led to his own spin-off series, *Benson*. Currently touring with own nightclub act. m. (dis.); three children. Hobbies: reading, piano, guitar, tennis. Address: c/o Phil Margo (Personal Management), Los Angeles, California. Birthsign: Sagittarius. **Favourite Place:** 'New York. I won a Tony for *Guys And Dolls* way back when and lived there for many years.'

GUINNESS, Sir Alec, CBE, D/Litt (Oxon), D/Fine Arts (Boston)
Actor, b. 2 April 1914 London. Advertising copy writer until scholarship to Fay Compton School of Dramatic Art. Member of John Gielgud's company and Old Vic. Theatre incl: *The Brothers Karamazov* (his own adaptation); *A Voyage Round My Father*; *The Old Country*; *The Merchant of Venice*. Films incl: *Great Expectations*; *Oliver Twist*; *Kind Hearts And Coronets*; *The Lavender Hill Mob*; *The Lady Killers*; *The Horse's Mouth*; *The Bridge On The River Kwai* (British Film Academy and Oscar awards); *Lawrence Of Arabia*; *Doctor Zhivago*; *Scrooge*; *Star Wars*; *The Empire Strikes Back*; *A Passage To India*. TV incl: *Tinker, Tailor, Soldier, Spy*; *Smiley's People*; *Edwin*; *Monsignor Quixote*. m. Merula Salaman; 1 s. Matthew. Address: c/o London Management. Birthsign: Aries.

GUTHRIE, Gwyneth
Actress, b. 28 April 1937 Ayr, Scotland. Trained at the Royal Scottish Academy of Music and Drama, Glasgow and won the James Bridie Silver Medal for best character acting work. Her stage debut at Ayr 1957, then Perth rep company. Theatre incl: *For Love Or For Money* (tour with Jimmy Logan); poetry readings at the Edinburgh Festival. Films incl: *Privilege*; *Years Ahead*. Played Mary Queen of Scots in radio serial. TV incl: *Sutherland's Law*; *Hill O' The Red Fox*; *Degree Of Uncertainty*; *The Lost Tribe*; *Behind The Green Door*; *The Reunion*; *The Prime Of Miss Jean Brodie*; *Something's Got To Give*; *Take The High Road*. m. John Borland; 3 d. Karen, Debbie, Olwen. Hobbies: writing, music. Address: c/o Mrs Freddie Young, Glasgow. Birthsign: Taurus. **Favourite Place:** 'In Ayrshire countryside when spring awakens.'

GUTTERIDGE, Lucy

Actress, b. 28 Nov 1956 London. Trained at Central School of Speech and Drama, London. Theatre incl: rep at Ipswich, Norwich and with the Royal Shakespeare Company; *The Real Thing*. Films incl: *The Greek Tycoon*; *Little Gloria*; *Christmas Carol*; *Merlin And The Sword*. Radio: *Antigone*. TV incl: *The Devil's Crown*; *The Marrying Kind*; *End Of Season*; *Betzy*; *Renoir My Father*; *Tales Of The Unexpected*; *Sweet Wine Of Youth*; *Love In A Cold Climate*; *Seven Dials Mystery*; *Nicholas Nickleby*; *Edge Of The Wind*. m. Andrew Hawkins; 1 d. Isabella. Hobbies: reading, walking, drawing, physical activities, people. Address: c/o Jeremy Conway, London. Birthsign: Sagittarius. **Favourite Place:** 'New York, because it's alive, and Italy, because it's warm, rich and beautiful. I love everything about it—food, people, landscape.'

GUYLER, Deryck

Actor, b. 29 April 1914 Wallasey, Cheshire. Started career with the Playhouse rep theatre in Liverpool. His creation of Frisby Dyke on radio (the first time the Liverpool accent had been used on air) in Tommy Handley's wartime show brought recognition. Other radio incl: *Just Fancy*; *Men From The Ministry*. Has appeared in numerous productions, notably on TV in *Please Sir!*; the Eric Sykes shows. Other TV incl: *Three Live Wires*; *That's My Boy*; *Best of Enemies*. Has also been a fanatical washboard player since his schooldays. m. former singer Paddy Lennox; 2 s. Peter, Christopher. Hobbies: model soldiers, collecting jazz 78 rpm records. Address: c/o Felix de Wolfe, London. Birthsign: Taurus. **Favourite Place:** 'The Conway Valley, north Wales where my wife and I spent our honeymoon.'

HAGMAN, Larry

Actor, b. 21 Sept 1930 Fort Worth, Texas. Trained at the Margo Jones Theatre-in-the-Round, Dallas. After professional debut in *The Taming Of The Shrew*, spent a year in regional theatre. Moved to England as a member of *South Pacific*. Stage incl: *Once Around The Block*; *Career*; *Comes A Day*; *The Beauty Part*. Films incl: *Fail-Safe*; *The Cavern*; *Stardust*; *Three In The Cellar*; *Harry And Tonto*; *The Eagle Has Landed*; *S.O.B.* TV incl: *Edge Of Night*; *I Dream Of Jeannie*; *Here We Go Again*; *Applause*; J R Ewing in *Dallas*. m. designer Maj Axelsson; 1 d. Kristina Mary, 1 s. Preston. Hobbies: skiing, backpacking, fishing, sailing, touring, collecting hats and flags. Address: c/o Lippin & Grant Inc, 8124 W Third St, Los Angeles, CA 90048. Birthsign: Virgo. **Favourite Place:** 'Our hot tub, overlooking the Pacific.'

HAID, Charles

Actor, b. 2 June Palo Alto, California. Directed plays in repertory before becoming an actor. Stage: *Elizabeth The First*. Films incl: *The Choirboys*; *Who'll Stop The Rain*; *Oliver's Story*; *Altered States*; *The House Of God*. TV incl: *A Death In Canaan*; *Divorce Wars*; *Hill Street Blues*. Co-produced the Emmy-winning *Who Are The Debolts And Where Did They Get 19 Kids?* Two Emmy nominations for *Hill Street Blues*. m. (1st) Penny, (2nd) actress Debi Richter; 2 d. Arcadia, Brittanny (from 1st m.). Hobbies: surfing, sailing, horse riding. Address: c/o Writers and Artists Agency, 11726 San Vincente Blvd, Los Angeles 90049. Birthsign: Gemini. **Favourite Place:** 'The beach. I love surfing and sailing.'

HAIG, Jack

Character actor/comedian, b. 5 Jan 1915 Streatham, South London. Was born into the theatre as both parents were in Variety. First appearance at the age of 12 was in his parents' revue. Played Buttons at 19 and became principal comedian in own shows at Ally Pally. Opened Tyne Tees TV in 1960 and stayed there for 10 years in own daily comedy show and weekly children's show. Stage incl: *Canterbury Tales*. Films incl: *'Arf A Sixpence*; *Oliver*; *Go For A Take*; *Emily*; *Passport To Pimlico*. TV incl: *Crossroads*; *'Allo 'Allo!* m. actress Sybil Dunn; 1 d. Suzanne. Hobbies: painting in oils, golf. Address: c/o W & J Theatrical Enterprises, London. Birthsign: Capricorn. **Favourite Place:** 'London, because it's where I spent my youth and is home, and Soto Grande Golf Course, Spain.'

HALL, Sam

TV reporter, b. 5 Sept 1936 Stockport, Cheshire. Before joining ITN as a scriptwriter in 1973 had been Reuter correspondent. He was also an announcer on Radio Sweden, News Editor of *Europa Magazine* and had worked for Visnews. Reporter for ITN since 1980. Reports incl: Nigerian-Biafran war; Turkish invasion of Cyprus; the Jeremy Thorpe trial; Northern Ireland; American hostages in Iran; Brixton riots; Beirut seige; and a C4 documentary, *Greenland: The Vikings Return*. m. Susanna; 1 d. Helen, 2 s. Jonas, Ben. Hobbies: photography, gardening, travel music, antique books, bonsai trees, Arctic. Address: c/o ITN, London. Birthsign: Virgo. **Favourite Place:** 'Melville Bay, Greenland, in May when the sun appears for the first time for nine months, bringing life to the whole Arctic region.'

HALLIWELL, Steve

Actor, b. 19 March 1946 Bury, Lancs. Trained at the Mountview Theatre School. Debut in *The Importance Of Being Earnest*. Other stage incl: *The Devils*; *Minyip*; *A Process Of Illumination*; the award-winning play, *The Only Way Out*. Also founder member/actor/writer/ director of the Interchange Theatre Project, Bury, Lancs. TV incl: the film special of *All Creatures Great And Small*; *Threads*; *Daft Mam Blues*; *The Gadfly*; *Crown Court*, *Coronation Street*; *Pickersgill People*; *The Practice*. m. Valerie; 2 step-s. John James, Nicholas, 1 d. Charlotte. Hobbies: pubs, writing, sketching, worrying. Address: c/o Libby Glenn, London. Birthsign: Pisces. **Favourite Place:** 'McDonalds, where two-year-old Charlotte can run riot whilst I read the Sundays.'

HAMEL, Veronica

Actress, b. Philadelphia. Worked as a model before becoming an actress. Films incl: *Beyond The Poseidon Adventure*; *When Time Ran Out*; *Cannonball*. TV incl: *The Rockford Files*; *Kojak*; *Dallas*; *The Gathering*; *79 Park Avenue*; *Hill Street Blues*. m. actor Michael Irving (dis.). Hobbies: tennis, cooking, gardening. Address: c/o Agency for the Performing Arts, Beverly Hills, California.

HAMILL, Desmond

TV reporter, b. 2 Nov 1936 Dublin. After service in the army (the Devonshire Regiment) and the 5th Bn the King's African Rifles in Kenya 1955–59, joined the Kenya Broadcasting Service, 1960–64, and then Rhodesian TV, 1964–66. Joined the BBC in 1966, then went to ITN in 1967. ITN political correspondent, European/Common Market correspondent, and crime correspondent. Books: *Bitter Orange*; *Pig In The Middle (The Army In Northern Ireland 1969–1984)*. m. Brigid; 1 s. Sean, 1 d. Sara. Address: c/o ITN, London. Birthsign: Scorpio.

HAMPSHIRE, Susan

Actress, b. 12 May 1942 London. Has been in over 50 plays and 30 films. TV incl: *What Katy Did*; *Andromeda*; *The Forsyte Saga*; *Vanity Fair*; *The First Churchills*; *The Pallisers*; *Barchester Chronicles*; *Dick Turpin*; *Leaving*. Books: *Susan's Story*; *The Maternal Instinct*; *Lucy Jane*. m. Eddie; 1 s. Christopher, 1 d. Victoria (dec.). Hobbies: gardening, writing. Address: c/o Chatto & Linnit, London. Birthsign: Taurus. **Favourite Place:** 'St Paul de Vence, out of season. Perfect climate, not too far from the UK. French speaking; I speak French and love France.'

HAN, Michelle

Presenter/reporter, b. 19 Nov 1954 New York. Joined Rediffusion Hong Kong as presenter/reporter. Moved to Television Broadcasting Ltd in same capacity. Produced own series for in-house cable TV, Hong Kong: *Hong Kong With Michelle*. Produced in-flight films for Cathay Pacific Airways. Worked for ABC/KGO-TV in San Francisco as reporter before joining ITN in London. m. Anthony Turner. Hobbies: water-skiing, shopping. Address: c/o ITN, London. Birthsign: Scorpio. **Favourite Place:** 'Old Wing Pier of Oriental Hotel, Bangkok, at sunset. Wonderful memories.'

HANDL, Irene

Actress/writer, b. 26 Dec 1902 London. Trained at the Embassy School of Acting and went straight into West End play, *George And Margaret*. Other stage incl: *Goodnight Mrs Puffin*; *Freeway*; *The Importance Of Being Earnest*; *Blithe Spirit*. Films incl: the *Carry On* films; *I'm All Right Jack*; *Brief Encounter*; *The Italian Job*; *On A Clear Day*; *Hedda Gabler*. Radio incl: *Hancock's Half-Hour*; *Educating Archie*. Recent TV incl: *For The Love Of Ada*; *Maggie And Her*; *Come Spy With Me*; *Metal Mickey*. With Peter Sellers on two of his albums in numbers she wrote: *Shadows On The Grass* and *Whispering Giant*. Books: *The Sioux*; *The Gold Tip Pfitzer*. Hobbies: cooking, gardening, films, art, dogs, having fun. Address: c/o Leading Artists, London. Birthsign: Capricorn. **Favourite Place:** Australia, 'Wonderland of incredible contrasts.'

HANDS, Jeremy
ITN reporter, b. 4 April 1951
Torquay. Before joining ITN he
worked on various newspapers
and for Westward TV and
Border TV. Joined ITN in 1978
and has since covered Northern
Ireland, the Falklands War and
Beirut, amongst other news
items. Has co-written two best-
selling books. m. Julia; 1 s.
Thomas, 1 d. Lucy. Hobbies:
writing, maritime history,
aardvarks. Address: c/o ITN,
London. Birthsign: Aries.
Favourite Place: Vanuatu,
South Pacific, 'The most beautiful
place on earth, and still without
television.'

HANN, Judith
Reporter/presenter, b. 8 Sept
1942 Littleover, Derby. BSc in
zoology at Durham University.
Trained as a journalist with
Westminster Press. Freelance for
BBC TV incl: *Tomorrow's World.*
Books incl: *But What About The
Children?*; *Family Scientist*; *The
Perfect Baby?*; *Judith Hann's Total
Health Plan.* Twice winner of the
Glaxo Award for science writers.
m. TV news editor John Exelby;
2 s. Jake, Daniel. Hobby:
cooking. Address: c/o BBC TV,
London. Birthsign: Virgo.
Favourite Place: 'The Cohn
Valley, Glos. Beautiful walking,
gentle countryside, Cotswold
stone villages.'

HANSON, Susan
Actress, b. 11 Feb 1946 Preston,
Lancs. Trained at the Webber
Douglas School of Dramatic Art,
followed by rep in Edinburgh,
Bristol Old Vic, The Mermaid in
London, and Newcastle. Other
theatre incl: *Dick Whittington*,
Cinderella. Films incl: *Catch Us If
You Can.* TV incl: *Crossroads*
(from 1965); *Nearest And
Dearest*; *Going For A Song*;
Glamour Girls; *Blankety Blank*;
Give Us A Clue. m. singer Carl
Wayne; 1 s. Jack. Hobbies:
collecting antiques, interior
design. Address: c/o Peter
Charlesworth, London.
Birthsign: Aquarius. **Favourite
Place:** 'Paris, Venice and Rome
for their beauty, culture and
atmosphere, not to mention
food!'

HARDY, Robert, CBE
Actor, b. 29 Oct 1925
Cheltenham. Began career with
the Royal Shakespeare Company.
First TV as David Copperfield,
Prince Hal and in *The
Troubleshooters.* Theatre incl:
Dear Liar. Films incl: *The Spy
Who Came In From The Cold*;
Ten Rillington Place; *Young
Winston*; *The Shooting Party*;
Robin Hood. TV incl: *Henry V*;
Coriolanus; *Elizabeth R*; *Upstairs,
Downstairs*; *The Duchess Of Duke
Street*; *Horses In Our Blood*; *All
Creatures Great And Small*;
Twelfth Night; *Fothergill*;
*Winston Churchill—The
Wilderness Years*; *The Demon
Lover*; *The Cleopatras*; *The Death
Of The Heart.* m. (1st) (dis.), (2nd)
actress Sally Cooper; 2 d. Emma,
Justine, 1 s. Paul. Hobbies: horses,
archery. Address: c/o Chatto &
Linnit, London. Birthsign:
Scorpio.

HARMON, Mark

Carpenter-actor, b. 2 Sept Los Angeles. Films incl: *Comes A Horseman* (debut); *Beyond The Poseidon Adventure*. TV incl: *Adam 12*; *Emergency*; *Police Woman*; *The Love Boat*; *Centennial*; *The Dream Merchants*; *Flamingo Road*; *Sam*; *240-Robert*; *Eleanor And Franklin*; *St Elsewhere*. Hobbies: carpentry, sports, films, collecting Gary Cooper memorabilia. Address: c/o Agency for the Performing Arts, 9000 Sunset Blvd, Los Angeles, CA 90069. Birthsign: Virgo. **Favourite Place:** loves the mountains.

HARRIS, Anita

Singer/actress, b. 3 June 1942 Midsomer Norton, Somerset. Won talent contest aged three, later learning ice-skating, the piano and dancing. Joined Charley Ballet in Italy, sang in Las Vegas 1959, joined the Granadiers and the Cliff Adams Singers. London theatre incl: London Palladium; Talk of the Town; *Peter Pan*; *CATS*. Many Guest appearances on TV and own programmes incl: *Anita In Jumbleland*; *The Anita Harris Show*. She has also made many records. 1982 named Concert Cabaret Performer of the Year by Variety Club. m. writer/director Mike Margolis. Hobbies: golf, fencing, yoga, skating, cooking, water-skiing. Address: c/o Impulse Recording Co, London. Birthsign: Gemini. **Favourite Place:** 'In the peace and shade of serried fishing boats at Olhos D'Agua, Algarve.'

HARRIS, Keith

Ventriloquist, b. 21 Sept 1947 Lyndhurst, Hants. Self-taught, he made his debut at 14 and began designing and making own characters; now has more than 100. First appeared in summer season at Rhyl in 1964, and has since appeared in numerous summer shows, pantomimes, cabaret and overseas tours. TV incl: *Let's Laugh* (debut); *Cuddles And Co*; guest spots on major variety shows and host of *Black And White Minstrel Show*, 1977 and 1978. *Royal Command Performance*, 1984. Own TV series, 1983–85, m. singer Jacqui Scott. Hobbies: DIY, eating good food. Address: c/o Billy Marsh, London. Birthsign: Virgo. **Favourite Place:** Barbados, 'Very sunny and just like the English countryside.'

HARRIS, Rolf, OBE

Entertainer/singer/songwriter/musician/artist/cartoonist, b. 30 March Perth, Australia. Started career by winning radio talent competition in 1949. Came to Britain in 1952. First stage appearance was in *One Under The Eight*; then *Talk Of The Town*; *Royal Variety Performance*. Returned to Australia to produce and star in children's series and own show. TV incl: *Hey Presto*, *It's Rolf*; *The Rolf Harris Show*; *Rolf On Saturday, OK?*; *Cartoon Time*. Records incl: *Tie Me Kangeroo Down, Sport*; *Two Little Boys*; *Jake The Peg*. m. sculptress Alwen Hughes; 1 d. Bindi. Hobbies: painting, making jewellery, collecting rocks, woodwork, photography. Address: c/o London Management, London. Birthsign: Aries. **Favourite Place:** 'Vancouver. The city and I have had a sort of mutual love affair since 1961.'

HARRISON, Jenilee
Actress, b. 12 June Glendale, California. Began her career in TV commercials. Film: *Tank*. TV incl: *Three's Company*; *Battle Of The Network Stars*; *Daredevil* Special; *Grand Prix All-stars*; *Bring 'Em Back Alive*; *The Love Boat*; *Fantasy Island*; *240-Robert*; *Mickey Spillane's Mike Hammer*; *Malibu*; now best known as Jamie Ewing in *Dallas*. Hobbies: investing, water-skiing, horse riding. Address: c/o Twentieth Century Artists, 3518 Cahuenga Blvd, Suite 316, Los Angeles, CA 90068. Birthsign: Gemini. **Favourite Place:** her land on the river in Kernville, California.

HART, Tony
Artist, b. 15 Oct 1925 Maidstone, Kent. After the Second World War he finished his art training and worked as a display designer in London. After going freelance he has worked as a graphic artist and TV presenter of *Saturday Special*; *Playbox*; *In Town Tonight*; *Vision On*; *Take Hart* (BAFTA Award, 1983); *Hartbeat*. m. Jean; 1 d. Carolyn. Hobbies: garden stonework, cooking, wine. Address: c/o Roc Renals, Crowthorne, Berks. Birthsign: Libra. **Favourite Place:** 'The bath—the place you *can* relax, preferably with a book and a B&S!'

HARTMAN, Kim
Actress, b. 11 Jan 1955 London. Training: ASM at Belgrade Theatre, Coventry, for a year before going to the Webber Douglas Academy. Stage incl: seasons at Chichester, Harrogate, Bristol Old Vic, Redgrave Theatre, Farnham; *The Cherry Orchard*; *Billy Liar*; *Hobson's Choice*; *Hay Fever*; toured Far and Middle East twice with *Move Over Mrs Markham*. Radio incl: *Lord Sky*; *Jamaica Inn*. TV incl: *The Peddlar* (Play For Today); *Kelly Monteith Show*; *'Allo 'Allo!*. m. John Nolan; 1 s. Tom, 1 d. Miranda. Hobbies: painting, gardening, walking the dog, croquet. Address: c/o Spotlight, London. Birthsign: Capricorn. **Favourite Place:** 'The banks of the River Avon on a hot summer's day.'

HARTY, Russell
TV journalist, b. 5 Sept 1934 Blackburn, Lancs. Lectured in US and Britain, a housemaster at Giggleswick before answering an ad for arts producer, which led to work on TV's *Aquarius* and own chat show, *Eleven Plus*. TV incl: *Russell Harty Plus*; *Saturday Night People*; *Russell Harty*; *Harty*; series for BBC Manchester *Russell Harty Goes To . . . Dublin . . . Newcastle . . . Oxford . . . Monaco*. Won Emmy for *Hello Dali* programme; Golden Harp Award for *Finnian Games*. Hobby: sitting down and looking at the wall. Address: c/o BBC TV, London. Birthsign: Virgo.

HASSELHOFF, David

Actor, b. 17 July 1953 Baltimore. Trained at the Academy of Dramatic Arts, New York, and California Institute of the Arts. Film: *Starcrash*. TV: *Police Story*; *Semi-Tough*; *Knightrider*; *Griffin & Phoenix*; *The Young And Restless*. Awards incl: Most Popular Actor on Daytime TV for *The Young And Restless*, 1980; People's Choice, 1983; US Magazine's Teen Idol, 1984; Hispanic Award for Best TV Actor, 1985. m. Catherine Hickland. Hobbies: singing, deep-sea diving, tennis, water-skiing, car racing, pumping iron. Address: c/o Paladino & Assocs, Los Angeles, California. Birthsign: Cancer. **Favourite Place:** home.

HATFIELD, Keith

Reporter, b. 18 Jan 1943 Sutton Coldfield. Travelled widely on all assignments for ITN but mainly in Northern Ireland, Europe, Africa, Middle East. m. Linette; 2 s. Alexander, Michael, 1 d. Dominique. Hobby: home affairs. Address: c/o ITN, London. Birthsign: Capricorn. **Favourite Place:** 'Venice out of season.'

HAVERS, Nigel

Actor, b. 6 Nov 1949 London. Broke family tradition of going into Law (father is Attorney General). Trained at Arts Educational Trust. Billy Owen in *The Dales* on radio, researcher *Jimmy Young Show* before TV in *Comet Among The Stars*. Title role *Nicholas Nickleby*. Theatre incl: *Man And Superman*; *Season's Greetings*. Films: *Chariots Of Fire*; *A Passage To India*. TV incl: *A Raging Calm*; *Upstairs, Downstairs*; *The Glittering Prizes*; *Pennies From Heaven*; *A Horseman Riding By*; *An Englishman's Castle*; *Coming Out*; *Goodbye Darling*; *Unity*; *Winston Churchill—The Wilderness Years*; *Nancy Astor*; *After The Party*; *Strangers And Brothers*; *The Death Of The Heart*; *Don't Wait Up*. m. Carolyn; 1 d. Katharine. Hobbies: golf, sport, reading. Address: c/o Leading Artists, London. Birthsign: Scorpio. **Favourite Place:** 'At home!'

HAWTHORNE, Nigel

Actor, b. 5 April 1929 Coventry. First professional appearance in London in 1951. Stage incl: *Privates On Parade*; *Uncle Vanya*; *Otherwise Engaged*; *Tartuffe*. Films incl: *Gandhi*; *Firefox*; *The Chain*; *Turtle Summer*. TV incl: *Yes, Minister*; *Mapp And Lucia*; *Jenny's War*; *The House*; *Marie Curie*; *The Knowledge*; *Tartuffe*. Awards incl: Clarence Derwent and SWET for *Privates On Parade*; Broadcasting Press Guild Award and BAFTA (1981 and 1982) for *Yes, Minister*. Hobbies: writing, painting, gardening, photography, sport. Address: c/o Ken McReddie, London. Birthsign: Aries. **Favourite Place:** 'The sea—having been lucky enough to have been brought up almost literally on a beach, I miss the sea terribly when I'm away from it.'

HAYES, Leila
Actress/entertainer, b. Victoria, Australia. Trained at the Jack White School of Music. Has worked in hotels and clubs throughout Australia. Appearances incl: *In Melbourne Tonight*; *Showcase*; *The Jimmy Hannon Show*; *Time For Terry*; *Penthouse*; *20 Good Years*; *Power Without Glory*; *Through The Looking Glass Darkly*; *Red Riding Hood*; *Sons And Daughters*. m. Ronald B Connelly; 1 d. Melissa-Jane. Hobbies: old movies, sketching, needlework, crochet, yoga, swimming, writing. Address: c/o Richard Stone, London. Birthsign: Capricorn. **Favourite Place:** 'There's a "special" beach at Blairgowrie, Victoria, which my thoughts often return to—open sea, sand, peace.'

HAYES, Melvyn
Actor, b. 11 Jan 1935 London. Started with the famous troupe, *Terry's Juveniles*. Rep incl: Chesterfield; Guildford; Leatherhead; Midland Theatre. London stage incl: *Apples Of Eve*; *South*; *Change For The Angel*; *Spring And Port Wine*. Recent work incl: *Run For Your Wife* (tour); *Wind In The Willows* (Sadlers Wells). Films incl: *Violent Playground*; *No Trees In The Street*; *The Young Ones*; *Summer Holiday*; *Wonderful Life*. TV incl: *Oliver Twist*; *The Unloved*; *The Silver Sword*; *It Ain't Half Hot Mum*. m. actress Wendy Padbury; 4 d. Sacha, Talla, Joanna, Charlotte, 1 s. Damian. Hobbies: breathing, meeting people in the street who ask questions like 'Didn't you used to be Melvyn Hayes?'. Address: c/o Richard Stone, London. Birthsign: Capricorn. **Favourite Place:** 'Home because the family live there.'

HAYES, Patricia
Actress, b. 22 Dec London. Trained at RADA. Has probably worked with more comics than any other British actress. Theatre incl: *Twelfth Night*; *Habeas Corpus*; *Liza Of Lambeth*; *Filumena*; *True West* and *Major Barbara* (both at the National Theatre). Films incl: *Love Thy Neighbour*; *The Never Ending Story*. TV incl: *Edna, The Inebriate Woman*; *Tea Ladies*; *Till Death Us Do Part*; *Spooner's Patch*; *The Lady Is A Tramp*; *Winter Sunlight*; *Marjorie And Men*; *Mr Pye*; *Mrs Capper's Birthday*. m. actor Valentine Brooke (dis.); 2 d. Teresa, Gemma, 1 s. actor Richard O'Callaghan. Hobbies: housework, gardening. Address: c/o Herbert de Leon, London. Birthsign: Sagittarius.

HEALY, Timothy
Actor/comedian, b. 29 Jan 1952 Newcastle-upon-Tyne. Recent TV incl: *The Jim Davidson Show*; *Highway*; *Tickle On The Tum* (children's programme); *Auf Wiedersehen Pet*. Hobbies: golf, snooker. Address: c/o Peter Browne, London. Birthsign: Aquarius. **Favourite Place:** Robin Hood's Bay, Yorkshire, 'A delightful, small, peaceful village by the sea. Best in winter—no one else is there.'

HEINEY, Paul
Presenter, b. 20 April 1949
Sheffield. Film: *Water*. Radio:
appearances on BBC Radios 1, 2
and 4. TV: *That's Life!*; *The Big
Time*; *In At The Deep End*; *The
Travel Show*. m. Libby Purves; 1
s. Nicholas, 1 d. Rose. Hobbies:
vegetable growing, sailing, horse
driving. Address: c/o Jo Gurnett,
London. Birthsign: Aries.
Favourite Place: 'At the helm
of a yacht or behind a team of
four horses.'

HENDERSON, Dickie, OBE
Comedian, b. 30 Oct 1922
London. Toured music halls with
his father, Dick Henderson. Stage
incl: *Wish You Were Here*;
Teahouse Of The August Moon;
When In Rome; *Come Live With
Me*; *And The Bride Makes Three*.
TV incl: *Face The Music* (debut,
1953); *Before Your Very Eyes*;
compèred *Sunday Night At The
London Palladium*; *The Dickie
Henderson Show*; *A Present For
Dickie*; *I'm Bob, He's Dickie And*

I'm Dickie—That's Show Business.
Now makes many working trips
abroad, incl: USA, Australia,
Canada, Hong Kong. Eight Royal
Command Performances. m. (1st)
Dixie Rose (dec.), (2nd)
Gwynneth; 1 d. Linda, 1 s. David
(both from 1st m.). Hobbies: golf
and most sports. Address: c/o
London Management, London.
Birthsign: Scorpio. **Favourite
Place:** 'Victoria Falls because
they represent all the splendour of
nature.'

HENDERSON, Don
Actor/author, b. 10 Nov 1932
London. Spent six years with the
Royal Shakespeare Company,
1966–72. Stage incl: *Campion's
Interview*; *The Orange Tree*; *The
Nerd*. Films incl: *A Midsummer
Night's Dream*; *Callan*; *Escape
From The Dark*; *The Voyage*; *Star
Wars*; *The Big Sleep*; *Brazil*. TV
incl: *Crown Court*; *Poldark*; *Van
Der Valk*; *Scorpio Tales*; *Annika*;
A Crack In The Ice; *The Odd
Couple*; *The Master Of Ballantrae*;

Squaring The Circle; *The Onedin
Line*; *The Captive Clairvoyant*;
Strangers; *Bulman*. m. (1st) Hilary
(dec.), (2nd) actress Shirley
Stelfox; 1 d. Louise, 1 s. Ian (from
1st m.), 1 step-d. Helena.
Hobbies: writing, painting,
lazing, thinking hard. Address:
c/o Associated International
Management, London. Birthsign:
Scorpio. **Favourite Place:**
'Home with my wife and
children.'

HENDLEY, Fiona
Actress/singer, b. 23 June 1959
Kingston-upon-Thames. Theatre
incl: *Guys And Dolls*; *The
Beggar's Opera*; *My Fair Lady*;
Elvis; *Not Now, Darling*; *Oh, Boy*;
Grease; *The Cherry Orchard*;
Charlie's Aunt. Film: *The Hawk*.
Radio: *Cast In Order Of
Disappearance* (Radio 4). TV incl:
Widows; *Jane In The Desert*;
Some Mothers Do 'Ave 'Em; *The
Manhood Of Edward Robinson*. m.
singer/actor Paul Jones. Hobbies:

music, mostly jazz, soul and
classical, sport, books, theatre.
Address: c/o Duncan Heath,
London. Birthsign: Cancer.
Favourite Place: 'Piazza San
Marco, Venice, sitting listening to
a small band playing whilst
sipping a bellini. It's beautiful,
peaceful and free from pollen (I
suffer from hayfever).'

HENRY, Lenny

Stand-up comedian/character actor, b. 29 Aug 1958 Dudley, Worcs. TV debut on *New Faces* in 1975 when he was 16. Has since appeared in venues all over the country. TV incl: *The Fosters*; *Tiswas*; award-winning *Three Of A Kind*; *OTT*; first British host of *Saturday Live*; *Royal Variety Performances*; *The Lenny Henry Show*. Debut album, *Stand Up, Get Down*. m. comedienne Dawn French. Hobbies: music and reading. Address: c/o Robert Luff Holdings, London. Birthsign: Virgo. **Favourite Place:** 'Sitting in the living room at home with my wife, Dawn.'

HENRY, Paul

Actor, b. 2 Feb 1947 Birmingham. Trained at the Birmingham School of Speech and Drama and took the part of Benny in TV's *Crossroads* in 1975 after eight years with Birmingham rep. Was also Peter Stevens in radio's *The Archers*. Theatre incl: *Funny Peculiar*; pantomimes incl *Dick Whittington* at Birmingham; *Run For Your Wife*. TV incl: *Roads To Freedom*, *A Midsummer Night's Dream*; *The Recruiting Officer*; *Ten Torry Canyons*; *Romeo And Juliet*; *The Sweeney*; *OTT*; *The Lenny Henry Show*. m. Sheila; 1 d. Justine, 1 s. Anthony. Hobby: golf. Address: c/o Richard Stone, London. Birthsign: Aquarius.

HENSON, Nicky

Actor, b. 12 May 1945 London. Trained at RADA as a stage manager. First London appearance was in a revue, *All Square*, followed by *Camelot* at Drury Lane. Has since played a variety of parts in revue, musicals and as a member of the Young Vic. Other theatre incl: *She Stoops to Conquer*; *Measure For Measure*; *Look Back In Anger*; *Man And Superman*; *Noises Off*; three seasons with the National Theatre; and most recently three productions with the RSC. Films incl: *There's A Girl In My Soup*; *The Bawdy Adventures Of Tom Jones*. TV incl: *Prometheus* series; *Seagull Island*; *Chains*; *Absurd Person Singular*. m. actress Una Stubbs (dis.); 2 s. Christian, Joe. Hobby: motocycling. Address: c/o Richard Stone, London. Birthsign: Taurus. **Favourite Place:** 'Bed.'

HICKSON, Joan

Actress, b. 5 Aug 1906 Kingsthorpe, Northampton. Stage debut 1927 in *His Wife's Children*; West End debut 1928 in *The Tragic Muse*. Since then has worked consistently in theatre, film and TV and is one of Britain's most distinguished character actresses. Recent theatre incl: *A Day In The Death Of Joe Egg*; *Forget Me Not Lane*; *The Card*; *Bedroom Farce* (also New York); *On The Razzle* (National Theatre). Films incl: *The Guinea Pig*; *Seven Days To Noon*; *Yanks*; *The Wicked Lady*. Numerous TV credits incl: *Nanny*; *Good Girl*; *Great Expectations*; *Poor Little Rich Girls*; *Time For Murder*; as Miss Marple in BBC Agatha Christie series. Address: c/o Plunket Greene, London. Birthsign: Leo. **Favourite Place:** 'The country, where I live.'

HILL, Benny

Comedian, b. 21 Jan 1925 Southampton. Started in working men's clubs and in variety and summer shows. Stage debut in 1941 in *Stars In Battledress*. Also *Paris By Night; Fine Fettle*. Films incl: *The Italian Job; Chitty Chitty Bang Bang; Those Magnificent Men In Their Flying Machines*. TV: own shows for which he writes all his own scripts and music. Elected to TV Hall of Fame, *TV Times*, 1978– 79. Voted Funniest Man on TV 1981–82 by *TV Times* readers. Hobbies: travel, spectator sports, show biz. Address: c/o Richard Stone, London. Birthsign: Aquarius. **Favourite Place:** St Catherine's Hill, Winchester: 'It's peaceful and a stone's throw away is a delightful city.'

HILL, Jimmy

Presenter, b. 22 July 1928 Balham, London. Began career in football, first as an amateur for Reading in 1949. Turned professional and joined Brentford. Went to Fulham in 1952; chairman of Professional Footballers' Association, 1957; worked as TV commentator and interviewer; manager of Coventry City, 1961; became head of London Weekend's sports unit, 1967; Deputy Controller of Programmes, 1971; joined BBC in 1973. TV incl: *World Of Sport; The Big Match; Grandstand; Match Of The Day*. m. (1st) Gloria (dis.), (2nd) Heather; 2 d. (one from each m.), 3 s. (2 from 1st m, 1 from 2nd m.). Hobbies: golf, riding, tennis, bridge. Address: c/o BBC TV, London. Birthsign: Leo/Cancer, **Favourite Place:** 'Looking over the Evenlode Vale in Gloucestershire.'

HILL, Rose

Actress/singer, b. 5 June 1914 London. Studied at the Guildhall School of Music and Drama. Theatre incl: *The Marriage Of Figaro; The Beggar's Opera; The Old Ones; End Game; Footfalls*; the award-winning *Nicholas Nickleby; On The Razzle*. Films incl: *Heavens Above; For The Love Of Ada; Every Good Home Should Have One; Footsteps*. TV incl: *Dad's Army; Happy Ever After; Born And Bred; Emergency Ward 10; Dixon Of Dock Green; The Barber of Stamford Hill; Take A Sapphire; Waterloo Sunset; The Wild Geese; Benbow Was His Name; The Three Sisters; Caring; 'Allo 'Allo!; Strangers*. m. J C Davis; 1 s. John. Hobbies: gardening, yoga, needlework. Address: c/o Richard Stone, London. Birthsign: Gemini. **Favourite Place:** 'Alone in the garden, on a warm sunny day, with the sound of birds and the rustling trees.'

HILL, Vince

Singer, b. 16 April 1937 Coventry. Started in local pubs and clubs. Became vocalist for Band of the Royal Signals, then Teddy Foster Band. Went solo with *The River's Run Dry*. First big hit was *Eidelweiss*. Other hits incl: *Roses Of Picardy; Look Around*. Wrote score for Radio 4 musical drama. Own Radio 2 series, *The Solid Gold Music Show*. TV incl: many top variety shows; presented *They Sold A Million; The Musical Time Machine*. Hosted 26-week TV series in Canada. Also international tours. m. Annie; 1 s. Athol. Hobbies: photography, gardening, travel, cooking, painting, boating. Address: c/o Mike Hughes, London. Birthsign: Aries. **Favourite Place:** 'The view of the Thames from my garden at Henley— beautiful, peaceful and very English.'

HILLERMAN, John

Actor, b. 20 Dec Denison, Texas. Trained at American Theater Wing, New York, and Theater Club, Washington. Films incl: *The Last Picture Show*; *Paper Moon*; *The Naked Ape*; *The Thief Who Came To Dinner*; *High Plains Drifter*; *Blazing Saddles*; *Chinatown*; *Sunburn*. TV incl: *Ellery Queen*; *One Day At A Time*; *Little Gloria . . . Happy At Last*; *Tales Of The Brass Monkey*; *Magnum PI*; and numerous guest appearances in series incl: *Kojak*; *Hawaii Five-O*; *The Love Boat*; *Hart To Hart*; *Lou Grant*; *Little House On The Prairie*. Hobbies: caviar, electronic toys. Address: c/o McCartt, Oreck, Barrett, 9200 Sunset Blvd, Los Angeles, CA 90069. Birthsign: Capricorn. **Favourite Place:** his penthouse apartment in Hawaii.

HINES, Frazer

Actor, b. 22 Sept 1944 Horseforth, Yorks. Started in the 'business' at the age of eight. By the time he was 15 had appeared in six films and served apprenticeship in theatre. Stage incl: *Heirs And Graces*; *No Trams*; *Happy Birthday*; *Hedda Gabler*; *On The Razzle*. Films incl: *Zeppelin*; *Last Valley*; *The Weapon*. TV incl: *Emmerdale Farm* (since its start in 1972); *Doctor Who*; *Duty Free*. m. actress Gemma Craven (dis.). Hobby: cricket for the Lord's Taverners. Address: c/o Peter Charlesworth, London. Birthsign: Virgo/Libra. **Favourite Place:** 'Monument Valley in Utah. I rode on the very place John Wayne made *Stagecoach* and other westerns.'

HINES, Ronald

Actor, b. 20 June 1929 London. Trained at RADA and then rep. Many theatre appearances incl with the National Theatre. Films incl: *Dunkirk*; *Whistle Down The Wind*; *Young Winston*; *Hot Property*. Numerous TV appearances, the most recent incl: *This Year, Next Year*; *The Last Romantic*; *We'll Meet Again*; *Shoestring*; *Bergerac*. m. Sheila; 2 d. Deborah, Stephanie, 1 s. Rupert. Hobbies: oil and watercolour painting, antiques. Address: c/o Leading Artists, London. Birthsign: Gemini.

HINGE (Dr Evadne) and BRACKET (Dame Hilda)

Partnership of female impersonators which came about by accident 1972 when Dr Evadne was engaged to accompany Dame Hilda. Since appeared in London's West End, on tour and in *Royal Command Performance*. Many guest appearances on TV and own series *Dear Ladies*. Address: c/o Noel Gay, London.

Patrick Fyffe (Dame Hilda) b. 23 Jan Stafford. Began as hairdresser who worked as an amateur. Hobbies: gardening, cooking, antiques, music, old houses. Birthsign: Aquarius. **Favourite Place:** 'In the garden.' **George Logan (Dr Evadne)** b. 7 July Glasgow. Formerly a computer programmer, but studied at the Royal Academy of Music. Hobbies: electronic music, computers, reading. Birthsign: Cancer. **Favourite Place:** 'In my shed.'

HIRD, Thora, OBE

Actress/comedienne, b. 28 May 1913 Morecambe, Lancs. Classic start in show business, having theatrical parents. At 16 she was making her mark in rep. Was an overnight success in her first London appearance in *Flowers For The Living* in 1944. Stage ranges from *Romeo And Juliet* to *No, No, Nanette*; *Me, I'm Afraid Of Virginia Woolf*; and *Afternoon Off*. Films incl: *The Entertainer*; *Over The Odds*; *Term Of Trial*; *Some Will, Some Won't*. TV incl: *Meet The Wife*; *The First Lady*; and more recently, *In Loving Memory* (four series); *Flesh And Blood*; *Praise Be* (ninth year); *Hallelujah!* (two series). m. James Scott; 1 d. actress Janette Scott. Hobbies: travel, reading. Address: c/o Felix de Wolfe, London. Birthsign: Gemini. **Favourite Place:** 'Our garden, there is so much to see, so much fantastic engineering.'

HODGE, Patricia

Actress, b. 29 Sept 1946 Cleethorpes, Lincs. Trained at LAMDA where she won the major award, the Eveline Evans Award, as best actress. Stage incl: *Rookery Nook* (West End debut). Film: *Betrayal*. TV incl: *The Naked Civil Servant*; *The Girls Of Slender Means*; *Target*; *Rumpole Of The Bailey*; *Edward And Mrs Simpson*; *Winston Churchill—The Wilderness Years*; *Holding The Fort*; *Jemima Shore Investigates*. m. musician Peter Owen. Hobbies: decorating, sewing, painting, music. Address: c/o ICM, London. Birthsign: Libra. **Favourite Place:** 'Home'.

HODSON, Charles

Reporter, *C4 News*, b. 20 July 1955 Bourton-on-the-Hill, Gloucestershire. BBC trainee from 1978 to 1979; Brussels journalist for BBC Radio News, 1979–82; *C4 News* scriptwriter, 1982–84. m. Ann Walton; 2 s. William, Thomas. Hobbies: the countryside, books, classical music, running. Address: c/o ITN, London. Birthsign: Cancer. **Favourite Place:** 'St Just-in-Roseland in Cornwall'.

HOLDERNESS, Sue

Actress, b. 28 May 1949 Hampstead, London. In 1967 went to Central School of Speech and Drama. Rep work incl: Manchester 69 Theatre Company; Oxford Playhouse; Chester; Perth; Harrogate; Sheffield. Stage incl: *Hay Fever*; *Edge Of Darkness*; *When The Lights Go On Again*; *Duet For One*; *Why Not Stay For Breakfast?*; and *Our Kid* (one-woman show). Films: *That'll Be The Day*; *It Could Happen To You*. TV incl: *Canned Laughter*; *The Sandbaggers*; *It Takes A Worried Man*; *The Brief*; *Only Fools And Horses*. Hobbies: dancing, horse riding, gymnastics. Address: c/o Bill Horne Personal Management, London. Birthsign: Gemini. **Favourite Place:** 'The Drum and Monkey in Harrogate, as it is, quite simply, the best fish restaurant I know.'

HOLLAND, Jools

Musician/songwriter/broadcaster, b. 24 Jan 1958 London. Made a name for himself initially as a member of the pop group Squeeze, which has since re-formed; followed by Jools Holland and The Millionaires. Co-presenter of *The Tube* on C4 TV. Also co-presenter *Baby, Baby*; *Rebellious Jukebox*. m. Mary; 1 s. George. Hobbies: motorcars and toy trains. Address: c/o Miles Copeland, London. Birthsign: Aquarius. **Favourite Place:** 'Romney, Hythe and Dymchurch Railway, Greatstone station because it means holidays start here.'

HOLMES, Michelle

Actress, b. 1 Jan 1967 Rochdale. While still at school she worked with the Oldham Theatre Workshop. Stage incl: *Zigger Zagger*; *Chalkie*. TV incl: *Juliet Bravo*; *Gathering Seed*; *The Road To 1984*; *Scully*; *In Loving Memory*. Now best known for her role in *The Practice*. Hobbies: keep-fit, singing, dancing, playing drums, elocution lessons. Address: c/o Granada TV, Manchester. Birthsign: Capricorn. **Favourite Place:** Rochdale Town Hall: 'It's a dream that one day I could own it. It's so very beautiful.'

HOLNESS, Bob

Radio/TV presenter, b. 12 Nov Vryheid, Natal. Stage and radio acting before leaving South Africa for Britain where he has worked on TV and radio. On radio he presented *Late Night Extra* for eight years as well as *Top Of The Form*; record programmes (for 16 years on BBC World Service); LBC's *AM Show*, which he co-presented for 10 years. TV incl: *Take A Letter*; *World In Action*; *Junior Criss Cross Quiz*; *What The Papers Say*; *Today*; *Blockbusters*. Variety Club Award for Joint Independent Radio Personality of the Year, 1979 and 1984. m. Mary Rose; 2 d. Carol Ann, Rosalind, 1 s. Jonathan. Hobbies: music, gardening. Address: c/o Spotlight, London. Birthsign: Scorpio. **Favourite Place:** the Plitvice Lakes in Northern Yugoslavia, 'Quite the most peaceful and beautiful spot I've visited in Europe.'

HOLTON, Gary

Actor/singer, b. 22 Sept 1952 London. Started acting at the age of 11 with Sadlers Wells and National Theatre companies. Stage incl: *Hair*; *Once A Catholic*; *There's A Girl In My Soup*; *Pump Boys And Dinettes*. Films incl: *Quadrophenia*; *Bloody Kids*; *Breaking Glass*. TV incl: *Shoestring*; *Gentle Touch*; *Minder*; *Auf Wiedersehen Pet*. Was lead singer and founder of the band Heavy Metal Kids. Formed Holton/Steel in Scandinavia where the duo enjoyed top recording success. Has recently released rock version of *Catch A Falling Star*, and is again writing music. Hobbies: model making, flying, sunbathing. Address: c/o Harwood-Bee Assocs, St Albans, Herts. Birthsign: Virgo. **Favourite Place:** Mijass, Spain. 'This quiet isolated community has become special to me and is the place I wish to live in someday.'

HONEYCOMBE, Gordon

TV presenter/writer, b. 27 Sept 1936 Karachi, British India. Started as a radio announcer in 1956, acted with the Royal Shakespeare Company, then joined ITN as scriptwriter and newscaster in 1965. Left to freelance in 1977, and joined TV-am as news presenter in 1984. Has also written plays, dramatisations and books. Stage incl: *The Redemption; Paradise Lost* (also radio); *A King Shall Have A Kingdom* (also radio). Radio: *Lancelot And Guinevere.* TV incl: *The Golden Vision; Time And Again; Something Special; The Late, Late Show; Family History.* Books incl: *Neither The Sea Nor The Sand* (also screenplay); *Adam's Tale; Royal Wedding; Selfridges.* Hobbies: genealogy, bridge, crosswords. Address: c/o Isobel Davie, London. Birthsign: Libra. **Favourite Place:** 'Any island when the sun shines.'

HOPKINS, Anthony

Actor, b. 31 Dec 1937 Port Talbot, Wales. Trained at RADA then worked at Phoenix Theatre, Leicester, Liverpool Playhouse and Hornchurch rep before successfully auditioning for Laurence Olivier to join the National Theatre at the Old Vic. 1974 appeared in *Equus* on Broadway and spent next 10 years working in US. Recent theatre: *The Lonely Road* (Old Vic); *Pravda* (National Theatre). Films incl: *The Lion In Winter; Magic; The Elephant Man; Bligh* in *The Bounty.* Most recent TV incl: *Othello; A Marrried Man; Hollywood Wives.* m. (1st) Petronella Barker (dis.), (2nd) Jennifer Lynton; 1 d. Abigail (from 1st m.). Hobbies: piano, reading history and philosophy, walking. Address: c/o Peggy Thompson Business Management, Richmond, Surrey. Birthsign: Capricorn.

HORDERN, Sir Michael, CBE

Actor, b. 3 Oct 1911 Berkhamsted, Herts. Started as ASM and understudy. London debut *Othello* in 1937. Two years in rep at Bristol's Little Theatre. After Royal Navy, returned to the stage. Stage incl: *King Lear; Richard II; Jumpers; The Tempest.* Films incl: *Alexander The Great; The VIPs; The Spy Who Came In From The Cold; Where Eagles Dare; Alice's Adventures In Wonderland; The Slipper And The Rose; The Missionary; Lady Jane.* TV incl: *The Browning Version; Tales Of The Unexpected; All's Well That Ends Well; The History Man; Trelawny Of The Wells.* m. former actress Eve Mortimer; 1 d. Joanna. Hobbies: fishing, gardening. Address: c/o ICM, London. Birthsign: Libra. **Favourite Place:** 'Dartmoor— the valley of the double Dart downstream from Dartmeet.'

HORSFALL, Bernard

Actor, b. Bishops Stortford, Herts. In 1950 enrolled at the Webber Douglas Academy of Dramatic Art. Toured with Dundee Rep Company and the Old Vic. Recent stage incl: *Who's Afraid Of Virginia Woolf?; Jumpers; Clouds; Master Builder; To Kill A King.* Films incl: *Shout At The Devil; Gold; Brass Target; Inside The Third Reich.* TV incl: *Dancers In Mourning; Death Of A Ghost; General Hospital; Big Boy Now; This Year, Next Year; Enemy At The Door; Minder; The Ladykillers; When The Boat Comes In.* m. Jane; 2 d. Hannah, Rebecca, 1 s. Christian. Address: c/o Michael Ladkin Personal Management, London. **Favourite Place:** 'The view of Cuillin Hills from Elgol on the Isle of Skye.'

HOUSEGO, Fred
Presenter and TV personality, b. 25 Oct 1944 Dundee. Former London taxi driver. Since winning the title of Mastermind in 1980 he has been much in demand for radio (*Start The Week*; *Just The Ticket*) and TV (*History On Your Doorstep*; *Blankety Blank*; *The Pyramid Game*; *This Is Your Life*; *The 6 O'Clock Show*), and as a speaker (Oxford and Cambridge Unions). He has also written articles for many periodicals and *Fred Housego's London*. Pye TV Personality of 1981 and is a registered London Tourist Board guide. m. Patricia; 2 d. Kate, Abigail. Hobbies: photography, history books, wine. Address: c/o Peter Charlesworth, London. Birthsign: Scorpio. **Favourite Place:** 'Smithfield, because it's one of London's oldest corners and it still functions as a community.'

HOWARD, Susan
Actress, b. 28 Jan Marshall, Texas. Trained with the Los Angeles Repertory Company. Films incl: *Moonshine County Express*; *Sidewinder I*. TV incl: *The Paper Chase*; *The Flying Nun*; *Bonanza*; *I Dream Of Jeannie*; *Petrocelli*; *Killer On Board*; *Man With A Gun*; *House On The Hill*; as Donna in *Dallas*. m. (2nd) film executive Calvin Chrane; 1 d. (from 1st m.) Lynn. Hobbies: jogging, health food. Address: c/o Herb Tobias and Assocs, 1901 Avenue of the Stars, Suite 840, Los Angeles, CA 90067. Birthsign: Aquarius. **Favourite Place:** her 65-acre ranch in Texas.

HOWERD, Frankie, OBE
Comedian, b. 6 March 1922 York. Stage debut at 13. Camp concerts during the war. Revue and stage shows incl: *Out Of This World*; *Pardon My French*; *Way Out In Piccadilly*; *Charley's Aunt*; *A Midsummer Night's Dream*; Palladium pantomimes, 1968 and 1973. Films incl: *Jumping For Joy*; *Further Up The Creek*; *Carry On Doctor*; *Carry On Up The Jungle*; *Up Pompeii* (also TV); *Up The Chastity Belt*; *Up The Front*; *The House In Nightmare Park*. TV incl: *Fine Goings On*; *The Frankie Howerd Show*; *Frankie Howerd Strikes Again*; *HMS Pinafore*; *Trial By Jury*. Many Royal Variety performances. Book: *Trumps*. Hobbies: tennis, swimming, music, reading. Address: c/o Tessa Le Bars Management, London. Birthsign: Pisces. **Favourite Place:** 'Any room filled with nice food, nice drink and, most especially, my friends.'

HUDD, Roy
Comedian, b. 16 May 1936 Croydon, Surrey. Began in 1957 in boys' clubs followed by holiday camp and summer shows. Stage incl: *Oliver!*; *Underneath The Arches*; and his touring show, *Roy Hudd's Very Own Music Hall*. Radio incl: *The News Huddlines*; '*Udds 'Our An' 'Arf*. TV incl: *Not So Much A Programme, More A Way Of Life* (TV debut 1964); *The Illustrated Weekly Hudd*; *The Roy Hudd Show*; *The 607080 Show*; *The Good Old Days*; *Look Who's Talking*; *Movie Memories*; various chat and variety shows. m. Ann; 1 s. Max. Hobbies: walking, sleeping, talking, music hall (history and songs). Address: c/o Aza Artistes, London. Birthsign: Taurus. **Favourite Place:** 'Any theatre designed by Frank Matcham, who designed dozens of music hall theatres. They are still the best in the country.'

HUGHES, Geoffrey
Actor, b. 2 Feb 1944 Liverpool. Trained with Stoke-on-Trent rep. London theatre incl: *Maggie May*; *Say Good Night To Grandma*. Films incl: *Virgin Soldiers*; *Adolf Hitler, My Part In His Downfall*; *The Bofors Gun*. Played Eddie Yeats in TV's *Coronation Street*. m. Susan. Hobbies: natural history, music. Address: c/o Richard Stone, London. Birthsign: Aquarius. **Favourite Place:** 'The music and people of the Shetland Islands—it's just a nice place to be.'

HUGHES, Nerys
Actress, b. 8 Nov 1941 Rhyl, Wales. Made a name for herself on TV in *The Liver Birds* followed by *The Merchant Of Venice*; *High Summer*; *Seasons*; *Diary Of A Young Man*; *How Green Was My Valley*; *Doctor Who*; *Jackanory*; *Play Away*; *Third Time Lucky*; *Alphabet Zoo*; *District Nurse*. Also presented a *QED* documentary on otters. m. Patrick Turley; 1 d. Mari-Claire, 1 s. Benjamin. Hobbies: playing with the children, gardening. Address: c/o Richard Stone, London. Birthsign: Scorpio. **Favourite Place:** 'View of Lake Mymbyr by Capel Curig. It's Wales. It's Snowdonia. It's beautiful.'

HULL, Rod
Entertainer/writer, b. 13 Aug 1935 Isle of Sheppey. Inseparable from Emu, which Rod hatched from an egg when he was in Australia running a breakfast-time chat show. In this country, they have made numerous TV appearances and had own shows. TV incl: *EBC*; *Emu's World*; *Michael Parkinson Show*; *This Is Your Life*; *Emu's World*; *Emu At Christmas*; *Emu All Live Pink Windmill Show*. Created, wrote and hosted first *Children's Royal Variety Performance 1981*. Pantomime: *Emu In Pantoland*. Book: *The Reluctant Pote*. m. (1st) (dis.), (2nd) Cheryl; 3 d. Danielle, Debbie (both from 1st m.), Amelia (from 2nd m.), 1 step-d. Katrina, 2 s. Toby, Oliver (both from 2nd m.). Hobbies: bee-keeping, golf. Address: c/o International Artists, London. Birthsign: Leo. **Favourite Place:** 'Home, I'm a great home bird.'

HUMPHRIES, Barry
Landscape painter/part-time actor and writer, b. 17 Feb 1934 Melbourne, Australia. Experience gained at Union Theatre, Melbourne, and Philip Street Theatre. Films incl: *Adventures Of Barry McKenzie*; *Barry McKenzie Holds His Own*; *The Getting Of Wisdom*. One-man shows incl: *A Nice Night's Entertainment*; *Excuse I*; *A Load Of Olde Stuffe*; *At Least You Can Say You've Seen It*; *Last Night Of The Poms*; *An Evening's Intercourse With The Widely Liked Barry Humphries*; TV chat shows. m. Diane Millstead; 2 d. Tessa, Emily, 2 s. Oscar, Rupert. Hobbies: travel, exploring the map of Tasmania, reading second-hand booksellers' catalogues in bed. Address: c/o William Morris Agency, London. Birthsign: Aquarius. **Favourite Place:** Adelaide, Australia: 'The Athens of the South.' (see also Everage, Dame Edna).

HUNNIFORD, Gloria
TV and radio presenter/
interviewer, b. 10 April 1940
Portadown, Co Armagh. Had
own radio programme in
Canada, 1959. For BBC in
Northern Ireland, *Up Country*
and *A Taste Of Hunni*. For BBC
World Service she did *A Taste of
Hunni—Irish Style* which has
been replaced by *Gloria
Hunniford*. Her daily Radio 2
programme began in 1982. TV

incl: *Good Evening Ulster*; *Val
Doonican Show*; *Les Dawson
Show*; *Karen Kay Show*; *The 6
O'Clock Show* (for LWT);
Sunday Sunday; *We Love TV*.
TV Times Top Female
Personality, 1984. m. Don
Keating; 1 d. Caron, 2 s. Paul,
Michael. Hobbies: antiques,
tennis. Address: c/o Jo Gurnett
Management, London. Birthsign:
Aries. **Favourite Place:** Lough
Erne, Co Fermanagh: 'Great
peace, no clocks to watch.'

HUNT, Gareth
Actor, b. 7 Feb 1943 London.
Trained at the Webber Douglas
Academy of Dramatic Art. Rep at
Ipswich, Bristol Old Vic,
Coventry, Royal Court in
London, and Watford before the
Royal Shakespeare Company and
the National Theatre. Stage incl:
Conduct Unbecoming; *Alpha Beta*;
Deathtrap. Films incl: *Licensed To*

Love And Kill; *The World Is Full
Of Married Men*; *The House On
Garibaldi Street*. TV incl: *Upstairs,
Downstairs*; *The New Avengers*;
That Beryl Marston . . .! m. (1st)
Carol (dis.), (2nd) Anette; 1 s.
Gareth (from 1st m.). Hobbies:
golf, keep-fit, squash, cricket.
Address: c/o ICM, London.
Birthsign: Aquarius. **Favourite
Place:** 'Standing on an empty
seashore looking out to sea: it
puts all the parking tickets into
perspective.'

HUNTER, Russell
Actor, b. 18 Feb 1925 Glasgow.
A former shipyard worker, began
acting as an amateur. Professional
debut with the Glasgow Unity
Theatre at the first Edinburgh
Festival 1947. Appeared all over
Scotland in one-man show, *Jock*.
Other theatre incl: *Lock Up Your
Daughters*. Worked with
playwright W Gordon Smith for
past 15 years creating series of
one-man plays. Due to play

Andrew Carnegie in a play
written to celebrate 150th
anniversary of the famous
philanthropist. Probably best
known on TV for part of Lonely
in series *Callan*. Other TV incl:
The Gaffer; *Play For Tomorrow*.
Hobby: collecting modern
paintings. Address: c/o Marjorie
Abel, London. Birthsign:
Aquarius. **Favourite Place:**
'The northern shore of Galilee,
where I feel more "at home" than
anywhere else in the world.'

ICKE, David
Presenter/commentator/reporter,
b. 19 April 1952 Leicester.
Formerly with Coventry City
and Hereford United football
clubs, but a football injury put
paid to his soccer career and he
went into journalism, first with
BBC Radio Leicester and BRMB,
then BBC TV. Member of BBC

sports team 1981–85. TV incl:
Grandstand; *Sportsnight*;
International Snooker; *Breakfast
Time*; *Saturday Superstore*. m.
Linda; 1 d. Kerry, 1 s. Gareth.
Hobbies: soccer, motor racing,
reading biographies, steam
railway preservation. Address:
c/o BBC TV, London. Birthsign:
Taurus. **Favourite Place:** 'So
many on the Isle of Wight—one
is the view from Blackgang
Chine along the coast to the
Needles.'

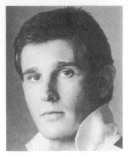

ILES, Jon

Actor, b. 17 May 1954 Ripon, Yorks. Trained at Rose Bruford College of Speech and Drama. Rep at Worthing, many tours incl: *Macbeth*; *Romeo And Juliet*; *Touch Of Spring*; *The Winslow Boy*; *A Murder Is Announced*. West End theatre incl: *Jungle Book*; *Dial M For Murder*. Film: *Those Glory, Glory Days*. TV incl: *The Bill*; *Crown Court*; *To The Manor Born*; Dick Emery series; *Happy Endings*; *Bognor*; *Supergran*; *CATS Eyes*. Hobbies: gym, writing, swimming, tennis, art. Address: c/o David Daly Personal Management, London. Birthsign: Taurus. **Favourite Place:** 'The gym. It concentrates the mind and expands the body! It's also a wonderful discipline.'

IMRIE, Celia

Actress, b. 15 July 1952 Guildford, Surrey. Theatre incl: Glasgow Citizens' Theatre; Royal Court Theatre, London; Bush Theatre, London; Traverse Theatre, Edinburgh; Royal Shakespeare Company world tour. Films incl: *The Wicked Lady*; *Assassin*; *The House Of Whipcord*; *Death On The Nile*. TV incl: *Cloud Howe*; *Bergerac*; *Upstairs, Downstairs*; *The Nightmare Man*; *To The Manor Born*; *Shoestring*; *Victoria Wood As Seen On TV*. Hobbies: Tae Kwondo, gardening, going to Italy. Address: c/o Larry Dalzell, London. Birthsign: Cancer. **Favourite Place:** 'Pulpit Rock—because it's secret.'

INGLE, Su

TV presenter, b. 23 April 1955 London. After taking a degree in botany, started career as a photographer in London and Los Angeles. Radio incl: *Living World*; *Nature Notebook*. TV incl: *Tomorrow's World*; *Wildtrack*; *Secrets Of The Coast*; *The Good Food Show*; *Motorfair*; *Don't Ask Me*; *Photo Assignment*; *Ten On Saturday*; *Craft, Design And Technology*. Hobbies: squash, tennis, microliting, skiing, windsurfing, listening to music, sailing, photography. Address: c/o Arlington Enterprises, London. Birthsign: Taurus. **Favourite Place:** 'In mid-air—I love flying—but if I have to be grounded, then Lye Rock in north Cornwall—a really savage coastline.'

INMAN, John

Actor, b. 28 June 1935 Preston, Lancs. One of his first jobs was as a window dresser in a London store. At 21 actor with Crewe rep. West End debut in *Anne Veronica*. Other theatre incl: *Salad Days*; *Let's Get Laid*; *Charley's Aunt*; summer shows; has played *Mother Goose* for nine consecutive years, incl West End at Victoria Palace. Overnight success in TV series *Are You Being Served?* Other TV incl: *Odd Man Out*; *Celebrity Squares*; *The Good Old Days*; *Take A Letter Mr Jones*. Hobby: work. Address: c/o Bill Robertson, London. Birthsign: Cancer. **Favourite Place:** 'Home, because there's no place like it.'

INNOCENT, Harold
Actor, b. 18 April 1935
Coventry, Warwicks. After
Birmingham School of Speech
Training and Dramatic Art, an
extensive career in theatre and
TV. Recent theatre incl: Royal
Shakespeare Company 1984
season; *On The Razzle; For
Services Rendered; Passion In Six
Days; The Triumph Of Death.*
Many West End plays incl:
*Donkey's Years; The School For
Scandal; A Month Of Sundays.* US
TV incl: *Gunsmoke; Have Gun—
Will Travel; Alfred Hitchcock
Presents; The Barbara Stanwyck
Show.* Other TV incl: *An
Englishman Abroad; A Tale Of
Two Cities; Minder; Diana;
Malice Aforethought; Ripping
Yarns; On The Razzle; Juliet
Bravo.* Hobbies: music,
particularly opera, travel, reading,
wit. Address: c/o Susan Angel
Assocs, London. Birthsign: Aries.
Favourite Place: 'Cities—
Bristol and Edinburgh.'

IRONS, Jeremy
Actor, b. 19 Sept 1948 Isle of
Wight. Trained at Bristol Old
Vic Theatre School and joined
Bristol Old Vic 1971. Theatre
incl: *Godspell; Diary Of A
Madman* (solo performance); *The
Caretaker; Much Ado About
Nothing; An Inspector Calls; Wild
Oats* (with Royal Shakespeare
Company); *The Rear Column;
An Audience Called Eduard; The
Real Thing* on Broadway. Films
incl: *Nijinsky; The French
Lieutenant's Woman;
Moonlighting; Blackout; Betrayal;
Swann In Love.* TV incl: *The
Voysey Inheritance; Langrishe Go
Down, Love For Lydia; Notorious
Woman; Churchill's People;
Brideshead Revisited.* Voted Best
Actor by *TV Times* readers 1981–
82. m. actress Sinéad Cusack; 1 s.
Samuel. Hobbies: walking,
sailing, skiing, riding. Address:
c/o Hutton Management,
London. Birthsign: Virgo.

JACKSON, Gordon, OBE
Actor, b. 19 Dec 1923 Glasgow.
Started in radio plays which
brought him to the attention of
Ealing Studios. Stage incl:
*Macbeth; Hamlet; Hedda Gabler;
What Every Woman Knows;
Noah; Twelfth Night; Cards On
The Table; Mass Appeal.* Films
incl: *Whisky Galore; Mutiny On
the Bounty; Those Magnificent
Men In Their Flying Machines;
The Prime Of Miss Jean Brodie;
Night Of The Generals; The
Shooting Party.* TV incl: *Dr
Finlay's Casebook; The Soldier's
Tale; Upstairs, Downstairs; The
Professionals.* m. actress Rona
Anderson; 2 s. Graham, Roddy.
Hobbies: music, gardening.
Address: c/o ICM, London.
Birthsign: Sagittarius. **Favourite
Place:** 'Lunch on the terrace of
the Gritti Palace Hotel on the
Grand Canal in Venice.
Breathtaking!'

JAMES, Geraldine
Actress, b. 6 July 1950 Berkshire.
Drama Centre training followed
by four years in rep at Exeter and
Coventry. Also worked at the
Bush Theatre, Oxford Playhouse,
Royal Court, Little Theatre, and
the Almost Free Theatre. Six
months in *Passion Of Dracula.*
Films incl: *Sweet William; Night
Cruiser; Gandhi.* TV incl: *The
Sweeney; Crown Court; Dummy*
(1978 Critics' Award for Best
Actress); *I Remember Nelson; The
History Man; Chains; The Jewel
In The Crown; Time And The
Conways; Blott On The Landscape.*
One child. Hobbies: piano,
clarinet, singing, gardening.
Address: c/o Leading Artists,
London. Birthsign: Cancer.
Favourite Place: Connemara,
Eire, 'Because I have been happier
there than anywhere.'

JAMES, John
Actor, b. 18 April Minneapolis, Minnesota. Trained at the American Academy of Dramatic Arts. Stage incl: *Butterflies Are Free*; *Suds*. TV incl: *Search For Tomorrow*; *The Love Boat*; *Fantasy Island*; the TV film, *He's Not Your Son*; *Dynasty*. Hobbies: skiing, scuba-diving, singing, playing the guitar. Address: c/o Kramer, Reiss, Patricola Public Relations, 9100 Sunset Blvd, Suite 240, Los Angeles, CA 90069.

Birthsign: Aries. **Favourite Place:** 'Beach hideaway in Santa Barbara, California.'

JAMES, Rachel
Actress, b. 29 Sept 1956 Cottingham, East Yorkshire. Studied English and drama before joining various theatre companies incl: Pumpkin Theatre, National Youth Theatre, Tricycle Theatre tour, Library Theatre. TV incl: *Juliet Bravo*; *Alive And Kicking*; *The Practice*. Hobbies: tennis, dog walking, travelling to unusual places. Address: c/o Robert MacIntosh, London. Birthsign: Libra. **Favourite Place:**

'Whitby on the east coast because it's bleak and beautiful and the dog likes it there!'

JAMES, Sally
TV presenter, b. 10 May 1950 Chiswick, London. After Arts Educational Trust education, she entered TV as an actress in series such as *Dixon Of Dock Green*; *Z Cars*; *Castlehaven*; *Two Ronnies*; *Wait Until Dark*. More recent TV as presenter incl: *Tiswas*; *Saturday Scene*; *Ultra Quiz*; *655 Special*. m. Mike Smith; 1 s. Adam James. Hobby: golf. Address: c/o Michael Cohen, London. Birthsign: Taurus.

Favourite Place: Scottsdale, Arizona. 'The most perfect place to relax.'

JAMESON, Brian
Actor, b. 31 Jan 1948 Fordingbridge, Hampshire. Started career as an ASM. Trained at RADA. Soon after leaving RADA he joined the National Theatre and the New Theatre. Has also worked at the Royal Court, Coventry, Leatherhead, Guildford and Windsor. Tours incl: *John, Paul, George, Ringo And Bert*; *Sisterly Feelings*. Film: *Birth Of The Beatles*. TV: regular presenter of *Playschool*. Other TV incl: *Z Cars*; *Warship*; *The Dawson Watch*; *Minder*; *Terry And June*; *Only Fools And Horses*; *Together*. m. Mandy Duckett; 2 s. Joe, Jack. Hobbies: gardening, making plans. Address: c/o Carole James Management, Richmond, Surrey. Birthsign: Aquarius. **Favourite Place:** 'The top of Mount Chaipaval on the Isle of Harris, Outer Hebrides. A wild place where eagles sit and admire the view.'

JANSON, David
Actor, b. 30 March 1950
London. Joined the Phildene
Stage School at the age of nine.
Stage debut in 1962 in *Oliver*.
Joined the Royal Shakespeare
Company in 1963 with *A
Midsummer Night's Dream*. Stage
incl: 1965 season at Stratford;
Hanky Park; *She Was Only An
Admiral's Daughter*; *Roll on Four O'Clock*; *Out Of The Crocodile*;
My Giddy Aunt; *Season's
Greetings*; *Taking Steps*; *The
Rivals*; *Don't Start Without Me*;
and various pantomimes. Film: *A
Hard Day's Night*. TV incl: *The
Newcomers*; *Get Some In*;
Grundy; *Don't Rock The Boat*.
Hobbies: wildlife, squash.
Address: c/o Barry Burnett,
London. Birthsign: Aries.
Favourite Place: Estuary of the
River Erme: 'Ever changing,
unspoilt Devon countryside.'

JARVIS, Martin
Actor, b. 4 Aug Cheltenham.
Trained at RADA. Stage incl:
Man And Superman; *The Prodigal
Daughter*; *The Rivals*; *Hamlet*;
The Woman I Love; *She Stoops To
Conquer* (Canada and Hong Kong
Arts Festival); *The Importance Of
Being Earnest*; *Other Places*. Films
incl: *The Last Escape*; *Ike*; *The
Circle*; *Caught In The Act*. Radio
incl: *War And Peace*; *Great
Expectations*; also readings and
author of several short stories. TV incl: *The Pallisers*; *After Liverpool*;
The Samaritan; *Zigger Zagger*;
David Copperfield; *Enemy At The
Door*; *Rings On Their Fingers*;
Doctor Who; *Mr Palfrey Of
Westminster*; *Oscar Wilde*;
Jackanory. m. actress Rosalind
Ayres; 2 s. Toby, Oliver.
Hobbies: music, Indian food,
movies, interior design. Address:
c/o Leading Artists, London.
Birthsign: Leo. **Favourite
Place:** 'Home! Well, "home *is*
where the heart *is*"!'

JASON, David
Comedy actor, b. 2 Feb 1940
London. Keen amateur actor
before his actor brother, Arthur,
helped him get his first
professional part in *South Sea
Bubble*. This was followed by rep
and then *Peter Pan*. A Dick
Emery season at Bournemouth
led to his role in *Do Not Adjust
Your Set*, which established him
on TV. Films incl: *The Odd Job*. Radio incl: *Week Ending*; *Jason
Explanation*. TV incl: *Hark At
Barker*; *Doctor In The House*;
Doctor At Large; *Doctor At Sea*;
*The Top Secret Life Of Edgar
Briggs*; *Lucky Fella*; *A Sharp
Intake Of Breath*; *Open All Hours*;
Only Fools And Horses. BBC TV
Personality of 1984. Hobbies:
gliding, skin-diving. Address: c/o
Richard Stone, London.
Birthsign: Aquarius. **Favourite
Place:** New Zealand, 'I love the
people, I love the place.'

JAY, Tracey
Actress, b. 29 May 1964
Cuckfield, Sussex. Attended
Formby School of Dance and
then Elliot Clarke College where
she studied drama. Now a
member of the cast of C4's
Brookside. Hobbies: horse riding,
dancing, stock cars. Address: c/o
Nigel Martin-Smith, Manchester
2. Birthsign: Gemini. **Favourite
Place:** 'Wherever I am with
friends enjoying myself.'

JEAVONS, Colin

Actor, b. 20 Oct 1929 Newport, Monmouthshire. Trained at the Old Vic Theatre School and his first stage appearance was with the Old Vic in 1951. His first film role was in 1962. Films incl: *The French Lieutenant's Woman*. TV incl: *Billy Liar*; *Hitch-Hiker's Guide To The Galaxy*; *Great Expectations*; *Reilly Ace Of Spies*; *Atlantis*; *Jury*; *Squaring The Circle*; *Travelling Man*; *Sherlock Holmes*; *Hitler's SS*; *Jackanory*. m. Rosie; 2 s. Barney, Saul. Hobbies: collecting 78 rpm records. Address: c/o London Management, London. Birthsign: Libra. **Favourite Place:** Watersmeet, North Devon, 'Because of memories of family holidays.'

JEFFREY, Peter

Actor, b. 18 April 1929 Bristol. No formal training but 12 years of theatre work, mostly with Bristol Old Vic and the Royal Shakespeare Company. Recent theatre incl: *The Merry Wives Of Windsor*; *Troilus And Cressida*. Many films incl: *The Odessa File*; *Midnight Express*. Recent TV incl: *Minder*; *All's Well That Ends Well*; *Nanny*; *Britannia Hospital*; *Bognor*; *The Jewel In The Crown*; *The Last Place On Earth*; *One By One*; *Yes, Minister*; *By The Sword Divided*; *Lace 2*. Hobby: golf. Address: c/o London Management, London. Birthsign: Aries.

JEFFRIES, Lionel

Actor/film director/producer/ screen writer, b. 10 June 1926 London. After training at RADA, rep at the David Garrick Theatre, Lichfield. Recent stage incl: *Hello Dolly*; *See How They Run*; *Two Into One*. Films incl: *The Colditz Story*; *Idle On Parade*; *The Wrong Arm Of The Law*; *The Spy With A Cold Nose*; *Chitty Chitty Bang Bang*; *The Prisoner Of Zenda*. TV incl: *Facts Of Life* (the first play on ITV); *Room At The Bottom*; *Cream In My Coffee*; *Shillingbury Tales*; *Father Charlie*; *Tom, Dick And Harriet*. Wrote and directed *The Railway Children*; also *The Amazing Mr Blunden*. Directed *Baxter*; *The Water Babies*; *Wombling Free*. m. Eileen; 2 d. Elizabeth, Martha, 1 s. Timothy. Hobby: looking at the garden. Address: c/o ICM. London. Birthsign: Gemini. **Favourite Place:** 'My study, lovingly gazing at TV residual cheques.'

JENSEN, David 'Kid'

Disc jockey/personality, b. 4 July Victoria, Canada. Started as a DJ at the age of 16 and worked for Canadian radio stations before joining Radio Luxembourg in 1968. After six years moved to Radio Trent and in 1975 to the BBC. Now has own daily programme with Capital Radio and is presenting the first networked commercial radio chart show on Sundays. TV incl: *Top Of The Pops*; *Pop Quest*; *Pop 45*; *Nationwide*; *Coast To Coast*; hosted *British Rock And Pop Awards*. m. Gudrun; 1 d. Anna-Lisa, 1 s. David. Hobbies: cooking, sport (QPR football supporter). Address: c/o John Miles Organisation, Bristol. Birthsign: Cancer. **Favourite Place:** Reykjavik, Iceland, 'Not only is it home for my wife, Gudrun, but I also regard it as my personal sanity base. It is clean, fresh and the people are very friendly.'

JEPHCOTT, Dominic
Actor, b. 28 July 1957 Coventry, Warwickshire. After studying at RADA he worked extensively in rep, incl: Sheffield, Cambridge, Watford, and tours through India and South East Asia. Joined the Royal Shakespeare Company, performing with it in London and Stratford. TV debut and film debut both in 1979 in *Enemy At The Door* and *All Quiet On The Western Front*. Since then TV and films have incl: *The Scarlet Pimpernel*; *Good And Bad At Games*; *The Aerodrome*; *Something In Disguise*; *Stalky & Co*; *The Jewel In The Crown*; *Oliver Twist*; *Getting On In Concorde*; *The Beiderbecke Affair*. Hobbies: tennis, playing the guitar. Address: c/o Richard Stone, London. Birthsign: Leo. **Favourite Place:** 'The first class deck on an outward bound 747 Jumbo Jet: a place which has comfort, a view and promise.'

JESSEL, David
TV journalist, b. 8 Nov 1945 Abingdon. Presenter/reporter of BBC Radio 4's *World At One*. TV presenting and reporting for programmes incl: *24 Hours*; *Midweek*; *Newsweek*; *Heart Of The Matter*; *Out Of Court*. 2 s. Benjamin, Robert. Hobbies: collecting 18th-century samplers, food, hypochrondria. Address: c/o BBC TV, London. Birthsign: Scorpio. **Favourite Place:** 'The Basilica at Torcello in the Venetian Lagoon. Peace, beauty, and a brilliant restaurant right next door.'

JEWEL, Jimmy
Actor/comedian, b. 4 Dec 1912 Sheffield. Started in the business with his father, also called Jimmy Jewel. Stage incl: *Sunshine Boys*; *Comedians*; *Death Of A Salesman*; *You Can't Take It With You*. Radio incl: *Up The Pole*. TV incl: *Spring And Autumn*, *Nearest And Dearest*; *Funny Man*; and many other TV plays and appearances. Won the Variety Club Special Award in 1984. m. Belle; 1 s. Kerry, 1 d. Piper. Hobby: golf. Address: c/o London Management, London. Birthsign: Sagittarius. **Favourite Place:** Juan-les-Pins, South of France.

JOHNSON, Andrew
Actor, b. 21 July 1959. Trained at the Central School of Speech and Drama and has since worked at the National Theatre, Coventry, Riverside Studios and Royal Court. Stage incl: *Map Of The World*; *The Trojan War Will Not Take Place*; *Talking Black*; *The Trail*. Film: *Majdhar*. Radio: *Bhowani Junction* for Radio 4. TV incl: *Come To Mecca*; *Salt On A Snake's Tail*; *Last Evensong*; *EastEnders*. Hobbies: cinema, reading biographies, literature, theatre, music, talking, visiting the coast. Address: c/o BBC TV, Borehamwood, Herts. Birthsign: Cancer. **Favourite Place:** 'A spot on the north bank of the Thames beside the Tower where I've found a bit of peace.'

JOHNSON, Don

Actor, b. Flatt Creek, Missouri. Won a drama scholarship to the University of Kansas and then went on to the American Conservatory Theater Group in San Francisco. Films incl: *The Magic Garden of Stanley Sweetheart* (debut); *The Harrad Experiment*; *A Boy And His Dog*; *Cease Fire*; *Zacharias*; *Return To Macon County*. TV incl: *The Rebels*; *From Here To Eternity*; *Elvis And Me*; *Revenge Of The Stepford Wives*; *Beulah Land*; *First You Cry*; *The Two Lives Of Carol Leitner*; *Miami Vice*. m. actress Patti D'Arbanville; 1 s. Jesse. Hobbies: song writing, music, fishing, golf. Address: c/o Belson and Klass Assocs, 211 South Beverly Blvd, Beverly Hills, CA 90212.

JOHNSON, Laura

Actress, b. 1 Aug Los Angeles. Studied at the University of California and graduated in the School of Fine Arts. Is best known in her role as Terry Hartford in the TV soap opera *Falcon Crest*. m. (1st) David Solomon (dis.), (2nd) actor Harry Hamlin. Hobbies: horse riding, swimming, camping, skiing, deep-sea fishing. Address: c/o Sandy Bressler & Assocs, 15760 Ventura Blvd, Encino, California 91436. Birthsign: Leo. **Favourite Place:** 'I spend all my free time at the stables training thoroughbred horses.'

JOHNSTON, Sue

Actress, b. 7 Dec 1943 Warrington. Trained at the Webber Douglas Academy of Dramatic Art. Worked in rep at Farnham, Salford, Lincoln, Manchester, Coventry. Also the Portable Theatre, Coventry's TIE, Bolton Octagon, and was a founder member of the M6 Theatre Company. TV incl: *Coronation Street*; *Brookside*. 1 s. Joel. Hobbies: cooking, walking, theatre, reading, music, playing the piano ('badly'). Address: c/o Brookside Productions, Liverpool. Birthsign: Sagittarius. **Favourite Place:** Borrowdale and Derwent Water: 'My grandparents came from the Lakes and I've inherited their love of a beautiful place.'

JONES, Freddie

Actor, b. 12 Sept 1927 Stoke-on-Trent. Trained at the Rose Bruford College of Speech and Drama, followed by rep and with the RSC. Stage incl: *Marat Sade* (and film); *Mister*. Films incl: *Far From The Madding Crowd*; *Otley*; *Goodbye Gemini*; *The Elephant Man*; *Firefox*; *Krull*; *Dune*; *Firestarter*; *And The Ship Sails On*. TV incl: *Sword Of Honour*; *Treasure Island*; *Cold Comfort Farm*; *Uncle Vanya*; *Sweeney Todd*; *The Ghosts Of Motley Hall*; *In Loving Memory*. Named world's best TV actor at Monte Carlo TV Festival 1969 for *The Caesars*. m. actress Jennifer Heslewood; 3 s. Toby, Rupert, Caspar. Hobbies: cooking, gardening. Address: c/o Duncan Heath, London. Birthsign: Virgo. **Favourite Place:** 'The Swan at Littlehaven, holding a pint and relating the restless sea outside to the restless sea within.'

JONES, Ken

Actor, b. 20 Feb 1930 Liverpool. Amateur actor before training at RADA and joining Joan Littlewood's Theatre Workshop in *The Hostage*. Considerable stage and TV work since. Films incl: *SWALK*; *File Of The Golden Goose*; *Sherlock Holmes*; *No Surrender*. TV incl: *Z Cars*; *Hunter's Walk*; *Go For Gold*; *Germinal*; *Her Majesty's Pleasure*; *First Class Friend*; *Last Of The Baskets*; *The Wackers*; *The Squirrels*; *Dead Ernest*; *Seconds Out*. m. actress/writer Sheila Fay. Address: c/o David White Assocs, London. Birthsign: Pisces. **Favourite Place:** 'The view from St George's Church, Everton. This looks out over the whole of Liverpool, across two estuaries to Wales.'

JONES, Paul

Actor/musician/writer/broadcaster, b. 24 Feb 1942 Portsmouth, Hampshire. Began career with the group Manfred Mann and as solo singer. Stage incl: *Guys And Dolls*; *Pump Boys And Dinettes*. Films incl: *Privilege*; *The Committee*. Radio incl: *Paul Jones On Music*; own programme World Service since 1982. TV incl: *Top Of The Pops*; *The Songwriters*; *A Matter Of Taste*; *The Sweeney*; *Jackanory*; *Great Big Groovy Horse*. Co-wrote BBC play, *They Put You Where You Are*. Also presenter of *Weekend* and *A Plus 4*. Albums incl: *Escalator Over The Hill*; *Evita*. m. Fiona Hendley; 2 s. Matthew, Jacob (from previous m.). Hobbies: books, records. Address: c/o Chatto & Linnit, London. Birthsign: Pisces. **Favourite Place:** 'Waterloo Bridge for the same reasons as Wordsworth's for Westminster Bridge.'

JONES, Peter

Actor/author, b. 12 June 1920 Wem, Shropshire. Radio incl: *In All Directions*; *Just A Minute*; *Hitch-Hiker's Guide To The Galaxy*. TV incl: *The Rag Trade*; *Beggar My Neighbour*; *Mr Digby Darling*; *One-Upmanship*; *Whoops Apocalypse*; *I Thought You'd Gone*; Recent TV plays incl: *Singles Weekend*; *The Agatha Christie Hour*. Also guest appearances on many quiz shows. m. American actress Jeri Sauvinet; 1 d. actress Selena Carey-Jones, 2 s. actor William Dare, Charles. Hobbies: cooking, restoring things, making plans, reading. Address: c/o Richard Stone, London. Birthsign: Gemini. **Favourite Place:** 'A hammock between two trees; no transistor within a mile, and my loved ones and a dry Martini close at hand.'

JONES, Simon

Actor, b. 27 July 1950 Charlton Park, Wilts. Started in rep before appearing in Peter Luke's *Bloomsbury* in 1974 (West End debut). Stage incl: *Privates On Parade*; *The Millionairess*; *Design For Living*; *Terra Nova*; *The Real Thing*. Films incl: *Sir Henry At Rawlinson End*; *Reds*; *Gyro City*; Monty Python's *Meaning Of Life*; *Privates On Parade*; *Brazil*. TV incl: *Rock Follies*; *Victorian Scandals—Hannah*; *Hitch-Hiker's Guide To The Galaxy*; *Brideshead Revisited*; *Fothergill*; *No Visible Scar*; *Muck And Brass*; *The Price*. m. Nancy. Hobbies: 19th-century watercolours, comics of the '50s; diary writing, auctions, watching re-runs of Perry Mason. Address: c/o Kate Feast Management, London. Birthsign: Leo. **Favourite Place:** 'Huntsham Court, Devon, Sneden's Landing, New York State. Most places where I happen to be.'

JONES, Steve
TV/radio presenter, b. 7 June 1945 Crewe, Cheshire. Became a radio DJ in 1972. DJ on Radio Clyde, 1973–78. Since 1979 has been with LBC and currently regular Radio 2 presenter. Voted Scottish Radio Personality of the Year, 1977. TV incl: *Battle Of The Comics*; *The Jones Boy*; *It's Friday*; *I'm Steve Jones*; *Sneak Preview*; *Steve Jones Illustrated*; *Watch This Space*; *Edinburgh Festival Show*; *Saturday Morning Show*; *Steve Jones Game Show*; *Search For A Star*; *The Pyramid Game*. m. Lolita; 3 s. Marc, Jason, Oliver. Hobbies: golf, swimming, tennis, current affairs. Address: c/o London Management, London. Birthsign: Gemini. **Favourite Place:** Lagos, Portugal, 'When your golf is bad, the view is good so it matters not!'

JUDD, Lesley
TV Presenter, b. 20 Dec 1946 London. After classical ballet and drama education, started on the stage as a dancer in such productions as *Half A Sixpence*; *Our Man Crichton*; *Twang!* Radio: *Woman's Hour* (Radio 4). TV incl: *Blue Peter*; *Adventure Game*; *Dance Crazy*; *The Great Egg Race*; *Threads*; *Horizon*; *Micro-Live*; *Holiday Talk*; *Pets In Particular*. m. A Relph; 1 s. Henry-Thomas. Hobbies: reading, accumulating old junk, interior design. Address: c/o Arlington Enterprises, London. Birthsign: Sagittarius.

JUNKIN, John
Actor/writer, b. 29 Jan 1930 Ealing. A schoolteacher turned scriptwriter, his more formal training took place at the Joan Littlewood Theatre Workshop. Devised and presented the radio panel game *Jump*. TV incl: *Sharon And Elsie*; *Blott On The Landscape*; *Ronnie Scott's First 25 Years*; *Countdown*; *Loose Ends*. Has written scripts for Leo Sayer and Karen Kay, and for a new series, *Langley Bottom*. Co-author of *Fosdyke Saga*. m. Jennil; 1 d. Annabel. Hobbies: crosswords, panel games, quizzes, surviving. Address: c/o Richard Stone, London. Birthsign: Aquarius. **Favourite Place:** 'Apart from home, a small local restaurant because we have had numerous long and hilarious lunches there with some of our best friends.'

KANALY, Steve
Actor, b. 14 March Burbank, California. A former US army radio operator. Films incl: *The Life And Times Of Judge Roy Bean*; *Fleshburn*; *The Wind And The Lion*; *Dillinger*; *Sugarland Express*; *Terminal Man*. TV films incl: *Young Joe, The Forgotten Kennedy*; *Melvin Purvis*; *The Lost*; *Amelia Earhart*; *To Find My Son*. Plays the part of Ray in TV's *Dallas*. Guest roles on TV incl: *Hotel*; *Police Woman*; *Police Story*; *The Love Boat*; *Hawaii Five-O*; *The Guest*; *Rafferty*. m. Brent; 1 d. Quinn Kathryn, 1 s Evan. Hobbies: hunting, fishing, tennis, jogging and is a silversmith. Address: c/o Paul Kohner Agency, 9169 Sunset Blvd, Los Angeles, California 90069. Birthsign: Pisces. **Favourite Place:** 'The outdoors, where I can hunt and fish.'

KANE, John
Actor/writer, b. 27 Oct 1945 Dundee. Trained at Glasgow College of Dramatic Art and spent seven years with the Royal Shakespeare Company. Entered TV in *Softly, Softly*. Other TV as an actor incl: *Doctor Who*; *Doctor On The Go*; *Play Away*; *Cymbeline*; *Devenish*; *Love's Labours Lost*; *Take The Stage*. As writer TV incl: *Scott On*; *Son Of The Bride*; *Black Beauty*; *The Kids From 47A*; *A Little Touch Of* *Wisdom*; *Feathered Serpent*; *Four Idle Hands*; *Cloppa Castle*; *The Vamp*; *Funny Ha-Ha*; *Terry And June*; *Happy Ever After*; *Me And My Girl*; *Never The Twain*; *Smuggler*; *All In Good Faith*. m. Alison Mary Hope Robine; 2 d. Alice, Susanna, 1 s. Simon. Hobbies: books, music, collecting movies. Address: c/o April Young, London. Birthsign: Scorpio. **Favourite Place:** 'Cavalaire-sur-Mer. We crash out there as a family every Easter.'

KAY, Charles
Actor, b. 3 Aug 1930 Coventry. Trained at RADA and has been a member of the Royal Shakespeare Company, and with the National Theatre and the Old Vic. Films incl: *Hennessey*; *Nijinsky*; *Amadeus*. Many TV appearances since 1972 incl: *The Duchess Of Malfi*; *The Merchant Of Venice*; *Microbe Hunters*; *Fall Of Eagles*; *Loyalties*; *I, Claudius*; *Target*; *The Devil's Crown*; *Lady Killers*; *To Serve Them All My Days*; *Bergerac*; *My Cousin Rachel*; *The Citadel*; *Magnox*; *King John*. Hobbies: reading, listening to music, watching TV, bridge. Address: c/o Marmont Management, London. Birthsign: Virgo. **Favourite Place:** 'The River Avon from Clopton Bridge. Pure nostalgia from boyhood.'

KAY, Karen
Singer/impressionist/entertainer, b. 18 July Blackburn, Lancs. Started in show business aged 15 in Blackpool summer season. Then in clubs, summer seasons in Britain and abroad. West End season 1980 *It's Magic*; *Royal Variety Show* 1982. TV incl: *Who Do You Do?*; *Punchlines*; *Wednesday At Eight*; *Blankety Blank*; *Max Bygraves Show*; *Des O'Connor Tonight*; *Russell Harty*; *Aspel And Co*; *The Vocal Touch*; *Bob Monkhouse Show*; *3-2-1*; *Look Who's Talking*; *The Karen Kay Show* (three series). Address: c/o London Management, London. Birthsign: Cancer. **Favourite Place:** 'The Cotswolds—marvellous scenery and tranquillity. A great place to get away from it all.'

KAYE, Gorden
Actor, b. 7 April 1941 Huddersfield, W Yorks. No formal training. Seasons at Bolton, Sheffield and Stratford East theatres in London. West End theatre incl: *Hobson's Choice*. US and Canada tour with National Theatre. Recent theatre incl: *Better Times*. Films incl: *Escape From The Dark*; *Porridge*; *Jabberwocky*; *Brazil*. Much TV ranging from *Coronation Street* to *Born And Bred*. Comedy series with Les Dawson, Marty Feldman and John Cleese. Other TV incl: *Fame Is The Spur*; *King John*; *Much Ado About Nothing*; *In The Secret State*; *Are You Being Served?*; *It Ain't Half Hot Mum*; *'Allo 'Allo!* Hobbies: food, travel, theatre, films. Address: c/o Plant & Froggatt, London. Birthsign: Aries. **Favourite Place:** 'San Francisco. Opened there in a US tour and began a love affair with America.'

KEAVENEY, Anna

Actress, b. 5 Oct 1949 Runcorn, Cheshire. Trained with Studio '68. Rep at Bolton, Oldham, Liverpool, Citizens' Theatre, Glasgow, Bristol Old Vic. Appeared in *Once A Catholic* and *Touched* at the Royal Court Theatre, London. Theatre also incl: *Translations* at Hampstead Theatre and later National Theatre; Victoria Wood's *Good Fun* at the King's Head, London. Numerous radio work and TV incl: *Enemy At The Door; Within These Walls; Widows*. She has played Marie Jackson in *Brookside* for two years. Hobbies: driving, eating out, going to the theatre. Address: c/o Louis Hammond Management, London. Birthsign: Libra. **Favourite Place:** 'London—I never tire of it. A really exciting city, with New York coming a close second.'

KEE, Robert

Journalist/presenter, b. 5 Oct 1919 Calcutta, India. Journalist on *Picture Post* 1948–51; *Observer* correspondent Suez Crisis; contributor to *The Sunday Times*; literary editor *The Spectator* 1957. Entered TV as reporter *Panorama* 1958–62. TV incl: *This Week; Looking For An Answer; Robert Kee Reports; Kee Interview*; ITN's *One O'Clock News* as presenter; *First Report*; General Election and Referendum programmes 1974– 75; *General Strike Report; Jubilee; Ireland—A TV History; Panorama*; TV-am; *Seven Days; The Writing On The Wall*. Books incl: *Ireland: A History*. m. (1st) Janetta (dis.), (2nd) Cynthia; 2 d. Georgina, Sarah, 2 s. Alexander, Benjamin (dec.). Hobbies: Irish history, swimming, cycling, music, writing. Address: c/o Anthony Sheil Assocs, London. Birthsign: Libra. **Favourite Place:** 'White Michelin roads in France.'

KEEL, Howard

Actor/singer, b. 13 April 1917 Gillespie, Illinois. Was an aircraft sales rep but began acting after winning singing scholarship. Has played most of the big singing roles in musicals. Theatre incl: *Carousel; Oklahoma!; No Strings; Camelot; South Pacific; On A Clear Day You Can See Forever; Kismet; Kiss Me, Kate*. Also variety and London Palladium. Films incl: *The Small Voice; Annie Get Your Gun; Showboat; Calamity Jane; Seven Brides For Seven Brothers*. Now best known as Clayton Farlow in TV's *Dallas*. m. (3rd) Judy; 2 d. Christina, Kaya, 1 s. Gunnar (from previous m.), 1 s. Leslie (from 3rd m.). Hobbies: golf, charity work. Address: c/o Lew Sherrell Agency, 7060 Hollywood Blvd, Suite 610, Los Angeles, California 90028. Birthsign: Aries. **Favourite Place:** 'London— England made me a star.'

KEEN, Diane

Actress, b. 29 July 1946 London. Brought up in Kenya—settled in England aged 19. Trained in rep but unknown until *The Cuckoo Waltz* on TV. Other TV incl: *Crossroads; Fall Of Eagles; Softly, Softly; Public Eye; The Legend Of Robin Hood; The Sweeney; The Feathered Serpent; Country Matters; Crown Court; The Sandbaggers; Rings On Their Fingers; The Shillingbury Blowers; The Shillingbury Tales; The Reunion; The Morecambe And Wise Show; Bruce Meets The Girls; Foxy Lady; Oxbridge Blues (Sleeps Six)*. TVTimes Top Ten Best Actress Award 1979. m. Neil Zeiger; 1 d. Melissa. Hobbies: reading, travel, DIY. Address: c/o William Morris Agency, London. Birthsign: Leo. **Favourite Place:** 'Amboseli Game Reserve looking at Mount Kilimanjaro, Kenya, to feel part of nature.'

KEITH, Penelope
Actress, b. 2 April Sutton, Surrey.
Trained at Webber Douglas
Academy of Dramatic Art, then
rep and the Royal Shakespeare
Company. Theatre incl: *Fallen
Angels; The Norman Conquests*
(and TV); *Donkey's Years* (and
TV); *The Apple Cart; The
Millionairess; Moving; Hobson's
Choice; Captain Brassbound's
Conversion; Hay Fever* (and TV).
Films incl: *The Hound Of The
Baskervilles; The Priest Of Love.*
TV incl: *Private Lives; The Good
Life; To The Manor Born; On
Approval; Spider's Web; Waters
Of The Moon.* Winner of
numerous awards incl: *TV Times*
Top Ten Award 1976–80;
Variety Club Award for BBC
TV Personality 1979. m. Rodney
Timson. Address: c/o Howes &
Prior, London. Birthsign: Aries.
Favourite Place: 'The
greenhouse, where I have free
range with my green fingers.'

KEITH, Sheila
Actress, b. 9 June 1920. Trained
at the Webber Douglas Academy
of Dramatic Art. Theatre incl:
Present Laughter; Mame (with
Ginger Rogers); *Banana Ridge;
Deathtrap; Anyone For Denis?;*
Liverpool rep, Coventry, Bristol
Old Vic. Films incl: *Ooh, You Are
Awful; House Of Whipcord;
Frightmare; The Comeback; House
Of The Long Shadows.* TV incl:
*David Copperfield; Moody And
Peg; Ballet Shoes; Within These
Walls; Angels; The Cedar Tree;
The Pallisers; Jubilee; Roof Over
My Head; Working Arrangements;
Heartland; Racing Game; Rings
On Their Fingers; Swing, Swing
Together; Agony; Bless Me Father;
The Other 'Arf; Drummonds.*
Hobbies: browsing in bookshops,
nature study, antique furniture.
Address: c/o Leading Players,
London. Birthsign: Gemini.
Favourite Place: 'After walking
the dog, the fireside on a cold wet
afternoon!'

KELLY, Barbara
TV personality/presenter, b. 5
Oct Vancouver. Began career in
CBC Radio, Canada, then in *The
Stage Series.* Arrived in Britain in
1949 and offered BBC Radio
series. Many TV appearances incl.
*Kelly's Eye; Criss Cross Quiz;
Leave Your Name And Number;*
joined *What's My Line?* team
1950 and appeared on and off for
12 years. m. Bernard Braden; 1 s.
Christopher, 2 d. Kelly, Kim.
Address: c/o Primer Performers,
London. Birthsign: Libra.
Favourite Place: 'A small town
called Nanyuki at the foot of
Mount Kenya.'

KELLY, Chris
Producer/writer/broadcaster, b.
24 April 1940 Cuddington,
Cheshire. Started career with
Anglia TV, then as a producer
with Granada before going
freelance. TV incl: *Clapperboard;
World In Action; The Royal Film
Performance; The Royal Academy
Summer Exhibition; I've Got A
Secret; Never Too Early, Never
Too Late; Friday Live; Folio;
Cinema Scrapbook; Food And
Drink; Wish You Were Here . . .?*
m. Vivien; 1 s. Nicholas, 1 d.
Rebecca. Hobbies: reading,
cooking. Address: c/o
Barry Burnett, London.
Birthsign: Taurus. **Favourite
Place:** 'By my old apple tree,
overlooking a cricket pitch.'

KELLY, David

Actor, b. 11 July 1929 Dublin. Worked in the theatre in Dublin, London, Paris, Berlin for 30 years. Became well known on TV in the part of the one-armed washer-up in *Robin's Nest*. Films incl: *Two By Forsythe*; *Ann Devlin*; *Pirates*. TV incl: *Cowboys*; *The Gentle Touch*; *Strumpet City*; *Whoops Apocalypse*; *A Comedy Of Errors*; *Late Starter*. m. actress Laurie Morton; 1 s. David, 1 d. actress Miriam. Hobby: painting. Address: c/o Joy Jameson, London. Birthsign: Cancer. **Favourite Place:** 'My garden—where I can't hear the phone.'

KELLY, Henry

Reporter/presenter, b. 17 April 1946 Dublin. Trained in daily journalism on the *Irish Times*, where he worked for eight years, travelling all over the world as a reporter. Joined Radio 4 in 1976 and has since done much radio work incl: *The World Tonight*; *Profile*; *Woman's Hour*; *Midweek*. He co-presented TV's *Game For A Laugh* for the first three years of the programme. Presenter of Saturday programme on TV-am. Also presenter of *Monkey Business* (BBC) and *Scene '85* (HTV West). Book: *How Stormont Fell* ('A political Mickey Spillane'). m. Marjorie; 1 d. Siobhan. Hobbies: golf, reading. Address: c/o TV-am, London. Birthsign: Aries. **Favourite Place:** 'The view, from in front of the stands, over Cheltenham racecourse.'

KELLY, Matthew

Actor, b. 9 May 1950 Manchester. First ten years spent working in theatre incl variety, rep and West End. Eight years on TV incl: *The Bonus*; *Pickersgill People*; *The Critic*; *Room Service*; *Holding The Fort* (three series); *Game For A Laugh* (three series); *Madabout* (two series); *The Sensible Show*; *Adventure Of A Lifetime*; *Relative Strangers*; *Kelly's Eye*. m. Sarah; 1 s. Matthew, 1 d. Ruth. Hobbies: travelling, swimming, dancing, talking, laughing. Address: c/o Regan Assocs, London. Birthsign: Taurus. **Favourite Place:** 'Nepal, because it's beautiful and so are the people.'

KELLY, Sam

Actor, b. 19 Dec 1943 Manchester. Trained at the London Academy of Music and Dramatic Art and in rep at St Andrews, Liverpool, Sheffield, Manchester, Coventry, Birmingham, Southampton and at the Young Vic, London. Has performed in numerous radio plays and was a presenter of *Listen With Mother*. TV incl: *Emergency Ward 10* (1967); *The Liver Birds*; *Porridge*; *Who's Who*; *Grown Ups*; *Days At The Beach*; *The Boys From The Black Stuff*; *Scully*; *Coronation Street*; *Bleak House*; *Now and Then*; *Jenny's War*; *'Allo, 'Allo!* Hobbies: watching cricket, classical music, barbershop singing. Address: c/o Richard Stone, London. Birthsign: Sagittarius. **Favourite Place:** 'The grandstand at Lord's. I can watch cricket, meet other actors and be happily out of work.'

KENDAL, Felicity
Actress, b. 25 Sept Birmingham. Taken to India when three months old by her parents, who were travelling actors. Grew up learning her art as a strolling player, eventually playing leading roles. Returned to Birmingham to live with her aunt. Break in a TV play with John Gielgud, *The Mayfly And The Frog*. Theatre incl: Regent's Park Open Air Theatre; *Kean*; *The Norman Conquests*; *Clouds*; *Amadeus*; *On The Razzle*; *The Second Mrs Tanqueray* and *Othello* (all for the National Theatre). Also in *The Real Thing* and *Jumpers* in the West End. Films: *Shakespeare Wallah*; *Valentino*. TV incl: *Crime Of Passion*; *The Woodlanders*; *The Dolly Dialogues*; *Love Story*; *Edward The Seventh*; *The Good Life*; *Solo*; *The Mistress*. Address: c/o Chatto & Linnit, London. Birthsign: Libra.

KENDALL, Kenneth
Presenter, b. 7 Aug 1924 South India, but brought up in Cornwall. Former schoolmaster and wartime Captain in the Coldstream Guards. Joined BBC 1948. Newsreader 1955–61, when he left to go freelance, but returned to BBC 1969. Voted best dressed newsreader by *Style International* and No 1 newscaster by *Daily Mirror* readers 1979. Left the BBC in 1981 and is now co-presenter of Channel 4's *Treasure Hunt*. Hobbies: racing, theatre, gardening, dogs. Address: c/o Lewis Joelle, London. Birthsign: Leo. **Favourite Place:** 'The cliffs at Chapel Porth in Cornwall for the magnificent views up and down the coast.'

KENNEDY, Cheryl
Actress, b. 29 April 1947 Enfield, Middx. Trained at the Corona Stage School. Theatre incl: *Half A Sixpence*; *The Boy Friend*; *1776*; *Time And Time Again*; *Absent Friends*; *Flowers For Algernon*; *My Fair Lady* (in US with Rex Harrison); *Time And The Conways* (Old Vic); *What A Way To Run A Revolution* (Young Vic). TV incl: Cliff Richard and Mike Yarwood shows; *That's Life!*; *Omnibus*; *Play For Today*; *Play Of The Month*; *The Sweeney*; *Target*; *The Professionals*; *Brookside*. m. (dis.); 1 d. Samantha. Hobbies: stamp collecting, tennis, swimming. Address: c/o Kate Feast Management, London. Birthsign: Taurus. **Favourite Place:** 'My bathroom, for relaxation, meditation and yoga.'

KENNEDY, Joyce
Actress, b. 3 Aug 1937 Leeds. Many TV appearances incl: *Leeds United*; *Spend, Spend, Spend!*; *Ready When You Are Mr McGill*; *The Evacuees*; *Crown Court*; *Coronation Street*; *Emmerdale Farm*; *All Creatures Great And Small*; *The Nearly Man*; *Nanny*; *PC Penrose*; *One Hundred And Eighty*; district nurse, Dorothy Fuller in *The Practice*. m. Trevor Ives; 1 d. Nicola. Hobby: knitting. Address: c/o ATS Casting, Leeds. Birthsign: Leo. **Favourite Place:** 'Harrogate: it ranges from luxurious to rural, picturesque and antique, quiet or busy, cultural and historic.'

KENNEDY, Kevin
Actor, b. 4 Sept 1961 Manchester. Trained at Manchester Polytechnic School of Theatre. Has appeared on stage in *Ducking Out* at the Greenwich Theatre and West End, London; and in *Hamlet* at the Crucible Theatre, Sheffield. Radio incl: *The Old Man Sleeps Alone*; *Metamorphosied Arkwright*. TV incl: *Dear Ladies*; *The Last Company Car*; *Keep On Running*; plays Curly Watts in *Coronation Street*. Hobbies: music, football, reading. Address: c/o Saraband Assocs, London. Birthsign: Virgo. **Favourite Place:** 'London. The West End has the best theatres in the world.'

KENNEDY, Ludovic
Writer/broadcaster, b. 3 Nov 1919 Edinburgh. Started writing as freelance journalist. TV incl: *Profile* 1955–56; ITN newscaster 1956–58; *Television Reporters International* 1963–64; *Time Out*; *World At One*; *The Nature Of Prejudice*; *Face The Press*; *24 Hours*; *Ad Lib*; *Midweek*; *Newsday*; *Tonight*; *Did You See . . .?*; *Obituary Of Lord Mountbatten*; *Great Railway Journeys Of The World*. Many films. His books incl: *Sub-Lieutenant*; *Ten Rillington Place*; *Pursuit*; *The Chase And Sinking Of The Bismarck*; *Menace*; *A Presumption Of Innocence*; *The Portland Spy Case*; *The British At War* (general editor); *Wicked Beyond Belief*; *The Lindburgh Case*; *The Framing Of Richard Hauptmann*. m. former ballerina Moira Shearer; 3 d. Ailsa, Rachel, Fiona, 1 s. Alastair. Address: c/o AD Peters, London. Birthsign: Scorpio.

KENNEDY, Sarah
Reporter/presenter, b. 8 July 1950 East Grinstead, Surrey. Worked in radio in Singapore and Germany before joining BBC Radio in London. Radio incl: *String Sound*; *Start The Week* with Richard Baker; *Colour Supplement*. TV incl: *Royale Progress*; *Chipperfield Safari*; *Game For A Laugh*; *60 Minutes*; *Daytime*. Hobbies: walking, sleeping, cooking. Address: c/o Bagenal Harvey, London. Birthsign: Cancer. **Favourite Place:** 'If I tell you, you'll be there, too.'

KERCHEVAL, Ken
Actor, b. 15 July Wolcottville, Indiana. Started acting at college and sang at military school. Appeared in summer theatres in California and in regional theatres; on Broadway in *Something About A Soldier* and *Fiddler On The Roof*. TV films incl: *Enemy Of The People*; *The Coming Asunder Of Jimmy Bright*. TV guest star in *Trapper John MD*; *Love Boat*. Best known as Cliff Barnes in TV's *Dallas*. Other TV incl: *The Defenders*; *Naked City*; *Secret Storm*; *Search For Tomorrow*. m. (dis.); 2 s. Aaron, Caleb, 1 d. Liza. Hobbies: chasing and collecting antiques, restoring Packard cars, collecting American regional art. Address: c/o ICM, 8899 Beverly Blvd, Los Angeles, California 90048. Birthsign: Cancer. **Favourite Place:** 'Any chance I get I run back home to my garden in Clinton, Illinois.'

KERSHAW, Richard
Presenter/reporter, b. 16 April 1934 London. Cambridge graduate and University of Virginia Graduate School. Spent 10 years as member of BBC TV's *Panorama* reporting team; then presenter of *Newsday*, *Newsweek* and *Nationwide*. Other TV incl: *This Week*; *Gallery*; *Tonight*; *Platform One*. Recent TV incl: *The World About Us* special reports on disasters. m. (dis.); two children. Hobby: sport, particularly cricket. Address: c/o Arlington Enterprises, London. Birthsign: Aries. **Favourite Place:** 'Bargemon, Var, France—the place I have been most happy.'

KEYS, Richard
Presenter, b. 23 April 1957 Coventry. Spent six years in independent local radio in Liverpool and Manchester and then worked as a journalist for a Fleet Street agency. Currently a presenter with TV-am. m. Julia; 1 d. Jemma. Hobbies: squash, golf, football, tennis. Address: c/o Bagenal Harvey, London. Birthsign: Taurus. **Favourite Place:** 'Corsica—Julia and I honeymooned there.'

KING, Jonathan
Presenter, b. 6 Dec 1948 London. Has worked as a pop entrepreneur and artist, producer, journalist, owner of a record company, consultant to a major record label, author. Own BBC TV series, *Entertainment USA*. Hobby: self. Address: c/o Carole Broughton, London. Birthsign: Sagittarius. **Favourite Place:** 'London, because I was born there and have lived there all my life. And New York.'

KINGSTON, Mark
Actor, b. 18 April 1934 London. Trained at the London Academy of Music and Drama and made his theatre debut in pantomime at Boscombe Hippodrome 1953, then rep seasons. First London appearance in *Caesar And Cleopatra* at Old Vic. Toured Russia, Poland, Australia and New Zealand with Old Vic Company. Many London appearances since incl: *The Mousetrap*; *The Cocktail Party*; *A Voyage Round My Father*; *Clouds*; *Educating Rita*. TV incl: *United*; *Beryl's Lot*; *Time Of My Life*; *Driving Ambition*; *Shine On Harvey Moon*. m. Marigold Sharman. Hobbies: music, golf. Address: c/o ICM, London. Birthsign: Aries.

KINNEAR, Roy

Actor, b. 8 Jan 1934 Wigan, Lancs. Trained at RADA and after rep at Nottingham, Glasgow, Edinburgh and Perth joined Joan Littlewood's Theatre Workshop in London. Then pantomime at London Palladium and with Royal Shakespeare Company. First came to the fore in TV's *That Was The Week That Was* and has appeared in many TV plays and series. Theatre incl: *The Clandestine Marriage*. Films incl: *Juggernaut; The Last Remake Of Beau Geste; Hammett; The Zany Adventures Of Robin Hood; Squaring The Circle*. TV incl: *A World Of His Own; A Slight Case Of . . .; Inside George Webley*. m. Carmel Cryan; 2 d. Karina, Kirsty, 1 s. Rory. Hobby: writing to the Inland Revenue. Address: c/o Richard Stone, London. Birthsign: Capricorn. **Favourite Place:** 'Home.'

KINNOCK, Neil, Rt Hon

Leader of the Opposition, b. 28 March 1942 Tredegar, Wales. Went to University College, Cardiff. From 1970–83 Labour MP for Bedwellty. Since 1983 Labour MP for Islwyn. 1974–75 Parliamentary Private Secretary to Rt Hon Michael Foot. 1979–83 Chief Opposition Spokesman on Education. 1980–82 member of Shadow Cabinet. Leader of the Labour Party and Leader of the Opposition since 1983. Been a member of the Labour Party since aged 15; member of T&GWU since 1966. m. Glenys; 1 s. Stephen, 1 d. Rachel. Hobbies: male voice choral music, reading, walking, watching and talking about sport, being with the family. Address: c/o House of Commons, London. Birthsign: Aries. **Favourite Place:** 'Home. It's where the heart, the kids, the books, the VTR and the best food in the world is.'

KIRKBRIDE, Anne

Actress, b. 21 June 1954 Oldham, Lancs. Trained at Oldham rep. TV incl: *Another Sunday; Sweet FA*; has played Deirdre in *Coronation Street* since 1972. Hobby: photography. Address: c/o Granada TV, Manchester. Birthsign: Cancer. **Favourite Place:** 'In the countryside on top of a hill, or any island will do.'

KITCHEN, Michael

Actor, b. 31 Oct 1948 Leicester. Worked with the National Youth Theatre, then a year as assistant stage manager before RADA. Appeared at London's Royal Court Theatre, Young Vic and at National Theatre, where plays incl: *On The Razzle; Bedroom Farce* (and TV); *Spring Awakening; Rough Crossing*. Other theatre incl: *Othello; Macbeth; Charley's Aunt*. Films incl: *Dracula Today; Breaking Glass; The Bunker; Out Of Africa*. TV incl: *King Lear; Churchill's People; Fall Of Eagles; Brimstone And Treacle; No Man's Land; The Misanthrope; The Long And The Short And The Tall; Caught On A Train; A Room For The Winter; The Best Of Everything; Freud; Love Song*. Hobbies: music, photography, sport. Address: c/o Plant & Froggatt, London. Birthsign: Scorpio. **Favourite Place:** 'A farmhouse in the Tuscan Hills, Siena.'

KLUGMAN, Jack
Actor, b. 27 April 1922
Philadelphia. After war service
made a living as a house painter
and post office employee before
studying drama with American
Theatre Wing in New York.
First breaks with Kim Stanley in
St Joan and with Rod Steiger in
Stevedore. Ten years in summer stock before a part in *Mr Roberts*
in New York, then opposite Ethel
Merman in *Gypsy* and on to
Hollywood. Appeared in *The
Odd Couple* in US and London
and on TV—for which he won
two Emmys. More than 400 TV
credits incl: *The Defenders*; *The
Virginian*; *The Fugitive*; *Harris
Against The World*. Since 1976
has played the unorthodox
pathologist in TV's *Quincy*. m.
actress Brett Somers; 2 s.
Birthsign: Taurus.

KNUTT, Bobby
Comedian/actor, b. 25 Nov 1945
Sheffield. Started in show business
as a member of The Whirlwinds
group and in working men's
clubs and cabaret. Had own TV
chat show on Yorkshire TV and a keep-fit series, *Inta Shape*. Other
TV incl: *Print Out*; *Price Of Coal*;
Coronation Street; Paul Squire
series; Marti Caine series;
Blankety Blank; own series *It's A
Knutthouse*. First British
entertainer to go to Falkland
Islands. m. (dis.). Hobbies: body-
building, cooking. Address: c/o
Johnnie Peller Enterprises,
Sheffield. Birthsign: Sagittarius.
Favourite Place: 'Top of
Mount Teide in Tenerife—a
great view and no phones.'

KOVE, Martin
Actor, b. 6 March 1947
Brooklyn, New York. Started
career at La Mama Theatre, New
York and with rep theatres.
Many films incl: *Capone*; *Death
Race 2000*; *White Line Fever*;
Savages; *The Four Deuces*; *Seven*;
The Red Tide; *Partners*; *First Blood
II*; *The Karate Kid*. TV films incl:
Captains And Kings; *City Of
Angels*; *The Yeagers*; *Donavon's
Kid*; *The Sky Trap*; *Cry For The
Stranger*. TV incl: *Code-R*; *We've* *Got Each Other*; *The Edge Of
Night*; *The Optimist*; plays
Detective Isbecki in *Cagney And
Lacey*. m. Vivienne; 1 step-s. Sean
Raymond. Hobbies: tennis,
scuba-diving, riding, skiing.
Address: c/o Troulman
Accountancy Corp, 11500 W
Olympic Blvd, Suite 300, Los
Angeles, California 90067.
Birthsign: Pisces. **Favourite
Place:** 'The Wild West. Places
where outlaws roamed —the
legends never die for me.'

KRAMER, Stepfanie
Actress, b. 6 Aug Long Beach,
California. Trained at the
American Academy of Arts/
West. Many guest roles on TV
incl: *Starsky And Hutch*; *Dynasty*;
Trapper John, MD; *Knot's
Landing*; *The A-Team*; *Riptide*; *Mickey Spillane's Mike Hammer*;
Bosom Buddies; *Fantasy Island*;
Vegas; *Operation Runaway*; *High
Performance*. TV series incl: *We
Got It Made*; *Hunter*. Hobbies:
dancing, writing and performing
country and rock 'n' roll music.
Address: c/o William Morris
Agency, 151 El Camino Drive,
Beverly Hills, California 90212.
Birthsign: Leo. **Favourite
Place:** 'The English countryside
and the Colorado Rocky
Mountains.'

THE KRANKIES

Husband and wife comedy team that began at Pavilion, Glasgow when Ian Tough was backstage electrician and Janet was in chorus line. Voted Comedy Act of the Year 1978 and made *Royal Variety Show* debut the same year. Starred in first *Children's Royal Variety Show* 1981 and several *Royal Shows* since, as well as summer seasons, pantomimes and tours. TV incl: *Crackerjack*; *The Krankies Klub*; specials for LWT; own series for BBC. **Ian Tough,** b. 26 March 1947 Glasgow. Hobbies: golf, fishing. Address: c/o International Artistes, London. Birthsign: Aries. **Favourite Place:** 'Shell Beach at Herm.'
Janet Tough, b. 16 May 1947 Queenzieburn, Stirlingshire. Hobbies: golf, swimming in the sea. Birthsign: Taurus. **Favourite Place:** 'From the clifftop overlooking Saints Bay in Guernsey.'

KWOUK, Burt

Actor, b. 18 July 1930 Manchester. Grew up in Shanghai, went to America and returned to England 1953. First break in a *Charlie Drake Show* and the film *The Inn Of The Sixth Happiness*. Well known as Peter Sellers' karate-mad houseboy in the *Pink Panther* films. Films incl: *A Shot In The Dark*; *Madam Sin*; *Deep End*; *The Most Dangerous Man In The World*; *Goldfinger*; *You Only Live Twice*; *The Return Of The Pink Panther*; *The Fiendish Plot Of Dr Fu Manchu*; *The Trail Of The Pink Panther*; *Plenty*; *The Curse Of The Pink Panther*. TV appearances incl: *Tenko*; *Hart To Hart*; *Supergran*; *Switch On To English*; *The Brief*; *The Lenny Henry Show*. Hobby: sport on TV. Address: c/o London Management, London. Birthsign: Cancer. **Favourite Place:** 'Old Shanghai, where I grew up.'

LA RUE, Danny

Actor/entertainer, b. Daniel Patrick Carroll 26 July Cork, Ireland. Brought to England aged six. While in the Royal Navy appeared in concert party and after went into rep. London debut at Irving Theatre, then cabaret. West End theatre incl: *Come Spy With Me*; *Queen Passionella And The Sleeping Beauty*; *At The Palace*; *The Danny La Rue Show* (also Canada); *The Exciting Adventures Of Queen Daniella*; numerous pantomimes; three *Royal Variety Shows*; first man to play Dolly Levi in *Hello Dolly!* Many awards incl: Entertainer of the Decade 1979. Film: *Our Miss Fred*. TV incl: *The Good Old Days*; *Charley's Aunt*; *Queen Of Hearts*; *Tonight With Danny La Rue*; *Come Spy With Me*; *The Ladies I Love*. Address: c/o Ann Zahl, London. Birthsign: Leo. **Favourite Place:** 'Sydney, Australia—it's become a second home to me.'

LACEY, Ronald

Actor/teacher/director, b. 28 Sept 1935 Harrow, Middx. Went to London Academy of Music and Drama after National Service. Theatre incl: *St Joan*. Films incl: *The Likely Lads*; *Charleston*; *Nijinsky*; *Betrayal*; *Raiders Of The Lost Ark*; *Firefox*; *Zulu Dawn*; *Sword Of The Valiant*; *Sahara*; *Red Sonja*; *Flesh And Blood*; *Buckeroo Banzai*; *Making The Grade*; *Invitation To The Wedding*. TV incl: *Tiny Revolutions*; *Aubrey Beardsley*; *Day Of The Janitor*; *Lady Killers*; *Rothko*; *Hart To Hart*; *Magnum PI*; *Masquerade*; *Scarecrow And Mrs King*. m. (1st) Mela (dis.), (2nd) Joann; 1 d. Rebecca, 2 s. David (both from 1st m.), Matthew (from 2nd m.). Hobby: photography. Address: c/o Joyce Edwards, London. Birthsign: Libra. **Favourite Place:** 'Pontypool, South Wales. A vibrant town with tough, genuine, kind, humorous people.'

LAINE, Cleo, OBE
Singer/actress, b. 28 Oct 1927 Southall. Started as hairdresser's apprentice then variety of jobs before introduced to John Dankworth after singing at Southhall British Legion Hall 1951. Signed up to sing with Dankworth band. Has appeared solo in cabaret, festivals and sung with London Philharmonic, Royal Philharmonic, Halle, Scottish National orchestras. Theatre incl: *Flesh To A Tiger*; *Under The Sun*; *The Trojan Women*; own one-woman show; *Showboat*; *Colette*. TV incl: *Cleo And John*; *Parkinson*. She and John awarded Honorary Music Degrees from Berkeley College of Music, Boston. m. (1st) George (dis.), (2nd) John Dankworth; 1 d. Jacqueline (from 1st m.), 2 s. Stuart (from 1st m.), Alex (from 2nd m.). Hobby: cooking. Address: c/o International Artistes, London. Birthsign: Scorpio.

LAMAS, Lorenzo
Actor, b. 20 Jan Los Angeles. The son of Arlene Dahl and the late Fernando Lamas, he trained with the Film Actors' Workshop. Best known for his role as Lance in the TV soap opera *Falcon Crest*. Films incl: *Body Rock*; *Grease*; *Tilt*; *Take Down*. Other TV incl: *California Fever*; *Secrets Of Midland Heights*. m. (1st) Victoria Hilbert (dis.), (2nd) Michele Smith; 1 s. Alvaro Joshua (from 2nd m.). Hobbies: surfing, karate, guitar, skiing, riding motorcycles. Address: c/o PMK Public Relations, 8642 Melrose Ave, Los Angeles, California 90069. Birthsign: Capricorn. **Favourite Place:** 'Catalina is my favourite get-away place.'

LANDEN, Dinsdale
Actor, b. 4 Sept 1932 Margate, Kent. At Florence Moore Drama School before National Service in RAF. Joined Worthing rep. Theatre incl: *Play On Love*; *The Philanthropist*; *Alphabetical Order*; *Plunder*; *The Merchant Of Venice*; *Bodies*; *On The Razzle*; *Uncle Vanya*; *Sufficient Carbohydrate*; *Loot*. Films incl: *The Valiant*; *We Joined The Navy*; *Mosquito Squadron*; *Every Home Should Have One*; *Morons From Outer Space*. Radio incl: *The Joke About Hilary Spite*. TV incl: *Devenish*; *Glittering Prizes*; *Pig In The Middle*; *Events In A Museum*; *Freud*; *This Office Life*; *Radio Pictures*; *Absent Friends*. m. actress Jennifer Daniel. Hobbies: golf, walking. Address: c/o Leading Artists, London. Birthsign: Virgo. **Favourite Place:** 'Oxwick, a tiny spot in Norfolk. This is where we live when not acting and gaze fondly at my collection of quacking ducks.'

LANDOR, Rosalyn
Actress, b. Oct 1958 Hampstead, London. Theatre incl: *Arms And The Man*; *Hay Fever*. Films incl: *The Devil Rides Out*; *Jane Eyre*; *The Amazing Mr Blunden*; *Divorce His/Divorce Hers*. TV films incl: *Hammer House Of Horror—Guardian Of The Abyss*; *Little Gloria, Happy At Last*; *Merlin And The Sword*. TV incl: *E Nesbit*; *The Need For Nightmares*; *Edgar Allen Poe*; *Z Cars*; *Dad*; *Little Girls Don't*; *Love In A Cold Climate*; *Rumpole Of The Bailey*; *Sherlock Holmes: The Speckled Band*; *CATS Eyes*. Hobbies: music, reading, shopping, travelling. Address: c/o William Morris Agency, London. Birthsign: Libra. **Favourite Place:** 'Phoenix, Arizona, USA. Wonderful landscapes, sunshine, humming birds, mega-size butterflies and the *best* cowboy boots!!'

LANEUVILLE, Eric G
Actor, b. 14 July New Orleans. Trained with the UCLA Theatre Group. Films incl: *A Piece Of The Action*; *A Force Of One*; *Backroads*; *Love At First Bite*. TV film: *Scared Straight*. Best known on TV for his role as orderly Luther Hawkins in *St Elsewhere*. Other TV incl: *Room 222*; *Hill Street Blues*. Has also directed five episodes of *St Elsewhere*. Hobbies: basketball, cars, all sport. Address: c/o Twentieth Century Artists,

3518 Cahuenga Blvd, Los Angeles, California 90068. Birthsign: Cancer. **Favourite Place:** 'Hawaii, Las Vegas and Dallas.'

LANG, Robert
Actor/theatre director, b. 24 Sept 1934 Bristol. Trained at Bristol Old Vic Theatre School then Bristol Old Vic Company, Nottingham rep, Chichester Festival. After RAF, National Theatre at Old Vic, London. Theatre incl: *Uncle Vanya*; *Dial M For Murder*; *Donkey's Years*; *The Medusa Touch*; *Rumpole And The Fascist Beast*. TV incl: *Emergency Ward 10*; *That Was The Week That Was*; *Not So*

Much A Programme, More A Way Of Life; *For Maddy With Love*; *1990*; *The Brack Report*; *King Lear*; *Antigone*; *The Father*; *Edward Lear*; *On The Edge Of The Sand*. m. actress Ann Bell; 1 d. Rebecca, 1 s. John. Hobbies: photography, gardening, pisciculture. Address: c/o Leading Artists, London. Birthsign: Libra. **Favourite Place:** 'Beside the Serpentine, where all the world comes to walk and time seems to go backwards.'

LANGFORD, Bonnie
Dancer/singer/actress, b. 22 July 1964 Hampton Court. Trained at Arts Educational and Italia Conti stage schools. At seven, played Bonnie Butler in West End musical *Gone With The Wind*, then Baby June in *Gypsy*. Other theatre incl: *Pirates Of Penzance*; *CATS*; *Cinderella*. Guest appearance in film *Bugsy Malone*. First TV on *Opportunity Knocks* then *Junior Show Time*. Other TV incl: *Just William*; *The Grace*

Kennedy Show; *The Video Entertainers*; *Live From Her Majesty's*; *On Safari*; *Sooty*; *The Adventure Game*; *The Main Attraction*; *Madabout*; *Saturday Royal*; *Royal Variety Show*; *Super Troupers*; *The Hot Shoe Show*; co-presenter *Saturday Starship*. Address: c/o Barry Burnett, London. Birthsign: Cancer. **Favourite Place:** 'London, New York and Los Angeles—centres of entertainment—full of life, vitality and fun.'

LARGE, Eddie
Impressionist/comedian, b. 25 June 1942 Glasgow. First ambition was to be a footballer before accident ended that career. Met Syd Little in a Manchester pub and teamed up as singing duo. Turned to comedy in northern clubs before winning *Opportunity Knocks* 1971. TV incl: *Who Do You Do?*; *Seaside Special*; *Wheeltappers And Shunters Social Club*; *Wednesday At Eight*; *Little And Large*

Tellyshow; *Little And Large Show*; *Disneytime*. Also wide experience cabaret, London Palladium, pantomimes and summer seasons. m. Patsy Ann; 2 d. Alison, Samantha, 1 s. Ryan. Hobbies: golf, keep-fit, supporting Manchester City FC. Address: c/o Peter Prichard, London. Birthsign: Cancer. **Favourite Place:** 'Watching Manchester playing at Maine Road from the trainer's bench.'

LATHAM, Bernard

Actor, b. 21 April 1951 Manchester. Trained at Bristol Old Vic Theatre School. Appeared on stage in Manchester, Stoke-on-Trent, Clwyd, Sheffield. Film: *The Lovers*. Acted in about 30 radio plays. TV incl: *Sally Ann*; *The Danedyke Mystery*; *Carrott Del Sol*; *Coronation Street*; *Crown Court*; *Great Expectations*; *Hard Times*; *Fox*; plays Kev Eccles in *The Practice*. 1 d. Emily Jane. Hobby: work. Address: c/o Michelle Braidman Assocs, London. Birthsign: Taurus. **Favourite Place:** 'Chagford, Devon—surrounded by Devonshire hills, this beautiful village speaks for itself.'

LATHAM, Philip

Actor, b. 17 Jan Leigh-on-Sea, Essex. After National Service, trained at RADA and in rep at Farnham. Most recent stage work incl tours of *The Letter*; *The Winslow Boy*. Films incl: *Spy Story*; *Force Ten From Navarone*; *Man From A Far Country*. TV incl: *Mogul*; *The Troubleshooters*; *Maigret*; *Whose Life Is It Anyway?*; *No Exit*; *Time-Lock*; *Good At Games*; *The Pallisers*; *The Cedar Tree*; *The Professionals*; *The Killers*; *Hammer House Of Horror*; *Name For The Day*; *Nanny*; *No 10* (Wellington), *The Fourth Arm*. He is also in demand for his religious readings. m. Eve; 1 d. Amanda, 1 s. Andrew. Hobby: golf. Address: c/o Bryan Drew, London. Birthsign: Capricorn. **Favourite Place:** 'Anywhere in England!'

LAWLEY, Sue

Broadcaster/journalist, b. 14 July 1946 Dudley, Worcs. After graduating from Bristol University, trained as a newspaper journalist 1967–70; joined BBC Plymouth as reporter/sub-editor/presenter 1970–72; presenter *Nationwide* (1972–75), *Tonight* (1975–76), *Nationwide* (1977–82). Newsreader *The Nine O'Clock News* (1983–84) and now for *The Six O'Clock News*—all BBC TV. Also presented Election and Budget specials. 1 s. Tom, 1 d. Harriet. Hobbies: cooking, walking, family. Address: c/o BBC TV, London. Birthsign: Cancer. **Favourite Place:** 'On top of Worcestershire Beacon in the Malvern Hills—fresh air, fantastic views and freedom.'

LAWRENCE, Patricia

Actress, b. 19 Nov Andover, Hants. Trained at RADA (she won the Bancroft Gold Medal); many parts in rep. West End theatre incl: *Funny Sunday/ Sometime Never*; *West Of Suez*; *Five Finger Exercise*; *Dead Ringer*. Films incl: *Tom Jones*; *The Hireling*. TV incl: *Our Mutual Friend*; *Love Story*; *Telford's Change*; *To Serve Them All My Days*; *Seven Faces Of Woman*; *Barriers*; *Brimstone And Treacle*; *Tenko*; *The Gentle Touch*. m. Greville Poke (vice-chairman English Stage Co, chairman LAMDA and Thorndike Theatre); 2 s. Christopher, James. Hobbies: pen and ink drawing, needlepoint. Address: c/o David White Assocs, London. Birthsign: Scorpio. **Favourite Place:** 'A hamlet in South West France— contemplation of that land and seascape restores my sense of proportion.'

LAWRENCE, Stephanie
Actress, b. 16 Dec 1955 Hayling Island. Trained at the Arts Educational School and made first London stage appearance aged 12 in the *Nutcracker*. West End debut in *Forget Me Not Lane*. Other West End incl: *Bubbling Brown Sugar*; the lead in *Evita*; *The Royal Variety Show* (also TV); as Marilyn Monroe in *Marilyn The Musical*. Variety Club Best Stage Actress of the Year. Latest West End musical: Pearl in *Starlight Express*.TV incl: *Night Music*; *Here And Now*; *Rod Argent Showcase*; *The David Frost End Of Year Show*; *The Two Ronnies*; her one-woman show *6.55*. Records incl: *You Saved My Life* (with Johnny Mathis); *Starlight Express*; *Only Me*. Hobbies: gardening, clothes shopping in Italy, waterskiing, music, riding. Address: c/o Susan James, London. Birthsign: Sagittarius. **Favourite Place:** 'My home, because I can put my feet up!'

LAWSON, Leigh
Actor, b. 21 July 1943 Atherstone, Warwicks. Trained at Mountview Theatre School and RADA. Worked extensively in rep and has appeared on stage in plays incl: *The Price Of Justice*; *A Touch Of Spring*; *The Cherry Orchard*; *The Second Mrs Tanqueray*; *From The Balcony*. Many films, the most recent incl: *Tess*; *The Sword Of The Valiant*. Most recent TV appearances incl: *Journey Into The Shadows*; *Black Carrian*; *Travelling Man*; *Lace*. Address: c/o ICM, London. Birthsign: Cancer.

LEACH, Rosemary
Actress, b. 18 Dec 1935 Shropshire. Trained at RADA and then rep. Recent theatre incl: *84, Charing Cross Road* (SWET Best Actress Award 1982); *Six For Gold* (musical). Films incl: *That'll Be The Day*; *SOS Titanic*; *The Bride*; *Turtle Summer*. Entered TV 1960 in *Z Cars*. Numerous TV appearances incl: three series with Ronnie Corbett, *No That's Me Over Here*; *Sadie It's Cold Outside* (own series); *Life Begins At Forty*; *Cider With Rosie*; *Birthday*; *Tiptoe Through The Tulips*; *The Velvet Glove*; *All's Well That Ends Well*; *Jackanory*; *Just Between Ourselves*; *The Jewel In The Crown*; *Displaced Persons*. m. Colin Starkey. Hobbies: cooking, gardening. Address: c/o William Morris, London. Birthsign: Sagittarius. **Favourite Place:** 'Richmond Park. I walk with my dog in the park and like to watch her swim.'

LEADER, Carol
Actress, b. 10 Nov Colchester, Essex. Studied drama at college and was a founder member of the Perspectives Theatre Co. Moved to do rep and TV work. London theatre incl: *Topokana Martyrs Day*; *Bazaar And Rummage*;*To Come Home To This*; *Whale Music*. TV incl: *Chocablock*; *Play School*; *Play Away*; *Flambards*; *Sally Ann*; *Honky Tonk Heroes*; *Young At Heart*; *Out Of Step*; *Getting On*; *Studio*; *Late Starter*. Hobbies: visiting standing stones, reading. Address: c/o Lou Coulson, London. Birthsign: Scorpio. **Favourite Place:** 'At the top of Glastonbury "Tor"—it has such a wonderful feel in the air up there—try it and see!'

LEE, Christopher
Actor/singer/author, b. 27 May 1922 London. Many appearances worldwide in theatre, radio and TV and in 162 feature films. His films incl: *The Private Life Of Sherlock Holmes*; *The Wicker Man*; *The Man With The Golden Gun*; *The Three Musketeers*; *The Four Musketeers*; *Airport '77*; *1941*. m. Gitte Kroencke; 1 d. Christina. Hobbies: golf, opera, travel. Address: c/o Duncan Heath, London. Birthsign: Gemini. **Favourite Place:** 'Finland and Holland. Unspoiled natural beauty, unchanged for centuries and very few people to ruin it.'

LEE, Maurice
Actor, b. 12 May 1946 Leeds. Probably best known as one of the Grumbleweeds. BBC Radio series: *The Grumbleweeds Radio Show*. Granada TV series: *The Grumbleweeds Radio Show*. m. Gillian; 2 s. James, Ben. Hobbies: painting, running, shooting. Address: c/o Times Artists, Oldham, Lancashire. Birthsign: Taurus. **Favourite Place:** 'St Lucia—it's warm, quiet, beautiful, tranquil and friendly. I think it's probably the prettiest of all the Caribbean islands.'

LEE, Rustie
Entertainer/singer, b. 22 May 1952 Portland, Jamaica. Was Head of Catering at Padgate Teachers' Training College. Entered show business as singer/entertainer in northern clubs. In 1980, with her husband, opened a Caribbean restaurant in Birmingham, where she entertains with cooking, singing and talent to amuse. TV debut on BBC's *Pebble Mill At One* and then became TV-am's cook. Other TV incl: co-presenter of *Game For A Laugh*; *Punchlines*; *Give Us A Clue*; *All Star Secrets*. Sang in LWT's *Night Of A Hundred Stars*. Book: *Rustie Lee's Caribbean Cookbook*. m. David Lees; 1 s. James Robert. Hobbies: cooking, badminton. Address: c/o International Management Group, London. Birthsign: Gemini. **Favourite Place:** 'My cottage in Bewdley, where peace and chaos live in harmony.'

LEEMING, Jan
TV newsreader/presenter, b. 5 Jan 1942 Kent. Fifteen years' experience in theatre, radio and TV in New Zealand and Australia before spending six years with HTV on news and women's programmes, then two years with Pebble Mill and a year with BBC Radio 2. BBC TV newsreader since 1980. Radio and TV Industries Club Newsreader of the Year Award 1981 and '82. Also PYE TV Personality of the Year 1982. 1 s. Jonathan. Hobbies: 'No time.' Address: c/o BBC TV, London. Birthsign: Capricorn. **Favourite Place:** 'A village in France, but I'm not saying where or everyone would want to go there!'

LEES, Michael
Actor, b. 5 Sept 1927 Bury, Lancs. Trained at RADA. Film: *Cuba*. TV incl: *People Like Us*; *Coronation Street*; *Emmerdale Farm*; *Pride And Prejudice*; *Stay With Me Till Morning*; *Ferry Ride Away*; *Spoils Of War*; *Nanny*; *A Fine Romance*; *Tenko*; *Mapp & Lucia*. Hobbies: trees, wine, Wagner. Address: c/o Roger Storey, London. Birthsign: Virgo. **Favourite Place:** 'The Round Pond, Kensington Gardens, for its variety of people, dogs and wonderful lighting effects.'

LENSKA, Rula
Actress, b. 30 Sept 1947 St Neots, Herts. Trained at Webber Douglas Academy of Dramatic Art. Theatre incl: *Suddenly At Home*; *Flare Path*; *Forget Me Not Lane*; *A Midsummer Night's Dream*; *Secretary Bird*; *Candle In The Wind*; *Abel—Where Is Your Brother?*; *Aladdin*; *Mr Fothergill's Murder*; toured Australia and New Zealand in *Same Time Next Year*. Films incl: *Soft Beds, Hard Battles*; *Alfie Darling*; *Royal Flash*. Well known for *Rock Follies* on TV. Other TV incl: *Special Branch*; *The Saint*; *Private Schultz*; *Minder*; *Watching Me, Watching You*; *Aubrey Beardsley*; *To The Manor Born*; *Take A Letter Mr Jones*; *Seven Dials Mystery*; *Conversations With A Stranger*; *Robin Of Sherwood*. m. (dis.); 1 d. Lara. Address: c/o Vernon Conway, London. Birthsign: Libra. **Favourite Place:** 'Our snooker room at home.'

LESTER, Anne
TV journalist/presenter, b. 25 July 1954 Wirral, Cheshire. Began career with Wirral newspapers, first as a reporter then as deputy editor. Moved to KOMU-TV in Missouri, US as reporter and presenter on news and current affairs programmes, also as news programme producer. Joined Granada TV as regional news reporter. Has worked as presenter for *Granada Reports*; as film reporter/presenter *Union World* (C4). Hobbies: theatre, music, reading, riding. Address: c/o Granada TV, Manchester. Birthsign: Leo.

LEUCHARS, Anne
Journalist, b. 2 Aug 1953 Kampala, Uganda. Trained on regional newspapers and regional TV news magazine programmes. Now a reporter with ITN. Hobbies: newspaper and magazine addict, theatre, gardening. Address: c/o ITN, London. Birthsign: Leo. **Favourite Place:** 'The Great Outdoors.'

LE VELL, Michael
Actor, b. 15 Dec 1964
Manchester. Theatre incl: *Kes*;
Joby; *No More Sitting On The Old School Bench*; *Dick Whittington*; *Jack And The Beanstalk*. TV incl: *My Son, My Son*; *Fame Is The Spur*; *The Last Song*; *The Hard Word*; *A Brother's Tale*; *One By One*; *Coronation Street*. Hobbies: football, pool, snooker, golf. Address: c/o Granada TV, Manchester. Birthsign: Sagittarius. **Favourite Place:** 'Australia, because it is so clean, good weather, very friendly people and lots of nice scenery.'

LEWIS, Martyn
Newscaster/reporter, b. 7 April 1945 Swansea. Started as freelance journalist. Later joined HTV and provided daily local news reports, documentaries and presented weekly *Welsh Scene*. Joined ITN 1970; became their first northern correspondent. Seven years later returned to London as senior correspondent and relief newscaster. Since 1981 *News At Ten* newscaster. Has reported for ITN from more than 30 countries. Member of first Western TV crew to enter Afghanistan after Soviet invasion. Author of *And Finally*. m. Liz; 2 d. Sylvie, Katie. Hobbies: photography, tennis, good food. Address: c/o ITN, London. Birthsign: Aries. **Favourite Place:** 'The Walnut Tree Inn, Llandewi Skirrid, Wales. Not only does it produce the finest *food* in the world, it is the only *place* where I can switch off and relax.'

LEWIS, Rhoda
Actress, b. 25 June 1933 Moseley, Birmingham. Trained at Birmingham School of Speech and Drama and then in rep at Bristol Old Vic, Nottingham, Birmingham, Edinburgh, Belgrade, Coventry, Old Vic, London. Films incl: *Under Milk Wood*; *The Accused*. Numerous TV plays incl: *Milton—Paradise Regained*; *Love Song*; *Rhino*. Many TV series incl: *Coronation Street*; *Lorna Doone*; *Doomwatch*; *Beryl's Lot*; *Sadie It's Cold Outside*; *The Nearly Man*; *Langley Bottom*. m. Norman Florence; 1 s. Peter. Hobbies: Open University, gardening, bread making, collecting recipes and records. Address: c/o St James Management, London. Birthsign: Cancer. **Favourite Place:** 'Sitting in the country with my back against a warm, sun-baked wall, listening to the peace.'

LILLICRAP, Christopher
Actor/writer/musician, b. 14 Feb 1949 Plymouth. Extensive rep incl: Nottingham, Canterbury, Cheltenham and Theatre in Education. A self-taught musician, he and his wife have a cabaret act. TV incl: *Playboard*; *Rose Of Puddle Fratrum*; *The Bands Played On*; *Canned Laughter*; two plays on Keats; *Love Story*; *Follow The Star*; *King Robert Of Sicily*; *Rainbow*. Presenter of *Playboard*; *We'll Tell You A Story*; *Flicks*; *Knock Knock*. Writer and performer of one-man children's BBC TV series *Busker*. Also author, with his wife, of several children's plays, notably *Christmas Cat And The Pudding Pirates*. m. actress Jeanette Ranger. Hobbies: golf, gardening. Address: c/o Aza Artistes, London. Birthsign: Aquarius. **Favourite Place:** 'Prawle Point, Devon.'

LINDEN, Jennie

Actress, b. 8 Dec 1940 Worthing, Sussex. Trained at Central School of Speech and Drama. Theatre incl: *On Approval*; *Hedda Gabler*; own one-woman shows *Sounds Entertaining* and *Twice Brightly*. Films incl: *Doctor Who And The Daleks*; *A Severed Head*; *Women In Love* (nominated for Academy Award for Best Newcomer). TV incl: *Lady Windermere's Fan*; *The Persuaders*; *Sister Mary*; *Little Lord Fauntleroy*; *Lillie*; *Charlie Muffins*; *Dick Turpin*; *Breadwinner*; *Degree Of Uncertainty*. m. antiques dealer Christopher Mann; 1 s. Rupert. Hobbies: music, gardening, antiques, reading, philosophy, UFO research, spiritualism. Address: c/o Roger Carey, London. Birthsign: Sagittarius. **Favourite Place:** 'In my garden after a day's work in a city, on a summer's day that's truly peaceful.'

LIPMAN, Maureen

Actress, b. 10 May 1946 Hull. Trained at London Academy of Music and Dramatic Art. Much stage experience incl: London's Royal Court Theatre; Old Vic; *Candida*; *The Ball Game*; Royal Shakespeare Company; founder member of Theatre of Comedy. Laurence Olivier Award 1984; Variety Club Award 1984. Films incl: *Up The Junction*; *Gumshoe*; *Educating Rita*; *Water*. Radio incl: *Delivery*; *Just A Minute*. TV incl: *Agony*; *Couples*; *The Lovers*; *The Evacuees*; *File It Under Fear*; *The Knowledge*; *Rogue Male*; *Absurd Person Singular*; *Absent Friends*; *Love's Labours Lost*; *On Your Way Riley*; *Smiley's People*. m. playwright Jack Rosenthal; 1 d. Amy, 1 s. Adam. Hobbies: writing, drawing. Address: c/o Saraband Assocs, London. Birthsign: Taurus. **Favourite Place:** 'Glasgow, because I spent six days there recently and fell in love with it all.'

LISTON, Ian

Actor/producer, b. 4 Aug 1948 Crosby, Liverpool. Has written for radio, produces and directs in the theatre and runs own production company, Hiss & Boo Productions, which tours plays and musicals. Films incl: *White Nights*; *Scum*; *A Bridge Too Far*; *Overlord*; *The Empire Strikes Back*. Many hundreds of TV appearances incl: *Brookside*; *Doctor Who*; *Secret Army*; *Juliet Bravo*; *The Professionals*; *Nelson*; *Warship*; *Coronation Street*; *Crossroads*. Hobbies: cricket, cooking and eating, golf, brass bands, music hall. Address: c/o Hiss & Boo Ltd, Walton-on-Thames. Birthsign: Leo. **Favourite Place:** 'Home—you enjoy it all the more when you spend a lot of time living out of a suitcase. Any island, particularly Guernsey. Islands always seem to be such relaxing places.'

LITTLE, Syd

Comedian, b. 19 Dec 1942 Blackpool. Solo guitarist and singer in Manchester pubs before teaming up with Eddie Large as singing duo. Turned to comedy in northern clubs before winning *Opportunity Knocks* 1971. TV incl: *Who Do You Do?*; *Seaside Special*; *Wheeltappers And Shunters Social Club*; *Wednesday At Eight*; *Little And Large Tellyshow*; *Little And Large Show*; *Disneytime*. Also wide experience cabaret, London Palladium, pantomimes and summer seasons. m. Sheree; 1 d. Donna, 1 s. Paul. Hobbies: making model boats, keep-fit. Address: c/o Peter Prichard, London. Birthsign: Sagittarius. **Favourite Place:** 'Gazing down on HMS Victory at Portsmouth and imagining I'm Lord Nelson.'

LLEWELYN-WILLIAMS, Peter

Actor, b. 21 March 1964 London. Trained for the stage as a member of the National Youth Theatre. Theatre incl: *Rosencrantz And Guildenstern Are Dead*; *No More Sitting On The Old School Bench*; *The Hired Man*. Film: *High Road To China*. TV incl: *To Serve Them All My Days*; *Robin Of Sherwood*. Hobbies: music, sailing, cars. Address: c/o JLM Management, London. Birthsign: Aries. **Favourite Place:** 'At home, on the settee, watching telly and roasting by the fire!'

LLOYD, Hugh

Comedy actor, b. 22 April 1923 Chester. Started as a journalist on the *Chester Chronicle*, then joined ENSA travelling worldwide entertaining the troops. Trained in variety, pantomime and summer seasons. Many West End appearances incl: *When We Are Married*; *Tonight At 8.30*; *No Sex Please, We're British*. TV incl: *Hancock's Half Hour*; *Hugh And I*; *Lollipop Loves Mr Mole*. TV drama incl: *A Visit From Miss Prothero*; *Say Something Happened*; *Who's Afraid Of Virginia Woolf—I Am* m Shân Elisabeth. Hobbies: snooker, bowls, soccer ('watching'), talking politics. Address: c/o Richard Stone, London. Birthsign: Taurus. **Favourite Place:** 'Chester and North Wales, as it is my native background.'

LLOYD, Kevin

Actor, b. 28 March 1949 Derby. Trained at East 15 Acting School, London. Stage debut in *The Importance Of Being Earnest* 1973. London debut *What The Butler Saw*. Appeared at Royal Court Theatre, London and member of Royal Shakespeare Company, also rep and Bristol Old Vic. Theatre incl: *Love Girl And The Innocent*; *Stiff Options*. Films incl: *Britannia Hospital*; *Trial By Combat*. TV incl: *Misfit*; *Coronation Street*; *Minder*; *Talent*; *Sounding Brass*; *Z Cars*; *Hazell*; *Midnite At The Starlite*; *Bergerac*; *By The Sword Divided*; *The Borgias*; *Foxy Lady*; *Young at Heart*; *Starting Out*; *The Last Company Car*. m. Lesley; 3 s. Mark, James, Henry, 2 d. Sophie, Poppy. Hobbies: football, cricket, tennis. Address: c/o Saraband Assocs, London. Birthsign: Aries. **Favourite Place:** 'St Ives, Cornwall. A lovely place to be on a hot summer day!'

LLOYD, Norman

Actor/director/producer, b. 8 Nov Jersey City, New Jersey. Trained with Eva Le Gallienne's Civic Repertory Theater and with the Mercury Theater. Appeared in *Noah* on Broadway. Films incl: *The Southerner*; *A Walk In The Sun*; *Scene Of Crime*; *The Light Touch*; *Limelight*; *FM*; *Audrey Rose*; *Saboteur*; *Spellbound*. TV film: *Harvest Home*. TV incl: *Alfred Hitchcock Presents* (producer, director, actor for eight years). Plays Dr Auschlander in TV's *St Elsewhere*. As producer, TV films incl: *The Bravos*; *What's A Nice Girl Like You?*; *Companions In Nightmare*; *Steambath* (also director). m. Peggy; 1 d. Suzanna, 1 s. Michael. Hobbies: tennis, reading (especially biographies). Address: c/o ICM, 8899 Beverly Blvd, Los Angeles, California 90048. Birthsign: Scorpio. **Favourite Place:** 'Home!'

LLOYD, Terry
TV reporter, b. 21 Nov 1952
Derby. Trained as a journalist
with Raymonds News Agency,
Derby. Reporter with ATV and
now ITN. Has reported for ITN
on Beirut, Libya, the Los Angeles
Olympics, Belfast and the miners'
strike. m. Lynn; 1 d. Chelsey.
Hobbies: 'No spare time.'
Address: c/o ITN, London.
Birthsign: Scorpio. **Favourite
Place:** 'Derbyshire: home sweet
home.'

LLOYD PACK, Roger
Actor, b. 8 Feb 1944 London.
Trained at RADA. Appeared in
rep and numerous stage
productions incl: *The Prime Of
Miss Jean Brodie*; *The Caretaker*;
Moving; *Caritas* (National
Theatre); *Noises Off* (West End);
Wild Honey (National Theatre);
directed own play *The End*. Films
incl: *The Virgin Soldiers*; *The Go-
Between*; *Hamlet*; *Bloody Kids*;
1984. TV incl: *Only Fools And
Horses*; *Making Good*; *Bouncing
Back*; *I Thought You'd Gone*;
Video Stars; *Miracles Take Longer*;
The Brief; *Moving*; *In A Secret
State*. m. Jehane Markham; 1 d.
Emily, 2 s. Spencer, Hartley.
Hobbies: reading, tennis, chess.
Address: c/o Kate Feast
Management, London. Birthsign:
Aquarius. **Favourite Place:** 'My
garden in Norfolk, where I am
king.'

LOCKE, Philip
Actor, b. 29 March 1928
London. Trained at RADA. Has
appeared in numerous
productions at London's Royal
Court Theatre, with the Royal
Shakespeare Company (incl
Richard III; *The Tempest*; *Julius
Caesar*; *Antony And Cleopatra*), in
Amadeus at the National Theatre.
First American appearance in the
Old Vic production of *A
Midsummer Night's Dream*. Films
incl: *Escape To Athena*; *Ivanhoe*;
And The Ship Sails On. TV incl:
Doctor Who; *Disappearance Of
Harry*; *Mill On The Floss*; *Dick
Turpin*; *Omega Factor*; *Oliver
Twist*; *Codename Icarus*; *Box Of
Delights*; *Trelawny Of The Wells*;
Connie. Hobby: painting.
Address: c/o Jeremy Conway,
London. Birthsign: Aries.
Favourite Place: 'My bed late
at night with a book.'

LOCKLEAR, Heather
Actress, b. 25 Sept 1961 Los
Angeles, California. Educated
UCLA. TV incl: *T J Hooker*;
Dynasty. Hobbies: sport,
needlepoint, reading. Address: c/o
ABC TV, 4151 Prospect Ave,
Los Angeles, California 90027.
Birthsign: Libra. **Favourite
Place:** 'My bedroom: I eat, sleep,
read, watch television,
needlepoint and play with my
dogs in that room—it's my
special place.'

LODGE, David
Actor, b. 19 Aug Rochester, Kent. Began career in *Gang Shows*, variety and concert party. Has appeared in over 120 films from *Cockleshell Heroes* to *The Pink Panther*. Many TV series and appearances incl: *Lovely Couple*; *Spike Milligan's Q8*; *Murder At*

The Wedding. Made a Freemason of the City of London 1982 for his charity work. m. Lyn. Hobbies: Grand Order of Water Rats, the Variety Club of Great Britain, organising charity events. Address: c/o Joan Gray Personal Management, Sunbury-on-Thames. Birthsign: Leo.
Favourite Place:
'Accompanying my French wife, who is a fashion agent, to Paris and sitting eating, watching the world go by.'

LOE, Judy
Actress, b. 6 March 1947 Manchester. Worked in rep at Chester and Crewe after university. Theatre incl: *Hair*; *A Game Called Arthur*; *No Sex Please, We're British*; *Middle-Age Spread*; *Illuminations*; *Class K*. Most recent TV: *Missing From*

Home; *Travelling Man*; *Letter Writing*. Other TV incl: *Ace Of Wands*; *General Hospital*; *Edward The Seventh*; *Woodstock*; *Man Of Straw*; *Z Cars*; *The Upchat Line*; *Couples*; *Ripping Yarns*; *Heartland*; *Visitors For Anderson*; *When The Boat Comes In*; *The Gentle Touch*; *Life After Death*; *Let There Be Love*. m. actor Richard Beckinsale (dec.); 1 d. Kate. Address: c/o Fraser & Dunlop, London. Birthsign: Pisces.

LONG, Shelly
Actress, b. 23 August Fort Wayne, Indiana. Trained with Chicago Second City Improvisational Troupe, summer stock theatre. Films incl: *Losin' It*; *Night Shift*; *Caveman*; *A Small Circle Of Friends*; *Irreconcilable Differences*. Best known on TV for *Cheers*, but also writer/associate producer and co-host of magazine show *Sorting It Out*.

TV films incl: *The Cracker Factory*; *A Promise Of Love*; *The Princess And The Cabbie* TV guest roles incl: *MASH*; *Family*; *Love Boat*. m. (2nd) stockbroker Bruce Tyson. Hobbies: writing, music, walking, collecting stuffed animals, cooking Italian food, travelling. Address: c/o William Morris Agency, 151 El Camino Drive, Beverly Hills, California 90212. Birthsign: Virgo.
Favourite Place: 'Anywhere I can take a nice long quiet walk.'

LONNEN, Ray
Actor, b. 18 May 1940 Bournemouth. Started as assistant stage manager in Belfast then rep at York, Worthing, Farnham, Bromley and Coventry. Also a stage tour of New Zealand. Guy Masterson in *Guys And Dolls* in Edinburgh. Films incl: *Zepplin*; *Lady Caroline Lamb*. TV debut 1965 in *Emergency Ward 10*, parts

followed in *The Power Game*; *Honey Lane*; *The Troubleshooters*; *Pathfinders*; *General Hospital*; *Z Cars*; *Hammer House Of Horror*; *The Gentle Touch*; *Sandbaggers*; *Glamour Girls*; *Harry's Game*; *Tales Of The Unexpected*. 1 d. Amy, 1 s. Thomas. Hobbies: cinema, music, tennis. Address: c/o CCA, London. Birthsign: Taurus. **Favourite Place:** 'The Grand Canyon, but I'd need many more than a few words to explain why.'

LOTT, Barbara
Actress, b. 15 May 1920 Richmond, Surrey. Trained at RADA and made first London appearance in *Love For Love*. Then Arts Theatre seasons and toured in *Major Barbara*; *Man And Superman*; *Richard III*. Many TV appearances incl: *Nightingale's Boys*; *Six Days Of Justice*; *Ballet Shoes*; *The Survivors*; *Sexton Blake*; *Kids*; *Rings On Their Fingers*; *Sorry!*; *Honeymoon*. m. Stuart Latham. Hobbies: walking, gardening, tapestry, music. Address: c/o Marmont Management, London. Birthsign: Taurus.

LOVE, Geoff
Bandleader/composer/arranger, b. 4 Sept Todmorden, Yorks. Was a motor mechanic but interested in music since aged 11 when he joined a local amateur orchestra. Professional at 17 when he joined a stage band with which he tap-danced and sang. After the war joined Harry Gold and his Pieces of Eight. Numerous gold and silver discs for his records, also platinum for *Western Movie Themes*. Also records as Manuel and his Music of the Mountains. Frequent radio and TV appearances but well known for his work with Max Bygraves on TV. m. Joy; 2 s. radio broadcaster Adrian, computer lecturer Nigel. Hobbies: water-skiing, power boats, windsurfing. Address: c/o Noel Gay, London. Birthsign: Virgo. **Favourite Place:** 'Prickly Bay, Grenada. The most beautiful and relaxing spot in the world.'

LOWE, John
Dart player, b. 21 July 1945 Chesterfield, Derbyshire. England dart captain and winner of over 1000 titles. The only player to date to win the World Professional, World Match Play, *News Of The World*, World Cup Singles and World Masters titles. The first American Champion of Champions. The winner of every major world title, some as many as seven times. The holder of a record eight World Cup Gold Medals. Only player to record a nine dart finish, the perfect game with scores of 180, 180, 141. m. Diana; 1 s. Adrian, 1 d. Karen. Hobbies: motor sport, gardening, golf. Address: c/o 4 Castle Blvd, Nottingham. Birthsign: Leo. **Favourite Place:** 'Home. When one travels 100,000 miles per year there can be no better place.'

LUCAS, William
Actor, b. 14 April 1925 Manchester. Trained at Bradford Theatre School after Royal Navy during the war. Rep incl: Liverpool. London theatre incl: *Amber For Anna*; *Ring Of Jackals*; *Dual Marriageway*. Films incl: *Sons And Lovers*; *The Professionals*; *Payroll*; *Bitter Harvest*. TV incl: *Portrait Of Alison*; *The Paragon*; *The Infamous John Friend*; *Rigoletto*; *A Flea Off Pepe*; *Champion Road*; *Flower Of Evil*; *Mogul*; *Warship*; *Black Beauty*; *The Spoils Of War*; *Doctor Who*; *The Two Ronnies*. 2 s. Daniel, Thomas. Hobbies: sailing, swimming. Address: c/o Joy Jameson, London. Birthsign: Aries. **Favourite Place:** 'Aboard a sailing boat anywhere at sea.'

LUCKHAM, Cyril
Actor, b. 25 July 1907 Salisbury, Wilts. Originally wanted career in Royal Navy but invalided out 1931. Trained with Arthur Brough Players and Folkestone Dramatic School. First part in *The Admirable Crichton*, Folkestone, then rep and member of Royal Shakespeare Company. West End theatre incl: *The Family Reunion*; *Photo Finish*; *You Never Can Tell*. Films incl: *The Naked Runner*; *Providence*. Numerous TV, the most recent incl: *Donkey's Years*; *To Serve Them All My Days*; *The Potting Shed*; *Strangers And Brothers*; *The Barchester Chronicles*. m. actress Violet Lamb; 1 s. opera singer Robert. Hobbies: music, cricket, ornithology. Address: c/o Howes & Prior, London. Birthsign: Leo. **Favourite Place:** 'The county of Dorset, where the Luckhams have lived for 460 years.'

LULU
Singer/actress, b. 3 Nov 1948 Lennoxtown, Stirlingshire. Started singing in concert party when she was nine. First record, *Shout*, in 1963. Has been in numerous pop and variety shows, twice playing Peter Pan, appearing in *Royal Variety Performance* and joint winner of the *Eurovision Song Contest* (1969). Recent theatre: *Guys And Dolls* in London's West End. Films incl: *To Sir With Love*. Numerous TV appearances incl: 10 series for BBC TV; *Some You Win*. m. (1st) Maurice Gibb (dis.), (2nd) hairdresser John Frieda; 1 s. Jordan (from 2nd m.). Hobbies: buying clothes, water-skiing. Address: c/o Marion Massey, London. Birthsign: Scorpio. **Favourite Place:** her villa in Ibiza.

LUMBLY, Carl W
Actor, b. 14 Aug 1952 Montego Bay, Jamaica. First professional experience in improvisational comedy. Over 30 stage performances ranging from *Sizwe Bansi Is Dead* to *River Niger*. Film: *Caveman*. TV incl: *Taxi*; *Lou Grant*; *Cagney And Lacey*. Hobbies: writing, painting (water colours), racquetball, basketball, running—a 'fitness freak'. Address: c/o Century Artists, 9744 Wilshire Blvd, Suite 308, Beverly Hills, California 90212. Birthsign: Leo. **Favourite Place:** 'Wakefield, Jamaica. My uncle's pond behind his house because it's got a tranquil beauty that stills my thoughts and my soul.'

LUMLEY, Joanna
Actress, b. 1 May 1946 Srinagar, India. A brief period in a craft and furniture shop followed by modelling course in London. After appearing in *Queen* magazine, her career as a model took off. Subsequently concentrated on acting. Theatre incl: *Don't Just Lie There, Say Something*; *Othello*; *Me Old Cigar*; *Hedda Gabler*. Films incl: *On Her Majesty's Secret Service*; *Tam Lin*; *The Breaking Of Bumbo*; *Games Lovers Play*. TV incl: *The Mark II Wife*; *Release*; *Two Girls*; *It's Awfully Bad For Your Eyes, Darling*; *Coronation Street*; *The Protectors*; *General Hospital*; *The New Avengers*; *Steptoe And Son*; *Sapphire And Steel*; *The Glory Boys*; *Oxbridge Blues*; *Mistral's Daughter*. m. Jeremy Lloyd (dis.); 1 s. James. Hobbies: collecting junk, painting, drawing, reading. Address: c/o MLR, London. Birthsign: Taurus.

LYNAM, Desmond
Journalist/broadcaster, b. 17 Sept 1942 Ennis, Co Clare, Eire. Wide experience of local and network radio and TV. Radio incl: presenting *Sport On 2*; *Sports Report*; *Today*; quiz programmes—*Forces Chance*, *Treble Chance*; *Midweek*; music programmes. Commentator for tennis and boxing. TV incl: presenting *Grandstand*; *Sports Review Of The Year*; *Sunday Grandstand*. Commentator for boxing and football. m. (dis.); 1 s. Patrick. Hobbies: all sport, theatre, poetry. Address: c/o BBC TV, London. Birthsign: Virgo. **Favourite Place:** 'The Cliffs of Moher, Co Claire. A stone's throw from where I was born. Spectacular and lonely.'

LYNDHURST, Nick
Actor, b. 20 April 1961 Emsworth, Hants. Left the Corona Academy in 1980 but has already appeared in many TV series incl: *Anne Of Avonlea*; *Heidi*; *The Prince And The Pauper*; *Going Straight*; *Butterflies*; *Only Fools And Horses*; *Spearhead*; *To Serve Them All My Days*; *Slimming Down* (play). Hobbies: surfing, scuba-diving. Address: c/o Chatto & Linnit, London. Birthsign: Aries. **Favourite** Place: 'Deep Water Bay, Hong Kong. It's very hot, very lonely and the bar sells cold beer for 20p a can.'

LYNN, Jonathan
Writer/director/actor, b. 4 March 1943 Bath. Started with Cambridge Footlights Revue, appearing on Broadway. Many rep roles, then London theatre incl: *When We Are Married*; *Dreyfus*. Artistic Director Cambridge Theatre Company 1977–81; also directed many London plays and short film *Mick's People*. As actor, TV incl: *Doctor In The House*; *The Liver Birds*; *My Brother's Keeper* (also co-writer); *Barmitzvah Boy*; *The Knowledge*; *Outside Edge*. Screenplay: *The Internecine Project*. Writer TV comedies incl: *Yes, Minister*, winner of three BAFTA awards. Books: *A Proper Man*; *Yes, Minister*; *The Complete Yes, Minister*. m. Rita Merkelis; 1 s. Edward. Hobbies: eating, drinking, dieting. Address: c/o AD Peters, London. Birthsign: Aries. **Favourite Place:** 'Home.'

MACARTHUR, Edith
Actress, b. 8 March 1926 Ardrossan, Ayrshire, Scotland. Began career with the Wilson Barrett Company at the Royal Lyceum Theatre, Edinburgh. Has since worked at the Edinburgh Gateway Theatre; Perth Repertory; Glasgow's Citizens' Theatre; York Theatre Royal; Bristol Old Vic; and with the Royal Shakespeare Company. Stage incl: *The Gazebo*; *The Prime Of Miss Jean Brodie*; *Mahler*; *The Douglas Cause*. Also many poetry recitals at the Edinburgh Festival; solo performance play, *Marie Of Scotland*; Scottish Theatre Company. TV incl: *Love Story*; *Heartland*; *The Sandbaggers*; *Sunset Song*; *The Borderers*; *Weir Of Hermiston*; *Take The High Road*; *Sutherland's Law*. Hobbies: music, reading, cat-watching. Address: c/o Larry Dalzell Assocs, London. Birthsign: Pisces. **Favourite Place:** Edinburgh.

McCALLUM, David

Actor, b. 19 March 1933 Glasgow. First acted with BBC Repertory Company, then went to RADA. Stage incl: *After The Prize*; *Alfie*; *Camelot*; *The Mousetrap*; *Donkey's Years*; *Night Must Fall*; *Sleuth*. Films incl: *A Night To Remember*; *Billy Budd*; *Dogs*; *Freud*; *The Great Escape*; *Mosquito Squadron*; *Three Bites Of The Apple*; *The Secret Place*; *Watcher In The Woods*. TV incl: *The Man From UNCLE*; *The Colditz Story*; *The File On Devlin*; *The Invisible Man*; *Kidnapped*; *Sapphire And Steel*. Directed *Charles Montague Doughty* (*The Explorers*) for the BBC in 1974. m. (1st) actress Jill Ireland (dis.), (2nd) interior designer Katherine Carpenter; 1 d. Sophie, 4 s. Paul, Jason, Valentine, Peter. Hobby: computers. Address: 40 East 62nd Street, New York 10021. Birthsign: Pisces. **Favourite Place:** 'On stage.'

McCASKILL, Ian

Weatherman, b. 28 July 1938 Glasgow. After the Royal Air Force attended the Meteorological Office College. Joined the BBC as a weather forecaster in 1978. Weatherman for Central TV, 1982–83. He has made many guest appearances on TV. m. Lesley; 2 d. Victoria, Kirsty. Hobbies: comic postcards, junk, swimming. Address: Beaconsfield, Bucks. Birthsign: Leo. **Favourite Place:** Paradise Bay, Malta, 'Friendly and comfortable. Nearly unspoilt and nearly paradise on earth.'

MacCORKINDALE, Simon

Actor/director/writer, b. 12 Feb 1952 Ely, Cambs. Trained with rep and with Studio 68 in London. As director, theatre incl: *The Merchant Of Venice*; *The Importance Of Being Oscar* (his own one-man show). Films incl: *Jaws 3-D*; *Death On The Nile*; *Riddle Of The Sands*. TV incl: *The Pathfinders*; *Just William*; *The Skin Game*; *I, Claudius*; *Romeo And Juliet*; *Wilfred Owens*; *The Mansions Of America*; *Jesus Of Nazareth*; *Three Weeks*. Own series *Manimal* and plays Greg Reardon in *Falcon Crest*. m. (1st) actress Fiona Fullerton (dis.), (2nd) actress Susan George Hobbies: photography, tennis, interior decorating, writing, producing feature and TV films. Address: c/o The Agency, 6380 Wilshire Blvd, Los Angeles, California 90048. Birthsign: Aquarius. **Favourite Place:** London.

MacCORMICK, Donald

TV journalist, b. 16 April 1939 Glasgow. Started with STV Glasgow then moved to Grampian TV, 1968–70. He then joined BBC Scotland. Since moving to BBC Current Affairs in London in 1975 he has worked on *Tonight*; *Newsweek*; *Twentieth Century Remembered*; *Newsnight*; *Question Time*. m. Liz, 1 d. Sarah 2 s. Donald, Niall (from previous m.), 1 d. Anna. Hobbies: theatre, tennis, wine, current events in all media. Address: c/o BBC TV, London. Birthsign: Aries. **Favourite Place:** 'Approaching Glasgow by air, with the first highlands flinging off to the right horizon.'

McCOWEN, Alec, OBE

Actor, b. 26 May 1925 Tunbridge Wells. Trained for the stage at RADA. Stage incl: his own one-man show; *St Mark's Gospel*; *Kipling*; *The Browning Version*; *Equus*. Extensive TV appearances incl: *All For Love*; *Private Lives*; *Family Dance*; *Twelfth Night*; *Mr Palfrey Of Westminster*. Hobby: gardening. Address: c/o Jeremy Conway, London. Birthsign: Gemini. **Favourite Place:** 'Sandakphu, Himalayan foothills, India. Because you can see most of the world.'

MACDONALD, Aimi

Actress/singer, b. 27 Feb Glasgow. Stage incl: *On The Town*; *The Mating Game*; *The Sleeping Prince*; *The Prime Of Miss Jean Brodie*; *Hi-Infidelity*; *Present Laughter*; *A Bedful Of Foreigners*. Films incl: *Vampira*; *Take A Girl Like You*; *Vendetta*; *No 1 Of The Secret Service*. Radio incl: *Just A Minute*; *Jump*; *The Law Game*. TV incl: *At Last The 1948 Show*; *The Saint*; *The Avengers*; *Man At The Top*; *Do You Come Here Often?*; *Definition*; *Rentaghost*; and many guest appearances. *Royal Variety Performance*, 1968 and 1983. Various pantomime roles. m. (dis.); 1 d. dancer Lisa Muldore. Hobbies: skating, writing. Address: c/o Peter Charlesworth, London. Birthsign: Pisces. **Favourite Place:** 'Home, because it's best.'

MacDONALD, Gus

TV journalist/executive, b. 20 Aug 1940 Larkhill, Scotland. Started career on *The Scotsman*. Joined Granada as reporter in 1967. TV incl: *Election 500*; *Devil's Advocate*; *Camera—Early Photography*; *Moving Pictures*; *Right To Reply*; *Union World*; *What The Papers Say*. Also live coverage of political party conferences. Former Editor of *World In Action*, Granada's Head of Current Affairs, Regional Programmes and Features, before becoming Controller of Programmes at Scottish TV. Founder chairman of the Edinburgh International Television Festival. m. Teen; 2 d. Jean, Tracy. Hobbies: swimming, 19th Century photographs, movies. Address: c/o Scottish TV. Birthsign: Leo. **Favourite Place:** 'Waverley Station, Edinburgh, and the first sight of the Old Town and castle at the start of another festival.'

McDONALD, Pat

Actress, b. 1 Aug Victoria, Australia. Started her career in live radio and the theatre. Has been awarded three Critics' Awards and four Logies, including the Gold Award which is for top personalities. One of most recent performances was in *Sons And Daughters*. Is national spokeswoman for the Muscular Dystrophy Association, and does 'talking books' for the Royal Blind Society. m. (dis); 1 s. Ian. Hobbies: music, reading, cooking, travel. Address: c/o June Gann Management, PO Box 1577, North Sydney 2060, Australia. Birthsign: Leo. **Favourite Place:** 'My own country because it *is* my own country.'

McDONALD, Trevor
Correspondent/presenter, b. 16
Aug 1939 San Fernando,
Trinidad. At 20 started reporting
for local radio stations in
Trinidad and went on to become
announcer, sports commentator
and assistant programme
manager. Joined Trinidad TV
1962. Came to London 1969 to
join BBC World Service. Joined
ITN as a reporter 1971 and later
as newscaster. *Channel Four News*
diplomatic correspondent and
presenter. Author of biographies
on Clive Lloyd and Viv Richards.
m. Beryl; 1 d. Joanne, 1 s.
Timothy. Hobbies: collecting
books (especially political
biographies), international
politics, philosophy. Address: c/o
ITN, London. Birthsign: Leo.

McEWAN, Geraldine
Actress, b. Old Windsor, Berks.
Began career at the Theatre
Royal, Windsor. Has played the
lead in many London plays incl:
Who Goes There?; *Summertime*;
The Member Of The Wedding;
The Entertainer; *The School For
Scandal*; *Dear Love*; *On Approval*;
Chez Nous; also member of
Royal Shakespeare Company and
National Theatre. Many TV roles
incl: *The Prime Of Miss Jean
Brodie*; *L'Elegance*; *The Barchester
Chronicles*; *Mapp And Lucia*. m.
Hugh Cruttwell; 1 s. Greg, 1 d.
Claudia. Address: c/o Marmont
Management, London. Birthsign:
Taurus.

McGEE, Henry
Actor, b. 14 May London.
Trained at Italia Conti School and
then spent several years in rep in
England and Australia. Stage incl:
the lead in *Uproar In The House*;
*The Man Most Likely To Be In
London*. TV: appeared in the
award-winning series of Feydeau
farces, *Paris 1900*; *The Worker*
(with Charlie Drake); *Let There
Be Love*; and his successful
association with Benny Hill
continues. Address: c/o Margery
Armstrong, London. Birthsign:
Taurus. **Favourite Place:** 'In a
light aircraft at 800 feet about a
mile from the main runway at
Biggin Hill and heading straight
towards it. This is a very
welcoming sight and it means
you have a fair chance of actually
reaching it.'

McGINTY, Lawrence
Reporter, b. 2 July 1948
Manchester. Before the start of
C4 in 1982, he worked for *New
Scientist* magazine as Technology
Editor, Health Correspondent
and then News Editor. Since
joining *Channel Four News*, he
has reported on scientific and
medical developments, including
exclusive filming of the process
behind test-tube babies and the
opening of Britain's biggest
telescope. m. Joan. Hobbies:
collecting old books about science
and natural history, eating,
drinking, cooking, walking.
Birthsign: Cancer. **Favourite
Place:** 'Observatorio Del Roque
De Los Muchachos, Las Palma,
Canaries. The astronomical
observatory with the best view in
the world.'

MacGRAW, Ali

Actress, b. 1 April 1938 Pound Ridge, New York. Films incl: *Goodbye Columbus*; *The Getaway*; *Convoy*; *Players*; *Just Tell Me What You Want*; *Love Story* (Golden Globe Award for Best Actress, and Academy Award nomination); *A Lovely Way To Die*. TV incl: *The Winds Of War*; *Dynasty*. m. (2nd) producer Bob Evans (dis.), (3rd) Steve McQueen (dis.); 1 s. Joshua (from 2nd m.). Hobbies: cooking, writing, illustrating. Address: c/o International Creative Management, 8899 Beverly Blvd, Los Angeles, CA 90048. Birthsign: Aries. **Favourite Place:** New York and Malibu.

MACKAY, Fulton, OBE

Actor, b. 12 Aug 1922 Paisley. Trained at RADA. Much theatre work incl: Citizens' Theatre, Glasgow; The Royal Lyceum, Edinburgh; Old Vic; National Theatre; Royal Shakespeare Company; Manchester's Royal Exchange. Films incl: *The Brave Don't Cry*; *Laxdale Hall*; *Gumshoe*; *Britannia Hospital*; *Local Hero*; *Water*. TV incl: *The Blind Man*; *Special Branch*; *Porridge*; *The Foundation*; *Clay*; *Three Tales Of Orkney*; *Ghosts*; *The Master Of Ballantrae*; *Going Gently*; *Songs Of A Sourdough*; *Mann's Best Friends*; *Fraggle Rock*. Has written several plays for TV under a pseudonym. Awarded OBE in 1984. m. Irish actress Sheila Manahan. Hobby: oil painting. Address: c/o Leading Players, London. Birthsign: Leo. **Favourite Place:** 'Painting studio in the garden.'

McKENZIE, Julia

Actress, b. 17 Feb 1942 Enfield, Middx. Trained at the Guildhall School of Music and Drama. Stage incl: *Guys And Dolls*. Extensive TV work incl: musical specials of Jerome Kern, Gershwin, Sondheim and Sheldon Harnick; guest on *The Two Ronnies*, and with Stanley Baxter, Harry Secombe, David Frost, Russell Harty and Mike Douglas (coast to coast in America); own TV series, *Maggie And Her* and *That Beryl Marston . . .!*; *Fresh Fields*; *Fame Is The Spur*; *Blott On The Landscape*; *Absent Friends*. m. actor/director Jerry Harte. Hobby: cooking. Address: c/o April Young, London. Birthsign: Aquarius. **Favourite Place:** 'My home.'

McKERN, Leo, AO

Actor/writer, b. 16 March 1920 Sydney, Australia. Came to England in 1946; spent three years with the Old Vic and two years with the Royal Shakespeare Company. Stage incl. *Rollo*; *Othello*; *A Man For All Seasons*; *Crime And Punishment*; *Uncle Vanya*; *Volpone*. TV incl: *The Prisoner*; *The Sun Is God*; *On The Eve Of Publication*; *The Tea Party*; *Rumpole of The Bailey*. m. actress Jane Holland; 2 d. Abigail, Harriet. Hobbies: sailing, swimming, ecology, environment preservation. Address: c/o ICM, London. Birthsign: Pisces. **Favourite Place:** 'On a replica of Joshua Slocum's boat hitting intended landfall on the nose.'

MacLAUGHLIN, Jack

TV presenter, b. 11 July 1943 Glasgow. Started broadcasting career 1966 with Radio Scotland, a pirate station closed down in 1967. He then worked in cabaret before TV job as announcer with Grampian TV. 1974 joined BBC Radio 2 as presenter, then programme controller Radio Victory. Also own radio shows on Radio Clyde. TV incl: *Thingummyjig*; *Funny You Should Say That*; *Now You See It*. Voted TV Personality of the Year by Scottish Radio Industries Club. Hobby: rebuilding cinema organs. Address: c/o Scottish TV, Glasgow. Birthsign: Cancer. **Favourite Place:** 'Deeside, Scotland. Beautiful scenery, good pubs and restaurants and a super golf course, on which I always seem to score well!'

McLAUGHLIN, Lise-Ann

Actress, b. 24 June 1958 Dublin. Started career with the Abbey Theatre, Dublin. Many stage appearances incl: *City Sugar*; *A Life*; *Nightshade*. Film: *Angel*. TV incl: many plays such as *Shadows On Our Skin*; *Katie—The Year Of A Child*; *Nobody's Property*; *2016*; *Teresa's Wedding*; *Friends And Lovers*; also the series *We'll Meet Again*; *The Irish RM*. In 1983 was awarded the *TV Times* Award for the Most Promising Newcomer to Television. Hobbies: music, food, reading. Address: c/o Kate Feast Management, London. Birthsign: Cancer. **Favourite Place:** Connemara, Western Ireland, 'Unchanging, wild, beautiful— whatever the weather!'

MACLEAN, Don

Comedian, b. 11 March 1944 Birmingham. Started in clubs and pubs, then holiday camps. Made acting debut in 1984 tour of the farce, *A Bedful of Foreigners*. Radio incl: *Maclean Up Britain*; *Wit's End*; *Keep It Maclean*. TV incl: *The Good Old Days*; *In All Directions*; *Jokers Wild*; *Out For The Count*; *The Greatest Show On The TV*; *A Frame With Davis*; *The Zodiac Game*. Has written several short stories for magazines, and made comedy records. m. Antoinette; 1 d. Rachel, 1 s Rory. Hobbies: making models of First World War aeroplanes, writing, squash. Address: c/o Paul Vaughan Assocs, Birmingham. Birthsign: Pisces. **Favourite Place:** 'Maroubra Beach in Sydney, Australia, where the surf comes at you from either side instead of straight on. It's a spectacular sight.'

McLEOD, Shelagh

Actress, b. 7 May Vancouver, Canada. Trained at the Corona Academy in London. Has made many TV appearances both here and in the US. Has worked on stage at the Theatre Upstairs, Royal Court, London as well as in Canada. Plays incl: *The Dresser*; *Love's Labours Lost*; *Much Ado About Nothing*. Films incl: *Success*; *Lady Oscar*. TV incl: *Cream In My Coffee*; *Keats*; *Camille*; *Street Think*; *Pygmalion* (with Peter O'Toole); *The Winning Streak*. Hobbies: music, travelling, swimming. Address: c/o Larry Dalzell, London. Birthsign: Taurus. **Favourite Place:** 'In my mother's garden in Surrey. It reminds me of chocolate milk, five cats and peanut butter sandwiches!'

McNALLY, Kevin
Actor, b. 27 April 1956 Bristol. Trained at RADA. Has worked in many plays at the Royal Court, the National and theatres in London's West End, the most recent being *Extremities*. Films incl: *The Spy Who Loved Me*; *Enigma*; *Masada*; *Inside Man*; *The Long Good Friday*; *Not Quite Jerusalem*. TV incl: *Praying Mantis*; *The Bad Sister*; *I, Claudius*; *Poldark*; *Doctor Who*; *Devil's Crown*; *Diana*; *Commitments*; *The Hard Word*; *Crown Court*; *A Brother's Tale*; *We'll Meet Again*; *The South Bank Show*. Also about to launch the rock band, O-BE-BIG in which he'll be songwriter and singer. Address: c/o Eric L'Epine Smith, London. Birthsign: Taurus. **Favourite Place:** 'Somewhere with loud music and a good pint of Guinness.'

MACNEE, Patrick
Actor, b. 6 Feb 1922 London. Won a scholarship to Webber Douglas Academy of Dramatic Art in 1939. Worked in rep before his first West End production, *Little Women*. Other stage incl: *Sleuth* (Broadway); *Made In Heaven*; *The Grass Is Greener*; *House Guest*. Films incl: *Hamlet*; *Three Cases Of Murder*; *The Sea Wolves*; *Young Doctors In Love*; *A View To A Kill*; *Shadey*. TV incl: *The Avengers*; *The New Avengers*; *For The Term Of His Natural Life*; *Vintage Quiz*; *Empire*. m. (1st) actress Barbara Douglas (dis.), (2nd) actress Catherine Woodville (dis.); 1 d. Jennie, 1 s. Rupert (both from 1st m.). Hobbies: tennis, walking, reading. Address: c/o John Redway & Assocs, London. Birthsign: Aquarius. **Favourite Place:** 'Wainscott, Long Island, or anywhere where agricultural land extends down to the sea.'

McPHEARSON, Patricia
Actress, b. 27 Nov Washington State. After achieving a Bachelor Degree in Art she turned to acting. Is now a regular member of the cast of *Knight Rider*, an American crime adventure series. Hobbies: horses, skiing, tennis, photography, loves animals of all kinds. Address: c/o NBC, 3000 West Alameda, Burbank, CA 91523. Birthsign: Sagittarius. **Favourite Place:** 'Rabbit field near my home.'

McROBERTS, Briony
Actress, b. 10 Feb 1957 Welwyn Garden City, Herts. Played at various theatres incl: National; Chichester; Citizens' Theatre, Glasgow; Liverpool Everyman. Stage performances incl: *Hay Fever*; *Browning Version*; *Charley's Aunt*; *Peter Pan*. Films incl: *Captain Nemo And The Underwater City*; *The Pink Panther Strikes Again*. TV incl: *Bachelor Father*; *Lucky Jim*; *Peter Pan*; *Malice Aforethought*; *Strangers*; *Diamonds*; *The Professionals*; *Kelly Monteith*; *Mr Palfrey Of Westminster*; *Butterflies*. m. David Robb. Hobbies: watching rugby, cooking, dancing. Address: c/o Barry Burnett, London. Birthsign: Aquarius. **Favourite Place:** 'The Sharrow Bay Hotel (Ullswater, Lake District)— beautiful food, stunning scenery, and truly romantic for me and my husband.'

McWHIRTER, Norris, CBE
Author/editor/publisher, b. 12
Aug 1925 London. Editor and
compiler of *Guinness Book Of
Records* since 1954 (209 editions
in 24 languages and over 51
million sales). Radio incl: *Desert
Island Discs*; *Any Questions*;
various radio shows during 1984
world tour. TV incl: co-presenter
of the *Record Breakers* (BBC TV).
Was athletics commentator for
BBC TV, 1951–72; *What's In
The Picture?* Books incl: *Get To
Your Marks* (co-author); *British
Athletics Record Book* (co-author);
Ross: Story Of A Shared Life;
Guinness Book Of Answers;
Guinness Book Of Origins. m.
Carole; 1 d. Jane, 1 s. Alasdair.
Hobbies: family, tennis, visiting
small islands, researching in
libraries. Address: c/o Guinness
Superlatives, Enfield. Birthsign:
Leo. **Favourite Place:** 'The
chapel tower rooms of Trinity
College, Oxford, where I was
with my late twin Ross.'

MADOC, Philip
Actor, b. 5 July 1934 Merthyr
Tydfil. First-rate linguist (seven
languages), his studies took him
to the University of Vienna
where he was the first foreigner
to win the Diploma of the
Institute of Interpreters. After
two years as an interpreter, he
went to RADA. TV incl: *Last Of
The Mohicans*; *Another Bouquet*;
*The Life And Times Of David
Lloyd George*; *Zina*. 1 d. Lowri, 1
s. Rhys. Hobbies: languages,
windsurfing, squash. Address:
c/o Hutton Management,
London. Birthsign: Cancer.
Favourite Place: 'Taormina,
summer, midnight, open-air café.
Above the glow of Etna in the
black sky. Divine.'

MADOC, Ruth
Actress/comedienne, b. 16 April
1943 Norwich. Best known on
TV as the love-sick Gladys Pugh
in BBC's *Hi-De-Hi!* Started
career with Nottingham Rep
Theatre as ASM before training
at RADA. Debut in *Under Milk
Wood* at Lyric, Hammersmith
(also film). Member of Black and
White Minstrels for three years
but left to work in *Man From La
Mancha* (London and S Africa),
Fiddler On The Roof (stage and
film) and pantomime. Also in
The Prince And The Pauper (film).
Other TV incl: *Hunter's Walk*;
Leave It To Charlie; *The Life And
Times Of David Lloyd George*. m.
(1st) actor Philip Madoc, (2nd)
manager John Jackson; 1 d.
Lowri, 1 s. Rhys (both from 1st
m.). Hobbies: home, children.
Address: c/o Richard Stone,
London. Birthsign: Aries.

MAGILL, Ronald
Actor, b. 21 April 1920 Hull.
Started his career during the
Second World War when he
toured with *Stars In Battledress*. A
year after demob joined a
travelling company, Arena, and
has since played most theatres
outside London. Actor and
director at Nottingham
Playhouse for nine years. Film:
Julius Caesar. TV: most well-
known as Amos Brearly in
Emmerdale Farm. Hobbies:
swimming, reading. Address: c/o
Bernard Gillman, London.
Birthsign: Taurus. **Favourite
Place:** 'Centre dress circle in any
theatre just before the curtain
goes up.'

MAGNUSSON, Magnus

Writer/presenter, b. 12 Oct 1929 Reykjavik, Iceland. Has lived in Scotland since he was nine months old. Started as reporter on the *Scottish Daily Express*, moved to *The Scotsman* as chief feature writer. TV incl: co-presenter of *Tonight* (1964–65); *Thereafter Chronicle*; *Checkpoint*; *Mainly Magnus*; *Mastermind*; *Living Legends*. Books incl: *Viking Expansion Westwards*; *Landlord Or Tenant?—A View Of Irish History*; *Magnus On The Move*; *Lindisfarne, The Cradle Island*; *Reader's Digest Book Of Facts*. m. journalist Mamie Baird; 3 d. Sally, Margaret, Anna, 1 s. Jon. Hobbies: translating Icelandic sagas and modern novels into English. Address: c/o BBC TV, London. Birthsign: Libra. **Favourite Place:** 'Thingvellir— the open-air lava arena where the Parliament of Iceland was created, and Iceland was born.'

MAJORS, Lee

Actor, b. 23 April Wyandotte, Michigan. Grew up in Kentucky when adopted by relatives after the death of his parents. A star athlete at school, might have been a pro footballer if not for a back injury. Idolised actor James Dean and went to California. Big break in TV series *Big Valley*, which ran for four years. Became well known for his role as Steve Austin in *The Six-Million Dollar Man*, and more recently in *The Fall Guy*. Other TV incl: *The Man From Shiloh*; *The Virginian*. Also films incl: *Will Penny*; *The Naked Sun*; *Piranha*. m. (1st) Kathy (dis.), (2nd) actress Farrah Fawcett (dis.); 1 s. Lee (from 1st m.). Hobbies: driving racing cars, flying a helicopter, hunting, fishing, golf, tennis, racquetball, basketball. Address: c/o Rogers & Cowan, 9665 Wilshire Blvd, Suite 200, Beverly Hills, California 90212. Birthsign: Taurus.

MANDEL, Howie

Actor, b. 29 Nov Toronto, Canada. Started his career as a stand-up comic at Los Angeles' The Comedy Store. Film: *A Fine Mess*. TV cinemax special: *Howie Mandel: Live From Carnegie Hall*. Guest appearances on TV incl: *The Tonight Show*; *Merv Griffin*; *Mike Douglas*; *HBO Special*; *Bizarre*. Regular member of the cast of *St Elsewhere*. m. Terry; 1 d. Jackelyn. Hobby: 'collecting pants from mail-order catalogues.' Address: c/o Triad Artists, 10100 Santa Monica Blvd, Los Angeles 90067. Birthsign: Sagittarius. **Favourite Place:** Las Vegas.

MANETTI, Larry

Actor, b. 23 July Pendleton, Oregon. Studied drama at Northwestern University and trained with Sal Dano. Film: *Two Minute Warning*. TV incl: *Emergency*; *Chase*; *Switch*; *Black Sheep Squadron*; *Battlestar Galactica*; *The Duke*; *Ten Speed And Brown Shoe*; *Fantasy Island*; *Quincy*; *Barnaby Jones*; *Magnum PI*. m. actress Nancy; 1 s. Lorenzo. Hobbies: tennis, bicycle riding, basketball. Address: c/o Rosenfield/Goldman Public Relations, 9229 Sunset Blvd, Los Angeles, CA 90069. Birthsign: Cancer. **Favourite Place:** 'Visiting friends and family back home in Chicago.'

MANN, Steven

Actor, b. 12 Feb 1958 Purley, Surrey. Trained at LAMDA. Stage incl: *The Country Girl*; *A Scent Of Flowers*; *Lady Audley's Secret*; *Romeo And Juliet*; *She Stoops To Conquer*; *Privates On Parade*; *Ruffian On The Stair*; *Liberty Hall*; *Ragman*; *Fiddler On The Roof*. TV incl: *Bless Me Father*; *Don't Wait Up*; *Lucky Jim*; *Codename Icarus*; *Let's Pretend*; *Visiting Day*; *My Father's House*; *Jemima Shore Investigates*; *Gems*. Hobbies: music, dancing, squash. Address: c/o Terry Gardner Management, London. Birthsign: Aquarius. **Favourite Place:** New York City, 'Because it is every bit as exciting as it's supposed to be.'

MANNING, Bernard

Comedian, b. 13 Aug 1930 Manchester. Worked in pubs and clubs, mainly in the north, until he was discovered in the TV series *The Comedians*. TV incl: *The Wheeltappers And Shunters Social Club*; *The Entertainers*; *Bernard Manning In Las Vegas*; *Bernard Manning*; *Under Manning*. Royal Command Performance, 1972, and Comic of the Year, 1982. m. Vera; 1 s. Bernard. Hobbies: reading, TV. Address: c/o The Embassy Club, Manchester. Birthsign: Leo. **Favourite Place:** 'Al Amin Restaurant—great curry.'

MANNING, Hugh

Actor, b. 18 Aug 1920 Birmingham. Trained at the Birmingham School of Speech Training and Dramatic Art. Joined Birmingham Rep in 1945 then Bristol Old Vic and London Old Vic. Stage incl: *Stalingrad*; *The Cherry Orchard*; *Paragraph For Mr Black*; *Uncle Vanya*; *A Woman Named Anne*; one-man play, *Song Of The Lion*. TV incl: *Mrs Thursday*; *Sergeant Cork*; *The Avengers*; *The Sullivan Brothers*; *The Venturers*; *Poldark*; *Emmerdale Farm*. Hobbies: gardening, tennis, bridge, travel. Address: c/o Plunket Greene, London. Birthsign: Leo. **Favourite Place:** 'My garden where I can relax.'

MANTLE, Clive

Actor, b. 3 June 1957 Barnet, London. Trained with the National Youth Theatre and at RADA. Stage incl: rep at Hornchurch and Southampton; *Of Mice And Men* (voted Most Promising Newcomer, 1984). Has also worked at the Bush Theatre; the Young Vic; the King's Head; the Shaw Theatre; the Roundhouse; the Jeanetta Cochrane Theatre; various national tours and the Edinburgh Festival. Films incl: *Party Party*; *The French Lieutenant's Woman*; *Orchard End Murder*. Radio: two series of the live comedy show, *In One Ear!* TV incl: *Minder*; *Jane*; *Robin Of Sherwood*. Hobbies: writing, sport. Address: c/o Marjorie Abel, London. Birthsign: Gemini. **Favourite Place:** 'The terraces at the shed end of Stamford Bridge watching Chelsea Football Club.'

MARINARO, Ed

Actor, b. 31 March New Milford, New Jersey. Played professional football with the Minnesota Vikings and the New York Jets. Studied acting with coaches Milton Katselas and Warren Robertson. Stage debut in *It Had To Be You*. Film: *Fingers*. TV incl: *Policewoman Centerfold*; *Three Eyes*; *Born Beautiful*; *Hill Street Blues*; plus guest appearances in *Eischeid*; *Laverne And Shirley*. Hobbies: all sports, exercising, golf, tennis, travel, racquetball, cooking. Address: c/o William Morris Agency, 151 El Camino Drive, Beverly Hills, CA 90212. Birthsign: Aries. **Favourite Place:** 'I love the sun in Mexico and Hawaii.'

MARKS, Alfred, OBE

Actor/comedian, b. 28 Jan 1921 London. Stage debut at the age of nine in a Boys' Brigade concert; first professional performance at the Kilburn Empire in 1946 in variety. Stage incl: *Where The Rainbow Ends*; *A Day In The Life Of...*; *Spring And Port Wine*; *The Entertainer*; *The Sunshine Boys*; *Fiddler On The Roof*. Films incl: *Desert Mice*; *There Was A Crooked Man*; *Frightened City*; *Scream And Scream Again*. TV incl: *Alfred Marks Time*; *The Good Old Days*; *Looks Familiar*; *Does The Team Think?*; *Maybury*; *Parkinson*; *Sunday Night At The London Palladium* (compère). m. actress Paddie O'Neil; 1 d. Danielle, 1 s. Gareth. Hobbies: target shooting, riding, stamp collecting. Address: c/o Barry Burnett, London. Birthsign: Aquarius. **Favourite Place:** 'Upwind of any good fish and chip shop.'

MARSDEN, Roy

Performer, b. 25 June 1941 London. Among his many TV appearances are: *The Sandbaggers*; *Airline*; *Goodbye, Mr Chips*; *Vanity Fair*; and the P D James crime books series playing Det Chief Sup Adam Dalgliesh. m. Polly Hemingway; 1 s. Joe. Hobbies: sailing, opera. Birthsign: Cancer. **Favourite Place:** 'The Victoria Palace Theatre: that's where I learnt my trade.'

MARSH, Reginald

Actor, b. 17 Sept 1926 London. Has worked in rep and for periods with the Royal Shakespeare Company and the National Theatre. Stage incl: *Thark*; *Relatively Speaking*; *Dance Of Death*; *Henry IV Part I*; *All For Oxford*; *My Brother's Keeper*. Author of a number of plays incl: *The Death Is Announced*; *The Man Who Came To Die*. Films incl: *The Sicilians*; *Shadow Of Fear*; *Jigsaw*; *Young Winston*; *Sky Pirates*. TV incl: *The Planemakers*; *The Power Game*; *The Ratcatchers*; *Bless This House*; *The Good Life*; *Terry And June*; *Nye*. Book: *Much More Than Murder*. m. Rosemary; twin d. Rebecca, Alison, 2 s. Adam, Alexander. Hobby: writing. Address: c/o Plunket Greene, London. Birthsign: Virgo. **Favourite Place:** Isle of Wight: 'Beautiful, peaceful, good weather, wonderful country, and all near the sea.'

MARTIN, Kiel
Actor, b. 26 July Pittsburgh, Pennsylvania. Studied drama at Trinity University, Texas, and the University of Miami. Worked in rep in New York and Miami, and for the National Shakespeare Company in San Diego. Films incl: *The Undefeated*; *The Catcher*; *Panic In Needle Park*; *Moonrunners*. TV incl: *Matt Houston*; *The Virginian*; *Dragnet*; *Ironside*; *Harry O*; *Kung Fu*; *The Edge Of Night*; *Hill Street Blues*; and TV films, *Trick Baby*; *The Log Of The Black Pearl*; *Raid On Short Creek*. 1 d. Jessie. Hobbies: softball, jogging, singing, racquetball, playing the guitar. Address: c/o Kubik Company, 9200 Sunset Blvd, Suite 531, Los Angeles, CA 90069. Birthsign: Leo. **Favourite Place:** 'I love my retreat—my house in Mexico.'

MATHIAS, Glyn
ITN Political Editor, b. 19 Feb 1945 South Wales. Educated at Llandovery College; Jesus College, Oxford, and Southampton University. Started his career as a reporter on the *South Wales Echo* before joining the BBC at Southampton. Political correspondent for ITN, 1973, and Home Affairs correspondent, 1979. Political Editor, 1981. m. Sian; 1 d. Megan, 1 s. Mathew. Hobbies: squash, walking, reading, talking. Address: c/o ITN, London. Birthsign: Pisces.

MATTHEWS, Francis
Actor, b. 2 Sept 1931 York. Started career at Leeds Rep at 17 and later at Oxford and Bromley. Recent stage incl: *The Business Of Murder*; *Middle-Age Spread*; *Aren't We All?* Films: *No Escape*; *Bhowani Junction*. Radio incl: *Not In Front Of The Children*; *Local Time*; *Stop The World*; *Double Trouble*. TV incl: probably best known as Paul Temple; *A Little Big Business*; *My Man Joe*; *Trinity Tales*; *Middlemen*; *Roof Over My Head*; *Don't Forget to Write*; *Morecambe And Wise Christmas Show*, 1971 and 1978; *Crowther Collection*; *Tears Before Bedtime*. Has also sung on *Saturday Night At The Mill* and on the *Marti Caine Show*. m. actress Angela Browne; 3 s. Paul, Dominic, Damien. Hobbies: writing, tennis. Address: c/o Jeremy Conway, London. Birthsign: Virgo. **Favourite Place:** 'Standing in the heart of Venice and just gazing.'

MAYNARD, Roger
Broadcaster/journalist, b. 3 Dec 1947 Eastbourne, Sussex. Started career with provincial newspapers and local radio. Began broadcasting with one of the first BBC local radio stations, Radio Brighton, in 1968. Has since had extensive radio and television experience as reporter and presenter. Radio incl: Capital Radio; Radio 4's *Today* programme; has made several documentaries for Radio 4. TV incl: BBC TV East; TV-am; *Look East*. Specialises in sport and leisure. m. Vivienne; 2 d. Corey, Zoe, 1 s. Thomas. Hobbies: tennis, walking, swimming. Address: c/o BBC TV, Norwich. Birthsign: Sagittarius. **Favourite Place:** the Suffolk coast, 'Unspoilt and still a closely guarded secret.'

MEDWIN, Michael
Actor, b. 18 July 1929 London.
Co-produced many West End
plays incl: *If...*; *Spring And Port
Wine*. Acted with the National
Theatre, 1977–78. Many films
both as an actor and producer
incl: (as actor) *For Them That
Trespass*; *The Lady Craved
Excitement*; *Boys In Brown*;
Curtain Up; *Above Us The
Waves*; *Heart Of A Man*; *Night
Must Fall*; *The Jigsaw Man*; (as
producer) *Charlie Bubbles*;
Gumshoe; *O Lucky Man!*; *Law
And Disorder*. TV incl: *The Army
Game*; *For The Love Of Mike*;
Three Live Wires; *Shoestring*. m.
(dis.). Hobby: golf. Address: c/o
London Management, London.
Birthsign: Cancer.

MELLINGER, Leonie
Actress, b. 24 June 1959 Berlin,
West Germany. Trained at the
Central School of Speech and
Drama. Stage incl: Royal
Shakespeare Company's
production of *A Winter's Tale*;
Titus Andronicus. Films incl:
Memoirs Of A Survivor; *Ghost
Dance*; *Memed, My Hawk*; *Zina*.
TV incl: *Sons And Lovers*; *Whale
Music*; *Infidelities*; *Dead Head*;
Paradise Postponed; *Mr Palfrey Of
Westminster*; *Summer Lightning*.
Hobbies: singing, water-skiing,
swimming, dancing. Address: c/o
London Management, London.
Birthsign: Cancer. **Favourite
Place:** 'Coming into Gozo
Harbour by boat at sunset—one
of the happiest moments of my
life.'

MELODY, Tony
Actor, b. 18 Dec London. Films
incl: *Yanks*; *Little Lord
Fauntleroy*; *Invitation To The
Wedding*; *Turtle Summer*; *Mr
Love*. TV incl: *Bergerac*; *Juliet
Bravo*; *Tom, Dick And Harriet*;
Crown Court; *Emmerdale Farm*;
Strangers; *Cost Of Loving*; *George
And Mildred*; *Home And Away*;
Comedy Playhouse; *Oranges And
Lemons*; *Steptoe And Son*; *The
Winning Streak*; *Let There Be
Love*; *Zigger Zagger*. m.
Margaret. Hobbies: golf, table
tennis, DIY. Address: c/o Felix de
Wolfe, London. Birthsign:
Sagittarius. **Favourite Place:**
'Home. Because I hate fighting
with strangers.'

MEO, Tony
Professional snooker player, b. 2
Oct 1959 Hampstead, London.
His success in the snooker
competition world has taken him
to success in the World
Professional Doubles, partnered
by Steve Davis, in 1982 and
1983; the Australian Masters
Tournament, 1981; and Pontins
Professional Tournament, 1984.
m. Denise; 1 d. Gina, 1 s. Tony.
Hobbies: horse racing and all
sports. Address: c/o Barry Hearn
Ltd, Romford. Birthsign: Libra.
Favourite Place: 'At home
with the family.'

MERCIER, Sheila
Actress, b. 1 Jan 1919 Hull.
Trained at the Stratford-on-Avon
College of Drama. Started career
with Sir Donald Wolfit's
company as did her brother,
Brian Rix. After the war she
joined Brian's Whitehall Theatre
company in 1955 and was with
him for 11 years. Has played
Annie Sugden in *Emmerdale Farm*
since its start in 1972. m.
theatrical manager Peter Mercier;
1 s. Nigel. Hobby: reading.
Address: c/o Yorkshire TV,
Leeds. Birthsign: Capricorn.
Favourite Place: Hornsea, East
Yorks, 'Because I spent wonderful
days of childhood there.'

MICHELMORE, Cliff, CBE
Commentator/presenter, b. 11
Dec 1919 Cowes, Isle of Wight.
Started with the British Forces
Network in Germany, 1947–49.
Joined BBC to produce, direct
and write for children's TV.
Sports commentaries from 1951
and a nightly interview
programme, 1955–57. TV incl:
Tonight; *24 Hours*; *Our World*;
Holiday; space programmes;
general elections; *Talkback*;
Wheelbase; *Chance To Meet*;
Across The Great Divide; *Let's
Pretend*; *A Ripe Old Age*; *People's
Choice*; *Fleet Air Arm*; *The
Thynne Inheritance*; *Day By Day*.
Still remembered as presenter of
Family Favourites. m. broadcaster
Jean Metcalfe; 1 d. Jenny, 1 s.
Guy. Hobbies: golf, sitting
around. Address: Reigate, Surrey.
Birthsign: Sagittarius. **Favourite
Place:** 'Either home or the
Canadian Rockies. Peaceful,
remote, lovely.'

MILLIGAN, Spike
Author/actor/comedian, b. 16
April 1918 Ahmaddnagar, India.
Stage incl: *For One Week Only*;
The Bed-Sitting Room (and film);
one-man shows. Films incl: *The
Last Remake Of Beau Geste*; *The
Life Of Brian*; *The Hound Of The
Baskervilles*; *History Of The
World, Part I*. Radio incl: *Crazy
People* (which became *The Goon
Show*); *The Last Goon Show Of
All*. TV incl: *Milligan's Wake*;
Q5 to Q10; *The Other Spike*; *The
Best Of British*. Records incl: *The
Ying Tong Song*; *The Goons*; *The
Snow Goose*. Books incl: *Puckoon*;
*Adolf Hitler: My Part In His
Downfall*; *The Spike Milligan
Letters*; *Monty: His Part In My
Victory*; *The Goon Show
Cartoons*; *Mussolini: His Part In
My Downfall*. m. (3rd) Shelagh
Sinclair; 3 d. Laura, Sile (from 1st
m.), Jane (from 2nd m.), 1 s. Sean
(from 1st m.). Hobbies: reading,
antiques. Address: c/o Norma
Farnes, London. Birthsign: Aries.

MILLS, Hayley
Actress, b. 18 April 1946 London.
Trained at the Elmhurst Ballet
School and made her first film,
Tiger Bay, when she was 12.
Made her stage debut in the title
role of *Peter Pan* in 1970. Other
stage incl: *The Three Sisters*; *The
Wild Duck*; *Rebecca*; *A Touch Of
Spring*; *The Summer Party*; *My
Fat Friend*; *Trelawney Of The
Wells*. Films incl: *Whistle Down
The Wind*; *The Chalk Garden*;
The Family Way; *Pretty Polly*;
Truth About Spring. TV incl:
Only A Scream Away; *Deadly
Strangers*; *The Flame Trees Of
Thika*. m. (dis.); 2 s. Crispian,
Jason. Hobbies: travel, reading,
studying philosophy. Address:
c/o James Sharkey Assocs,
London. Birthsign: Aries.
Favourite Place: 'Anywhere
that is naturally beautiful,
peaceful and in harmony with
everything else around it.'

MILLS, Royce
Actor, b. 12 May 1941 Tetbury, Glos. Trained at the Guildhall School, where he was the Major Open Scholar in drama, Shakespeare Prizeman and the Gold Medallist. Also won BBC Sound Repertory Prize. Spent three years with Yvonne Arnaud Theatre before joining the Old Vic. Stage incl: *The Boy Friend*; *The Bed Before Yesterday*; *The Streets Of London*; *Run For Your Wife*; *See How They Run*; *The Seven Year Itch*. Films incl: *Up Pompeii*; *Sunday Bloody Sunday*; *History Of The World, Part I*. TV incl: *Charley's Aunt*; *Sir Yellow*; *Rules, Rules, Rules*; *Rings On Their Fingers*; *The Knowledge*; *Tears Before Bedtime*; *The Old Boy*. m. Una Morriss; 2 d. Samantha, Miranda. Hobbies: painting, pondering, prevaricating. Address: c/o Roger Storey, London. Birthsign: Taurus. **Favourite Place:** Beachy Head.

MITCHELL, Warren
Actor, b. 14 Jan 1926 London. Trained at RADA and went on to become a household name for his role as Alf Garnett in BBC TV's *Till Death Us Do Part*. Theatre incl: *Death Of A Salesman*; *The Caretaker* (both at the National Theatre). Films incl: *Knights And Emeralds*; *The Chain*. Other TV incl: *The Merchant Of Venice*; *The Caretaker*; *Moss*. m. actress Constance Wake; 2 d. Rebecca, Anna, 1 s. Daniel. Hobbies: tennis, sailing, clarinet, supporting Spurs FC. Address: c/o ICM, London. Birthsign: Capricorn ('I don't believe in it'). **Favourite Place:** 'Beaulieu River. Why? Go and have a look.'

MOLLISON, Fiona
Actress, b. 9 Jan 1954 Duakarta, Indonesia. Trained at the Central School of Speech and Drama. Has played at many theatres countrywide incl: Oxford Playhouse, Nuffield Theatre, Derby Playhouse, Liverpool Playhouse, Windsor and various theatres in London's West End. Films incl: *Sweeney II*. TV incl: *Spaghetti Two-Step*; *Hazell*; *Minder*; *Strangers*; *Fallen Hero*; *A Day In The Life . . .*; *Lytton's Diary*. m. David Gilmore; 1 s. Charles. Hobby: cooking. Address: c/o Michael Ladkin Management, London. Birthsign: Capricorn. **Favourite Place:** Loch Eck, Argyllshire, 'My father's family home, where we go to get away from it all.'

MONKHOUSE, Bob
Entertainer, b. 1 June 1928 Beckenham, Kent. Trained as cartoon film animator. Later became the BBC's first contract comedian. Formed script-writing team with Denis Goodwin and together they wrote thousands of scripts for radio and TV. Stage incl: *Bob Monkhouse Startime*; *Come Blow Your Horn*; *Boys From Syracuse*. Films incl: *Dentist In The Chair*; *Weekend With Lulu*; *She'll Have A Go*. TV incl: *Candid Camera*; *Sunday Night At The London Palladium*; *The Golden Shot*; *Celebrity Squares*; *I'm Bob—He's Dickie*; *Family Fortunes* (1980–83); *The Bob Monkhouse Show*; *Bob's Full House*. m. (1st) Elizabeth (dis.), (2nd) Jacqueline; 1 d. Abigail, 2 s. Gary, Simon. Hobbies: collecting vintage films and artwork by great cartoonists. Address: c/o Peter Prichard, London. Birthsign: Gemini. **Favourite Place:** 'A cinema seat.'

MONTAGUE, Bruce
Actor/writer, b. 24 March 1939 Deal, Kent. After National Service as aerial photographer and finishing his RADA training, he started at Birmingham Rep, followed by the Old Vic. Numerous TV roles incl: *Dimensions Of Fear*; *The Saint*; *Public Eye*; *Undermind*; *Butterflies*; *Whoops Apocalypse*; and guest appearances in programmes such as *Secret Army*; *Fresh Fields*. Has written many radio plays and stage plays incl *Die Laughing* and *A Bird In The Hand*. m. Barbara Latham; 1 s. Sam, 1 d. Kate. Hobbies: music, barbeques, *The Times'* Portfolio. Address: c/o London Management, London. Birthsign: Aries. **Favourite Place:** Montmartre: 'Great licensing hours and I cannot understand a word anybody says.'

MONTEATH, Alec
Actor, b. 22 May Doune, Perthshire. Trained at the Royal Scottish Academy of Music and Drama. Has worked in theatre seasons at Glasgow's Citizens', Edinburgh Gateway, Pitlochry Festival, Perth, Edinburgh Lyceum and with the Scottish Theatre Company. Stage incl: *Brief Glory*; *Journey's End*; *Swansong*; *The Birthday Party*; *Mr Bolfry*; *Ringo*; *Battle Royal*. His TV experience started as an announcer/newsreader, 1965–76. Other TV incl: *Omega Factor*; *Doom Castle*; *Hess*; *Take The High Road*. m. Linna Skelton; 2 s. actor David, Alasdair. Hobbies: Scottish history and heraldry, swimming, cycling, fishing, clay pigeon shooting. Address: c/o STV, Glasgow. Birthsign: Gemini. **Favourite Place:** 'Pass of Killiecrankie—steeped in history. Happy memories of living there over several seasons at Pitlochry Theatre.'

MONTEITH, Kelly
Comedian/actor/writer, b. 17 Oct 1942 St Louis, Missouri. Trained at the Pasadena Playhouse College of Theater Arts. Has since made regular appearances in major nightclubs and hotel/casinos in Las Vegas, Reno and Nevada. TV in America incl: summer show on CBS; *The Kelly Monteith Show*; *No Holds Barred*. Since working in Britain he has had a seven-week one-man show in London's West End, *Kelly Monteith In One*; three national tours; six years of the BBC2 comedy series *Kelly Monteith*. Hobbies: reading, writing, travel. Address: c/o John Redway & Assocs, London. Birthsign: Libra. **Favourite Place:** 'A beach house overlooking the Pacific Ocean in the Malibu area. It's tranquil and the unrelenting persistence of the ocean is inspiring.'

MOONE, Maggie
Singer/actress, b. 5 July 1953 Aston, Birmingham. Made her debut as a member of the famous Bluebell Girls. Winner of TV's *New Faces*; runner-up in *Song For Europe*. Now resident singer on *Name That Tune*. Other TV incl: *Mike Yarwood In Persons*; *The Morecambe And Wise Show*; *Starburst*; *London Night Out*. m. Colin Davies. Hobbies: driving, music. Address: c/o Mike Hughes Entertainments, Liverpool. Birthsign: Cancer. **Favourite Place:** 'My home in Solihull. It's nice to get back there and relax with Colin.'

MOORE, Bill
Actor, b. 19 April Birmingham. Started his career with the Birmingham Repertory Company. Considerable theatre work incl: the Pitlochry Festival; Dundee and Swansea theatres. Taught for several years at the Bristol Old Vic Theatre School. Appeared in London's West End in *When We Are Married*. TV incl: *Dad's Army*; *Middlemarch*; *South Riding*; *The Bröntes*; *The Cedar Tree*; *Coronation Street*; *Sorry!*; *Dombey And Son*. m. actress Mollie Sugden; 2 s. (twins), Robin, Simon. Hobbies: reading and writing poetry. Address: c/o Joan Reddin, London. Birthsign: Aries. **Favourite Place:** Grasmere, Cumbria, 'Happy memories of times spent there in my youth and later on family holidays, introducing my sons to the joys of fell walking and climbing.'

MOORE, Brian
Commentator, b. 28 Feb 1932 Benenden, Kent. Journalistic experience with *World Sports*, *Exchange Telegraph* and *The Times* before joining the BBC and then LWT. Compère of *The Big Match* and various ITV sports programmes. Also major sporting documentaries for ITV. m. Betty; 2 s. Christopher, Simon. Hobbies: family life, animals, all sport. Address: c/o LWT, London. Birthsign: Pisces. **Favourite Place:** 'In the fields behind Farnborough Church in Kent— dogs at heel, problems a million miles away!'

MOORE, Patrick, OBE
Author/astronomer/TV presenter and personality, b. 4 March 1923 Pinner, Middx. TV incl: BBC's longest-running programme, *The Sky At Night*, which celebrates 28 years this year; *One Pair Of Eyes*; coverage of various space shots and guest appearances incl *Face The Music*; *Blankety Blank*; *It's A Celebrity Knockout*. Guest xylophonist in 1981 *Royal Command Performance*. Has written many books incl: boys' novels; science fiction; science fact; the best-selling *The Unfolding Universe*; *Atlas Of The Universe*. Also a regular contributor to magazines and journals. Hobbies: astronomy, cricket, music, tennis. Address: c/o BBC TV, London. Birthsign: Pisces. **Favourite Place:** 'The rose garden outside the bay window of my study. It gives me a sense of peace and contentment. I wouldn't leave it for anything!'

MOORE, Roger
Actor, b. 14 Oct 1927 London. Trained at RADA and soon became a film and TV star. Many films incl: *The Man Who Haunted Himself*; *Gold*; *Shout At The Devil*; *The Wild Geese*; *Escape From Athena*. Has played James Bond, first in 1970 in *Live And Let Die* and subsequently in: *The Man With The Golden Gun*; *The Spy Who Loved Me*; *Moonraker*; *Octopussy*; *For Your Eyes Only*; *A View To A Kill*. TV incl: *Ivanhoe*; *The Alaskans*; *Maverick*; *The Saint*; *The Persuaders*. m. (1st) Doorn van Steyn (dis.), (2nd) Dorothy Squires (dis.), (3rd) Luisa Mattioli; 2 s. Geoffrey, Christian, 1 d. Deborah. Hobbies: skiing, tennis, backgammon. Address: c/o London Management, London. Birthsign: Libra.

MORANT, Jane

Actress, b. 27 Sept Shipston-on-Stour, Warwicks. Trained at Central School of Speech and Drama and at Guildford. Theatre incl: *Noah*; *The Stranger*; *Hello From Bertha*; *The Killing Of Sister George*; *The Unvarnished Truth*; *Amadeus*; *Verdict*; *Friends*. TV incl: *Renoir My Father*; *The Dancing Years*; *All Creatures Great And Small*; *Talisman*; *The Winning Streak*. Address: c/o Libby Glenn Assocs, London. Birthsign: Libra. **Favourite Place**: 'The terrace of my home overlooking the hills towards the Mediterranean—perfect peace and tranquillity.'

MORGAN, Garfield

Actor, b. 19 April 1931 Birmingham. After attending Birmingham Drama School went to the Arena Theatre, Birmingham. Was Director of Productions at Marlowe Theatre, Canterbury, 1957–58, and at Manchester's Library Theatre, 1959–60. Associate Director, Northcott Theatre, 1976–78, and Nottingham Playhouse, 1978–80. Stage and films incl: *The Pumpkin Eater*; *The Story Of Private Pooley*; *Perfect Friday*. TV incl: *Softly, Softly*; *Randall and Hopkirk (Deceased)*; *Dear Mother . . . Love Albert*; *The Sweeney*; *Shelley*; *One By One*. Hobbies: golf, photography, showjumping and eventing. Address: c/o Michelle Braidman Assocs, London. Birthsign: Aries. **Favourite Place**: 'Venice in late September and early October because of the light.'

MORIARTY, Paul

Actor, b. 19 May 1946 London. Has worked at a variety of theatres countrywide, incl: Coventry, Bolton, Liverpool, Bristol, Royal Shakespeare, National Theatre, Royal Court, London. Stage incl: *The Contractor* in the West End. Also founder member of the Enemy Within theatre group. Film: *Quest For Love*. TV incl: *Holly*; *Pelham*; *Coronation Street*; *Z Cars*; *Minder*; *The Sweeney*; *Jackanory*; *Love Story*; *Troilus And Cressida*; *The Gentle Touch*. m. Teresa; 1 d. Jessica, 1 s. Matthew. Hobbies: reading, music, rugger, mooching about. Address: c/o Ken McReddie, London. Birthsign: Taurus. **Favourite Place**: 'Tony's Cafe, Golders Hill. It reminds me of my children and my own childhood.'

MORRIS, Beth

Actress, b. 19 July 1949 Gorseinon, South Wales. Trained at the Cardiff College of Music and Drama, followed by rep at Northampton, Colchester, Bristol and Birmingham before appearing in London's West End and with the Royal Shakespeare Company. Stage incl: *Man And Superman*; *Banana Ridge*; *Travesties*; *Passion Of Dracula*; *Mrs Grabofskies Academy*. TV incl: *Play Of The Week*; *Play Of The Month*; *Jude The Obscure*; *Minder*; *Z Cars*; *Softly, Softly*; *Armchair Thriller*; *I, Claudius*; *David Copperfield*. m. actor Stephen Moore. Hobby: reading. Address: c/o Ken McReddie, London. Birthsign: Cancer. **Favourite Place**: 'The mountain road through the Brecon Beacons because it's so beautiful and it makes me proud of my country.'

MORRIS, Mike
Presenter, b. 26 June 1947 Harrow, Middlesex. Educated at St Paul's School, London, and Manchester University. Journalistic background working for Reuters, United Newspapers, and then Thames TV. Now presenter of TV-am's *Good Morning Britain*, where he started as the sports presenter. m. Alison; 2 d. Sarah, Helen. Hobbies: books, sport, boozing. Address: c/o TV-am, London. Birthsign: Cancer. **Favourite Place:** 'My toilet—it's the only place I can get some peace and quiet.'

MORSE, David
Actor, b. 11 Oct Hamilton, Massachusetts. Worked with the Boston Repertory Company and the Circle Repertory Company in New York. Drama Logue Award for his performance in the Los Angeles production *Of Mice And Men*. Films: *Inside Moves*; *Invasion From Mars*. TV incl: *Family Business*; *Prototype*; *Shattered Vows*; *St Elsewhere*. m. actress Susan Wheeler Duff. Hobbies: oil painting, drawing, running, charity work. Address: c/o Yvette Bikoff Agency, 9120 Sunset Blvd, Suite A, Los Angeles, CA 90069. Birthsign: Libra. **Favourite Place:** 'A retreat in the mountains of Idylwild, California.'

MOSES, Billy
Actor, b. 11 Nov 1959 Los Angeles, California. Went to the University of Southern California and Wesleyan University before starting successful acting career. Now well known for his role as Cole Gioberti in the TV soap opera *Falcon Crest*. Hobbies: basketball, swimming, running, fixing up his house. Address: c/o Agency for the Performing Arts, 9000 Sunset Blvd, Los Angeles, California 90069. Birthsign: Scorpio. **Favourite Place:** 'My ranch in Ojai, California.'

MOSLEY, Bryan
Actor, b. 25 Aug 1931 Leeds. Trained at the Esme Church Northern Theatre School. Rep at St Andrews, Perth, Derby, Harrogate, York. Films incl: *Get Carter*; *Charlie Bubbles*; *Far From The Madding Crowd*; *A Kind Of Loving*; *This Sporting Life*; *Rattle Of A Simple Man*. TV incl: *The Saint*; *Z Cars*; *The Avengers*; *No Hiding Place*; *Crossroads*; *Coronation Street*. Expert swordsman and arranges fights for stage, films and TV. Has toured and directed several stage plays. m. Norma; 3 d. Jacqueline, Simone, Helen, 3 s. Jonathan, Bernard, Leonard. Hobbies: painting, drawing, fencing, walking, swimming, reading, films, theatre. Address: c/o Granada TV, Manchester. Birthsign: Virgo. **Favourite Place:** 'San Francisco, because there is access to so many places of beauty and interest.'

MOSLEY, Roger E

Actor, b. Los Angeles. Best known for his role as TC, an ex-Vietnam war helicopter pilot, who assists Tom Selleck in the title role of TV's *Magnum PI.* He was a champion wrestler while at college and a founder member of the Watts Repertory Company. m. (1st) (dis.); 5 children. Hobbies: collecting cowboy boots, tennis, basketball (coaches a basketball league in Hawaii and created an all-girl basketball team). Address: c/o Aimee Entertainment, 13743 Victory Blvd, Van Nuys, California 91401. **Favourite Place:** 'Being home in LA—I need a daily dose of smog.'

MOWER, Patrick

Actor, b. 12 Sept Pontypridd. Trained at RADA. Stage incl: *House Of Cards; Alfie; John Gabriel Borkman; A Boston Story; Night And Day; Country Girl; The Seven Year Itch.* Films incl: *The Devil Rides Out; Doctors Wear Scarlet; The Smashing Bird I Used To Know; The Cry Of The Banshee; One Away; The Devil's Advocate; Catch Me A Spy; Escape From El Diablo; Czech Mate.* TV incl: *Haunted; Front Page Story; Callan; Special Branch; Target.* Plus many guest appearances in series such as *The Sweeney; Minder.* 1 d. Claudia, 1 s. Sam. Address: c/o London Management, London. Birthsign: Virgo. **Favourite Place:** 'On an English lawn listening to a test match, drinking Krystal champagne with a beautiful girl.'

MUIR, Frank

Scriptwriter/performer, b. 5 Feb 1920 Broadstairs, Kent. Started writing seriously in 1946. In 1947 teamed up with Denis Norden in *Navy Mixture.* Together for 17 years during which they wrote *Take It From Here; Bedtime With Braden;* and TV series *And So To Bentley; Whack O!; The Seven Faces Of Jim; Brothers-In-Law.* Radio incl: *My Word!; My Music.* TV incl: *Sound Of Laughter; Call My Bluff; How To Be An Alien; We Have Ways Of Making You Laugh.* BBC's Head of Comedy, 1963; LWT's Head of Light Entertainment, 1966–69. Books: *You Can't Have Your Kyak And Heat It* (with Denis Norden); *The Frank Muir Book.* m. Polly; 1 d. Sarah, 1 s. James. Hobby: collecting books. Address: c/o April Young, London. Birthsign: Aquarius.

MURPHY, Brian

Actor, b. 1933 Ventnor, Isle of Wight. After National Service with the RAF trained at RADA. Became a stalwart of Joan Littlewood's Theatre Workshop. Stage incl: *On Your Way Riley;* a season with the Royal Shakespeare Company in 1984. TV incl: *Man About The House; George And Mildred; The Incredible Mr Tanner; Lame Ducks.* m. Carol; 2 s. Trevor, Kevin. Hobby: collecting vintage films. Address: c/o Saraband Assocs, London. Birthsign: Libra. **Favourite Place:** 'To sit, a glass of Nuit St George in hand, gazing across Loch Lomond. I feel peaceful and it satisfies the romantic in me.'

MURRAY, Bryan

Actor, b. 13 July 1949 Dublin, Ireland. Trained at the Abbey Theatre School in Dublin. Went on to become a member of the Abbey Theatre Company where he played many leading parts, directed and co-wrote two musicals performed by the Company. Joined the National Theatre Company in 1977. Also a member of the RSC. TV incl: *Strumpet City*; *Bread Or Blood*; *Year Of The French*; *Rifleman*; *The Irish RM*; as George Bernard Shaw in *Oscar*. m. Angela Harding; 1 d. Laura. Hobbies: squash, music, movies. Address: c/o Brunskill Management, London. Birthsign: Cancer. **Favourite Place:** 'Walking by the sea anytime, anywhere, and hearing the waves. I find it comforting, calming and inspiring!'

NADER, Michael

Actor, b. 18 Feb St Louis, Missouri. Trained at the Actor's Studio, New York, at Herbert Berghoff Studios, New York and in workshop productions. Also worked as a model. Started acting career in 'beach movies' in 1960s and on TV in *Gidget*. He appeared on stage in several off-Broadway productions and in regional theatre in Hawaii; also in *Vieux Carré* at the Beverly Hills Playhouse. In TV soap opera *As The World Turns* for three years. Now best known as Dex Dexter in TV's *Dynasty*. m. Robin Weiss; 1 d. Lindsay Michelle. Hobbies: surfing, skiing, workshop productions, restoring Porches and Volkswagens, his pedigree Australian cattle dog. Address: c/o Lippin & Grant Inc, 8124 West Third St, Suite 204, Los Angeles, California 90048. Birthsign: Aquarius. **Favourite Place:** 'The Californian beaches.'

NETTLETON, John

Actor, b. 5 Feb 1929 London. Trained at RADA and spent many years with the Royal Shakespeare Company, National Theatre and Old Vic. Recent theatre incl: *Anyone For Denis?*; *When The Wind Blows*. Films incl: *A Man For All Seasons*; *And Soon The Darkness*; *Black Beauty*. TV incl: *The Tempest*; *Crown Court*; *The Citadel*; *The Flame Trees Of Thika*; *Brideshead Revisited*; *The Happy Apple*; *Yes, Minister*. m. Deirdre Doone; 3 d. Sarah, Joanna, Jessica. Hobby: listening to music. Address: c/o Marmont Management, London. Birthsign: Aquarius. **Favourite Place:** 'Venice, for its inexhaustible beauty.'

NEWMAN, Nanette

Actress/author, b. Northampton. Trained at RADA and went straight into films incl: *The L-Shaped Room*; *The Whisperers*; *The Wrong Box*; *The Love Ban*; *Man At The Top*; *The Stepford Wives*; *The Raging Moon*; *International Velvet*. TV incl: *Prometheus*; *Fun Food Factory* (own series); *London Scene*; *Stay With Me 'Til Morning*; *Let There Be Love*; *Jessie* (title role). As an author, sales over one million. Books incl: *God Bless Love*; *My Granny Was A Frightful Bore*; *The Christmas Cookbook*. m. film director/author Bryan Forbes; 2 d. Sarah, Emma. Hobbies: painting, needlepoint. Address: c/o ICM, London. Birthsign: Gemini. **Favourite Place:** 'London and New York.'

NICHOLAS, Paul
Actor/singer, b. 3 Dec 1945
Peterborough. Former rock 'n'
roll piano player, started acting
1969 in original London
production of *Hair*. Followed by
Jesus Christ Superstar and *Grease*.
Joined Young Vic and Prospect
Theatre Company. Theatre incl:
Cats; *Blondel*; *The Pirates of
Penzance*. Films incl: *Tommy*;
Stardust; *Lisztomania*; *Sergeant
Pepper's Lonely Hearts Club Band*;
The World Is Full Of Married
Men; *Yesterday's Hero*; *Alice*; *The
Jazz Singer*; *Nutcracker*; *Invitation
To A Wedding*. TV incl: *Season
Of The Witch*; *Two Up Two
Down*; *Chips*; *The Lady Killers*;
The Boys From Ipanema; *A Little
Rococo*; *Just Good Friends*;
Doubting Thomas. m. Linzi; 1 d.
Natasha, 2 s. Oscar, Alexander.
Hobby: posing. Address: c/o
Duncan Heath, London.
Birthsign: Sagittarius. **Favourite
Place:** 'Bed, it has everything
that one could possibly want.'

NICHOLLS, Sue
Actress, b. 23 Nov 1943 Walsall,
W Midlands. Trained at RADA
and then worked in rep and
cabaret in England and abroad.
Appeared in *London Assurance* on
Broadway. Film: *Expresso
Splahso!* TV incl: *Crossroads*; *The
Fall And Rise Of Reginald Perrin*;
Solo; *The Professionals*; *Pipkins*;
Rentaghost; *Tycoon*; *Not On Your
Nellie*; *Heartlands*; *Coronation
Street*; *Up The Elephant And
Round The Castle*. Hit record
with *Where Will You Be*.
Hobbies: music, singing, dancing,
sauna, films, eating out. Address:
c/o Barry Brown Management,
London. Birthsign. Sagittarius.
Favourite Place: 'Breakfast in
bed. Sitting up in my bedroom
with a lovely tray of tea and toast
and newspapers—and on Sunday
the omnibus *Archers*!'

NICHOLSON, Michael
Newscaster, b. 9 Jan 1937
Romford, Essex. As foreign
reporter for ITN has covered
more wars and conflicts than any
other reporter. Nominated for
Emmy Award 1969 for his
reports from Biafra. In 1974
received Special Award by
British Broadcasting Press Guild
for his war coverage in Cyprus;
his *Battle For Newport Bridge*, the
last battle in South Vietnam, won
him Silver Nymph at Cannes
Film Festival 1976; Reporter of
the Year 1979. His reporting of
Falklands War won him many
awards, incl BAFTA Richard
Dimbleby Award 1982.
Appointed newscaster for ITN
1982. Books: *The Partridge Kite*;
Red Joker; *December Ultimatum*;
Across The Limpopo. m. Diana; 2
s. Tom, Will. Hobbies: novel
writing, classic cars. Address: c/o
ITN, London. Birthsign:
Capricorn. **Favourite Place:**
Ullswater.

NIMMO, Derek
Actor/writer, b. 19 Sept 1933
Liverpool. First job at the
Hippodrome, Bolton at £4 a
week. Many West End
appearances incl: *The Amorous
Prawn*; *Duel Of Angels*; *Charlie
Girl*; *Why Not Stay For
Breakfast?*; *A Friend Indeed*; *See
How They Run* (also TV). Also
tours in Australia and the Far
East. Film: *One Of Our Dinosaurs
Is Missing*. TV incl: *All Gas And
Gaiters*; *Oh Brother!*; *O Father!*;
My Hon Mrs; *Sorry I'm Single*;
Life Begins At Forty; *Third Time
Lucky*. m. Patricia; 1 d. Amanda,
2 s. Timothy, Piers. Hobbies:
sailing, collecting English 17th
and 18th century furniture.
Address: c/o Barry Burnett,
London. Birthsign: Virgo.
Favourite Place: 'Kashmir and
in particular Lake Nagir—
kingfishers on every bow, lotus
blossom, houseboats and the
snow-capped Himalayas beyond.'

179

NOAKES, John

Actor/presenter, b. 6 March 1934 Halifax, Yorks. Trained at the Guildhall School of Music and Drama. First job in a Cyril Fletcher pantomime 1960. Other theatre incl: rep at Bournemouth, Harrogate, York, Manchester, Sheffield, Worthing, Leatherhead; summer show with Cyril Fletcher; Children's Theatre tour; *Chips With Everything* (on Broadway). On TV has been in plays for ITV and BBC. He joined BBC TV's *Blue Peter* as a presenter in 1966 and left in 1979. TV also incl: *Go With Noakes* series 1975–81; *Country Calendar*. Has appeared in pantomimes and currently chartering his 45-foot boat in Balearics. m. Victoria; 1 s. Mark. Hobby: sailing. Address: c/o Arlington Enterprises, London. Birthsign: Pisces. **Favourite Place:** 'Mallorca, where I am skipper chartering my boat.'

NOLANS, The

International singing group, made up of four sisters—their parents were both singers. Have appeared in a *Royal Command Performance*, on a European tour with Frank Sinatra and at the Montreux Music Festival. Winners of Grand Prix Tokyo Festival 1981. Had nine hit records in British charts and sold over three million records in Japan. **Anne,** b. 12 Nov 1950 Dublin. m. Brian Wilson; 1 d. Amy. Hobbies: music, sport. Birthsign: Scorpio. **Bernadette,** b. 17 Oct 1960 Dublin. Hobbies: sport, travel. Birthsign: Libra. **Coleen,** b. 12 March 1965 Blackpool. Hobby: riding. Birthsign: Pisces. **Maureen,** b. 14 June 1954 Dublin. Hobbies: fashion, clothes design. Birthsign: Gemini. Address: c/o Mel Bush Organisation, Bournemouth. **Favourite Places:** The Lake District, Florida and the Caribbean.

NORDEN, Denis

Scriptwriter/performer, b. 6 Feb 1922 Hackney, London. Originally a theatre manager 1939–42. Wrote for troop shows in RAF then scriptwriter for variety. Teamed up with Frank Muir 1947–64 and they wrote for radio: *Take It From Here* and *Bedtime With Braden*. For TV: *And So To Bentley*; *Whack-O!*; *The Seven Faces of Jim*; *Brothers-In-Law*; *The Glums.* Solo writer 1964 and film scripts incl: *Bueno Sera, Mrs Campbell*; *The Statue*; *Every Home Should Have One*; *The Water Babies.* Radio incl: *My Word!*; *My Music.* TV incl: *The Name's The Same*; *How To Be An Alien*; *Looks Familiar*; *It'll Be Alright On The Night*; introduced 1982 BAFTA Awards. m. Avril; 1 d. TV producer Maggie, 1 s. Nick. Hobbies: reading, loitering. Address: c/o April Young, London. Birthsign: Aquarius.

NORMAN, Barry

Writer/presenter, b. 21 Aug 1933 London. A journalist, mostly with *Daily Mail* until made redundant. 1972 joined BBC 2's *Late Night Line-Up*; this led to *Film* series 1972–81 and *The Hollywood Greats.* 1982 presented *Omnibus* for BBC 1 before returning to *Film 83, 84, 85.* TV incl: *The British Greats*; *Barry Norman In Chicago*; *Barry Norman's Hong Kong Quest*; *Barry Norman On Broadway*; *Barry Norman's London Season*; *Barry Norman In Celebrity City*; *The Rank Charm School.* Won BAFTA Richard Dimbleby Award 1984. Books incl: *The Movie Greats*; *Have A Nice Day*; *Sticky Wicket*; *The Film Greats.* m. Diana; 2 d. Samantha, Emma. Hobby: cricket. Address: c/o BBC TV, London. Birthsign: Leo. **Favourite Place:** 'The Hong Kong landscape seen from the Star Ferry, Kowloon Harbour.'

NORVELLE, Duncan
Comedian, b. 2 April 1958
Loughborough, Leicestershire.

Learned his art as a comedian while performing in cabaret across the country. Has made many TV appearances incl: *Saturday Royal*; *Mike Reid And Friends*; *The Bob Monkhouse Show*; various guest appearances. Hobbies: golf, squash, football. Address: c/o AMA, 140 Beckett Rd, Doncaster, S Yorks. Birthsign: Aries. **Favourite Place:** 'Any golf course—it's good exercise, while enjoying the countryside.'

OBERMAN, Claire
Actress, b. 21 Feb 1956 New Zealand. Dutch by birth, brought up in New Zealand and trained at the National Drama School there. Joined a theatre group, created own one-woman show. Break in New Zealand TV series *Hunter's Gold*. Theatre incl: *The Taming Of The Shrew*; *Twelfth Night*; *Kennedy's Children*; *Pygmalion*; *Time And Time Again*; *Just Between Ourselves*; *The Merchant Of Venice*; *Tick Tock*. Female lead in New Zealand's most successful film, *Goodbye Pork Pie*. Came to London and worked in theatre and then on TV as Kate Norris in *Tenko*. Also roles in *Hi-de-Hi!* and *Paradise Postponed*. Hobbies: reading, music, swimming, running, cycling. Address: c/o Barry Burnett, London. Birthsign: Pisces. **Favourite Place:** 'Engelberg, Switzerland, because it fills me with pure air and is an utter delight.'

O'BRIEN, Eileen
Actress, b. 4 Dec 1945 Liverpool. After working in Children's Theatre and Theatre in Education, rep in Manchester and seasons at Scarborough in Alan Aykbourn's *Absent Friends*, *Bedroom Farce* and *Confusions*. Other theatre incl: *Breezeblock Park*; *Funny Peculiar*; *A Doll's House*; *Skirmishes*; *Dracula*; *Alfie*. Films incl: *The Nation's Health*, *Runners*; *A Private Function*. Numerous plays for radio. TV incl: *The Crezz*; *The Sheikh Of Pickersgill*; *One In A Thousand*; *The Boys From The Black Stuff*; *The Last Company Car*; *Coronation Street*; as Carol Stansfield in *The Practice*. m. writer Stephen Mallatratt; 1 d. Hannah. Address: c/o The Actors' Group, Manchester. Birthsign: Sagittarius. **Favourite Place:** 'The lane where I live in spring after six months of hard, Pennine winter when new life appears.'

O'BRIEN, Richard
Actor/writer, b. 25 March 1942 Cheltenham, Glos. Brought up in New Zealand, but had no formal training as an actor. Theatre performances incl: *Gulliver's Travels*; *Hair*; *Jesus Christ Superstar*; *The Unseen Hand*; *The Hostage*; *The Rocky Horror Show* (also as writer); *The Tooth Of Crime*; *T Zee* (also as writer); *Disaster* (also as writer); *They Used To Star In Movies*; *Eastwood Ho!*; *Top People* (also as writer/director). Films incl: *Carry On Cowboy*; *Fighting Prince Of Donegal*; *The Odd Job Man*; *Flash Gordon*; *Shock Treatment*. TV incl: *A Hymn For Jim*. m. Jane Elizabeth Moss-O'Brien; 2 s. Linus, Joshua. Hobbies: drawing, music, cooking. Address: c/o Chatto & Linnit, London. Birthsign: Aries. **Favourite Place:** 'Around a dinner table with friends—preferably in a kitchen.'

O'BRIEN, Simon

Actor, b. 19 June 1965 Garston, Liverpool. Attended Highfield Comprehensive in Liverpool and had no formal acting training—says he's 'a natural'. Plays the role of Damon Grant in C4's soap opera set in Liverpool, *Brookside*. Hobbies: watching and supporting Everton FC, playing football. Address: c/o Brookside Productions Ltd, Liverpool. Birthsign: Gemini. **Favourite Place:** 'Scotland—it's sound.'

O'CONNOR, Des

Entertainer, b. 12 Jan Stepney, London. Joined RAF at 18. A former Butlin's Red Coat, professional debut Palace Theatre, Newcastle 1953. Has since starred in many *Royal Variety Shows* and in 1972 made his 1,000th performance at London Palladium. Appeared in Canada, America, Australia. Many TV appearances incl: *Spot The Tune*; *Sunday Night At The London Palladium*; *The Des O'Connor Show*; *Des O'Connor Tonight*; *Des O'Connor Now*. Many hit records incl: *Careless Hands*; *I Pretend*; *One Two Three, O'Leary*. Gold discs for albums *Just For You* and *Des O'Connor Now*. *TV Times* Favourite Male TV Personality from 1969–73. Hobbies: show business, golf, all sport. Address: c/o London Management, London. Birthsign: Capricorn. **Favourite Place:** 'The Den at Millwall—on a Saturday afternoon.'

O'CONNOR, Tom

Comedian, b. 31 Oct 1940 Bootle, Merseyside. Originally a maths and music teacher at St Joan of Arc School, Bootle; also performed in working men's clubs while still a teacher. Appeared in the second series of *The Comedians* on TV and became a full-time entertainer 1974. *Opportunity Knocks* and a summer season at Blackpool were followed by *The Tom O'Connor Show*; *Wednesday At Eight*; *Royal Variety Performance 1976*; *Tom O'Connor At The Casino*; *London Night Out*; *Gambit*; *The Zodiac Game*; *I've Got A Secret*. Also many pantomimes and summer seasons. m. former teacher Pat; 3 d. Ann, Frances, Helen, 1 s. Stephen. Hobbies: golf, snooker, football. Address: c/o Clifford Elson, London. Birthsign: Scorpio.

ODDIE, Bill

Writer/performer, b. 7 July 1941 Rochdale, Lancs. Was a member of Footlights at Cambridge University 1960–63. Writer/performer for *I'm Sorry I'll Read That Again* on radio. Co-writer for *Doctor In The House*, *The Astronauts* on TV. As writer/performer TV incl: *That Was The Week That Was*; *Twice A Fortnight*; *Broaden Your Mind*; *The Goodies*; various ornithological programmes for TV incl *Oddie In Paradise*. Has written and sung on various Goodie hit records and is the author of several bird books. m. Laura Beaumont (also co-writer of recent books and TV); 2 d. Kate, Bonnie (from previous m.). Hobbies: ornithology, music, especially jazz, painting birds. Address: c/o Roger Hancock, London. Birthsign: Cancer. **Favourite Place:** 'Flying into Lundy Island in the helicopter—the promise of peace.'

O'FARRELL, Maureen
Actress/dancer/educationalist, b. 8 Jan 1952 London. Studied drama and dance at Dartington College and education at Rolle College. Theatre incl: *Helen Jives*; *Audience*; season with Stir About Theatre Company. Radio incl: *Jonathan Wilde*. TV incl: *The Fourth Arm*; *Widows* (two series); *Minder*; *The Comic Strip Presents*; *Shine On Harvy Moon*; *Dempsey And Makepeace*; *CATS Eyes*. 1 s. Thomas. Address: c/o Alan Mitchell Assocs, London. Birthsign: Capricorn. **Favourite Place:** 'Upper Egypt—because it's full of everything we've lost.'

OGILVY, Ian
Actor, b. 30 Sept 1943 Woking, Surrey. Started backstage at London's Royal Court Theatre before RADA. Rep at Colchester, Canterbury and Northampton Theatre incl: *The Waltz Of The Toreadors*; *The Millionairess*; Chichester Festival. Films incl: *Stranger In The House*; *The Sorcerers*; *Witchfinder General*; *The Invincible Six*; *Waterloo*; *Wuthering Heights*; *Fengriffin*; *No Sex Please, We're British*; *Design For Living*. TV incl: *The Liars*; *Upstairs, Downstairs*; *Catherine (Affairs Of The Heart)*; *A Walk With Destiny*; *The Return Of The Saint*; *Tom, Dick And Harriet*; *TVTimes* Award Most Compulsive Character 1978–79. m. former model Diane; 1. step-d. Emma, 1 s. Titus. Address: c/o Leading Artists, London. Birthsign: Libra. **Favourite Place:** 'London still the most civilised place on the globe.'

OLIVIER, Lord Laurence, OM
Actor/director/manager, b. 22 May 1907 Dorking. Founder Director National Theatre (1963–73). Stage debut 1922 as Katherine in *Taming Of The Shrew*. With Old Vic until 1938; co-director Old Vic 1944. Shakespeare Company 1955 season. Films incl: *Wuthering Heights*; *Rebecca*; *Henry V*; *Hamlet* (Oscar); *Richard III*. Most recent TV incl: *Brideshead Revisited*; *A Voyage Round My Father*; *Mr Halpern And Mr Johnson*; *A Talent For Murder*; *The Ebony Tower*. Knighted 1947; Baron 1970 m (1st) Jill Esmond (dis.), (2nd) Vivien Leigh (dis.), (3rd) Joan Plowright; 2 s. Tarquin (from 1st m.), Richard (from 3rd m.), 2 d. Tamsin, Julie-Kate (both from 3rd m.). Hobbies: swimming, gardening. Address: c/o Temple, Gothard & Co, London. Birthsign: Gemini.

OLSEN, Gary
Actor, b. 3 Nov 1957 London. Theatre incl: *The Rocky Horror Show*; *Bentley*; *Saved*; *The Pope's Wedding*; *Welcome Home*; *Cut And Thrust*; *Cabaret*. Films incl: *The Birth Of The Beatles*; *The Sender*; *Party Party*; *Underworld*; *Loose Connections*; *Bloody Kids*; *Winter Flight*; *Outland*; *The Wall*. TV incl: *The Day Of The Triffids*; *The Bill*; *Prospects*. Hobbies: softball, snooker, pool, music. Address: c/o Lou Coulsen, London. Birthsign: Scorpio. **Favourite Place:** 'My living room, in front of the TV, with a constant supply of Budweiser beer.'

O'SHEA, Kevin

Actor, b. 7 March 1952 Enfield, Middx. Trained with the National Youth Theatre and at Bristol Old Vic Theatre School. Theatre incl: at Glasgow Citizens' Theatre; *Much Ado About Nothing*; *The Lion In Winter*; *The Caretaker*; with the Royal Shakespeare Company; *Romeo And Juliet*; directed *As You Like It* in US. Films incl: *SOS Titanic*; *Black Joy*; *Woman On A Roof*; *Inseminoid*. TV incl: *Thank You Comrades*; *We Think The World Of You*; *Secret Army*; *Spearhead*; *The Professionals*; *The Gentle Touch*; *The Scarlet Pimpernel*; *Kelly Monteith*. m. (sep.). Hobbies: film-making, computers, cinema. Address: c/o London Management, London. Birthsign: Pisces. **Favourite Place:** 'The seaside. Perhaps it's because I'm Pisces—I just love the sea.'

O'SULLIVAN, Richard

Actor, b. 7 May 1944 Chiswick, London. Child actor in many films incl: *Stranger's Hand*; *Dangerous Exile*; *Cleopatra*; in many Cliff Richard musicals. Theatre incl: *The Government Inspector*; *Boeing-Boeing*; panto at London Palladium. TV incl: *Doctor At Large*; *Doctor In Charge*; *Father, Dear Father* (and film); *Alcock And Gander*; *Man About The House*; *Robin's Nest*; *Dick Turpin*; *Me And My Girl*. Hobby: soccer (plays for charity matches). Address: c/o Al Mitchell Assocs, London. Birthsign: Taurus.

OULTON, Brian

Actor, b. 11 Feb 1908 Liverpool. Trained at RADA and began career in rep at Liverpool Playhouse. Theatre incl: *The National Health*; *Forty Years On*. Films incl: several *Carry On . . .* films; *The Thirty-Nine Steps*; *I'm All Right, Jack*; *Very Important Person*; *On The Buses*; *Gandhi*; *The Young Sherlock Holmes*. Numerous TV appearances, the most recent incl: *The Old Curiosity Shop*; *Brideshead Revisited*; *The Young Ones*; *Alice In Wonderland*. m. actress Peggy Thorpe-Bates; 1 d. Jennifer, 1 s. Nicholas. Hobby: writing plays and novels. Address: c/o Patrick Freeman, London. Birthsign: Aquarius. **Favourite Place:** 'My desk in the country because I write there and look out on the garden, which my wife designed.'

OWEN, David, Rt Hon, MD

Member of Parliament, b. 2 July 1938 Plympton, Devon. After Cambridge University, qualified as a doctor at St Thomas's Hospital, London 1962. Elected to Parliament as Labour member for Plymouth 1966. Became Foreign Secretary 1977–79. Founder member of the Social Democratic Party 1981 and became Leader of the Party 1983. Author: *The Politics Of Defence*; *In Sickness And In Health*; *Human Rights*; *Face The Future*; *A Future That Will Work*. m. literary agent Deborah Schabert; 2 s. Tristan, Garath, 1 d. Lucy. Hobbies: sailing, tennis. Address: c/o The House of Commons, London. Birthsign: Cancer. **Favourite Place:** 'The River Yealm looking out towards the Mewstone, a rocky island three miles from Plymouth where I have sailed, fished and swam ever since I was a small boy.'

OWEN, Nicholas

TV correspondent, b. 10 Feb 1947 London. Has worked as a journalist since 1964. With BBC TV as a reporter before joining ITN as a correspondent in 1984. m. Brenda Owen; 1 d. Rebecca, 1 step-d. Justine, 1 s. Anthony, 1 step-s. Daniel. Hobbies: reading, walking, sleeping. Address: c/o ITN, London. Birthsign: Aquarius. **Favourite Place:** 'Reigate Heath in Surrey. My home.'

OWEN, Nick

TV presenter, b. 1 Nov 1947 Berkhamsted, Herts. Newspaper journalist (*Doncaster Evening Post* and *Birmingham Post*) and local radio experience (BBC Radio Birmingham) before joining ATV/Central 1978 to present news and sport programmes.

Presenter of *Good Morning Britain* for TV-am. m. Jill; 2 s. Andrew, Timothy. Hobbies: playing squash, watching football and cricket, keeping up with his children. Address: c/o Paul Vaughan Assocs, Birmingham. Birthsign: Scorpio. **Favourite Place:** 'After two and a half years of breakfast television—bed. Also Long Mynd, Church Stretton, Shropshire—beautiful, tranquil, full of boyhood memories, still a delight for a family outing.'

OXENBERG, Catherine

Actress, b. New York City. Is the daughter of Princess Elizabeth of Yugoslavia. Pursued a successful career as a model on both sides of the Atlantic before studying acting with Stanley Zaraff in New York. Started her career on TV as Lady Diana Spencer in *The Royal Romance Of Charles And Diana* and in *The Love Boat* and *Cover Up*. Plays Amanda Bedford in TV's *Dynasty*. Hobbies: reading, travelling, skiing, tennis. Address: c/o Contemporary-Korman, 132 Lasky Drive, Beverly Hills, California 90212. **Favourite Place:** her new home in Los Angeles.

PAGE, Frank

Journalist/broadcaster, b. 16 April 1930 London. A journalist for over 30 years, specialising in motoring and sailing. TV incl: many scripts and voice overs for *The World About Us*; contributor to *Drive-In*; reporter/presenter BBC's *Top Gear* from 1979. m. Samantha; 3 d. Lucasta, Georgina, Hermione. Hobbies: music, sport, pictures. Address: c/o BBC TV, London. Birthsign: Aries. **Favourite Place:** 'Tortola, British Virgin Isles—some of the most idyllic sailing waters in the world.'

PAGE, Tim

Actor/singer, b. 23 Feb 1947 Wellington, New Zealand. Trained at the Wellington Repertory Drama School. Made his debut 1959 in *The Merry Wives Of Windsor*. Joined New Zealand Opera Company 1966–71. Moved to Australia 1973 and appeared in *A Little Night Music*. Joined Australian Opera 1973–83. Recent theatre incl: *The Actor's Nightmare*; *Sister Mary Ignatious*; *The Caretaker*; *The Golden Pathway Annual*; *The Three Sisters*. Musicals incl: *The Labours Of Hercules*; *Candide*; *Camelot*. TV incl: *The Young Doctors*; *Case For The Defence*; *Possession*; *Certain Women*; *La Bohème*. Hobbies: music making, swimming, writing. Address: c/o Kevin Palmer Management, 20 Prospect St, Surrey Hills 2010, Australia. Birthsign: Pisces. **Favourite Place:** 'Sparkling water, beaches and yachts. Beautiful.'

PALMER, Geoffrey

Actor, b. 4 June 1927 London. No formal training but worked as unpaid trainee assistant stage manager at the Q Theatre, London. Most recent theatre incl: *A Friend Indeed*; *Tishoo*; *St Joan*. Films incl: *O Lucky Man*; *The Outsider*; *The Honorary Consul*. Many radio plays and is one of the busiest actors on TV. TV incl: *The Fall And Rise Of Reginald Perrin*; *Butterflies*; *A Midsummer Night's Dream*; *The Last Song*; *Absurd Person Singular*; *Radio Pictures*; *Fairly Secret Army*. m. Sally; 1 s. Charles, 1 d. Harriet. Hobbies: squash, gardening, bird watching. Address: c/o Marmont Management, London. Birthsign: Gemini. **Favourite Place:** 'My home, then Venice, then Hong Kong.'

PARKIN, Leonard

Journalist/broadcaster, b. 2 June 1929 Thurnscoe, Yorks. Reporter for *Wakefield Express* series, *Yorkshire Observer*, Bradford *Telegraph* and *Argus* and *Yorkshire Evening News*. Joined BBC Radio *Newsreel* and TV news 1954; correspondent in Canada 1960, Washington DC 1963–65; *Panorama* and *24 Hours* 1965–67. ITN roving reporter and *News At Ten* newscaster since 1967. Has presented all ITN news programmes; political interviewer ITN election specials. Anchorman for special programmes incl coverage Brighton bombing. m. Barbara; 1 s. Jeremy. Hobbies: fly fishing, shooting, collecting antiques. Address: c/o ITN, London. Birthsign: Gemini. **Favourite Place:** 'A bed of nettles on a river bank in East Yorkshire. It's from there I cast the first fly to the first rising trout of the season.'

PARKINSON, Michael

TV presenter/interviewer, b. 28 March 1935 Ludworth, Yorks. Entered journalism via local paper, *The Guardian, Daily Express* and as columnist for *The Sunday Times*. TV incl: Granada's *Scene*; *Granada In The North*; *World In Action*; *What The Papers Say*; *24 Hours*; executive producer sporting documentaries with LWT; *Cinema*; presenter *Tea Break* with his wife Mary. Joined BBC TV to present own chat show *Parkinson*. In Australia 1979–81. Recent TV incl: *Good Morning Britain*; *Give Us A Clue*. Author of many books incl: *Cricket Mad*; *Parkinson's Lore*. m. TV presenter Mary Parkinson; 3 s. Andrew, Nicholas, Michael. Hobbies: cricket, loafing, cinema. Address: c/o Mark McCormack, London. Birthsign: Aries.

PARRY, Alan
Journalist/broadcaster, b. 20 Aug
1948 Liverpool. Started in
newspapers incl the Liverpool
Weekly News; *Evening Post*,
Wigan; Mercury Press Agency.
He then worked for Radio
Merseyside and BBC Radio
before joining BBC TV and then
ITV as a sports journalist. m.
Barbara; 2 s. Simon, Mark.
Hobbies: football, golf,
'drinking!'. Address: c/o John
Hockey Assocs, London.
Birthsign: Leo. **Favourite
Place:** 'On the Thames—a bit of
peace and quiet.'

PARSONS, Nicholas
Actor/compère/presenter, b. 10
Oct 1928 Grantham, Lincs.
Engineering apprentice, then
variety in Glasgow. Rep followed
by cabaret and revues in London.
Many film comedies in the 60s;
also much radio work incl
chairman for 18 years *Just A
Minute*. TV incl: Eric Barker
series (50s); straightman to
Arthur Haynes (60s); host of *Sale
Of The Century* since 1971.
Producer/director short film *Mad
Dogs And Cricketers*, also *A Fair
Way To Play* and *Relatively
Greek*. One-time holder after
dinner speech record of 11 hours.
Author of *Egg On The Face*. m.
actress Denise Bryer; 1 d. Suzy, 1
s. Justin. Hobbies: photography,
gardening, sport. Address: c/o
Richard Stone, London.
Birthsign: Libra. **Favourite
Place:** 'The Cotswolds. It
embodies in scenery, architecture
and character so much that is
typically English.'

PASCO, Richard, CBE
Actor, b. 18 July 1926 Barnes,
London. Began as student stage
manager at the Q Theatre,
London 1943. After war trained
at Central School of Speech and
Drama. With the Old Vic, Sir
Barry Jackson's Birmingham Rep
Company, Brook/Scofield
Hamlet Company, English Stage
Company, then Bristol Old Vic
and Theatre Royal, the RSC.
Films incl: *Room At The Top*;
Yesterday's Enemy; *Wagner*. TV
incl: *Let's Run Away To Africa*;
Pythons On The Mountains;
Sorrell & Son; *Arch Of Triumph*;
Drummonds. m. (1st) Greta
Watson (dis.), (2nd) actress
Barbara Leigh-Hunt; 1 s.
William (from 1st m.). Hobbies:
music, gardening, walking.
Address: c/o Leading Artists,
London. Birthsign: Cancer.
Favourite Place: 'I am drawn
to the Cornish coast to
contemplate the state of our
existence.'

PAXMAN, Jeremy
Presenter/reporter/writer, b. 11
May 1950 Leeds. After
Cambridge University, reporter
for BBC News, Northern
Ireland, then reporter for *Tonight*
and *Panorama* (1979–84).
Presenter *The Six O'clock News*
since 1984. TV incl: *The Bear
Next Door*. Film: *Called To
Account—How Roberto Calvi
Died*. Won Royal TV Society
Award for International Current
Affairs 1984. Books: *A Higher
Form Of Killing* (with Robert
Harris); *Through The Volcanoes*.
Hobbies: fly fishing, travel in
remote places, skiing. Address:
c/o BBC TV, London. Birthsign:
Taurus. **Favourite Place:** 'A
couple of miles on the upper
banks of the River Wharfe when
the trout are rising and the sun is
going down and the pub awaits.'

PECK, Lee

TV presenter/producer, b. 13 July 1953 Scarborough, Yorks. Worked on a pig farm, then in insurance and then as a journalist—edited *Wetherby News* aged 21. Joined Radio Tees then Radio Trent, producing and presenting. Joined TVS in Southampton 1981 as a news reporter, then co-presenter of *DJ*. Other TV incl: *No 73*; *Coast To Coast*; *Game For A Laugh*. m. (dis.). Hobbies: most sports, music, the company of close friends, travel. Address: c/o MPC Management, London. Birthsign: Cancer. **Favourite Place:** 'Lone Pine, Sierra Nevada. Desert—this is where the "great" Westerns were made. I had one of the best meals of my life there in real cowboy country, in the company of close mates.'

PEEL, John

Presenter, b. 31 Aug 1939 Heswall, The Wirral. Started career as a disc jockey for US radio and later joined BBC Radio 1, presenting his own show, and also worked for BBC World Service. Currently hosts *John Peel*, his thrice-weekly late night show on Radio 1. Has regularly hosted *Top Of The Pops* on TV. m. Sheila; 2 s. William, Thomas, 2 d. Alexandra, Florence. Hobbies: music, cycling. Address: c/o Shurwood Management, Woking. Birthsign: Virgo. **Favourite Place:** 'Anfield Road.'

PENHALIGON, Susan

Actress, b. 3 July 1949 Manila, Philippines. Brought up in England and trained at the Webber Douglas Academy of Dramatic Art. Wide rep experience incl Worthing, Manchester, Guildford, Brighton, Bromley and Open Space, London. Films incl: *No Sex Please, We're British*; *The Land That Time Forgot*; *Nasty Habits*; *Under Milk Wood*; *Leopard In The Snow*; *Private Road*; *Patrick*. TV incl: *Public Eye*; *Country Matters*; *Bouquet Of Barbed Wire*; *Fearless Frank*; *Call My Bluff*; *Give Us A Clue*; *The Taming Of The Shrew*; *A Fine Romance*; *A Kind Of Loving*; *Heather Ann*; *Remington Steele*; *A Kind Of Living* (presenter). 1 s. Truan. Hobby: acting. Address: c/o Jeremy Conway, London. Birthsign: Cancer. **Favourite Place:** 'The top of the island in St Ives–good view of the Atlantic, the rocks and St Ives.'

PENTELOW, Arthur

Actor, b. 14 Feb 1924 Rochdale. A cadet clerk in the police, but amateur dramatics in spare time. After Royal Navy during the war became a student teacher. Joined Bradford Civic Theatre School to train as an actor, then rep at Bristol Old Vic. In Orson Welles' *Othello* in London. Best known on TV as Henry Wilkes in *Emmerdale Farm*, which he has played since the series began in 1972. Films incl: *Privilege*; *Charlie Bubbles*; *United!* Other TV incl: *Z Cars*; *Armchair Theatre*; *The Troubleshooters*; *Coronation Street*; *Play For Today*. m. pottery teacher Jacqueline, 2 s. Nicholas, Simon. Hobbies: the countryside, gardening, tennis, music. Address: c/o Green & Underwood, London. Birthsign: Aquarius. **Favourite Place:** 'A garden with croquet mallets, a rural wood for bird watching–or a rural stream.'

PEPPARD, George
Actor, b. 1 Oct Detroit,
Michigan. Appeared on
Broadway in *Girls Of Summer*
and *The Pleasure Of His Company*.
His film career began in the 60s
in *Home From The Hill* and *Pork
Chop Hill*. Among his 25 films
are *Breakfast At Tiffany's*; *The
Carpetbaggers*; *The Blue Max*;
How The West Was Won; *Fall
Down Dead*; *Five Days From
Home*. His TV career incl: *Little
Moon Of Alban*; *Guilty Or*
Innocent; *The Sam Sheppard
Murder Case*; *Banacek*; *Doctor's
Hospital*. Plays John 'Hannibal'
Smith in *The A-Team*. m. artist
Alexis. Hobbies: fishing, hunting.
Address: c/o Rogers & Cowan,
7083 Hollywood Blvd,
Hollywood, California 90028.
Birthsign: Libra. **Favourite
Place:** 'I love to be in my new
home in Los Angeles with my
wife. I have such a wonderful
settled life now, I can't think of
any place I'd rather be.'

PERERA, Shyama
Producer/presenter/journalist, b.
4 March 1958 Moscow, Russia.
Started career at Fleet Street news
agency as a junior reporter.
Worked through local papers and
Daily Star before joining *The
Guardian* in 1981. Home news
journalist for two years. Presenter
and researcher for *Eastern Eye* for
C4; associate producer *Black On
Black* for C4. Presenter of LWT's
The Six O'Clock Show. Also
appeared on *What The Papers
Say*; *Loose Talk*; *Sunday Sunday*.
Hobbies: writing, reading, eating,
drinking, dancing, cinema.
Address: c/o LWT, London.
Birthsign: Pisces. **Favourite
Place:** 'Tintagel, Cornwall.
Wonderful cliffs, beautiful sea,
great for daydreaming an
afternoon away.'

PERLMAN, Rhea
Actress, b. 31 March Brooklyn,
New York. Took a degree in
drama and trained in off-
Broadway productions. Best
known for her role as Carla in
TV's *Cheers* but has also appeared
in *Taxi* and has made TV films
incl: *Mary Jane Harper Cried Last
Night*; *I Want To Keep My Baby*;
Intimate Strangers; *Having Babies
II*; *Drop Out Father*. m. actor
Danny DeVito; 1 d. Lucy Chet.
Hobbies: roller-skating, watching
films and TV, babies, vegetarian
cooking. Address: c/o Shapiro-
West and Assocs, 141 El Camino
Drive, Beverly Hills, California
90212. Birthsign: Aries.
Favourite Place: 'Our new
Hollywood Hills home, the first
we've ever owned.'

PERTWEE, Bill
Actor/comedian, b. 21 July 1926
Amersham. First ambition was to
be a cricketer, but entered show
business in concert party tours,
then variety tour with Jon
Pertwee. Stooged for comics incl
Beryl Reid, Charlie Chester, Dick
Emery. Numerous stage farces
incl: *There Goes The Bride*; *See
How They Run*; *Run For Your
Wife*. Radio: *It Sticks Out Half A
Mile*. TV: played Air Raid
Warden Hodges in *Dad's Army*.
m. Marion; 1 s. Jonathan.
Hobbies: cricket, DIY. Address:
c/o Richard Stone, London.
Birthsign: Leo. **Favourite
Place:** 'Anywhere in the home.
I'm a home bird and proud of it.'

PERTWEE, Jon

Actor/comedian, b. 7 July 1919 London. Trained at RADA, then rep incl Jersey and Brighton. War service in Royal Navy then radio. Recent theatre: *Irene*. Films incl: *A Funny Thing Happened On The Way To The Forum*; *The Ugly Duckling*; *Nearly A Nasty Accident*; *The House That Dripped Blood*; *Mr Drake's Duck*; *One Of Our Dinosaurs Is Missing*; *There's A Girl In My Soup*; *Oh Clarence*. TV incl: *Three Of A Kind*; *Doctor Who*; *Whodunnit?*; *Worzel Gummidge*. Noted for his range of accents and voices. m. (1st) actress Jean Marsh (dis.), (2nd) Ingeborg Rhoesa; 1 d. Dariel, 1 s. Sean (both from 2nd m.). Hobby: skin-diving. Address: c/o Richard Stone, London. Birthsign: Cancer.

PETTIFER, Julian

Presenter/reporter, b. 21 July 1935 Malmesbury, Wilts. Started with Southern TV 1958; joined *Tonight* 1962; war correspondent for *24 Hours* 1965 and moved to *Panorama* 1969. As BBC reporter been to Vietnam, Aden, Hong Kong, the Suez Canal zone and Northern Ireland. Documentary programmes incl: *90 South*; *War Without End*; *Millionaire*; *Vietnam—The Other World*; *The Regiment*; *The Country Game*; *The World About Us*; *The China Programme*; *The History Of Civil Aviation*; *Nature Watch*. Most recent TV incl: *Automania*; *Busman's Holiday*. Hobby: travel. Address: c/o Curtis Brown, London. Birthsign: Cancer. **Favourite Place:** 'A cottage overlooking a small, deserted beach with no telephone and no traffic—and I'm not saying where it is!'

PHILBIN, Maggie

Broadcaster, b. 23 June 1955 Manchester. After taking a degree in English and Drama, has appeared on TV incl: *Swap Shop*; *The Show Me Show*; *Tomorrow's World*; *The Saturday Picture Show*; *The Quest*. m. TV presenter Keith Chegwin. Hobbies: riding, reading, eating, films. Address: c/o Dave Winslett Entertainments, Purley. Birthsign: Cancer. **Favourite Place:** 'Home—on a good day when the roof isn't leaking, or anywhere hot when I haven't got anything to do!'

PHILLIPS, Sian

Actress, b. 14 May Carmarthenshire. Began career in Wales, then joined BBC Repertory Company and Arts Council National Company (Welsh). Then trained at RADA and in rep. West End incl: *You Never Can Tell*; *Pal Joey*; *Dear Liar*; *Peg*; *Love Affair*. Films incl: *Goodbye, Mr Chips*; *Murphy's War*; *Clash Of The Titans*; *Dune*. TV incl: *How Green Was My Valley*; *I, Claudius*; *Tinker, Tailor, Soldier, Spy*; *Crime And Punishment*; *Winston Churchill—The Wilderness Years*; *Smiley's People*; *Barriers*; *Language And Landscape*; *A Painful Case*; *George Borrow*. Hon Doc Litt University of Wales. m. (1st) actor Peter O'Toole (dis.), (2nd) Robin Sachs; 2 d. Kate, Pat (both from 1st m.). Hobby: gardening. Address: c/o Saraband Assocs, London. Birthsign: Taurus. **Favourite Place:** 'The Black Mountain foothills.'

PHILLIPS, Stephen J
Arts Correspondent, b. 28 May 1947 Eastbourne, East Sussex. Reporter, feature writer and critic for *Yorkshire Post*. TV and theatre critic for *Daily Express*. Joined BBC TV North as reporter/presenter. Became administrator Prospect Theatre Company; director of various theatre productions and chairman of Janet Smith and Dancers and Tricycle Theatre, London. From 1982, been Britain's first arts correspondent on a news programme, for *C4 News* at ITN. Hobbies: photography, travel, work. Address: c/o ITN, London. Birthsign: Gemini. **Favourite Place:** 'The view of the Nile from the terrace of the Cataract Hotel in Aswan–this year anyway.'

PHILPOTT, David
Weather presenter, b. 21 March 1930 Birmingham. After attending Birmingham University, spent over 30 years providing weather information to the Royal Navy. Has presented weather bulletins for TV-am since its beginning in 1983. m. Margaret; 2 d. Hilary, Suzannah, 4 s. Richard, Jonathon, Jeremy, Oliver. Hobbies: meteorology, walking, gardening, finance, music. Address: c/o TV-am, London. Birthsign: Aries. **Favourite Place:** 'Tresco, Isles of Scilly–no cars, few people, a variation of landscape from tropical garden, heath, beach to moor in two square miles.'

PHOENIX, Patricia
Actress/writer, b. 26 Nov 1923 Manchester. Started career in radio plays at 11, went into theatre at 19. With Manchester Arts Theatre Company and rep. Theatre incl: *Suddenly Last Summer; The Miracle Worker; The L-Shaped Room*. TV incl: *Coronation Street* (from first episode in 1960, with a two-year break, until 1983). Since leaving *Coronation Street*, has toured in theatre, appeared on chat shows and on TV-am. m. (1st) Peter Marsh (dis.), (2nd) Alan Browning (dec.). Hobbies: work, travel, reading, tapestries. Address: c/o Saraband Assocs, Manchester. Birthsign: Sagittarius. **Favourite Place:** 'Anywhere near the sea—islands and Cornwall.'

PICKERING, Ronald
Commentator/compère/journalist, b. 4 May 1930 London. Attended Carnegie College of Physical Education and Leicester University. Spent six years teaching, six years as National Athletic Coach, then Recreation Director Lee Valley Park. TV journalist for 20 years: Five Olympic Games for BBC; *The Superstars; We Are The Champions*. TV documentaries: *African Runner; Cuba Sport And Revolution; China–The Long Wait Of The Dragon; South African Sport And Apartheid*. m. former Olympic and European long jump champion Jean Desforges; 1 d. Kim, 1 s. Shaun. Hobbies: golf, photography. Address: c/o Bagenal Harvey, London. Birthsign: Taurus. **Favourite Place:** 'A sauna bath at the end of my usual 70 hour week.'

PICKLES, Christina
Actress, b. 17 Feb Yorkshire. The niece of actor Wilfred Pickles, she trained at RADA and pursued her career in the US, appearing on Broadway and at the Joe Papps Shakespeare Festival. Is best known as Nurse Helen Rosenthal in TV's *St Elsewhere*. Other TV incl: *Lou Grant*; *The Andros Targets*; *The White Shadow*; *The Guiding Light*; *Another World*. Hobbies: running, tennis, gardening, reading, cooking pasta. Address: c/o J Michael Bloom Agency, 9200 Sunset Blvd, Suite 1210, Los Angeles, California 90069. Birthsign: Aquarius. **Favourite Place:** New England State.

PIGOTT-SMITH, Tim
Actor, b. 13 May 1946 Rugby. Trained at Bristol Old Vic Theatre School and appeared with the company. Rep at Nottingham, Birmingham and Cambridge and with the Prospect Company, London. Member of the Royal Shakespeare Company 1972–75. Recent theatre: *Bengal Lancer*. Films incl: *Clash Of The Titans*; *Escape To Victory*; *Richard's Things*. TV incl: *Eustace And Hilda*; *Lost Boys*; *Measure For Measure*; *Henry IV (I)*; *No, Mama, No*; *Hannah*; *Winston Churchill—The Wilderness Years*; *Fame Is The Spur*; *I Remember Nelson*; *The Jewel In The Crown* (for which he won the *TV Times* Top Ten Actor Award 1984); *Struggle*; *Man In A Fog*. m. Pamela Miles; 1 s. Tom. Hobbies: reading, music, yoga. Address: c/o Jeremy Conway, London. Birthsign: Taurus. **Favourite Place:** 'Bed.'

PIVARO, Nigel
Actor, b. 11 Dec 1959 Manchester. Trained at RADA and has since appeared on stage at the Theatre Royal, Stratford-upon-Avon and in *Rich And Famous* at Community Theatre. Now appears regularly in Granada TV's *Coronation Street*. Hobbies: international travel, most fitness sports. Address: c/o Peter Graham at Crouch Assocs, London. Birthsign: Sagittarius. **Favourite Place:** 'The Tomb of the Seven Sleepers, Ephesus, Turkey. The essence of time encapsulated.'

PLANER, Nigel
Actor/writer/comedian, b. 22 Feb 1953 London. Trained at LAMDA and has appeared on stage at Traverse Theatre, Leeds Playhouse, Young Vic. In original cast of *Evita*. Co-founder of London's Comic Strip and original Comedy Store comedian. As actor, films incl: *Yellowbeard*; *Brazil*; *Supergrass*. TV incl: *Shine On Harvey Moon*; *The Young Ones*; *The Comic Strip Presents . . .*; *Roll Over Beethoven*. As writer/comedian creator of 'Neil' character in *The Young Ones* on TV, and numerous live appearances as Neil incl Hammersmith Odeon in London. Hit single: *Hole In My Shoe*. Co-author: *Neil's Book Of The Dead*. Sketch material for TV's *Not The Nine O'Clock News*. Co-author: *The Comic Strip* film. Address: c/o Fraser & Dunlop, London. Birthsign: Pisces, Aquarius rising.

PLUMB, Gwendoline Jean, MBE

Actress/announcer, b. Sydney, Australia. Professional stage debut 1948 in *See How They Run*. Numerous theatre appearances incl: *Entertaining Mr Sloane*; *Blithe Spirit*; *Steaming*. Own radio programme for 26 years covering major events and interviewing celebrities. Starred in *Blue Hills*, Australia's longest-running radio serial, and in TV's *The Young Doctors*. Also own TV show and many guest appearances. Hobbies: swimming, reading, travel, entertaining. Address: c/o ICS, 147A King St, Sydney 2001 Australia. Birthsign: Leo. **Favourite Place:** 'My sundeck—to sunbathe, look out at the sea, read and feed the wild birds.'

POLLARD, Su

Actress/comedienne/singer, b. 7 Nov 1949 Nottingham. Numerous cabaret appearances and concerts. In an all-girl singing group Midnight News. Theatre incl: *The Desert Song*; *Rose Marie*; *Godspell*; *Big Sin City*; *Oh Mr Porter*; *Grease*. Also many pantomimes incl *Aladdin* at Manchester. TV debut *Opportunity Knocks*. TV since incl: *Summer Royal*; *The Comedians*; *Golden Gala*; *Get Set For Summer*; *Clock On*; *The Saturday Show*; *Two Up Two Down*; as Peggy in *Hi-De-Hi!* (also on stage). m. teacher Peter Keogh. Hobbies: talking, dancing, Mills & Boon books. Address: c/o Richard Stone, London. Birthsign: Scorpio. **Favourite Place:** 'I haven't got one. I like everywhere!'

PORTER, Eric

Actor, b. 8 April 1928 London. Started career at Stratford-upon-Avon then with companies run by Lewis Casson, Donald Wolfit, Barry Jackson and John Gielgud before Bristol and London Old Vics. Appeared in nearly all of Shakespeare's plays. Many films incl: *The Belstone Fox*; *Callan*; *Little Lord Fauntleroy*. Fame aged 40 as Soames in TV's *The Forsyte Saga*. Other TV incl: *Anna Karenina*; *Why Didn't They Ask Evans?*; *Churchill And The Generals*; *Hamlet*, *The Crucible*; *Winston Churchill—The Wilderness Years*; *The Jewel In The Crown*; *Oliver Twist*. Hobbies: woodwork, gardening. Address: c/o London Management, London. Birthsign: Aries. **Favourite Place:** 'A calm anchorage at sunset after a quiet day's sail.'

POWELL, Peter

Disc jockey, b. 24 March 1951 Stourbridge, West Mids. Organised school concerts, appeared on local radio and ran a mobile disco before joining Radio Luxembourg, where he stayed for three and a half years. Joined BBC Radio 1977 and presenter of weekend breakfast show on Radio 1. Is a regular presenter of *Top Of The Pops*. Other TV incl *Seaside Special* and *ORS 85*. Is a director of the charity Radio Lollipop and vice president of National Assoc Youth Clubs. Hobbies: driving power boats, water-skiing, squash, tennis, football, photography, driving a Porsche. Address: c/o BBC Radio 1, London. Birthsign: Aries. **Favourite Place:** 'The village of Aberdovey in Wales – in particular the wharf, where I used to fish as a youngster.'

POWELL, Robert

Actor, b. 1 June 1944 Salford, Lancs. Theatre incl: *Travesties*; *Terra Nova*; *Private Dick*. Films incl: *Mahler*; *Tommy*; *The Thirty-Nine Steps*; *Harlequin*; *Jane Austen In Manhattan*; *Imperative*; *The Jigsaw Man*. Since appearing in *Doomwatch* in 1970, TV incl: *Shelley*; *Jude The Obscure*; *Mr Rolls And Mr Royce*; *Looking For Clancy*; *Jesus Of Nazareth*; *Mrs Warren's Profession*; *You Never Can Tell*; *Pygmalion*; *Frankenstein*. m. Barbara; 1 s. Barnaby, 1 d. Katherine. Hobbies: cricket, tennis, golf. Address: c/o ICM, London. Birthsign: Gemini. **Favourite Place:** 'The snooker room at the Eccentric Club. Quietest place in London. That and Lord's.'

PRAED, Michael

Actor, b. 1 April 1960 Glos. Trained at the Guildhall School of Music and Drama, London. Theatre incl a season at Southampton and at Civic Theatre, Chesterfield. Played leading role in West End production *The Pirates Of Penzance* for a year, and in *Abbacadabra* at Lyric Theatre, Hammersmith. Also in *The Three Musketeers* on Broadway. TV incl: *The Gentle Touch*; *The Professionals*; *Rothko*; *Video Entertainers*. Played Robin in *Robin Of Sherwood* and is Prince Michael of Moldavia in TV's *Dynasty*. Address: c/o London Management, London. Birthsign: Aries.

PRESLEY, Priscilla Beaulieu

Actress, b. 24 May Brooklyn, New York. Attended school in Germany, where she lived until moving to US to marry Elvis Presley. Studied acting with Milton Katselas and co-hosted TV series *Those Amazing Animals*. Now well known as Jenna in TV's *Dallas*. Book: *Elvis And Me*. m. Elvis Presley (dis. 1973); 1 d. Lisa Marie. Hobbies: karate (a brown belt), modern jazz, exercising. Address: c/o William Morris Agency, 151 El Camino Drive, Beverly Hills, California 90212. Birthsign: Gemini. **Favourite Place:** 'I love the wilderness—the outback of Australia, safaris in Africa.'

PRICE, Andy

Presenter/reporter/researcher, b. 17 Aug 1943 Woking, Surrey. Joined Westward TV, then BBC TV South. Spent 12 years with BBC Radio 4 incl *Today* and *You And Yours*. TV incl: *The 6 O'Clock Show*; *Wheeltracks*. m. Larraine; 2 s. Sam, Joe, 1 d. Anna. Hobbies: reading modern fiction, riding bicycles ferociously. Address: c/o PVA Management, London. Birthsign: Leo. **Favourite Place:** 'The view from the Royal Kennels in Windsor Great Park—"essential England"—passed during my training run near my home.'

PRINCIPAL, Victoria
Actress/authoress, b. 3 Jan 1950
Fukuoka, Japan. Brought up in
Ruislip, Middx, where her father
was stationed with US Air Force.
Studied ballet at Royal Academy,
London and spent her teens in
London before going to
Hollywood, where she studied
law. A former Miss Miami, films
incl: *The Life And Times Of Judge
Roy Bean*, *Earthquake* and
Vigilante Force until she lost
interest. Tempted back to acting
by a part in *Fantasy Island* on TV
which led to her role of Pam in
Dallas. Other TV incl: *The
Pleasure Palace*; *Not Just Another
Affair*; *Love American Style*.
Books: *The Body Principal*; *The
Beauty Principal*. m. Christopher
Skinner (dis.). Hobbies: business,
real estate, exercise, swimming.
Address: c/o ICM, 8899 Beverly
Blvd, Los Angeles, California
90048. Birthsign: Capricorn.
Favourite Place: 'Europe—
Paris, London, Gstaad.'

PRINGLE, Bryan
Actor, b. 19 Jan 1935 Glascote,
Staffs. Trained at RADA and was
with the Old Vic 1955–57, rep at
Birmingham, Nottingham. West
End theatre incl: *Long And The
Short And The Tall*; *Fings Aint
What They Used To Be*; *One
More River*; *Big Soft Nellie*; *Lower
Depths*; *The Birthday Party*; *End
Game*; *Billy*; *The Passion*. Films
incl: *Saturday Night, Sunday
Morning*; *HMS Defiant*; *The Boy
Friend*; *Bullshot*; *Brazil*. TV incl:
Portsmouth Defence; *Dustbinmen*;
On Giant's Shoulders; *Love Story*;
Still Waters; *Diary Of A Nobody*;
Paradise Postponed; *Auf
Wiedersehen Pet*. m. actress Anne
Jameson; 1 d. Kate, 1 s. Craster.
Address: c/o Plant & Froggatt,
London. Birthsign: Capricorn.
Favourite Place: 'The Lake
District, wet or dry.'

PROSKY, Robert
Actor, b. 13 Dec Philadelphia.
Trained at the American Theater
Wing School and Arena Stage,
Washington DC. Films incl:
Thief; *Christine*; *The Keep*; *The
Lords Of Discipline*; *The Natural*.
TV film: *Carney Case*. TV mini
series: *World War II*; *Adams
Chronicles*. Best known as Sgt
Stan Jablonski in TV's *Hill Street
Blues*. m. Ida; 3 s. Hobby:
restoring old houses and
furniture. Address: c/o Smith,
Freedman and Assocs, 123 N San
Vincente Blvd, Beverly Hills,
California 90211. Birthsign:
Sagittarius.

PYNE, Frederick
Actor, b. 30 Dec 1936 London.
Started as a farmer in Cheshire
and Cambridgeshire. He signed
on with the RAF and became
interested in the theatre. Trained
at RADA, then rep and four years
at the National Theatre at the Old
Vic 1966–70. TV incl:
Crossroads; *Dixon Of Dock Green*;
Justice; *Emmerdale Farm*. Hobbies:
music, gardening, foreign travel.
Address: c/o Yorkshire TV,
Leeds. Birthsign: Capricorn.
Favourite Place: 'Durham
Cathedral–the most perfect
Norman building on a fantastic
site.'

QUAYLE, Anna

Actress/writer, b. 6 Oct 1937 Birmingham. Trained at RADA after touring in Douglas Quayle's Company (her actor/producer father) for whom she made stage debut aged four. Theatre incl: *Full Circle* (which she wrote); *Out Of Bounds*; *Pal Joey*; *Kings And Clowns*; Old Vic season 1984; *The Boy Friend*. Films incl: *Chitty Chitty Bang Bang*; *SOS Titanic*; *The Seven Per Cent Solution*; *Towers Of Babel*. TV incl: *Henry V*; *Brideshead Revisited*; *Father Charlie*; *Rolling Home*; *Marjorie And Men*; *Mapp And Lucia*. m. Donald Baker; 1 d. Katy Nova. Hobbies: collecting books, exploring old buildings, Siamese cats (she has five). Address: c/o Green & Underwood, London. Birthsign: Libra. **Favourite Place:** 'St Ives, Cornwall, because it is beautiful, relaxing and I'm always happy there. A source of inspiration and peace.'

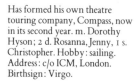

QUAYLE, Sir Anthony, CBE, KBE

Actor, b. 7 Sept 1913 Ainsdale, Lancs. Trained at RADA. Numerous theatre appearances, the most recent incl: *The Clandestine Marriage*; *After The Ball Is Over*. Films incl: *The Guns Of Navarone*; *Ice Cold In Alex*; *Lawrence Of Arabia*; *Anne Of A Thousand Days* (Oscar nomination); *The Tamarind Seed*. TV incl: *Moses The Lawgiver*; *Masada*; *The Testament Of John*. Has formed his own theatre touring company, Compass, now in its second year. m. Dorothy Hyson; 2 d. Rosanna, Jenny, 1 s. Christopher. Hobby: sailing. Address: c/o ICM, London. Birthsign: Virgo.

QUAYLE, John

Actor, b. 21 Dec 1938 Lincoln. Trained at RADA and has worked extensively in rep. London theatre incl: *Habeas Corpus*; *When We Are Married*; *Watch On The Rhine*; *Noises Off*. Films incl: *Charles And Diana*; *Privates On Parade*. TV incl: many comedy series; *Upstairs, Downstairs*; *The Duchess Of Duke Street*; *Jumbo Spencer*; *The King's Dragon*; *Nanny*; *Pig In The Middle*; *Jane*; *This Office Life*; *Marjorie And Men*. m. Petronell. Hobbies: horses, donkeys, post and railing paddocks. Address: c/o Barry Burnett, London. Birthsign: Sagittarius. **Favourite Place:** 'A bench under an oak tree in Dorset, overlooking my lake.'

QUICK, Diana

Actress, b. 23 Nov 1946 Kent. Member of National Youth Theatre aged 16. Has appeared at London's Royal Court Theatre; Bristol Old Vic; Open Space; Royal Exchange; Soho Poly; Lyric, Hammersmith; Greenwich; West End. Also National Theatre and Royal Shakespeare Company. Films incl: *Nicholas And Alexandra*; *The Duellists*; *The Big Sleep*; *The Odd Job*; *Ordeal By Innocence*; *1919*. TV incl: *Christ Recrucified*; *Complete And Utter History Of Britain*; *At Last It's Friday*; *Napoleon And Love*; *Mr Garrick And Mrs Woffington*; *Hanging On*; *Brideshead Revisited*; *The Woman In White*. Hobbies: reading, writing, gardening, cooking, skiing, restoring furniture. Address: c/o James Sharkey, London. Birthsign: Scorpio. **Favourite Place:** 'Macchu Picchu, Peru. The most haunting place I've ever been.'

QUILLEY, Denis

Actor, b. 25 Dec 1927 London. Trained with Birmingham rep, where he made his debut 1945. Numerous theatre appearances, the most recent incl: *Death Trap*; *Sweeney Todd*; *Antony And Cleopatra*. Films incl: *Life At The Top*; *Anne Of The Thousand Days*; *Evil Under The Sun*; *King David*; *Privates On Parade*. TV incl: *Murder In The Cathedral*; *Contrabandits* (Australia); *The Crucible*; *Honky-Tonk Heroes*; *Sunday Thriller*; *Tales Of The Unexpected*; *Gladstone In No 10*; *Masada*; *A D*; *Murder Of A Moderate Man*. m. Stella Chapman; 2 d. Sarah, Joanna, 1 s. David. Hobbies: piano, flute, cello, walking. Address: c/o Leading Players, London. Birthsign: Capricorn. **Favourite Place:** 'Hampstead Heath—an oasis of beauty only minutes from the West End of London.'

QUINTEN, Christopher

Actor, b. 12 July Middlesbrough. Went to a secondary modern school. He has played the part of Brian Tilsley in Granada TV's *Coronation Street* since Dec 1978. Hobbies: golf, fitness training and gymnastics, reading. Address: c/o Granada TV, Manchester. Birthsign: Cancer. **Favourite Place:** 'A golf course on a summer's day. It's so peaceful and whatever pressures you have seem to just disappear.'

QUIRKE, Pauline

Actress, b. 8 July 1959 London. Drama training at Anna Scher Theatre and while still at school appeared on TV in *Dixon Of Dock Green*; *Kids About Town*; *Days Of Hope* and *You Must Be Joking*. Turning point in her career as the autistic child in *Jenny Can't Work Any Faster*. Other TV incl: *Pauline's Quirkes*; *Pauline's People*; *Baby Talk*; *A Name For The Day*; *The Story Of The Treasure Seekers*; *Shine On Harvey Moon*; *Angels*. Hobbies: reading autobiographies, watching plays, decorating, eating out. Address: c/o Anna Scher Theatre Management, London. Birthsign: Cancer. **Favourite Place:** 'London and—Tipperary, because it's where my family live.'

RAGIN, John S

Actor, b. Newark, New Jersey. Won a scholarship to study acting at the Old Vic and then Central School of Speech and Drama in London. He also studied acting in New York under Lee Strasberg. Many appearances on stage, incl on Broadway: *Hostage*; *JB*. Films incl: *Earthquake*; *Paralax View*; *Marooned*; *Doctor's Wives*; *Bob And Carol And Ted And Alice*; *Alice B Toklas*. TV incl: *Cannon*; *Name Of The Game*; *Ironside*; *The Killer Bees*; *Old Man Who Cried Wolf*; as Dr Asten in *Quincy*; *Sons And Daughters*. m. Frances. Hobbies: fishing, singing. Address: c/o Talent Agency, 261 S Robertson Blvd, Beverly Hills, Los Angeles, California. Birthsign: Taurus. **Favourite Place:** 'Shark River, Manasquan, New Jersey. A lovely and exciting place to fish, with youthful memories.'

RANTZEN, Esther

TV journalist, b. 22 June 1940 Berkhamsted, Herts. Went to Oxford University and started career in radio studio management, TV research and production. First appeared on TV as a reporter on *Braden's Week* and went on to produce and present *That's Life!* (since 1973) and *That's Family Life*. Also producer/reporter for *The Big Time*. m. independent TV producer/writer Desmond Wilcox; 2 d. Emily, Rebecca, 1 s. Joshua. Address: c/o Noel Gay, London. Birthsign: Cancer. **Favourite Place:** 'The New Forest.'

RAT, Roland

Actor/singer/songwriter/dancer/ genius, b. 12 March under King's Cross Station, London. No formal training or education but a natural performer and has appeared on TV-am in *Rat On The Road*; *Roland's Winter Wonderland*; *Roland Goes East*; *Roland Rat In Cinderella*. Hobbies: reading his fan mail, watching videos of himself. Address: c/o TV-am, London. Birthsign: Pisces. **Favourite Place:** 'Hollywood. I've never been, but it's crying out for new talent like me.'

RAVENS, Jan

Actress/comedienne/broadcaster/ director, b. 14 May 1958 Bebington, Merseyside. Trained as a drama teacher at Cambridge and was a member of Cambridge Footlights (first woman president). Co-wrote and performed in *Ha Bloody Ha* theatre revue and has directed a musical revue for Chichester Festival. Started in radio as a producer for BBC Radio comedy, then as a performer incl: *Extra Dry Sherrin*; *Just A Minute*; *Good Timing*. Has appeared on TV in *Just Amazing*; *Getting In Shape*; *Carrots Lib*; *The Lenny Henry Show*; *The Kenny Everett Show*; *Friday People*; voices for *Spitting Image*. m. comedy singer/ songwriter Steve Brown. Hobbies: music, dance, reading. Address: c/o Richard Stone, London. Birthsign: Taurus. **Favourite Place:** 'Any out of season English seaside town.'

RAWLE, Jeff

Actor/writer, b. 20 July 1951 Birmingham. Worked at Sheffield Playhouse until he went to the London Academy of Dramatic Art. A few weeks after leaving, chosen to play Billy Liar in TV series. West End theatre incl: *Equus*; *Once A Catholic*; *Bent*; *Butley*. Has worked in radio incl *Still Life*, *The Morning Story*. TV incl: *Beryl's Lot*; *The Cost Of Loving*; *Van Der Valk*; *Send In The Girls*; *Wilde Alliance*; *Leave It To Charlie*; *Singles*; *Juliet Bravo*; *Whose Child*; *Angels*; *Bergerac*; *Doctor Who*; *Singles Weekend*; *Country And Irish*. Hobbies: playing musical instruments, filling in VAT forms. Address: c/o Louis Hammond Management, London. Birthsign: Cancer. **Favourite Place:** 'Crackington Haven, St Gennys, Cornwall. Apart from being a beautiful place, my family has lived there since 1485.'

RAY, Robin

Writer/presenter, b. London. Trained at RADA and extensive experience in radio and TV. Radio incl: classical music programmes on Radio 3 and 4 such as *A Touch Of Genius*; first classical music programme on commercial radio, *The Robin Ray Collection*, for Capital. TV (more than 500 shows for BBC) incl: *Face The Music*; *The Movie Quiz*; *Music In Camera*; *Masters Of The Keyboard*; *The Lively Arts*; *Robin Ray's Picture Gallery*; *Cabbages And Kings*; *Film Buff Of The Year*. Also written and presented documentaries. Stage work incl *Tomfoolery*, and is associate director Meadowbank Theater, Detroit, US. Several books incl: *Words On Music*. m. Susan Stranks; 1 s. Rupert. Hobbies: cinema, music, TV. Address: c/o Roger Hancock, London. Birthsign: Virgo. **Favourite Place:** 'By the sea.'

RAYNER, Claire

Journalist/agony aunt/author, b. 22 Jan 1931 London. Trained as an SRN and midwife. Radio incl: *Woman's Hour*; *Schools*; *Today*; *Contact*; a regular spot on the *Michael Aspel Show*, Capital Radio. TV incl: Family Advice slot on *Pebble Mill*; co-presenter *Kitchen Garden*; *Claire Rayner's Casebook*; *Breakfast Time*. Author of 70 books incl medical subjects, childcare and fiction. Agony aunt for *Woman's Own* and *The Sunday Mirror*. m. Desmond Rayner; 1 d. Amanda, 2. s. Adam, Jason. Hobbies: cooking, party-giving, reading, talking, swimming. Address: c/o Box 125, Harrow, Middx HA1 3XE. Birthsign: Aquarius. **Favourite Place:** 'A hot, bubble-filled bath. Beside the bath a pile of warm, fluffy towels. There is also a control panel for radio/record player. Thus equipped I can spend up to an hour in peace and comfort.'

REARDON, Ray, MBE

Professional snooker player, b. 8 Oct 1932 Tredegar, Gwent. Turned professional in 1967 and has won all of the top snooker titles, apart from Coral UK. World Professional Snooker Champion for six years. Welsh champion 1984. m. Susan; 1 d. Melanie, 1 s. Darren. Hobbies: golf, music, collecting unusual seals. Address: c/o WPBSA Headquarters, Bristol. Birthsign: Libra. **Favourite Place:** 'Old Beams Restaurant, Waterhouses, Staffs. Marvellous food, superb setting.'

REED, Donna

Actress, b. 27 Jan 1921 Denison, Iowa. Started her successful film career in 1941 in *The Get-Away*. Many films since incl: *It's A Wonderful Life*; *The Stratton Story*; *The Picture Of Dorian Gray*; *Shadow Of The Thin Man*; *The Courtship Of Andy Hardy*; *From Here To Eternity* (Academy Award Best Supporting Actress 1953); *The Last Time I Saw Paris*; *Ransom*. Joined the cast of TV's *Dallas* as the new Miss Ellie. Other TV incl: *The Donna Reed Show*; *The Best Place To Be*; *The Love Boat*. m. (1st) make-up artist Bill Tuttle, (2nd) producer Tony Owen, (3rd) Grover Asmus; 2 d. Penny, Mary, 2 s. Timothy, Tony. Hobbies: geneology, photography. Address: c/o Triad Artists, 10100 Santa Monica Blvd, Los Angeles, California 90067. Birthsign: Aquarius. **Favourite Place:** 'I love Paris, and going back to see family and friends in Iowa.'

REES, Ken

TV correspondent, b. 26 Jan 1944 Cardiff, Wales. Worked as a newscaster for HTV Wales, then reporter with HTV Bristol. He joined ITN in 1978 and became their northern correspondent 1979–82, Washington correspondent 1985. m. Lynne; 1 d. Samantha, 1 s. Christian. Hobbies: work, old films, reading on planes. Address: c/o ITN, London. Birthsign: Aquarius. **Favourite Place:** 'Anywhere in Wales with my family and friends, because there really is no place quite like home.'

REES, Roger

Actor, b. 5 May 1944 Aberwystwyth, Wales. Trained as a fine artist at Slade School of Fine Art in London before taking up acting. Royal Shakespeare Company debut 1966 in *The Taming Of The Shrew*. Numerous other plays incl: *Much Ado About Nothing*; *Othello*; *Major Barbara*; *Macbeth*; *Cymbeline*; *Twelfth Night*; *The Suicide*; *The Birthday Party*; *She Stoops to Conquer*; *The Importance Of Being Earnest*. Played title role of *Nicholas Nickleby* in RSC production in London, New York (where he won a Tony Award) and on TV. Recent theatre incl: *A Christmas Carol*; *Hamlet*. Films incl: *Star 80*. TV incl: *Under Western Eyes*; *Bouquet Of Barbed Wire*; *Saigon*; *Imaginary Friends*; *The Ebony Tower*. Hobby: riding. Address: c/o ICM, London. Birthsign: Taurus. **Favourite Place:** 'The back of my neck—I've not got a sight of it yet.'

REGALBUTO, Joe

Actor, b. 14 Aug 1949 Brooklyn, New York. Trained at the Academy of Dramatic Arts, in regional theatre and in the New York Shakespeare Festival. Best known for his role in TV's *Street Hawk*. Films incl: *Missing*; *Lassiter*; *Star Chamber*; *Six Weeks*. TV incl: *The Associates*; *Barney Miller*; *Mork And Mindy*. m. Rosemary; 2 s. Nicholas, Michael, 1 d. Gina. Hobbies: photography, cooking Italian food. Address: c/o Triad Artists, 10100 Santa Monica Blvd, Los Angeles, California 90067. Birthsign: Virgo. **Favourite Place:** 'Rome.'

REGAN, Brian

Actor, b. 2 Oct 1957 Liverpool. Went to Yewtree Comprehensive School. Trained at the Liverpool Playhouse. Appeared in many productions at the Liverpool Playhouse and on TV in *Murphy's Mob* and as Terry Sullivan in C4's soap opera *Brookside* since 1983. Hobbies: shooting, football (has played for Liverpool FC), classical music. Address: c/o Brookside Productions Ltd, Liverpool. Birthsign: Libra. **Favourite Place:** 'Greece, because it's cheap and hot and it's got loads of booze.'

REID, Beryl

Actress, b. 17 June 1920 Hereford. First appearance in a concert party in Bridlington 1936. Well known as Monica in radio's *Educating Archie*. Worked in TV, radio, clubs, variety and revues before first serious stage play, *The Killing Of Sister George* (1965) then *Entertaining Mr Sloane*. Recent theatre incl: *School For Scandal*; *Gigi*. Films incl: *The Belles Of St Trinian's*; *Yellowbeard*; *Doctor And The Devils*. TV incl: *The Rivals*; *Father, Dear Father*; *Smike*; *The Apple Cart*; *When We Are Married*; *Tinker, Tailor. Soldier, Spy*; *Minder*; *Late Starter*. m. (1st) Bill Worsley (dis.), (2nd) musician Derek Franklin (dis.). Hobbies: gardening, cooking, driving. Address: c/o Eric Braun, Twickenham. Birthsign: Gemini. **Favourite Place:** Honeypot Cottage on the Thames, described in her autobiography *So Much Love*.

REITEL, Enn

Actor, b. 21 June Forfar, Scotland. Trained at Central School of Speech and Drama. TV incl: *Misfits*; *The Further Adventures Of Lucky Jim*; *The Optimist*; *Mog*; *Spitting Image*. Hobby: cartooning. Address: c/o James Sharkey Assocs, London. Birthsign: Gemini. **Favourite Place:** 'Sandown Park–the first racecourse I ever went to, and I love going racing.'

RICE, Anneka

TV presenter/journalist, b. 4 Oct 1958 Cowbridge, Wales. From 1979–82 worked in Hong Kong in radio, on TV as a newscaster and producer and edited a children's book on Hong Kong. She also worked as a copy writer and PR consultant. In the UK, TV has included numerous guest appearances and presenter on programmes incl: *CBTV*; *Treasure Hunt*; *Sporting Chance*; *Show Business*; *Family Trees*; *Wish You Were Here . . .?*; *Names And Games*; *Driving Force*; *World Circus Championships*. Hobbies: tennis, running, weight-training, theatre. Address: c/o Arlington Enterprises, London. Birthsign: Libra. **Favourite Place:** 'The garden of New Oriental Hotel, Sri Lanka—a luxuriant jungle surrounding a crystal-clear swimming pool.'

RICHARD, Cliff, OBE

Singer, b. 14 Oct 1940 Lucknow, India. Came to England aged seven. On leaving school worked as a clerk. First TV *Oh Boy!* series in 1958 with The Shadows. Films incl: *Serious Charge*; *Expresso Bongo*; *The Young Ones*; *Summer Holiday*; *Wonderful Life*; *Finders Keepers*; *Two A Penny*; *Take Me High*; *His Land*. Has had over 100 hit records. First record: *Move It* (1958). No 1 hit: *We Don't Talk Anymore*. Gold discs: *Living Doll*; *The Young Ones*; *The Next Time*; *Lucky Lips*; *Congratulations*; *Power To All Our Friends*; *Devil Woman*; *We Don't Talk Anymore*. Has 30 silver discs. Hobbies: swimming, tennis, photography. Address: c/o Gormley Management, Esher. Birthsign: Libra. **Favourite Place:** 'My cottage in North Wales—I love the peace and quiet!'

RICHARD, Eric

Actor, b. 27 June 1940 Margate, Kent. Acted with many rep companies incl: Nottingham, Liverpool, Sheffield, Birmingham and Manchester. Two years touring with Paines Plough. In London has performed at the Royal Court Theatre, E15 and The Bush. TV incl: *Shoestring*; *The Onedin Line*; *Mitch*; *Angels*; *Juliet Bravo*; Mike Leigh's *Home Sweet Home*; *Made In Britain*; *Games Without Frontiers*; *Shogun*; as Sgt Bob Cryer in *The Bill*. m. Christine; 1 s. Richard, 1 d. Frances. Hobby: motorcycling. Address: c/o Louis Hammond Management, London. Birthsign: Cancer. **Favourite Place:** 'A sunny day, riding a large motorcycle along the Mountain Mile, Isle of Man.'

RICHARD, Wendy

Actress, b. 20 July Teesside. Trained at the Italia Conti Stage School. Theatre incl: *No Sex Please, We're British*; *Blithe Spirit*. Films incl: *On The Buses*; *Bless This House*; *Doctor In Clover*. TV drama incl: *The Newcomers*; *Harpers West One*; *No Hiding Place*; *Joe Nobody*; *West Country Tales*; *Nurses Do*; *Making Of Jericho*; *Z Cars*; *EastEnders*. Comedy incl: *Please Sir!*; *Fenn Street Gang*; *Spooner's Patch*; *Hog's Back*; *Both Ends Meet*; *Not On Your Nellie*; *Hugh And I*; *Dad's Army*; *Are You Being Served?* (also stage and film). Hobbies: collecting frogs, clowns and pierrots, antique glass, tapestry. Address: c/o John Mahoney Management, London. Birthsign: Cancer. **Favourite Place:** 'Probably the West Country. Having worked there, and returned for visits, I love the friendliness of the people, as well as the scenery and cream teas!'

RICHARDS, Clare

Actress, b. 21 Dec. 1930 Edinburgh. Rep experience, incl Glasgow, Aberdeen and Perth, of 20 years. Returned to theatre in *Hay Fever* at Theatre Royal, York. Much TV experience incl: *Heather On Fire*; *Redgauntlet*; *Cesar Birotteau*; *Revenue Men*; *High Living*; *A Place Of Her Own*; *Toy Princess*; *Last Love*; Stanley Baxter series; *That's My Boy*. m. Sonnie Whyatt-Parr. Hobby: reading. Address: c/o Joan Reddin, London. Birthsign: Sagittarius. **Favourite Place:** 'Our cottage in the mountains near Balmoral, all that remains of what once was a village.'

RICHARDS, Stan

Actor, b. 8 Dec Barnsley, Yorks. Best known on TV as Seth Armstrong in *Emmerdale Farm*. Has been a successful entertainer in northern clubs for over 30 years. Began as a dance band pianist after studying at Trinity College of Music, London. In 1952 formed Melody Maniacs, a comic quartet, and went solo in 1968. Other TV incl: *The Price Of Coal*; *Coronation Street*; *The Cuckoo Waltz*; *Crown Court*; *All Creatures Great And Small*; *Last Of The Summer Wine*. m. Susan; 3 d. Joan, Dawn, June, 3 s. Alan, Keith, Irvine. Address: c/o Yorkshire TV, Leeds. Birthsign: Sagittarius. **Favourite Place:** 'Barnsley—it's where I was born.'

RICHARDS, Tom

Actor/cartoonist, b. Brisbane, Australia. Trained in theatre in Queensland. Films incl: *Raw Deal*; *Dawn*. TV incl: *Matlock Police*; *The Box*; *Chopper Squad*; *Sons And Daughters*. Hobbies: drawing cartoons. Address: c/o Lee Leslie, Sydney, Australia. Birthsign: Aries. **Favourite Place:** 'Anywhere, as long as the air is clear, the mind at peace— and lots of good food and friends.'

RIDLEY, Joanne

Actress/comedienne, b. 23 March 1970 London. Trained at the Arts Educational School and at Guildhall School of Music and Drama. Appeared in the film *The World Is Full Of Married Men* aged six. Has appeared on TV in *A Question Of Guilt* and *Makenzie*. Plays Samantha in LWT's *Me And My Girl*. Hobbies: photography, ice-skating, parties, tennis. Address: c/o Emanco Management, London. Birthsign: Aries. **Favourite Place:** 'Hampstead Heath in autumn. I love to take long walks, all wrapped up warm, over the heath.'

RIGGANS, Mary

Actress/broadcaster, b. 19 July Glasgow. Was a child actress with the BBC and studied at Glasgow University Drama Society. Theatre incl: *Sailor Beware*; *Till A' The Seas Gang Dry* (a play about Robert Burns which led to a radio production and won her award of Radio Actress of the Year 1983). Much radio work incl: presenter *Twelve Noon*; *Saturday Night Theatre* etc. TV incl: *Sunset Song*; *Weir Of Hermiston*; *Annals Of The Parish*; *Maggie*; *Take The High Road*. m. Malcolm Taylor; 1 d. Samantha. Hobbies: tennis, swimming, reading biographies, knitting. Address: c/o STV, Glasgow. Birthsign: Cancer. **Favourite Place:** 'Andros, a Greek island where you can meet warm people in a kind and beautiful climate.'

RIX, Debbie

Newsreader/presenter/reporter, b. 28 April 1956 Bromley, Kent. Joined BBC as a secretary at 18 in Radio Science Unit. Became production assistant in Children's and Schools' TV, later on *Everyman*. Joined BBC TV's *Breakfast Time* at its start in Jan 1983 as newsreader. TV also incl: *Making Waves*; *Game For A Laugh*. Hobbies: cooking, painting, sleeping. Address: c/o LWT, London. Birthsign: Taurus.

ROACH, Pat

Actor, b. 19 May 1937 Birmingham. Films incl: *Robin Hood*; *Adventures Of The Spaceman And King Arthur*; *Clash Of The Titans*; *Red Sonja*; *Monster Club*; *Clockwork Orange*; *Barry Lyndon*; *Conan The Destroyer*; *Rising Damp*; *Raiders Of The Lost Ark*; *Indiana Jones And The Temple Of Doom*; *Never Say Never Again*. TV incl: *Auf Wiedersehen Pet*; *The Last Place On Earth*. Hobby: running a health club. Address: c/o Peter Charlesworth, London. Birthsign: Taurus. **Favourite Place:** 'Britain, for the seasons and the overall beauty of the four countries. And for its democracy and freedom of speech. It's just good to be British.'

ROACHE, William

Actor, b. 25 April 1932 Ilkeston, Derbyshire. After five years in the army, in which he reached the rank of captain in the Royal Welsh Fusiliers, went into rep at Nottingham and Oldham. Films incl: *Behind The Mask*; *His And Hers*; *Queen's Guards*. Has played Ken Barlow in *Coronation Street* since it began in 1960. Runs a production company with his wife presenting plays and chat shows. m. Sara; 1 d. Verity. Hobby: golf. Address: c/o Spotlight, London. Birthsign: Taurus. **Favourite Place:** 'Home with Sara, Verity, nine cats and two dogs, because I feel at home!'

ROËVES, Maurice

Actor/theatre director/writer, b. 19 March Sunderland, Co Durham. Trained at the Royal College of Drama, Glasgow. Theatre incl: *Macbeth*; *Othello*; *Tunes Of Glory*; *Carnegie*; *There Was A Man*. Directed many stage plays incl: *City Sugar*; *Doo Lally Tap*. Films incl: *Young Winston*; *A Day At The Beach*; *The Eagle Has Landed*; *Transfusion*; *When Eight Bells Toll*; *SOS Titanic*; *Escape To Victory*. TV incl: *Danger UXB*; *Twelfth Night*; *Journal Of Bridgitt Hitler*; *On The Line*; *Inside The Third Reich*; *Heather Ann*; *Magnum PI*; *Remington Steele*; *The Quest*; *Lytton's Diary*. m. Annie; 1 d. Sarah. Hobbies: five-mile runs, seven-card stud poker, looking for work. Address: c/o London Management, London. Birthsign: Pisces. **Favourite Place:** 'The view of the Mediterranean from Kantara Castle, Cyprus.'

ROBB, David

Actor, b. 23 Aug 1947 London. Brought up in Edinburgh and trained at Central School of Speech and Drama in London. Theatre incl: *Cowardy Custard*; *Betzi*; *She Stoops To Conquer*. Films incl: *Conduct Unbecoming*; *The Four Feathers*. Recent TV incl: *Fanny By Gaslight*; *Ivanhoe*; *The Last Days Of Pompeii*; *Wallenberg*; *Off-Peak*; *Dangerous Corner*. m. Briony McRoberts. Hobbies: watching rugby, riding, military history. Address: c/o William Morris Agency, London. Birthsign: Leo/Virgo cusp. **Favourite Place:** 'Yosemite National Park, California. It's the most impressive and beautiful place I've ever visited.'

ROBBIE, Sue
Presenter, b. 5 July 1949 London. Before working in television taught English in a comprehensive school for four years; worked with the Richmond Fellowship rehabilitating ex-psychiatric patients and drug addicts, and was also an air stewardess with British Airways for four years. TV presenter for programmes incl: *First Post*; *Hold Tight*; *Sneak Preview*; *Cartoon Crackers*; *Connections*. Hobbies: riding, fell walking, yoga, cinema, theatre. Address: c/o Granada TV, Manchester. Birthsign: Cancer. **Favourite Place:** 'On the back of a horse or the top of a fell— good for the soul!'

ROBERTSON, Cliff
Actor/writer/director, b. 9 Sept 1925 La Jolla, California. Trained at the Actors' Studio, New York and then appeared on Broadway. Numerous films incl: *Picnic*; *Charly* (won an Oscar); *Three Days Of The Condor*; *Star 80*; *Class*; *Brainstorm*. Plays Dr Michael Ranson in TV's *Falcon Crest*. Other TV incl: *The Game*; *Days Of Wine And Roses*; *Washington: Behind Closed Doors*; *The Twilight Zone*. m. (1st) actress Cynthia Stone, (2nd) actress Dina Merrill; 2 d. Stephanie (from 1st m.), Heather (from 2nd m.). Hobbies: flying vintage aircraft, air and balloon races, collecting WWII and older planes. Address: c/o ICM, 8899 Beverly Blvd, Los Angeles, California 90048. Birthsign: Virgo. **Favourite Place:** 'East Hampton Beach on Long Island, New York.'

ROBINSON, Robert
Commentator, b. 17 Dec 1927 Liverpool. First trained as a journalist after National Service in the West African Army Corps. First broadcast 1955. Radio incl: *Today* (1971–74); *Stop The Week*; *Brain Of Britain*. TV incl: *Points Of View*; *Ask The Family*; *Call My Bluff*; *The Fifties*; *Robinson's Travels*; *The Book Programme*; *Word For Word*; *The Book Game*; *Robinson Country*. Books incl: *Conspiracy*; *Landscape With Dead Dons*; *Inside Robert Robinson*; *The Dog Chairman*; *Everyman Book Of Light Verse*. m. Josephine; 2 d. Lucy, Suzy, 1 s. Nicholas. Address: c/o BBC TV, London. Birthsign: Sagittarius. **Favourite Place:** 'Bed.'

RODGERS, Anton
Actor/director, b. 10 Jan 1933 Wisbech, Cambs. Trained at Italia Conti Stage School and was a child actor before rep and going to the London Academy of Dramatic Art. Has appeared in and directed many stage plays. Most recent appearances incl: *St Joan*; *Two Into One*; *Windy City*; *Passion Play*. Films incl: *Rotten To The Core*; *The Man Who Haunted Himself*; *Scrooge*. TV incl: *The Organisation*; *Zodiac*; *Rumpole Of The Bailey*; *Lillie*; *Flaxborough Chronicles*; *Fresh Fields* (three series); *The Gay Lord Quex*. m. (2nd m.) Elizabeth Garvie; 1 d. Talia, 1 s. Adam (both from 1st m.), 2 s. Barnaby, Dominic (both from 2nd m.). Hobbies: fly fishing, antique collecting. Address: c/o Leading Artists, London. Birthsign: Capricorn.

ROGERS, Jean

Actress, b. 2 Feb Perivale, Middx. Trained at Guildford School of Music and Drama. Appeared in rep, a year at the National Theatre and two seasons at Chichester Festival Theatre. Has made over 1500 radio broadcasts and has also been a presenter and writer for *Listen With Mother*. Played the part of Dolly Skilbeck in Yorkshire TV's *Emmerdale Farm* since 1980. Before joining *Emmerdale Farm*, TV incl: *George And Mildred*; *Callan*; *Comedy Playhouse*; *General Hospital*; *The Harry Worth Show*; *Charge*; *Emergency Ward 10*; *Crossroads*; *Watch* (presenter). m. (dis.); 1 d. Justine, 1 s. Jeremy. Hobbies: cooking, wine-making, gardening, badminton, yoga. Address: c/o Margery Armstrong, London. Birthsign: Aquarius. **Favourite Place:** 'By the sea—the sea relaxes me mentally and emotionally.'

ROGERS, Paul

Actor, b. 22 March 1917 Plympton, Devon. Trained at the Michael Chekhov Theatre Studio, Dartington Hall. Debut in London 1938. At Stratford-upon-Avon 1939, also in rep before serving in the Royal Navy during the war. Has acted with Bristol and London Old Vics, the Royal Shakespeare Company and National Theatre. Plays incl: *Plaza Suite*; *Sleuth*; *Othello*; *Heartbreak House*; *Madras House*; *Volpone*; *Tales From The Vienna Woods*; *The Importance Of Being Earnest*; *Other Places*. Films incl: *Billy Budd*; *The Homecoming*. TV incl: *The Three Sisters*; *Butterflies Don't Count*; *The Executioner*; *Barriers*; *Edwin*; *Connie*. m. (1st) Jocelyn Wynne (dis.), (2nd) Rosalind Boxall; 2 s. Jan, Piers (from 1st m.), 2 d. Lucy, Emma (from 2nd m.). Address: c/o London Management, London. Birthsign: Aries.

ROGERS, Ted

Comedian, b. 20 July 1935 London. Started in bookshops and reached star status the hard way, via touring, guest appearances, cabaret and winning a talent contest. After National Service in the RAF became a Butlin's Redcoat. On stage he has played both the London Palladium and Savoy Hotel 11 times and has appeared in Las Vegas, New York, Miami, Toronto, Hong Kong and Sydney. Started in TV 1963 in *Billy Cotton's Band Show* and had own show, *Ted On The Spot*. Other TV incl: *Sunday Night At The London Palladium*; *3-2-1*. His first radio series was in 1979. m. (1st) Margie (dis.), (2nd) Marion; 2 d. Dena, Fenella. Hobby: playing polo at Cowdray Park, Sussex. Address: c/o Yorkshire TV, Leeds. Birthsign: Cancer. **Favourite Place:** 'La Jolla, California, where I have a holiday apartment.'

ROSE, Clifford

Actor, b. 24 Oct 1929 Hamnish, Herefordshire. Began career with Elizabethan Theatre Company, then rep and 10 years with the Royal Shakespeare Company. Films incl: *The Marat/Sade*; *Work Is A Four-Letter Word*; *The Wall*; *The Cold Room*. TV incl: *Roads To Freedom*; *Callan*; *The Pallisers*; *How Green Was My Valley*; *The Lady From The Sea*; *The Devil's Crown*; *Secret Army*; *Buccaneer*; *Kessler* (title role); *A Married Man*; *Reilly Ace of Spies*; *Strangers And Brothers*; *Oxbridge Blues*; *Love's Labours Lost*; *One By One*. m. actress Celia Ryder; 1 d. Alison, 1 s. Jonathan. Hobbies: music, travel, Russian. Address: c/o ICM, London. Birthsign: Scorpio. **Favourite Place:** 'Ludlow, Shropshire. A perfect jewel of a town in a unique setting.'

ROSE, David
Political correspondent, b. 11 Feb 1941 Herts. Trained as a journalist on *The Scotsman* and then worked for Border TV on *Lookaround*; BBC Scotland and *Current Account* and Southern TV *Day By Day*. Joined ITN as a reporter in 1972 and has been their political correspondent since 1974. m. Rosalind (sep.); 2 s. Jeremy, Christopher, 2 d. Isobel, Elinor. Hobbies: books, keeping fit. Address: c/o ITN, London. Birthsign: Aquarius. **Favourite Place:** 'My own back garden, with my feet up, watching the fruit swell.'

ROSE, Phil
Actor, b. 2 May 1952 Manchester. Trained at Old Rep Theatre, Birmingham and then worked in rep. Film: *Memed My Hawk*. TV incl: *Backs To The Land*; *Gaskin*; *Threads*; *Robin Of Sherwood*. Hobbies: swimming, astrology, walking. Address: c/o Felix De Wolfe, London. Birthsign: Taurus. **Favourite Place:** 'The Highlands of Scotland—the most beautiful place in the world.'

ROSITA, Sharon
Actress, b. 4 June 1959 Guyana, South America. Trained at the Barbara Speake Stage School. Theatre incl: *Sherry And Wine*; *Short Sleeves In The Summer*; *Rain*; *Banana Box*. Radio incl: *Liz*; *Some Cold Night Air*; *One Nine For A Lady Breaker*. TV incl: *The Fosters*; *Angels*; *Lytton's Diary*; *Brookside*. Hobbies: tennis, backgammon, entertaining friends. Address: c/o Don Baker, London. Birthsign: Gemini. **Favourite Place:** 'Warm and at peace, with the duvet over my head, my bed is my favourite place. I love it!'

ROSS, Nick
Broadcaster/journalist/presenter, b. 7 Aug 1947 London. Began broadcasting while at university in Belfast, reporting for and presenting BBC TV Northern Ireland's news and current affairs programmes, moving to network radio and to national TV. Radio incl: *The World At One*; *The World This Weekend*; *The World Tonight*; *Newsdesk*; *You The Jury*; *Any Questions*. TV incl: *Man Alive*; *Out Of Court*; *Fair Comment*; *Did You See?*; *Sixty Minutes*; *Horizon*; *Breakfast Time*; *Crimewatch UK*; *Watchdog*. TV producer for programmes incl: *The Fix*; *The Cure*; *The Biggest Epidemic Of Our Times*. m. Sarah. Hobby: skiing. Address: c/o Jon Roseman Assocs, London. Birthsign: Leo. **Favourite Place:** 'Northern Ireland: beautiful, friendly and much maligned.'

ROSSINGTON, Jane

Actress, b. 5 March 1943 Derby. Amateur acting experience and training at Rose Bruford College of Speech and Drama before joining radio's *The Archers* as Monica Downs. Rep at Sheffield and York, various tours and TV work. Played Nurse Ford in *Emergency Ward 10* and has played Jill Harvey in *Crossroads* since it started. m. (1st) TV director Tim Jones (dis.), (2nd) chartered surveyor David Dunger; 1 d. Sorrel, 1 s. Harry. Hobbies: tapestry, gardening. Address: c/o Leading Players, London. Birthsign: Pisces. **Favourite Place:** 'Salcombe, Devon.'

ROSSINGTON, Norman

Actor, b. 24 Dec 1928 Liverpool. Originally an office boy at Liverpool Docks, but started acting as an amateur and trained at Bristol Old Vic Theatre School. An original cast member of *Salad Days*. Has acted with the Royal Shakespeare Company, London Old Vic. Recent theatre incl: *Guys And Dolls.* Films incl: *Saturday Night And Sunday Morning*; *The Longest Day*; *A Hard Day's Night*; *Tobruk*; *Double Trouble*; *The Charge Of The Light Brigade*; *Digby The Biggest Dog In The World*; *Man In The Wilderness*; *Young Winston.* TV incl: *Hunter's Walk*; *Crime Of Passion*; *Comedy Playhouse*; *Armchair Theatre*; *Village Hall*; *Budgie*; *Follow That Dog*; *Spooner's Patch*; *Big Jim And The Figaro Club.* Hobbies: woodwork, skiing, golf, languages. Address: c/o Peter Charlesworth, London. Birthsign: Capricorn.

ROTHWELL, Alan

Actor/director, b. 9 Feb 1937 Oldham, Lancs. Trained at RADA and many appearances on stage in rep. Films incl: *Linda*; *Nothing But The Best*; *Zeppelin.* Played David Barlow in *Coronation Street* until 1968. Other TV incl: *Top Secret*; *Picture Box*; *Brookside*; *Crown Court.* m. Maureen; 2 s. Tobe, Ben. Hobbies: music, literature, philosophy, cinema. Address: c/o Elspeth Cochrane Agency, London. Birthsign: Aquarius. **Favourite Place:** 'The world as seen from outer space.'

ROWAN, Nick

TV reporter, b. 24 Nov 1960 Canterbury, Kent. Joined Yorkshire TV as a trainee researcher. TV since incl: *Ad Lib*; *Rowan's Report*; *Run It Again*; *ORS 84* and *85*; *Friday People*; *Saturday Picture Show.* Hobbies: windsurfing, youth hosteling, hiking. Address: c/o BBC TV, London. Birthsign: Sagittarius. **Favourite Place:** 'BBC TV Centre canteen—the best egg sandwiches I know outside ITV!'

ROWE, Alan

Actor, b. 14 Dec 1926
Palmerston North, New Zealand.
Worked in rep and radio in New
Zealand and came to England in
1948. Worked in rep incl with
Sir Barry Jackson's Birmingham
Repertory Theatre. Films incl: 55
Days At Peking; Say Hello To
Yesterday; A Taste Of Excitement;
Very Like A Whale. Numerous
TV credits, most recent incl:
Tales Of The Unexpected; The
First Modern Olympics 1896;
Morgan's Boy; Mr Palfrey Of
Westminster; Paradise Postponed.
Hobbies: modern British art,
gardening. Address: c/o Annette
Stone Assocs, London. Birthsign:
Sagittarius. **Favourite Place:**
'Waterloo Bridge, where I
realised a childhood dream to be
in London.'

ROWLANDS, Patsy

Actress, b. 19 Jan 1940 London.
Trained at the Guildhall School
of Music and Drama and her first
professional appearance was in the
chorus as a singer. Played in
pantomimes and summer seasons
until her big break in Valmouth.
Recent theatre incl: Shut Your
Eyes And Think Of England; The
Bed Before Yesterday. Films incl:
Tess; Little Lord Fauntleroy,
several Carry On films. TV incl:
Bless This House; The Squirrels;
Ladies; The History Of Mr Polly;
Hallelujah; George And Mildred;
Robin's Nest; In Loving Memory.
m. Malcolm Sircom (dis.); 1 s.
Alan. Hobbies: painting,
collecting anything Victorian.
Address: c/o David White Assocs,
London. Birthsign: Capricorn/
Aquarius. **Favourite Place:**
'The view of Bolton Bridge,
North Yorkshire, is one of my
favourite places, especially to
paint.'

RUSHTON, William

Actor/writer/comedian, b. 18
Aug 1937 London. After
National Service, a solicitor's
articled clerk before becoming a
freelance cartoonist, helping to
found and edit Private Eye.
Theatre incl: The Private Eye
Revue; Pass The Butler. Films incl:
Those Magnificent Men In Their
Flying Machines; The Bliss Of Mrs
Blossom; Adventures Of A Private
Eye. TV incl: That Was The
Week That Was; Not So Much A
Programme, More A Way Of Life.
Many guest appearances on TV
panel shows. Recent TV incl: The
Cobblers Of Umbridge; The Kenny
Everett Show. Many books incl:
Great Moments In History;
Ffrench Letters; WG Grace's Last
Case. m. actress Arlene Dorgan; 1
s. Tobias, 2 step-s. Matthew, Sam.
Hobbies: ping pong, cricket.
Address: c/o Roger Hancock,
London. Birthsign: Leo.

RUTTER, Barrie

Actor, b. 12 Dec 1946 Hull,
Yorkshire. Trained with the
National Youth Theatre 1964
and became a leading player
1966, when he was voted Most
Promising Actor by London
Critics for Apprentices. Theatre
incl seasons at Nottingham
Playhouse, with the Royal
Shakespeare Company and at the
National Theatre. TV incl:
Apprentices; Queenie's Castle; Our
Kid; Bavarian Nights; Astronauts;
The Oresteia; The Big H. m. Dr
Carol Rutter (author/university
lecturer); 1 d. Bryony Rose.
Hobbies: rugby league, making
wine. Address: c/o ICM, London.
Birthsign: Sagittarius. **Favourite
Place:** 'A field planted with 160
trees in memory of Harry
Michael Rutter, our son, aged 14
and a half weeks.'

RYAN, Christopher

Actor b. 25 Jan 1950 London. Trained at E15 Acting School, London. Began career with Glasgow Citizens' Theatre and has since worked in rep throughout the UK. Spent one year with Shared Experience Theatre in *Bleak House*. West End theatre incl: *Can't Pay? Won't Pay!* Films incl: *Santa Claus—The Movie*. TV incl: *Angels*; *Target*; *Fox*; *The Olympian Way*; *A Turn For The Worse*; *Days At The Beach*; *Carrott's Lib*; *The Lenny Henry Show*; *Inside Out*; *The Tempest*; as Mike in *The Young Ones*. Hobbies: reading, listening to music. Address: c/o Kerry Gardner Management, London. Birthsign: Aquarius. **Favourite Place:** 'When I'm hungry it's the kitchen, when I'm tired it's my bed. And the Cornish coast.'

RYAN, Helen

Actress, b. 16 June 1938 Liverpool. After RADA, stage debut Ipswich rep. Other rep incl: Birmingham, Manchester. Theatre incl: *Twelfth Night* with New Shakespeare Company; *The Ginger Man*; *Madras House* and *The Cherry Orchard* with the National Theatre; *Dark Lady Of The Sonnets*; *Terra Nova* at Chichester. Films incl: *The Elephant Man*; *A Clash Of Loyalties*; *The Misunderstood*. TV incl: *Love Story*; *Crimes Of Passion*; *Edward The Seventh*; *My Father's House*; *Hannah—Miss Mole*; *Fathers And Families*; *My Brother Jonathan*. m. Guy Slater (dis.); 1 s. Daniel, 1 d. Rebecca. Hobbies: reading, cooking, music, knitting, tennis. Address: c/o Joyce Edwards, London. Birthsign: Gemini. **Favourite Place:** 'The Villa Moraitis on Skiathos—the most spectacular view of the Aegean.'

SACHS, Andrew

Actor/writer, b. 7 April 1930 Berlin, Germany. Came to England just before the war. Rep at Worthing and Liverpool, and with Brian Rix on tour and in London's West End. Other stage incl: *A Voyage Round My Father*; *No Sex Please, We're British*; *Not Now, Darling*; *Jumpers*. TV incl: *Fawlty Towers* (Variety Club Award for Most Promising Artist, 1977); *James And The Giant Peach*; *Rising Damp*; *The Tempest*; *The History Of Mr Polly*; *There Comes A Time*; *The Galactic Garden*. Has written frequently for radio and TV, and several stage plays incl: *Made In Heaven*. m. actress Melody Lang; 1 d. Kate, 2 s. Bill, John. Hobbies: wildlife, photography, art. Address: c/o Richard Stone, London. Birthsign: Aries. **Favourite Place:** 'Africa; anywhere remote, beautiful countryside, animals, decent food, no telephone.'

SADLER, Brent

News correspondent, b. 29 Nov 1950 Manchester. Trained at the National Council for the Training of Journalists. Before entering TV, worked for the *Harrow Observer* and the Reading *Evening Post*. Reporter/news producer for Southern TV; reporter/presenter for Westward TV; presenter/reporter for HTV's *Report West* and *Report Extra*. Joined ITN as a reporter in 1981. m. (dis.); 1 d. Nicola. Hobbies: snow-skiing, sailing, water-skiing, riding, travel. Address: c/o ITN, London. Birthsign: Sagittarius. **Favourite Place:** 'Booby's Bay, Cornwall, when the surf is up. A place of great beauty and excitement when surfing.'

ST CLAIR, Isla
Singer/entertainer, b. 2 May 1952 Buckie, Scotland. Made her stage debut at the age of three, her TV debut at 12, and her radio debut at 13 when she hosted her own show. In 1971 she recorded her first LP, *Traditional Scottish Ballads*, for which she was named Best Female Folk Singer by the *New Musical Express*. From there her professional career took off. Stage incl: Maria in *The Sound Of Music*; *Alladin*. TV incl: *Isla's Island*; *Birthday Honours*; co-host of *The Generation Game* (Pye TV Award for Best Female Personality); *The Farm On The Hill*; *The Song And The Story* (which she also devised); *Saturday Show*; and many guest appearances on light entertainment shows and panel games. Hobbies: walking, animals, riding, films, reading. Address: c/o Kramer Organisation, London. Birthsign: Taurus.

SALEM, Pamela
Actress, b. 22 Jan Bombay, India. Trained at the Central School of Speech and Drama. Stage incl: rep at Chesterfield, York and Palmers Green; English tours of *Secretary Bird*, *Salad Days*, and *Linden Tree*; and foreign tours of *The Constant Wife*; *Romantic Comedy*, and *Phoenix Too Frequent*. Films incl: *The First Great Train Robbery*; *The Bitch*; *Never Say Never Again*; *After Darkness*. TV incl: *The Onedin Line*; *Doctor Who*; *Carnforth Practice*; *Early Life Of Stephen Hind*; *Into The Labyrinth*; *All Creatures Great And Small*; *The Professionals*; *Tripods*; *Lytton's Diary*; *Ever Decreasing Circles*; *Thirteen At Dinner*. m. actor Michael O'Hagan. Hobbies: tropical fish, shell collecting. Address: c/o Marina Martin Management, London. Birthsign: Aquarius. **Favourite Place:** 'A deserted tropical palm-fringed beach at sunset, because I feel completely happy there.'

SALIH, Nejdet
Actor, b. 23 Dec 1958 London. Although he has had no official training, his acting career is progressing successfully. Stage appearances incl: *Old Tyme Music Hall*; puppeteering for TIE. TV incl: *The Brief*; *Auf Wiedersehen Pet*; *West*; and the BBC soap opera, *EastEnders*. Hobbies: reading, music, horse riding. Address: c/o David Raphael Management, Twickenham, Middlesex. Birthsign: Capricorn. **Favourite Place:** 'I love the countryside; just to be surrounded by greenery is wonderful.'

SALLIS, Peter
Actor, b. 1 Feb 1921 Twickenham. Studied at RADA. Recent stage incl: *Sisterly Feelings*; *Run For Your Wife*. Films incl: *Sarah*; *Julie*; *The VIPs*; *Full Circle*; *The Divine Sarah*; *Witness For The Prosecution*. Radio incl: *End Of Term* (a play he wrote himself). TV incl: *Into The Dark*; *How To Murder Your Wife*; *The Pallisers*; *Softly, Softly*; *Yanks Go Home*; *A Crowded Room*; *Tales Of The Unexpected*; *The Lady Killers*; *You're Not Watching Me, Mummy*; *She Loves Me*; *Strangers And Brothers*; and perhaps his best known role as Cleggy in *Last Of The Summer Wine*. m. actress Elaine Usher; 1 s. Crispian. Hobbies: painting, gardening. Address: c/o London Management, London. Birthsign: Aquarius. **Favourite Place:** 'Standing in the centre of Holmfirth wondering if it will stop raining.'

SALTHOUSE, John

Actor, b. 16 June 1951 London. Trained at LAMDA after retiring from professional football. Stage incl: seasons at Lancaster, Liverpool's Everyman, Leicester, Stratford East, Sheffield's Crucible; *Man Is Man*; *Abigail's Party*; *Ten Times Table*. Then four years with the National Theatre. Appearances there incl: *The Long Voyage Home*; *The Iceman Cometh*; *Shoemaker's Holiday*; *Red Saturday*. Films incl: *The Spy Who Loved Me*; *A Bridge Too Far*; *An American Werewolf In London*; *Give My Regards To Broad Street*. TV incl: *Man Above Men*; *Not Quite Cricket*; *The Bill*. m. actress Heather Tobias; 1 s. William. Hobbies: cricket, music, most sports. Address: c/o Louis Hammond, London. Birthsign: Gemini. **Favourite Place:** Aberaeron, Wales, 'Peaceful, beautiful, and the local people make you very welcome.'

SAMMARCO, Gian

Actor, b. 30 Jan 1970 Northampton. Made stage debut at the Royal Theatre, Northampton, in *The Innocents*. Other stage appearances incl: *David Copperfield*; *Great Expectations*. TV incl: *Space Station Milton Keynes* (TV debut); the lead in *The Secret Diary of Adrian Mole Aged 13¾*. Hobbies: writing, girlfriend, playing the piano. Address: c/o Thames TV, London. Birthsign: Aquarius. **Favourite Place:** 'Teddington Lock—it's peaceful, quiet, and is a pleasant environment.'

SANDERSON, Joan

Actress, b. 24 Nov 1912 Bristol. Trained at RADA and went on to work in repertory. Toured North Africa and Italy during the war and then returned to rep. Stage incl: *See How They Run*; *The Bad Seed*; *Let's Get A Divorce*; *A Lady Mislaid*; *Anyone For Denis?*; *Semi-Detached*; *Doctor At Sea*; *The Mousetrap*. Has also worked with the National Theatre and the Old Vic. TV incl: *Please Sir!*; *Mixed Blessings*; *The Fainthearted Feminist*; *Me And My Girl*; *Fawlty Towers*; *Rising Damp*; *Ripping Yarns*; *Upstairs, Downstairs*. m. Gregory Scott. Hobbies: gardening, reading, prowling round antique shops and going to auction sales. Address: c/o Bryan Drew, London. Birthsign: Sagittarius. **Favourite Place:** 'My cottage in the Cotswolds because the countryside is so beautiful and very peaceful.'

SANDS, Leslie

Actor/writer/playwright, b. 19 May 1921 Bradford, Yorks. Professional stage debut Lyceum, Sheffield in 1941; London debut in *Antony And Cleopatra* in 1946. Acted with Bristol Old Vic, the Royal Shakespeare Company and National Theatre. Theatre incl: *Hobson's Choice*; *Measure For Measure*; *Ducking Out*. Films incl: *The Deadly Affair*; *One More Time*; *The Ragman's Daughter*. TV incl: *Z Cars*; *Cluff*; *Three Days In Szcecin* (drama/doc); *Very Like A Whale*; *For Services Rendered*; *My Brother's Keeper*; *The Winning Streak*. Written extensively for TV incl: *Z Cars*; *Planemakers*; *A Family At War*; *Something To Hide*. m. actress Pauline Williams; 1 d. Joanna. Hobby: gardening. Address: c/o Fraser & Dunlop, London. Birthsign: Taurus. **Favourite Place:** 'My study—where I can be myself.'

SAVALAS, Telly

Actor, b. 21 Jan 1925 Garden City, New York. Has appeared in numerous films and TV programmes. Films incl: *The Birdman Of Alcatraz*; *The Slender Thread*; *Beau Geste*; *The Dirty Dozen*; *On Her Majesty's Secret Service*; *The Border*. On TV he is probably best known for his part in the title role of *Kojak*. Won Peabody Award for Your Voice of America; nominated twice for Best Actor and twice for Best Director for *Kojak*, won for the 1973–74 season. m. Julie; 2 d. Christina, Candace, 2 s. Nicholas, Christian. Hobbies: reading, sports, race horses. Address: c/o ICM, 8899 Beverly Blvd, Los Angeles, CA 90048. Birthsign: Aquarius. **Favourite Place:** 'The world, wherever things are happening. New York, Los Angeles and London are favourite cities.'

SAYLE, Alexei

Comedian/actor, b. 7 Aug 1952 Liverpool. Went to Southport and Chelsea Schools of Art and had odd jobs, drifting into cabaret and then stand-up comedy. Films incl: *The Secret Policeman's Other Ball*; *Gorky Park*; *The Bride*; *Supergrass*. Radio incl: *Alexei Sayle Community Detective* in *Alexei Sayle And The Fish People*. TV incl: OTT; *The Young Ones*; *Arena*; *Doctor Who*; *Comic Roots*; *Whoops Apocalypse*. Record: *'Ullo John, Gotta New Motor?* Book: *Train To Hell*. m. Linda. Hobbies: drinking, cycling. Address: c/o ICM, London. Birthsign: Leo. **Favourite Place:** 'The Skinner's Arms—it's the nearest pub to my flat.'

SCALES, Prunella

Actress, b. 22 June Sutton Abinger, Surrey. Trained at the Old Vic Theatre School and the Herbert Berghof Studio, New York. Stage incl: *Big In Brazil*; *Buried Treasure*; her one-woman show, *An Evening With Queen Victoria*. Films incl: *Hound Of The Baskervilles*; *Boys From Brazil*; *Wagner*. TV incl: *Fawlty Towers*; *Target*; *Bergerac*; *Jackanory*; *An Evening With Queen Victoria*; *Never The Twain*; *Slimming Down*; *Mapp & Lucia*. m. actor Timothy West; 2 s. Samuel, Joseph. Hobbies: gardening, languages, listening to music. Address: c/o Jeremy Conway, London. Birthsign: Cancer. **Favourite Place:** 'The English canals. No telephone, no television.'

SCANNELL, Tony

Actor, b. 14 Aug 1945 Kinsale, Co Cork, Eire. Trained at the E15 Acting School and Theatre Workshop, followed by rep at Oxford, Leicester, Newcastle, Exeter, Frinton, Stratford East. Films incl: *Flash Gordon*; *Blue Money*. TV incl: *The Professionals*; *Armchair Thriller*; *The Gentle Touch*; *The Bill*. m. (dis.); 1 s. Sean. Hobby: golf. Address: c/o Harbour & Coffey, London. Birthsign: Leo. **Favourite Place:** 'Any golf course, playing better than my handicap.'

SCHULTZ, Dwight
Actor, b. 24 Nov Baltimore.
Stage incl: *The Screens* (debut);
The Tempest; *The Seagull*;
Twelfth Night; *Tiny Alice*;
Indians; *Happy Birthday, Wanda
June*; *Man With Bags*; *The Crazy
Locomotive*; *The Water Engine*;
The Crucifier Of Blood
(Dramalogue Critics Award for
Outstanding Achievement);
Night And Day; *Funeral For A
One-Man Band*. Co-produced
Mary Rose. Films incl: *The Fan*;
Alone In The Dark. TV incl:
When Your Lover Leaves; *Dial M
For Murder*; *Bitter Harvest*; *Thin
Ice*; *The A-Team*. Founder and
Artistic Director, Baltimore
Theatre Ensemble. m. actress
Wendy Fulton. Hobbies: theatre,
running, sound reproduction.
Address: c/o Lippin & Grant,
8124 West 3rd St, Los Angeles,
CA 90048. Birthsign: Sagittarius.
Favourite Place: 'Wherever I'm
given the opporunity to act. I
love to perform.'

SCOTT, Brough
Sports presenter, b. 12 Dec 1942
London. Was professional
National Hunt jockey, 1962–71.
Joined ITV commentary team in
1977. Radio incl: *The
Thoroughbred*. TV incl: *Something
To Brighten The Morning*; *The
Derby Stakes* (writer and
presenter); *The Challenge Of The
Sexes*; *Sporting Chance*; *Thames
Sport*; *George Stubbs The Painter*;
Breeders Cup (NBC). *Sunday
Times*' racing correspondent.
Racing Journalist of the Year,
1977; Sports Council Award,
1983; Sports Journalist of the
Year, 1983. Books: *The World Of
Flat Racing*; *On And Off The
Rails*. m. former British skier
Susie McInnes; 2 d. Sophie, Tessa,
2 s. Charlie, Jamie. Hobby:
making bonfires. Address: c/o
Ewhurst, Surrey. Birthsign:
Sagittarius. **Favourite Place:**
Brooke Cliff, Isle of Wight,
'Whatever loot is left is there—
and the cliff is crumbling.'

SCOTT, Selina
TV journalist, b. 13 May 1951
Yorkshire. Trained as a journalist
with DC Thomson Publications
in Dundee before joining
Grampian TV in Aberdeen as an
announcer in 1978. Made
documentary *Fall Out At
Pentland*. Became one of ITN's
newscasters in 1981, and was
involved in ITN's coverage of the
wedding of Prince Charles.
Joined BBC TV's *Breakfast Time*
at its outset in 1983 as co-
presenter. Hobby: antiques.
Address: c/o BBC TV, London.
Birthsign: Taurus.

SCOTT, Terry
Comedian, b. 4 May 1927
Watford. Began in rep in Grange-
over-Sands, then worked in clubs,
pubs, summer shows and
pantomime before teaming up
with Bill Maynard for *Great
Scott, It's Maynard*. Stage incl:
The Mating Game; *A Bedful Of
Foreigners*. Films incl: *The Bridal
Path*; several of the *Carry On*
films incl: *Up The Jungle*; *Up The
Khyber*. TV incl: *Hugh And I*;
The Gnomes Of Dulwich; *The
Scott On . . .* series; *Son Of The
Bride*; *Happy Ever After*; *Terry
And June*. m. (2nd) former ballet
dancer Margaret Pollen; 4 d.
Sarah, Nicola, Lindsay,
Alexandra. Hobbies: gardening,
chickens. Address: c/o Richard
Stone, London. Birthsign:
Taurus. **Favourite Place:**
Marrakech, 'Particularly the open
market with snake charmers,
belly dancers and story tellers.'

SEABROOK, Peter

Horticulturist, b. 22 Nov 1935 Chelmsford, Essex. Trained in commercial horticulture, production and marketing. Started broadcasting for the BBC in 1969, first to present *Dig This!* and then presenter of *Gardeners'* *World*. Author of several books, incl: *Peter Seabrook's Vegetable Gardener* (published in 10 languages); *Peter Seabrook's Book Of The Garden*. Also gardening correspondent for the *Sun* and *Family Circle*. m. Margaret; 1 d. Alison, 1 s. Roger. Hobby: gardening. Address: c/o BBC, Pebble Mill, Birmingham. Birthsign: Scorpio. **Favourite Place:** 'Anywhere in the English countryside especially in spring and autumn.'

SECOMBE, Sir Harry, CBE

Actor/singer/comedian, b. 8 Sept 1921 Swansea. Forces shows during the war (served in the army), and the Windmill Theatre on demob. First break on radio in *Variety Bandbox*, then *Welsh Rarebit* and *Educating Archie* before *The Goon Show*. Numerous variety shows, stage musicals and guest appearances worldwide. TV incl: *Highway*. Books incl: *Twice Brightly*; *Goon For Lunch*; *Katy And The Nurgla*; *Welsh Fargo*. Knighted in Birthday Honours, 1981. m. Myra; 2 d. Jennifer, Katy, 2 s. Andrew, David. Hobbies: reading, photography, golf, cricket. Address: c/o 46 St James's Place, London SW1. Birthsign: Virgo. **Favourite Place:** 'Home because it's where the heart is.'

SELBY, David

Actor, b. Morgantown, W Virginia. Many films incl: *Rich And Famous*; *Up The Sandbox*; *Super Cops*; *Rich Kids*; *Raise The Titanic*. Now best known for TV soap opera *Falcon Crest*. Other TV incl: *Dark Shadows*; *The Waltons*; *Kojak*; *Family*; *Washington: Behind Closed Doors*; *Flamingo Road*. m. Chip; 1 s. Todd, 2 d. Brooke, Amanda. Hobby: all outdoor sports. Address: c/o William Morris Agency, 151 El Camino Drive, Beverly Hills, California 90212. **Favourite Place:** New York.

SELBY, Tony

Actor, b. 26 Feb 1938 London. Trained at the Italia Conti Stage School and made stage debut in 1950 in *Peter Pan*. Other stage incl: *Living For Pleasure*; *Alfie*; *Saved*; *Sometime Never*; *Enemy*; *Flashpoint*; *Man And Superman*. TV incl: *Three Clear Sundays*; *Up The Junction*; *Silent Song*; *A* *Night Out*; *Another Day Another Dollar*; *Shine A Light*; *Ace Of Wands*; *Moody And Peg*; *Get Some In*; *Antigone*; and numerous guest appearances in drama series. m. (dis.); 1 d. Samantha, 1 s. Matthew. Hobbies: football, swimming. Address: c/o Aza Artistes, London. Birthsign: Pisces. **Favourite Place:** 'Many favourite places but Beachy Head must come first. I had so many happy holidays in Eastbourne as a child.'

SELLECCA, Connie

Actress, b. 25 May Bronx, New York. Began as a fashion and commercials model; took acting classes in New York. TV incl: *The Greatest American Hero*; *Flying High*; *Beyond Westworld*; *Somebody's Killing The World's Greatest Models*; *The Bermuda Depths*; *Captain America*; *Hotel*. m. Gil Gerard; 1 s. Gilbert Vincent. Hobby: working out. Address: c/o Lippin & Grant, 8124 West 3rd St, Suite 204, Los Angeles, CA 90048. Birthsign: Gemini. **Favourite Place:** spending time with her family and their two dogs.

SELLECK, Tom

Actor, b. 29 Jan 1945 Detroit, Michigan. Studied drama at Valley College and started his career in TV commercials. Films incl: *Seven Minutes*; *Midway*; *Coma*; *Myra Breckenridge*; *High Road To China*; *Lassiter*; *Runaway*. TV incl: *The Sacketts*; *Bracken's World*; *The Young And The Restless*; *The Rockford Files*; *Magnum PI*; and the TV films *Returning Home*; *Divorce Wars*. Emmy Award Best Actor for *Magnum*. m. Jacki Ray (dis.); 1 s. Kevin (adopted from Jacki Ray's previous m.). Hobbies: swimming, volleyball, basketball, softball, making furniture, restoring antiques. Address: c/o McCartt, Oreck, Barrett, 9200 Sunset Blvd, Suite 1009, Los Angeles, CA 90069. Birthsign: Aquarius.

SERLE, Chris

Journalist, b. 13 July 1943 Bristol. Former actor (with the Bristol Old Vic), radio producer (*Petticoat Line*; *Brain Of Britain*), and TV director. A former presenter of BBC TV's *That's Life!* Other TV incl: *Medical Express*; *The Computer Programme*; *Greek Language And People*; *60 Minutes*; *In At The Deep End*. m. Anne; 1 s. Harry. Hobbies: gliding, jazz drumming, staring into space. Address: c/o Curtis Brown, London. Birthsign: Cancer. **Favourite Place:** 'One particular Greek island—quiet, welcoming. Just sun, sea, tranquillity, fresh fish and good wine.'

SHANE, Paul

Actor/comedian, b. 19 June 1940 Rotherham. Worked for 20 years as a stand-up comic in northern clubs and playing small character parts on TV. Stage incl: *Hi-De-Hi!*; *Spring And Port Wine*. TV incl: *Hi-De-Hi!*; *Sounding Brass*; *Turtle's Progress*; *Muck And Brass*; *The Generation Game*; *Punchlines*; *Swop Shop*; *Saturday Night At The Mill*; *Russell Harty*; *Tiswas*; *3-2-1*; *This Is Your Life*. m. Dorry; 3 d. Janice, Andrea, Gillian. Hobbies: golf, fishing, gardening, greyhound racing. Address: c/o ATS City Varieties, Leeds. Birthsign: Gemini. **Favourite Place:** 'Owlerton stadium. Greyhound racing with my wife and seeing all our friends and, of course, hoping to have a few winners.'

SHANNON, Johnny
Actor, b. 29 July 1932 London. Made his acting debut in the Warner Brothers' film, *Performance*. Other films incl: *That'll Be The Day*; *The Great Rock And Roll Swindle*; *Flame*; *Runners*. TV incl: *Gold Robbers*; *Beryl's Lot*; *XYY Man*; *Watch All Night*; *Give Us A Break*; *Big Deal*; *The Dick Emery Show*; *Never Mind The Quality, Feel The Width*; *Minder*; *The Sweeney*; *The Professionals*; *The Morecambe And Wise Show*; *Supergran*; *The Kenny Everett Show*; *Keep It In The Family*. m. Rose; 1 s. Gary, 1 d. Terry. Hobbies: watching boxing, horse racing. Address: c/o Chatto & Linnit, London. Birthsign: Leo. **Favourite Place:** 'The Friendly Eight, a Chinese restaurant in Bromley, for its lovely food and very friendly atmosphere.'

SHARROCK, Ian
Actor, b. 20 Dec 1959 Darley, near Harrogate. Trained at the Corona Academy of Music and Dramatic Art. Has appeared in more than 20 films, incl: Walt Disney's *Candleshoe*. Has acted in over 30 radio plays, incl: the award-winning *Equus* with Peter Barkworth. TV incl: *Smike*; *Peter Pan*; *Games*; and since 1980 *Emmerdale Farm*. Hobbies: motorcycling, spending time with friends, eating out, parties. Address: c/o Yorkshire TV, Leeds. Birthsign: Sagittarius. **Favourite Place:** 'My front room, curled up in front of the fire with a good book.'

SHATNER, William
Actor, b. 22 March 1931 Montreal, Canada. Started his career with the Canadian Repertory Company. Appeared in the Stratford Shakespeare Festival, Ontario. Films incl: *Star Trek I, II, III, IV*; *The Brothers Karamazov*; *The Explosive Generation*; *The Intruder*; *The Outrage*; *Big Bad Mama*; *Judgement At Nuremberg*; *Airplane II*. TV incl: *Go Ask Alice*; *The Horror At 37,000 Feet*; and the series *Barbary Coast*, *TJ Hooker*; *Star Trek*. m. (1st) Gloria Ranel, (2nd) Marcy Lafferty; 3 d. Leslie, Lisabeth, Melanie (all from 1st m.). Hobbies: horse riding, raising champion Dobermans, tennis, scuba-diving, jogging. Birthsign: Aries. **Favourite Place:** Equestrian Centre, Griffith Park, Los Angeles.

SHAW, Martin
Actor, b. 21 Jan 1945 Birmingham. Trained at LAMDA; rep at Hornchurch, Bromley and Bristol Old Vic. Stage incl: *Look Back In Anger*; *The Contractor*; *Cancer*; *Saturday, Sunday, Monday*; *A Streetcar Named Desire*; *Miss Julie*; *Teeth 'N' Smiles*; *They're Playing Our Song*; *Are You Lonesome Tonight?* Films incl: *Macbeth*; *Operation Daybreak*. TV incl: *Travelling Light*; *Doctor At Large*; *Helen—A Woman Of Today*; *Electra*; *The Professionals*; *Cream In My Coffee*; *The Last Place On Earth*. m. Maggie; 2 s. Luke, Joe, 2 d. Sophie, Kate. Hobbies: walking, reading, strumming the guitar. Address: c/o Hutton Management, London. Birthsign: Aquarius. **Favourite Place:** 'My cottage in Galloway, for peace, quiet and solitude.'

SHELTON, Deborah

Actress, b. 21 Nov Washington DC. Started as a model; studied acting at Lee Strasberg's Actors' Studio and with coach Warren Robertson. Film: *Body Double*. TV incl: *Yellow Rose*; *The Yeagers*; as Mandy in *Dallas*; and guest appearances on *TJ Hooker*; *Kate Columbo*. m. (1st) (dis.), (2nd) musician/writer/record producer Shuki Levy; 1 s. (from 1st m.), 1 d. (from 2nd m.). Hobbies: foreign languages, needlepoint, writing song lyrics (collaborates with her husband and together they have written over 100 songs, incl: *Sad*, a million-seller for Andy Williams; and *Magdalena*, recorded by Julio Iglesias). Address: c/o William Morris Agency, 151 El Camino Drive, Beverly Hills, CA 90212. Birthsign: Scorpio. **Favourite Place:** Helmsley Palace, New York City.

SHEPHERD, Jack

Actor/director/writer, b. 29 Oct 1940 Leeds. Acted with the Royal Court Theatre, 1965–69. Stage incl: *Saved*; *Twelfth Night*; *Narrow Road To The Deep North*; *Early Morning*; *Glengarry Glen Ross* (Actor of the Year, 1983). Films incl: *The Virgin Soldiers*; *The Bedsitting Room*. TV incl: *All Good Men*; *Occupations*; *Through The Night*; *Bill Brand*; *All*; *A Room For The Winter*. Founder member of the Actors' Company. Wrote and directed *The Sleep Of Reason*; also *Real Time*. National Theatre, 1978–85. m. (1st) Judy Harland (dis.), (2nd) Ann Scott; 1 d. Jan, 1 s. Jake (both from first m.), 2 twin d. Victoria, Catherine, 1 s. Ben (all from 2nd m.). Hobbies: photography, sports, playing the saxaphone. Address: c/o Green & Underwood, London. Birthsign: Scorpio. **Favourite Place:** Snowdonia, North Wales.

SHERIDAN, Dinah

Actress, b. 17 Sept Hampstead Garden Suburb, London. Trained at Italia Conti School and made her debut in *Where The Rainbow Ends* 1932. Retired from acting but returned 1967. Films incl: *Irish And Proud Of It*; *Where No Vultures Fly*; *Genevieve*; *The Railway Children*; *The Mirror Cracked*. Recent TV incl: *Doctor Who*; *Swish Of The Curtain*; *Don't Wait Up* (three series); *Winning Streak*. m. (1st) actor Jimmy Hanley (dis.), (2nd) John Davis (dis.); 1 s. Jeremy, 1 d. actress/presenter Jenny. Hobbies: tapestry, gardening. Address: c/o John Mahoney, London. Birthsign: Virgo.

SHERIDAN, Michael

Reporter for ITN, b. 12 Dec 1957 London. After studying history at Cambridge University, he joined Reuters in 1980. Reuters correspondent in Rome, 1981–83, and in Beirut, Damascus, Tehran, Baghdad, Amman, Khartoum and Cyprus, 1983–84. Now a reporter for ITN. Also freelance writer for *The Sunday Times, New Statesman* and *Spectator*. Hobbies: reading, swimming, photography. Address: c/o ITN, London. Birthsign: Sagittarius. **Favourite Place:** Piazza Navona, Rome.

SHODIENDE, Shope
Actress, b. 21 March 1957 London. Read drama at

Manchester University. Theatre experience incl: *Circumstantial Evidence*; with the Black Theatre Co-op Productions in *Welcome Home Jacko* and *Mama Dragon*; *The Warp*. Films incl: *Sailor's Return*; *In Search Of Eden*. TV incl: *In A Secret State*; *Intensive Care* (by Alan Bennett and starring Julie Walters); *Watch All Night* (children's series). Hobbies: music, film. Address: c/o Morgan & Goodman, London. Birthsign: Pisces/Aries.

SIKES, Cynthia
Actress/singer, b. 2 Jan Coffeyville, Kansas. Studied drama at the American Conservatory Theater Company

in San Francisco. Films incl: *All Washed Up*; *Goodbye Cruel World*; *The Man Who Loved Women*. TV incl: *His Mistress* (TV film); *Falcon Crest*; *The Fall Guy*; *Archie Bunker's Place*; *Hart To Hart*; *Flamingo Road*; *St Elsewhere*. Hobbies: singing, dancing, scuba-diving, travel, river rafting. Address: c/o Triad Agency, 10100 Santa Monica Blvd, Los Angeles, CA 90067. Birthsign: Capricorn. **Favourite Place:** New York and Tahiti.

SIKKING, James
Actor, b. 5 March Los Angeles, California. BA in Theatre Arts from UCLA. Films incl: *Capricorn One*; *The New Centurions*; *The Terminal Man*; *Outland*; *Von Ryan's Express*; *Scorpio*; *The Magnificent Seven*; *The Electric Horseman*; *Ordinary People*; *Star Chamber*; *Star Trek III*. TV incl: guest appearances in *Charlie's Angels*; *The Incredible*

Hulk; *Starsky And Hutch*; *MASH*. Other TV incl: *Turnabout*; *General Hospital*; *Hill Street Blues*; and the TV films, *Jesse Owen's Story*; *First Steps*. m. Florine; 1 s. Andrew, 1 d. Emily. Hobbies: golf, skiing, racquetball, collecting wine, cooking. Address: c/o McCartt, Oreck, Barrett Agency, 9200 Sunset Blvd, Los Angeles, CA 90069. Birthsign: Pisces. **Favourite Place:** 'Wherever the skiing is good!'

SILVERA, Carmen
Actress, b. Toronto, Canada. Trained in classical ballet, then studied drama at LAMDA. Stage incl: *Serious Charge*; *Let's Get A Divorce*; *El Baille*; *People Are Living There*; *On The Rocks*; *Torrents Of Spring*; *Waters Of The Moon*; *Hobson's Choice*; *A Coat Of Varnish*; *The Unexpected Guest*; *The Cherry Orchard*; and many guest appearances in provincial theatres. TV incl: *Compact*; *Dad's Army*; *Beggar My*

Neighbour; *New Scotland Yard*; *Within These Walls*; *Maggie And Her*; *The Gentle Touch*; *Two Women*; *Lillie*; *Tales Of The Unexpected*; '*Allo, 'Allo!*. Hobbies: antiques, interior decor, reading, bridge and Scrabble, golf. Address: c/o Barry Burnett, London. Birthsign: Gemini. **Favourite Place:** 'Constantly changing—currently I think it would be north-east Majorca, wonderful weather and not too crowded!'

SINDEN, Donald, CBE

Actor, b. 9 Oct 1923 Plymouth. Fellow of the Royal Society of Arts. Trained at the Webber Douglas School of Dramatic Art and first appeared on TV in *Bullet In The Ballet* in 1948. Films incl: *The Cruel Sea*; *Mogambo*; *Doctor In The House*; *Doctor At Large*; *Eyewitness*; *Twice Round The Daffodils*; *Decline And Fall*; *The Day Of The Jackal*; *The Island At The Top Of The World*. TV incl: *The Organisation*; *Our Man From St Marks*; *Two's Company*; *Never The Twain*; *Discovering English Churches*. Books: *A Touch Of The Memoirs*; *Laughter In The Second Act* (autobiographies). m. Diana Mahony; 2 s. Jeremy, Marcus. Hobbies: theatrical history, ecclesiology, serendipity. Address: c/o Leading Artists, London. Birthsign: Libra. **Favourite Place:** 'Ditchling in Sussex—because I was brought up there.'

SINDEN, Jeremy

Actor, b. 14 June 1950 London. Trained at LAMDA. Spent 1969 season at Pitlochry; 1970–72 with the RSC; 1975 at Chichester. Stage incl: *Conduct Unbecoming*; *French Without Tears*; *Journey's End*; *The Jungle Book*; *Lady Harry*; *The Winslow Boy* (as director). Films incl: *Star Wars*; *Ascendency*; *Chariots Of Fire*. TV incl: *The Expert*; *The Sweeney*; *Crossroads*; *Soldiers Talking Cleanly*; *Brideshead Revisited*; *Old Glad Eyes*; *Holding The Fort*; *Never The Twain*; *Squadron*; *The Far Pavilions*; *Fairly Secret Army*; *Lytton's Diary*; *Two Up, Two Down*. m. Delia Lindsay; 2 d. Kezia, Harriet. Hobbies: walking, photography, tree climbing, travel. Address: c/o ICM, London. Birthsign: Gemini. **Favourite Place:** 'A house in Kent where I spent happy times in my childhood—and now my children are doing the same.'

SINER, Guy

Actor/singer, b. 16 Oct 1947 New York City. Trained at the Webber Douglas Academy and in 1971 won the Rodney Millington Award. Has worked with various repertory companies incl: Bristol Old Vic, Cambridge Theatre Company, Oxford Playhouse, Leicester Haymarket, Brighton, Worthing and Windsor. Stage incl: *Cowardy Custard* (debut); *Biograph Girl*; *Nickelby And Me*; *Off The Peg*; *Toad Of Toad Hall*; and tours of *Barefoot In The Park*; *Sunshine Boys*. TV incl: *'Allo, 'Allo!*; *I, Claudius*; *Life At Stake*; *Doctor Who*; *Secret Army*; *Softly, Softly*; *Z Cars*. He also appeared in cabaret at the Ritz. Hobbies: dining out, photography, collecting hippos. Address: c/o Barry Burnett, London. Birthsign: Libra. **Favourite Place:** New York Harbour, 'For its atmosphere and childhood memories.'

SINGLETON, Valerie

TV journalist, b. 9 April 1937 Hitchin. Won scholarship to RADA, went into rep and worked on TV advertising magazines before joining the BBC as an announcer. Joined *Blue Peter* in 1962. Other TV incl: *Blue Peter Special Assignments*; *Blue Peter Royal Safari*; *Val Meets The VIPs*; *Nationwide*; *Tonight*; *The Money Programme*. Hobbies: looking at London, riding, water and snow skiing, prowling round sale rooms, photography, travel, reading. Address: c/o BBC TV, London. Birthsign: Aries. **Favourite Place:** 'Too many to mention, but one that never fails to satisfy is a library on a wet, cold Saturday afternoon.'

SISSONS, Peter
Newscaster, b. 17 July 1942
Liverpool. Joined ITN as trainee
in 1964 and has been reporting
since 1967. Has covered Middle
East War. Wounded during the
Nigerian civil war in 1968. Was
made industrial editor in 1974.
Presenter of *News At One*, 1978,
and now of Channel Four's news
and analysis programme. In
March 1985 was awarded the
Broadcasting Press Guild Award,
1984, for Outstanding
Contribution to Television in
front of the Cameras. m. Sylvia; 1
d. Kate, 2 s. Michael, Jonathan.
Hobbies: amusing the kids,
giving spiritual support to
Liverpool FC. Address: c/o ITN,
London. Birthsign: Cancer.

SLEEP, Wayne
Ballet dancer/actor, born in
Plymouth but brought up on
Tyneside. Won a scholarship to
the Royal Ballet School aged 12,
joined the Royal Ballet in 1966
and became principal dancer in
1973. Because of his height (5ft
3in) he felt he had to diversify so
combines stage, film and TV
work. Theatre incl: *The Tempest*;
Winnie The Pooh; *The Servant Of
Two Masters*; *The Point*; *Aladdin*;
CATS; *Dash* (world tour).
Films: *Virgin Soldiers*; *The First
Great Train Robbery*. TV incl:
The Hot Shoe Show; *This Is Your
Life*; *Celebration*. Choreographed
ballet *Adam's Rib*, for BBC TV.
Record: *Man To Man*. Hobbies:
parachute jumping, watching TV
videos. Address: c/o London
Management, London.
Favourite Place: 'Anywhere
that has no phone.'

SLOANE, Doreen
Actress, b. 24 Feb 1934
Birkenhead, Wirral. Trained at
the Theatre School, Liverpool,
and the Student Playhouse,
Liverpool. Various repertory
seasons incl: Liverpool, Chester,
Preston. Films incl: *Yanks*;
Chariots Of Fire. TV incl:
Coronation Street (four different
parts); *Emmerdale Farm* (two
parts); *Victorian Scandals*; *Nearest
And Dearest*; *Life For Christine*;
All For Love; *How We Used To
Live*; *Brookside*. m. (1st) (dis.),
(2nd) Len; 2 s. Angus, Bruce, 2 d.
Sarah, Jane. Hobbies: horse
riding, *Telegraph* crossword,
reading. Address: c/o Brookside
Productions, Liverpool.
Birthsign: Pisces. **Favourite
Place:** 'A bank of bright yellow
daffodils. All flowers are
beautiful, especially yellow
ones—I just adore bright yellow.'

SMETHURST, Jack
Actor/producer, b. 9 April 1932
Blackley, Manchester. Many TV
appearances, incl: *The Casualties*;
No Hiding Place; *Plane Makers*; *Z
Cars*; *Coronation Street*; *Parables*;
Love Thy Neighbour, and *For The
Love Of Ada*; both made into
films. His most recent TV role in
BBC's comedy series *Hilary*. m.
Julie; 3 d. Pardita, Merry, Jane
Louise, 1 s. Adam. Hobbies:
supporting Manchester United
FC, collecting medals, avoiding
gardening. Address: c/o Richard
Stone, London. Birthsign: Aries.
Favourite Place: Garden-office:
'peaceful rural surroundings with
my books, music and theatrical
memorabilia.'

SMITH, Giles
ITN Industrial Editor, b. 23 May 1944 Beaconsfield, Bucks. Started in journalism on the *Harrow Observer*. Specialising in industrial matters, he became industrial correspondent for the *Western Mail*, Cardiff, and later joined *The Times* as industrial reporter and then the BBC in the same capacity before moving to ITN in 1974. m. Gladwyn; 3 d. Sian, Georgia, Alex. Hobbies: cricket, squash, Bob Dylan. Address: c/o ITN, London. Birthsign: Gemini. **Favourite Place:** 'Datchet Cricket Club, where I want my ashes to be put on the square when I die.'

SMITH, Mel
Comedy actor/director, b. 3 Dec 1952 Chiswick, London. Devoted to drama at school and while at Oxford chose to produce *The Tempest* rather than take his degree. This led to an invitation to join Royal Court Theatre production team in London. He then joined Bristol Old Vic, the Young Vic in London and for two years was associate director Sheffield's Crucible Theatre. Recent theatre incl: *Not In Front Of The Audience*, which he directed. Films incl: *Morons From Outer Space*; *Slayground*; *Number One*. Became well known on TV for *Not The Nine O'Clock News*. Other TV incl: *Muck And Brass*; *Smith And Goody*; *Alas Smith And Jones*. Hobby: horses. Address: c/o Peter Brown, London. Birthsign: Sagittarius. **Favourite Place:** 'Bed.'

SMITH, Mike
Broadcaster, b. 23 April 1955 Hornchurch, Essex. Began his career with hospital and commercial radio. Award-winning presenter for Capital Radio and Radio 1. Member of BBC *Breakfast Time* presenting team. Other TV incl: *Greatest Hits*; *Family Trees*; *TV Times Star Family Challenge*; *Show Business*; *Friday People*; *Top Of The Pops*; *Speak Out*; *Driving Force*; *Royal Tournament*. Founder/director of Charity Projects, which organises shows in aid of youth unemployment: First International Nether Wallop Arts Festival. Hobbies: car racing, scuba diving, theatre and film going, laughing. Address: c/o Bagenal Harvey Organisation, London. Birthsign: Taurus. **Favourite Place:** 'Anywhere—provided Sarah Greene is there as well!'

SNOW, Jon
ITN Washington Correspondent, b. 28 Sept 1947 Ardingly, Sussex. TV journalist of considerable experience. Won the Royal Television Society's Journalist of the Year Award, 1980–81, for his reports on Iran, Iraq and Afghanistan. Started as a radio reporter for LBC/IRN, 1973–76. He then joined ITN for whom he has reported most of the major news events from all parts of the world, including from the Falklands, before becoming Washington Correspondent. Address: c/o ITN, London. Birthsign: Libra.

SNOW, Peter
Reporter, b. 20 April 1938
Dublin. Joined ITN in 1962 and
was successively sub-editor,
reporter and then newscaster.
Diplomatic and defence
correspondent for ITN, 1966.
Joined BBC's *Newsnight* as
presenter/reporter, 1980. Book:
Hussein (biography). m. (1st)
Alison (dis.), (2nd) Anne
Macmillan (of Canadian TV); 3
d. Shuna, Rebecca, Katherine, 2 s.
Shane, Daniel. Hobbies: sailing,
writing books, photography.
Address: c/o BBC TV, London.
Birthsign: Aries.

SPALL, Timothy
Actor, b. 27 Feb 1957 London.
Trained at RADA where he was
awarded the Bancroft Gold
Medal. Stage incl: *Merry Wives
Of Windsor*; *Nicholas Nickelby*;
Knight Of The Burning Pestle;
Baal (all with the RSC); *Saint
Joan*; *Dauphin*; *Aunt Mary*; *Man
Equals Man*. Films incl: *The
Missionary*; *The Bride*; *The
Sinking Of The Titanic*; *Predator*.
TV incl: *Auf Wiedersehen Pet*;
Brylcream Boys; *Cotswold Death*;
Home Sweet Home; *Three Sisters*;
The Cherry Orchard;
Remembrance; *Vanishing Army*.
m. Shane; 1 d. Pascale, 1 s. Rafe.
Hobbies: cars, take-away food,
watching TV. Address: c/o Plant
& Froggatt, London. Birthsign:
Pisces. **Favourite Place:**
'Hastings in mid-winter because
of the desolation and the chips are
cheaper!'

SPANO, Joe
Actor, b. 7 July San Francisco.
Started his career with the
Berkeley Repertory Company,
and with the Wing and the
Committee improvisational
workshops in San Francisco.
Films incl: *American Graffitti*; *The
Enforcer*; *Northern Lights*; *Roadie*;
The Incredible Shrinking Woman.
TV incl: *Lou Grant*; *Tenspeed
And Brownshoe*; *Paris*; *Trapper
John*; *Fighting Back*; *Hill Street
Blues*. m. Joan. Hobbies: running,
skiing, Italian cooking, gardening.
Address: c/o Smith, Freedman &
Assocs, 123 North San Vicente
Blvd, Beverly Hills, CA 90211.
Birthsign: Cancer.

SPEAR, Bernard
Actor, b. 11 Sept 1919 London.
Started show business career in
music halls and in cabaret. Film:
Yentl (with Barbra Streisand).
TV incl: *The Kelly Monteith
Show*; *Never Mind The Quality,
Feel The Width*; *The Lenny Henry
Show*; *Target*; *Barmitzvah Boy*;
The Schoolmistress; *3-2-1*. m.
Mary Logan; 1 s. Julian. Hobbies:
playing golf, travelling in France.
Address: c/o Leading Players
Management, London. Birthsign:
Virgo. **Favourite Place:** The
City of London: 'Dr Johnson said
it all.'

SPINETTI, Victor

Actor, b. 2 Sept 1933 Cwm, South Wales. Trained at the Cardiff College of Music and Drama. Stage incl: *Expresso Bongo*; *Make Me An Offer*; *Every Man In His Humour*; *The Hostage*; *Fings Ain't Wot They Used T'Be*; *Oh! What A Lovely War*; *Jesus Christ Superstar*; *Windy City*. Also a stage director, incl: *Deja Revue*; *Let's Get Laid*; *Yes, We have No Pyjamas*; *In His Own Write* (co-author); *King Rat*.

Films incl: all the Beatles' films; *The Taming Of The Shrew*; *The Pink Panther*; *The Voyage Of The Damned*. TV incl: *Two In Clover*; *Take My Wife*; *The Sea*; *Superted*; many guest appearances. Hobbies: writing, talking, learning. Address: c/o Howes & Prior, London. Birthsign: Virgo. **Favourite Place:** 'On the mountains of South Wales: Brecon Beacons; mountains around Cwm. Great up there, feel young there!'

SPOUND, Michael

Actor, b. 8 April Santa Monica, California. Stage incl: *Sweet Charity*; *Brigadoon*; *1776*; *Design For Living*; *Six Rooms Rive Vu*; *The Gingerbread Lady*; *Sing Out, Sweet Land*. TV incl: *Hotel*; *Family Ties*; *The Love Boat*; *Fantasy Island*; *Laverne And Shirley*; *Happy Days*; *Teachers Only*; the TV special, *All-American College Comedy Show*; and the TV film, *Emergency Room*. Hobbies: basketball, touch football, tennis, softball, writing, skiing. Address: c/o Abrams, Harris & Goldberg, 9220 Sunset Blvd, Suite 101B, Los Angeles, CA 90069. Birthsign: Aries. **Favourite Place:** 'My hometown.'

SPRIGGS, Elizabeth

Actress, b. 18 Sept 1929 Buxton, Derbyshire. Trained for opera at Royal School of Music but turned to acting, first with Birmingham rep, then Royal Shakespeare Company (assoc member). Joined National Theatre 1976. Films incl: *An Unsuitable Job For A Woman*. TV incl: *We, The Accused*; *The Kindness Of Mrs Radcliffe*; *Bognor*; *Sergeant Cribb*; *Richard's Things*; *Shine On Harvey Moon* (three series); *Frost In May*; *The Haunting Of Cassie Palmer*; *The Merry Wives Of Windsor*. m. musician Murry Manson; 1 d. Wendy. Hobbies: people, animals. Address: c/o Harbour and Coffey, London. Birthsign: Virgo.

SQUIRE, Paul

Entertainer, b. 11 July 1950 Stoke on Trent. Started performing aged nine with his brother and sister as The Millionaires and became well known in northern clubs and cabaret for 18 years. Went solo, toured UK and Australia and has appeared in many pantomimes incl *Babes In The Wood*, *Mother Goose* and *Cinderella*. Royal Variety Performance 1980. TV incl: *Search For A Star* (came second); *The Paul Squire Show*; *PS It's Paul Squire*; *Paul Squire Esq.* m. Linda; 1 s. Ben. Hobby: golf. Address: c/o Forrester George, Brighton. Birthsign: Cancer. **Favourite Place:** 'The golf club near where I live – it's so very peaceful.'

STAFF, Kathy
Actress, b. 12 July 1928
Dukinfield, Cheshire. Started
career with a touring company in
Scotland and then rep. Films incl:
A Kind Of Loving; *The Family
Way*; *The Dresser*. On TV she is
well-known in *Crossroads*; *Open*
All Hours; and in *Last Of The
Summer Wine*. Other TV incl:
Castle Haven; *Within These
Walls*; *Hadleigh*; *Coronation
Street*; Les Dawson's *Sez Les*
series; *Separate Tables*; *The Benny
Hill Show*. m. John; 2 d.
Katherine, Susan. Hobbies: choral
singing, church work. Address:
c/o Fraser & Dunlop, London.
Birthsign: Cancer. **Favourite
Place:** 'Sitting in my garden
watching the fish in the pond. I
find this very relaxing.'

STAGG, Lindsey
Actress, b. 23 Feb 1970
Northampton. Trained with
Sally-Ann Tollitt School of
Speech and Drama. Although still
at school, has appeared on stage in
The Innocents; *David Copperfield*;
Great Expectations (all at Royal
Theatre, Northampton). Appears
on TV in *The Secret Diary Of
Adrian Mole*. Hobbies: studying
the past, collecting rubbers,
walking. Address: c/o Thames
TV, London. Birthsign: Pisces.
Favourite Place: 'Busy bric-a-
brac stalls like in Petticoat Lane,
and beautiful, mature summer
gardens.'

STANDING, John
Actor, b. 16 Aug 1939 London.
Real name Sir John Leon, the
fourth baronet. Acting in his
family seven generations (his
mother was actress Kay
Hammond), but wanted to be an
artist until decided he wasn't good
enough and joined the Royal
Shakespeare Company. London
theatre incl most recently: *The
Biko Inquest* (Riverside); *Rough
Crossing* (National Theatre).
Films incl: *The Eagle Has Landed*;
The Elephant Man; *The Sea
Wolves*. TV incl: *Rogue Male*;
Sinking Of HMS Victoria; *Home
And Beauty*; *Tinker, Tailor,
Soldier, Spy*; *The Other 'Arf*; *All
The World's A Stage*; *The Young
Visiters*. m. (1st) actress Jill
Melford (dis.), (2nd) Sarah
Forbes; 1 s. Alexander (from 1st
m.). Hobbies: travelling,
painting. Address: c/o William
Morris Agency, London.
Birthsign: Leo.

STEEL, David, Rt Hon
Member of Parliament, b. 31
March 1938 Kirkcaldy, Scotland.
Was first elected to Parliament in
March 1965 for Roxburgh,
Selkirk and Peebles, and was the
youngest member of that
Parliament. Became the Liberal
Party Leader in July 1976. m.
Judy; 3 s. Graeme, Rory, Billy, 1
d. Catriona. Hobby: vintage cars.
Address: c/o The Liberal Party
Headquarters, 1 Whitehall Place,
London SW1, or House of
Commons, London. Birthsign:
Aries. **Favourite Place:** 'The
riverbank at Ettrick Bridge:
beautiful and peaceful.'

STEELE, Tommy, OBE

Actor, b. 17 Dec 1936 London. Was discovered while playing in the Two I's Coffee Bar in London. Within 10 weeks was a teenage idol. Stage incl: variety shows; pantomime; *She Stoops To Conquer*; *Half A Sixpence*; *The Servant Of Two Masters*; *Meet Me In London*; *Hans Andersen*; *An Evening With Tommy Steele*; *Singin' In The Rain*. Films incl: *Half A Sixpence*. TV incl: *The Tommy Steele Show*; *Twelfth Night*; *In Search Of Charlie Chaplin*; *A Special Tommy Steele*; *Tommy Steele And A Show*; *Quincy's Quest*. m. former dancer Ann Donoghue; 1 d. Emma. Hobbies: squash, painting. Address: c/o Talent Artists, London. Birthsign: Sagittarius. **Favourite Place:** 'Home.'

STENNETT, Stan, MBE

Comedian/actor, b. 30 July 1927 Cardiff, Wales. First big break as resident comic on radio's *Welsh Rarebit*, then *Show Band* and *The Black And White Minstrels*. Film: *Possessions*. TV incl: *Stan At Ease*; *Road Show*; *The Good Old Days*; *Those Wonderful TV Times*; *The Golden Shot*; *Celebrity Squares*; *Top Town*; *Leeds United*; *What A Performance*; *Cries From A Watchtower*; a trilogy of plays written by his son, Roger, *1, 2, 3*; now a regular on *Crossroads*. Administrator for Roses Theatre, Tewkesbury, and New Hereford Theatre, Hereford; also runs cinemas. m. Betty; 2 s. Roger, Ceri. Hobbies: most sports, especially soccer, flying. Address: c/o Geo Bartram Enterprises, Birmingham. Birthsign: Leo. **Favourite Place:** 'The view from the TV room of my house—looking across the fir trees to the Wenallt Hills. A real slice of my native Wales.'

STEPHENSON, Pamela

Comedienne, b. 4 Dec Auckland, Australia. Trained at the Australian National Institute of Dramatic Art. Came to England in 1976. Stage incl: *Charles Charming's Challenges*; *Not In Front Of the Audience*; *The Pirates Of Penzance*. Films incl: *History Of The World, Part I*; *The Secret Policeman's Other Ball*; *Superman III*; *Finders Keepers*. TV incl: *Not The Nine O'clock News* (which won an Emmy and BAFTA Award, 1981); *The New Avengers*; *Target*; *Hazell*; *Funny Man*; *Behind The Scenes With . . .*; and in America, NBC's *Saturday Night Live*; *The Johnny Carson Show*. 1 d. Daisy Stephenson-Connolly. Hobbies: travel, parties, playing outrageous practical jokes. Address: c/o ICM, London. Birthsign: Sagittarius. **Favourite Place:** Kathmandu: '"For the wildest dreams of Kew are the facts of Kathmandu"— Kipling.'

STEVENS, Ronnie

Actor/director, b. 2 Sept 1930 London. Trained at RADA and PARADA. Began in revue, his earliest successes being *Intimacy At 8.30*; *For Amusement Only*; *The Lord Chamberlain Regrets*. Other stage incl: *King Lear*; *Twelfth Night*; seasons at New Shakespeare Company and the Bristol Old Vic; *St Joan*; *Romeo And Juliet*; *The Government Inspector*; *Arms And The Man*; *The Beggar's Opera*; *84 Charing Cross Road*; *A Patriot For Me*; *Time And The Conways*. Films incl: several of the *Doctor* series; *I'm All Right Jack*; *A Home Of Your Own*. TV incl: *Twelfth Night*; *Cover Her Face*; *Roll Over Beethoven*; *Bulman*. m. Ann Bristow; 2 s. Paul, Guy. Hobbies: painting, music, yoga. Address: c/o Larry Dalzell Assocs, London. Birthsign: Virgo. **Favourite Place:** 'Anywhere it is quiet in the English countryside.'

STEVENSON, Jeff
Comedian, b. 3 March 1961 London. Trained at the Barbara Speake Stage School. Film: *Bugsy Malone*. TV incl: *The Thora Hird Show*; *Citizen Smith*; *Get Some In*; *Search For A Star*; *Knees Up*; *Chas And Dave's Knees Up*; *Live From Her Majesty's*; *The Entertainers*; *Entertainment Express*; *Freddie Star Showcase*; *Punchlines*; *Blankety Blank*; *Late, Late Breakfast Show*; *The Laughter Show*. Hobbies: travel, golf, cooking, keep-fit. Address: c/o Derek Block Artists, London. Birthsign: Pisces. **Favourite Place**: 'The Canary Isles, especially Tenerife. To see the top of Mount Teide on a clear day is a beautiful sight.'

STEVENSON, Parker
Actor, b. 4 June 1952 US. After studying at Princeton, he entered show business via commercials. Well known for his role in TV's *Falcon Crest*. Films incl: *A Separate Place*; *Our Time*; *Stroker Ace*. Other TV incl: *The Hardy Boys Mysteries*; *Gunsmoke*; *The Streets Of San Francisco*; *Shooting Stars*. m. actress Kirstie Alley. Hobbies: auto racing, tennis, rowing, soccer, hockey. Address: c/o McCartt, Oreck, Barrett, 9200 Sunset Blvd, Suite 1009, Los Angeles, California 90069. Birthsign: Gemini. **Favourite Place**: 'Cabo San Lucas, Mexico.'

STEWART, Alastair
ITN newscaster/reporter, b. 22 June 1952 Emsworth, Hampshire. Began career with Southern TV. Worked on the award-winning magazine programme *Day By Day*; *Southern Report*; *People Rule!*; *Your Westminster*; *Energy: What Crisis?* Moved to ITN in 1980. Industrial Correspondent, 1980–82. Has presented *News At One*; *News At 5.45*; *News At Ten*; *Channel 4 News*. Reported on the Liberals in the 1983 General Election; 1984 European Elections; the Pope's visit to Britain; the Royal wedding; first live TV from House of Lords. m. TV production assistant Sally; 2 d. Alexandra, Clementine. Hobbies: food, wine, reading, writing. Address: c/o ITN, London. Birthsign: Cancer. **Favourite Place**: 'A stream in the Hampshire village of Arlesford: ducks, trout, clean air, no telephones.'

STEWART, Allan
Comedian/impressionist/singer, b. 30 July 1950 Glasgow. Having made his first record at the age of 10, he began working in clubs and theatres even before he left school. On stage he's appeared at the London Palladium and in Royal shows as well as in summer seasons and pantomime. Has made many appearances for STV and BBC Scotland, and has also had his own radio show. TV incl: *The Allan Stewart Tapes*; *Hello, Good Evening, Welcome*; *Go For It*. Has also had success in America, Canada and on the Continent. Address: c/o Richard Stone, London. Birthsign: Leo. **Favourite Place**: 'The white sandy beaches of the Caribbean.'

STILGOE, Richard

Presenter/writer/performer, b. 28 March 1943 Camberley, Surrey. A product of the Cambridge Footlights revue. Has since had wide experience in radio and TV incl: *A Class By Himself*; *Nationwide*; *And Now The Good News*; *That's Life!*; *Finders Keepers*; *Stilgoe's Around*; *Royal Variety Performance*, 1982. Wrote *Starlight Express* with Andrew Lloyd Webber. Plays 14 instruments, sings in opera and tours Britain with his one-man show. m. Annabel; 2 d. Jemima, Holly, 3 s. Rufus, Jack, Joe. Hobbies: sailing, DIY. Address: c/o Noel Gay Artists, London. Birthsign: Aries. **Favourite Place:** 'SX 765389—Because hardly anyone can find it.'

STOCK, Nigel

Actor, b. 21 Sept 1919 Malta. Studied at RADA and acted until the war; became a major at 23. Has acted in nearly 50 films incl: *The Lion In Winter*; *Cromwell*; *The Mirror Cracked*; *The Young Sherlock Holmes*. His many stage and TV appearances incl: *And No Birds Sing*; *Owen MD*; *The Doctors*; *Churchill's People*; *Tinker, Tailor, Soldier, Spy*; *Wingate*; *London Assurance*; *Van Der Valk*; *Flesh And Blood*; *A Tale Of Two Cities*; *Dear Brutus*; *The Union*; *Yes, Minister*; *A Man Called Intrepid*; *Pickwick Papers*; *Oscar*; *Barretts Of Wimpole Street*. m. (1st) Sonia Williams (dis.), (2nd) Richenda Carey; 2 d. Penny, Polly, 1 s. Robin (all from 1st m.). Hobbies: ornithology, stamps. Address: c/o DGLA, London. Birthsign: Virgo. **Favourite Place:** Scilly Isles, 'Because they are beautiful, unique, the place for bird migrations.'

STOPPARD, Miriam, MB, BS, MD, MRCP

Doctor/medical reporter, b. 12 May 1937 Newcastle-upon-Tyne. Worked in clinical medicine, specialising in dermatology. Joined pharmaceutical industry, became research director, then managing director. TV incl: *Don't Ask Me*; *Don't Just Sit There*; *Where There's Life*; *The Health Show*; *So You Want To Stop Smoking*. Books incl: *Miriam Stoppard's Book Of Babycare*; *Mirian Stoppard's Book Of Healthcare*; *The Face And Body Book*; *Marks & Spencer Book Of Babycare*; *Marks & Spencer Book Of Childcare*. Also regular contributor to magazines. m. playwright Tom Stoppard; 2 step-s. Oliver, Barnaby, 2 s. William, Edmund. Hobbies: family, gardening, photography. Address: c/o Yorkshire TV, Leeds. Birthsign: Taurus.

STOURTON, Edward

TV news reporter, b. 24 Nov 1957 Lagos, Nigeria. Joined ITN as graduate trainee in 1979. Has worked on *News At One*, *News At 5.45*, *News At Ten*, and has contributed to ITN Specials incl: *The Royal Wedding*; *The Papal Visit*. Founder member of *Channel Four News* team and has since been writer, Home News Editor and Chief Sub-Editor. Now full-time reporter for *Channel Four News*, covering foreign and domestic news and specialist coverage of religious affairs. m. Margaret McEwen; 1 s. Ivo, 1 d. Eleanor. Hobbies: tennis, 19th Century novels. Address: c/o C4 TV, London. Birthsign: Sagittarius. **Favourite Place:** 'The Brompton Oratory, for the best sung Mass in London.'

STRAULI, Christopher
Actor, b. 13 April 1946
Harpenden, Herts. Trained at
RADA before joining the Old
Vic in Bristol in 1970. Has
worked in rep, and West End
appearances incl: *The Licentious
Fly*; *Season's Greetings*. TV break
came with the part of Bunny in
Raffles. Other TV incl: *Harriet's
Back In Town*; *Owen MD*;
Family At War; *Warship*; *Angels*;
For Tea On Sunday; *Gentle Folk*;

Measure For Measure; *Romeo And
Juliet*; *Only When I Laugh*;
Edward The Seventh; *Eustace And
Hilda*; *Dempsey And Makepeace*;
Lytton's Diary; *Full House*; *A
Crack In The Ice*. m. Lesley; 2 d.
Belinda, Hanneli, 1 s. Barnaby.
Hobbies: DIY, computers,
gardening, games, music, golf.
Address: c/o Michael Ladkin,
London. Birthsign: Aries.
Favourite Place: 'Crystal Palace
Restaurant, Walt Disney World,
Florida.'

STREET-PORTER, Janet
Presenter/producer, b. 27 Dec
1946 London. Wide journalistic
experience on magazines and
newspapers (*Daily Mail*, *London
Evening Standard*, *Observer*) and
commercial radio. Presented
London Weekend Show for five

years; *Saturday Night People* with
Clive James and Russell Harty;
produced two series of *Twentieth
Century Box*; co-presenter of *The
Six O'Clock Show*; currently
producing a series of short films
for Channel 4. Books: *The British
Teapot*; *Scandal!* and is now
writing a book on British taste.
m. director Frank Cvitanovich.
Address: c/o Hatton & Baker,
London. Birthsign: Capricorn.
Favourite Place: 'Lying in the
bath after work!'

STRIDE, John
Actor, b. 11 July 1936 London.
Trained at RADA; professional
debut at Liverpool Rep in 1957
before joining the army. On
demob went to the Old Vic. Five
years with the National Theatre
before his TV break. Films incl:

Bitter Harvest; *Brannigan*;
Macbeth; *Juggernaut*; *The Omen*;
A Bridge Too Far. TV incl: *The
Main Chance*; *Wilde Alliance*;
Love Among The Artists; *Henry
VIII*; *Diamonds*; Lloyd George in
Number 10. m. actress April
Wilding; 3 d. Philippa, Lindsay,
Eleanor. Address: c/o Hatton &
Baker, London. Birthsign:
Cancer. **Favourite Place:** 'A
good dining table: likely to meet
more happy hedonists there than
anywhere.'

STRONG, Gwyneth
Actress, b. 2 Dec 1959 London.
Made stage debut in the Royal
Court production of *Live Like
Pigs*, at the age of 11. Other stage
incl: *Shout Across The River*;

Heroes; *Care*; *Sugar And Spice*;
Strangers In The Night; *Glad
Hand*; *Voyzeck*; *Loving Women*.
TV incl: *Edward The Seventh*;
The Story Of Ruth; *Rainy Day
Women*; *Mr Right (Love Story)*;
It's A Lovely Day Tomorrow;
Inside Out; *Paradise Postponed*.
Hobbies: theatre, swimming.
Address: c/o Plant & Froggatt,
London. Birthsign: Sagittarius.
Favourite Place: 'As yet I have
not found one, but hope that very
soon I do.'

STUBBS, Una
Actress/dancer, b. 1 May 1937 London. Trained as a dancer at La Roche Dancing School, Slough, and made her stage debut in *A Midsummer Night's Dream* at the Theatre Royal, Windsor. Other stage incl: *Grab Me A Gondola*; *On The Brighter Side*; *The Knack*; *The Soldier's Tale*; *Cowardy Custard*; *Oh, Mr Porter*; *Baggage*. Films incl: *Summer Holiday*; *Wonderful Life*. TV incl: *Cool For Cats*; Cliff Richard series; *Till Death Us Do Part*; *Fawlty Towers*; *Give Us A Clue*; *Worzel Gummidge*. m. (1st) actor Peter Gilmore (dis.), (2nd) actor Nicky Henson (dis.); 3 s. Jason, Christian. Joe. Hobby: embroidery. Address: c/o Richard Stone, London. Birthsign: Taurus. **Favourite Place:** 'My home, especially when it's quiet.'

STUYCK, Joris
Actor, b. 23 April 1952 Orpington, Kent. Took part in many of the productions that were staged while he was studying at McGill University, Montreal, Canada. Film: *The Shooting Party*. TV incl: *We'll Meet Again*; *Reilly Ace Of Spies*; *A Woman Of Substance*; *Tender Is The Night*. Hobbies: music, languages, swimming, sailing, long trips to unfamiliar places. Address: c/o Kate Feast Management, London. Birthsign: Taurus. **Favourite Place:** 'Any country I haven't seen before or the cinema when the house lights go down.'

SUCHET, John
ITN reporter/newscaster, b. 29 March 1944 London. Began career with Reuters, followed by the BBC. ITN's Washington correspondent, 1981–83. Has covered major news events incl: Iran Revolution; Soviet Occupation of Afghanistan. m. (dis.); 3 s. Damian, Kieran, Rory. Hobbies: classical music, photography, traditional jazz, playing the trombone. Address: c/o ITN, London. Birthsign: Aries. **Favourite Place:** 'On the settee with Beethoven and *The Times* crossword.'

SUGDEN, Mollie
Actress, b. 21 July Keighley, Yorks. Trained at the Guildhall School of Music and Drama, and has recently been made a Member. Spent eight years in rep. TV incl: *Hugh And I*; *Please Sir!*; the *Doctor* series; *For The Love Of Ada*; *The Liver Birds*; *Coronation Street*; *Whodunnit?*; *Come Back Mrs Noah*; *That's My Boy*; and perhaps her best-known role in *Are You Being Served?* m. William Moore; twin s. Robin, Simon. Hobby: gardening. Address: c/o Joan Reddin, London. Birthsign: Cancer. **Favourite Place:** 'Home. Like most Cancerians, I love to travel but always want to get back to my home and my loved ones.'

SULLIVAN, Susan
Actress, b. 18 Nov New York.
Trained at American Academy of
Dramatic Arts. Probably best

known for her role as Maggie
Gioberti in TV soap opera *Falcon
Crest*. Other TV incl: *Swat; Julie
Farr, MD; It's A Living; Having
Babies; Rich Man, Poor Man; The
Incredible Hulk; Breaking Up Is
Hard To Do; The New Maverick;
The Ordeal Of Dr Mudd*. Hobbies:
collecting art, literature, music,
travel, skiing, charity work.
Address: c/o STE Representation,
211 Beverly Drive, Beverly Hills,
California 90212. Birthsign:
Scorpio.

SUMPTER, Donald
Actor, b. 13 Feb 1943
Northampton. Trained at
RADA, followed by two years at
Nottingham rep. Stage incl:
*Cowboy Mouth; The Entertainers;
Sky Blue Life; Next Time I'll Sing
To You; Edward II; Mary Barnes;
Much Ado About Nothing; Bastard
Angel; Hedda Gabler; Mrs
Gauguin; An Honourable Trade*.
Films incl: *The Lost Continent;*

*The Walking Stick; Stardust;
Sunday Bloody Sunday; The Curse
Of The Pink Panther; Unstable
Elements*. TV incl: *A Pig And A
Poke; Doctor Who; Hadleigh;
Justice; The Look; Target; Antony
And Cleopatra; Bergerac; Bleak
House; Oscar Wilde; Time
Trouble*. Hobbies: sailing, lying.
Address: c/o Kate Feast
Management, London. Birthsign:
Aquarius. **Favourite Place:** 'My
most comfortable armchair with
a copy of the *TV Times*.'

SUTCLIFFE, Albert
Comedian, b. 22 Dec 1940 Leeds,
Yorks. One of the
Grumbleweeds. Broke their
record with three years at Opera
House Theatre, Scarborough.

Then BBC Radio series and TV
incl: *Children's Royal Variety
Show; Grumbleweeds Radio Show*
(own TV series). m. Marie
Josephine; 3 s. Stephen, John,
Andrew. Hobbies: jogging,
watching snooker, reading,
music, writing songs, working as
a hospital porter. Address: c/o
Time Artistes, Oldham.
Birthsign: Capricorn. **Favourite
Place:** 'A night in with my wife
having a meal, because I don't get
many (nights in, not meals).'

SUTTON, Dudley
Actor/writer/director, b. 6 April
1933 East Molesley, Surrey.
Trained at the Joan Littlewood
Theatre Workshop; failed at

RADA. Stage incl: author of
Quack-Quack; directed *Fanshen;
Oh! What A Lovely War; Curse
Of The Starving Class*. Films incl:
*The Devils; Casanova; The House;
Lamb; Chain Reaction*. TV incl:
*Widows; Juno And The Paycock;
The Beiderbecke Affair*. m. (dis.); 2
s. Peter, Barnaby, 1 d. Fanny.
Hobby: music. Address: c/o Plant
& Froggatt, London. Birthsign:
Aries. **Favourite Place:** 'The
middle of London because it isn't
dead.'

SWIFT, Clive
Actor, b. 9 Feb 1936 Liverpool. Started in rep at Nottingham before joining the Royal Shakespeare Company. Also directed at LAMDA and RADA. Films incl: *Catch Us If You Can*; *Frenzy*; *Excalibur*; *A Passage To India*. Many TV plays and series incl: *South Riding*; *Clayhanger*; *Roll On Four O'Clock*; *Waugh On Crime*; *Churchill: The Wilderness Years*; *Lucky Jim*; *The Barchester Chronicles*; *The Gentle Touch*; *Pickwick Papers*. Books incl: *The Job Of Acting*; *The Performing World Of The Actor*. m. writer Margaret Drabble (dis.); 1 d. Rebecca, 2 s. Adam, Joseph. Hobbies: music, The Actors' Centre (of which he was originator). Address: c/o ICM, London. Birthsign: Aquarius. **Favourite Place:** 'Lords on a sunny day. Fresh air, beautiful cricket, and it's near home!'

SYKES, Eric
Comedian/writer, b. 4 May 1923 Oldham, Lancs. On stage he has toured extensively with Jimmy Edwards in *Big Bad Mouse* and with his own show, *A Hatful Of Sykes*. Films incl: *The Bargee*; *One Way Pendulum*; *Those Magnificent Men In Their Flying Machines*; *Rotten To The Core*; *Spy With A Cold Nose*; *The Plank* (scripted, directed and acted in); *Shalako*; *Monte Carlo Or Bust*; *Rhubarb*; *Theatre Of Blood*; *Ghost In The Noonday Sun*. Radio scripts incl: *Educating Archie*; *Variety Bandbox*; own shows. TV incl: *Saturday Spectaculars*; *Curry And Chips*; *Charley's Aunt*; own shows. Book: *Sykes Of Sebastopol Terrace*. m. Edith Milbrandt; 3 d. Catherine, Susan, Julie, 1 s. David. Hobby: golf. Address: c/o Paul Elliott, London. Birthsign: Taurus.

SYMS, Sylvia
Actress, b. 6 Jan 1936 London. Trained at RADA and first play was *The Apple Cart* 1953. Much theatre experience incl: *Peter Pan*; *Not Now Darling*; *In Praise Of Love*; *An Ideal Husband*; *The Vortex*; *Entertaining Mr Sloane*; *Ghosts*. Film debut in 1956 *My Teenage Daughter*. Other films incl: *The World Of Suzie Wong*; *Operation Crossbow*; *The Tamarind Seed*; *There Goes The Bride*; *Run Wild, Run Free*. TV credits incl: *My Good Woman* (with Leslie Crowther); *The Life Of Nancy Astor*; *A Murder Is Announced*; *Time For Murder*. m. Alan Edney; 1 s. Benjamin, 1 d. Beatrice. Hobbies: gardening, horse riding. Address: c/o Marmont Management, London. Birthsign: Capricorn. **Favourite Place:** 'The Isabella plantation, Richmond Park, as it has wonderful memories of when my children were very young.'

T, Mr
Actor, b. Chicago, Illinois. Born Lawrence Tureaud, he excelled in athletics and as a wrestling champion and football player. After serving as a military policeman, became a bodyguard. Best known for his role as B A (for Bad Attitude) Baracus in TV's *The A-Team*. Films incl: *Penitentiary*; *D C Cab*; *Rocky III*. Other TV incl: *Mr T*. Hobbies: working out, being with children. Address: c/o Triad Artists, 7083 Hollywood Blvd, Hollywood, California 90028. Birthsign: Gemini. **Favourite Place:** 'Either at home in Chicago with my family, or visiting children who are less fortunate than others.'

TANDY, Mark
Actor, b. 8 Feb 1957 Athlone, Ireland. Read drama at Bristol University, then trained at Webber Douglas Academy. Theatre incl: with the RSC, incl *Nicholas Nickleby*; *Major Barbara* at the National Theatre; *The Lucky Chance*, Royal Court. TV incl: *Aubrey Beardsley*; *The Jewel In The Crown*; *Nicholas Nickleby*; *Gems*. Address: c/o Hattan & Baker, London. Birthsign: Aquarius.

TARBUCK, Jimmy
Comedian/entertainer, b. 6 Feb Liverpool. Started career at 18 as a compére with a rock 'n' roll show, then as a Butlin's Redcoat. Turned professional 1963 working in clubs in Liverpool and Manchester. TV debut 1963 *Comedy Bandbox*. Other TV incl: *Sunday Night At The London Palladium*; *It's Tarbuck*; *Tarbuck's Back*; *Winner Takes All*; *Live From Her Majesty's*; *Tarby And Friends*; *Bring Me Sunshine*; *This Is Your Life* (1983) Books incl: *Tarbuck On Golf*. m. Pauline; 2 d. Lisa, Cheryl, 1 s. James. Hobbies: golf, football, all sports. Address: c/o Peter Prichard, London. Birthsign: Aquarius. **Favourite Place:** 'Anfield Stadium watching Liverpool FC . . . there's no greater place on earth.'

TARMEY, William
Actor, b. 4 April 1941 Manchester. No formal training, but now well known for his role as Jack Duckworth in Granada TV's *Coronation Street*. m. Alma; 1 s. Carl, 1 d. Sara. Hobbies: golf, singing. Address: c/o Granada TV, Manchester. Birthsign: Aries. **Favourite Place:** 'Home, because I like it.'

TAYLFORTH, Gillian
Actress, b. 14 Aug 1955 London. Trained as a secretary before taking up acting at evening classes with the Anna Scher Theatre. First professional part in a BBC TV *Play For Today*. Film: *The Long Good Friday*. TV incl: *Zigger Zagger*; *The Rag Trade*; *Phyllis Dixey*; *Thunder Cloud*; *Little Girls Don't*; *Watch This Space*; *Hi-De-Hi!*; *Big Jim And The Figaro Club*; *Sink Or Swim*; *On Safari*; *The Gentle Touch*; *EastEnders*; *Minder*. Hobbies: dancing, any sport, swimming, reading, driving, keep-fit. Address: c/o Anna Scher Theatre Management, London. Birthsign: Leo. **Favourite Place:** 'My mum and dad's place on Sundays, because of the family atmosphere and Sunday lunch!'

TEWSON, Josephine

Actress, b. 26 Feb London. Trained at RADA then rep at Darlington, Salisbury, Bristol Old Vic. In London at the Mermaid and West End theatres her plays have incl: *The Real Inspector Hound*; *Habeas Corpus*; *Rookery Nook*; *Noises Off*. Film: *The Hound Of The Baskervilles*. On TV has been the foil for comedians incl: Ronnie Barker; Ronnie Corbett; Dick Emery; Jimmy Tarbuck; Bruce Forsyth; Les Dawson; Frankie Howerd; Charlie Drake. Other TV incl: *Lord Rustless Entertains*; *Son Of The Bride*; *Odd Man Out*; *Shelley*. m. (1st) the late actor Leonard Rossiter (dis.), (2nd) (dec.). Hobbies: watching cricket, music. Address: c/o International Artists, London. Birthsign: Pisces. **Favourite Place:** 'Nothing more relaxing than sitting in the Mound Stand at Lords in the sunshine watching a county match.'

THATCHER, Margaret Hilda, Rt Hon

Prime Minister, b. 13 Oct 1925 Grantham, Lincs. Oxford University and called to the Bar 1954. Conservative MP for Finchley 1959. Secretary of State for Education and Science 1970. Elected Leader of the Conservative Party 1975 and Leader of the Opposition. Britain's first woman Prime Minister after General Election 1979. m. Denis; 1 s. Mark, 1 d. Carol (twins). Hobbies: walking, reading, gardening, music. Address: c/o 10 Downing St, London. Birthsign: Libra. **Favourite Place:** 'The garden around the ruin of Scotney Castle in Kent. It is especially beautiful in spring, full of rhododendrons and azaleas. The whole atmosphere is so peaceful—it's a different world. One can walk around the garden just looking at nature and feel overwhelmed by the joy of being alive.'

THAW, John

Actor, b. 3 Jan 1942 Manchester. Trained at RADA. Stage debut 1960 Liverpool Playhouse in *A Shred Of Evidence*. London debut at Royal Court Theatre 1961 in *The Fire Raisers*. Recent theatre incl: *Henry VIII*; *Pygmalion*. Film debut: *The Loneliness Of The Long Distance Runner*. Other films incl: *Sweeney*; *Sweeney 2*. TV incl: *Redcap*; *The Younger Generation*; *Thick As Thieves*; *The Sweeney*; *Drake's Venture*; *Killer Waiting*; *Mitch*; *Home to Roost*. m. (1st) Sally Alexander (dis.), (2nd) actress Sheila Hancock; 2 d. Melanie (from 1st m.), Joanna (from 2nd m.). Hobbies: music, reading. Address: c/o John Redway, London. Birthsign: Capricorn.

THIRKETTLE, Joan

Reporter, b. 14 Sept 1947 Kent. Started career with Associated-Rediffusion as a trainee researcher; left to join Radio Caroline as a researcher. Then worked for the *Daily Mail* and *The Sunday Times*. Radio reporter for BBC and British Forces Broadcasting, and London Broadcasting. Joined ITN as a reporter in 1976. 1 d. Daisy, 1 s. Michael. Address: c/o ITN, London. Birthsign: Virgo. Virgo. **Favourite Place:** 'A secret. If everyone knew, they'd all want to go there.'

THOMAS, Betty
Actress, b. 27 July St Louis, Missouri. Started as a waitress, then joined the Second City Improvisational Theater in Chicago. Films incl: *Loose Shoes*; *Used Cars*; *Tunnelvision*; *Jackson County Jail*. TV incl: plays Lucy Bates in TV's *Hill Street Blues*. Other TV incl: *Outside Chance*; *Nashville Grab*. Hobbies: photography, flying helicopters, riding motorcycles, target practice, weight lifting, painting, fishing, improvisational theatre. Address: c/o SGA Representation Inc, 12750 Ventura Blvd, Suite 102, Studio City, California 91604. Birthsign: Leo.

THOMAS, Gareth
Actor. Trained at RADA and theatre experience at Yvonne Arnaud Theatre, Guildford; Liverpool Playhouse; Derby Playhouse; with the Royal Shakespeare Company and Welsh Actors' Company. Most recently on stage at Theatre Royal, Windsor. TV incl: *How Green Was My Valley*; *Who Pays The Ferryman?*; *Blake's Seven*; *Hammer House Of Horror*; *The Bell*; *The Citadel*; *Love And Marriage*; *Sherlock Holmes*; *Dog Food Dan And The Carmarthen Cowboy*; *By The Sword Divided*; *Morgan's Boy*. Address: c/o Leading Artists, London. **Favourite Place:** Glencoe.

THOMAS, Philip Michael
Actor, b. 26 May Columbus, Ohio. Started career in off-Broadway and Broadway plays. Theatre incl: *No Place To Be Somebody*; *Reggae*; *Selling Of The President*; *Hair*. Films incl: *Stigma*; *Sparkle*; *Book Of Numbers*; *Coonskin*. TV incl: *This Man Stands Alone*; *Starsky And Hutch*; *Medical Center*; *Roots: The Next Generation*; *Police Woman*; *Wonder Woman*. Now best known for his role as Detective Ricardo Tubbs in TV's *Miami Vice*. Has written a musical, *The Legend Of Stacker Lee*, and is president of his own music company PMT International. m. (dis.). Hobbies: composing songs, photography, painting, fixing up cars. Address: c/o Exclusive Artists Agency, 4040 Vineland Ave, Studio City, California. Birthsign: Gemini.

THOMPSON, Derek
Racing and sports presenter, b. 31 July 1950 Stockton, Co Durham. Presents racing on ITV. Also *Stunt Challenge*; *Extra Time* (Tyne Tees weekly sports programme); racing correspondent Central TV. Also partner in Derek Thompson Assocs, which deals in sports promotion and PR. m. Janie (daughter of BBC rugby commentator Bill McLaren); 2 s. James, Gordon. Hobbies: family, keep-fit. Address: c/o Derek Thompson Assocs, London. Birthsign: Leo. **Favourite Place:** 'Riding out on a racehorse on a summer morning— preferably at Newmarket.'

THOMSON, Gordon
Actor, b. 2 March Ottawa, Canada. Trained at the Shakespearian Festival, Ontario. Theatre incl: *Loot*; *The Fantasticks*; *King John*; *Godspell*. Films incl: *Explosion*; *Leopard In The Snow*; *Acts Of Love*; *The Intruder*. Well known on TV for his portrayal of Adam in *Dynasty*. Other TV incl: *Flappers*; *The Great Detective*; *Secret Lover*; *Fantasy Island*. m. Maureen (dis.). Hobbies: cooking, gardening, animals, swimming, reading. Address: c/o William Morris Agency, 151 El Camino Drive, Beverly Hills, California 90212. Birthsign: Pisces. **Favourite Place:** 'The beach, any beach, anywhere.'

THORBURN, Cliff
Snooker player, b. 16 Jan 1948 Victoria, BC, Canada. Turned professional 1973 when he first came to England. Has won 10 Canadian Championships; two Australian Masters; two English Masters; one World Championship. Holds the World Championship break record 147 points. m. Barbara; 1 s. Jamie. Hobbies: golf, reading. Address: c/o Robert Winsor, St Audrey Lane, St Ives, Cambs. Birthsign: Capricorn. **Favourite Place:** 'Victoria, BC. I wish I could have appreciated it more as a youngster.'

THORNTON, Frank
Actor, b. 15 Jan 1921 London. Started in Sir Donald Wolfit's company and has recently returned to Shakespeare on stage. Served as RAF officer during the war. Theatre incl: *Twelfth Night* (with the Royal Shakespeare Company); *The Doctor's Dilemma*; *Me And My Girl*. Well known as Captain Peacock in TV's *Are You Being Served?* Other TV incl: *It's A Square World*; *The World Of Beachcomber*; *Steptoe And Son*; *The Taming Of The Shrew*. m. actress Beryl Evans; 1 d. Jane. Hobbies: music, photography. Address: c/o Annie Clough Management, London. Birthsign: Capricorn. **Favourite Place:** 'Home! I've done a lot of touring.'

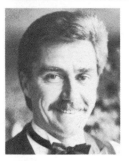

THORP, Richard
Actor, b. 2 Jan Purley. Started TV career as Dr Rennie in *Emergency Ward 10*. Is now best known as Alan Turner in YTV's *Emmerdale Farm*. Theatre incl: *Murder In The Vicarage*; *Moving*. Films incl: *The Dam Busters*; *The Barretts Of Wimpole Street*; *The Good Companions*. Other TV incl: *Family At War*; *The Cedar Tree*; *To The Manor Born*; *Strangers*; *Where Are They Now?* m. (1st) Maureen Moore, (2nd) Noola; 1 d. Kate, 2 s. Douglas Stephen (all from 1st m.), 1 step-d. Sarah. Hobbies: motorcycling, gardening. Address: c/o Jean Drysdale Management, London. Birthsign: Capricorn. **Favourite Place:** 'The country—I'm torn between Sussex and the Yorkshire countryside.'

THORPE-BATES, Peggy
Actress. b. 11 Aug 1914 London.
Professional debut Croydon rep
1934; then Memorial Theatre,
Stratford-upon-Avon; rep at
Harrogate, Birmingham, Bristol.
West End debut *Country Wife*
1938. With ENSA during the
war. Countless radio and West
End roles. Films incl: *Georgy
Girl*; *Mosquito Squadron*; *A Touch
Of Love*. First TV: *Little Dry*

Thorn at Alexandra Palace. More
recent TV incl: *Richard II*;
Timeslip; *The Glittering Prizes*;
Two's Company; *The Saint*; *Tales
Of The Unexpected*; *Rumpole Of
The Bailey*; *Rumpole's Return*; *The
Young Ones*. m. actor Brian
Oulton; 1 d. actress Jenny, 1 s.
Nicholas. Hobbies: house and
garden renovation. Address: c/o
Patrick Freeman, London.
Birthsign: Leo. **Favourite
Place:** 'Dining with my husband
at his lovely club, The Garrick.'

THRELFALL, David
Actor, b. 12 Oct 1953
Manchester. Trained at
Manchester Polytechnic School
of Theatre. Many theatre credits
incl: *Bed Of Roses*; *Not Quite
Jerusalem*. With the Royal
Shakespeare Company incl: *Julius*

Caesar; *Nicholas Nickleby*; *The
Party*. TV incl: *Scum*; *The Kiss Of
Death*; *Red Monarch*; *Rolling
Home*; *The Gathering Seed*;
Nicholas Nickleby; *Dog Ends*;
King Lear (Olivier's); *The
Daughter-In-Law*; *Paradise
Postponed*. Hobby: keeping fit.
Address: c/o James Sharkey
Assocs, London. Birthsign: Libra.
Favourite Place: 'By the sea
playing music through a personal
stereo headset, because I feel
happy.'

TILBURY, Peter
Actor/scriptwriter, b. 20 Oct
1945 Redruth, Cornwall. Started
as assistant stage manager and
acting at Chelmsford rep. Later
with Welsh Drama Co, Royal
Shakespeare Company and
National Theatre. As actor, films
incl: *Our Day Out*; *Breaking
Glass*; *Those Glory Glory Days*.
As TV actor incl: *The Expert*;
Shadow Of The Tower; *Perils Of*

Pendragon; *Dixon Of Dock Green*;
My Son Reuben; *Whodunnit?* As
writer TV incl: *Sprout* (with
Anthony Matheson), *Sorry, I'm A
Stranger Here Myself*; *Shelley*; *It
Takes A Worried Man* (in which
he starred); an episode of *Never
The Twain*. Hobbies: listening to
music, collecting Art Deco.
Address: c/o Jill Foster, London.
Birthsign: Libra. **Favourite
Place:** 'Hampstead Heath. The
heart of the countryside, but close
to several decent pubs.'

TIMOTHY, Christopher
Actor, b. 14 Oct 1940 Bala,
North Wales. Trained at Central
School of Speech and Drama,
then New York. Acted with the
National Theatre and Young Vic.
West End theatre incl:
*Rosencrantz And Guildenstern Are
Dead*; *Underneath The Arches*.
Most recent theatre: *The Real
Thing*. Films incl: *Othello*
(Olivier's); *Here We Go Round
The Mulberry Bush*; *The Virgin
Soldiers*. TV incl: *Some Mothers*

Do 'Ave 'Em; *The Kitchen*;
Murder Most English; *All
Creatures Great And Small*. m.
(1st) (dis.), (2nd) Annie Swatton;
2 d. Tabitha, Kate, 4 s. Simon,
Nicholas, Robin, David (all from
1st m.), 1 d. Grace (from 2nd m.).
Hobbies: reading, writing,
swimming. Address: c/o Plant &
Froggatt, London. Birthsign:
Libra. **Favourite Place:** 'The
garden of our flat on a hot, sunny
day with Annie and all or some of
my kids.'

TODD, Bob

Actor, b. 15 Dec 1921 Faversham, Kent. A cattle breeder whose business failed at the age of 42. Turned to acting and made his TV debut 1963 in *Citizen James*. Been foil to top comics incl: Dick Emery; Marty Feldman; Michael Bentine; Des O'Connor; Benny Hill. Own TV series: *In For A Penny*. Other TV incl: *What's On Next?*; *Alan Stewart Show*; *The Generation Game*; *Steam Video Show*; *Rhubarb*; *Give Us A Clue*; *This Is Your Life*. m. Monica; 1 d. Anne, 2 s. John, Patrick. Address: c/o International Artists, London. Birthsign: Sagittarius.

TODD, Richard

Actor, b. 11 June 1919 Dublin. Trained at Italia Conti School and made his debut in 1936 in *Twelfth Night* at the Open Air Theatre, Regent's Park. Rep experience before and after the war. From 1948–65 worked mostly in films incl: *Robin Hood*; *The Dam Busters*; *The Longest Day*. Later films incl: *The Big Sleep*; *Jenny's War*. Numerous theatre appearances incl *The Business Of Murder*. In 1970 formed Triumph Theatre Productions. TV incl: *Wuthering Heights*; *The Brighton Mesmerists*. Awarded Hollywood Golden Globe, Best Actor Oscar nomination for *The Hasty Heart*. m. (1st) Catherine Grant-Bogle, (2nd) Virginia Mailer; 1 s. Peter, 1 d. Fiona (both from 1st m.), 2 s. Andrew, Seumas (both from 2nd m.). Hobbies: shooting, farming, gardening, working. Address: c/o Richard Stone, London. Birthsign: Gemini.

TOMLINSON, Ricky

Actor, b. 26 Sept 1939 Blackpool. No formal training, but well known as Bobby Grant in C4's *Brookside*. Other TV incl: *United Kingdom*. m. Marlene; 2 s. Clifton, Gareth, 1 d. Kate. Hobby: converting an old church into a children's drama workshop. Address: c/o ART Casting, Liverpool. Birthsign: Libra. **Favourite Place:** 'My house—I love to spend all my time with my wife and kids.'

TONG, Jacqueline

Actress, b. 21 Feb 1950 Bristol. Trained at Rose Bruford College of Speech and Drama. Many theatre appearances incl: *The Winter's Tale* at Royal Exchange Theatre; *The Dresser* and *The Man Who Fell In Love With His Wife* in London. TV incl: *Voyage In The Dark*; *Upstairs, Downstairs*; *Hard Times*; *Phyllis Dixey*; *Spearhead*; several *Plays For Today* incl *Out Of Step*, written for her by Carol Bunyan; *Coronation Street*; *The Climber*; *Bazaar And Rummage*. m. Gordon Nicholas. Hobbies: Open University ('hardly a hobby!'), gardening, reading, walking in natural surroundings. Address: c/o Annie Clough, London. Birthsign: Pisces. **Favourite Place:** 'A small beach beside Crummock Water, Cumbria. Beautiful for views and cooking on an open fire.'

TRAVANTI, Daniel J
Actor, b. 7 March Kenosha, Wisconsin. Trained at Yale Drama School and Bucks County Playhouse. Theatre incl: *Who's Afraid Of Virginia Woolf?*; *Othello*; *Twigs*; *The Taming Of The Shrew*. TV films incl: *A Case Of Libel*; *Adam*; *Aurora*. Plays Captain Frank Furillo in TV's *Hill Street Blues* and is also a regular cast member of *General Hospital*. TV guest roles incl: *The Defenders*; *Route 66*; *Kojak*; *The FBI*; *Hart To Hart*; *Knot's Landing*. Hobbies: cooking, sports, working on his new home. Address: c/o Bauman, Hiller and Assocs, 9220 Sunset Blvd, Suite 202, Los Angeles, California 90069. Birthsign: Pisces. **Favourite Place:** New York.

TREACHER, Bill
Actor, b. 6 June London. Trained at Webber Douglas Academy of Dramatic Art and worked in rep until West End debut 1963 in *Shout For Life*. Joined Brian Rix Theatre of Laughter 1967–69 when appearances incl *Let Sleeping Wives Lie* and *Uproar In The House*. In *Murder At The Vicarage* 1977–79 at Fortune Theatre, London. Many tours and summer seasons. TV incl: *Bless This House*; *Angels*; *Maggie And Her*; *Grange Hill*; *Agatha Christie Hour*; *Fanny By Gaslight*; *Sweet Sixteen*; *The Bright Side*; *Who Sir? Me Sir?*; *EastEnders*. m. actress Kate Kessey, 1 s. Jamie, 1 d. Sophie. Hobbies: sailing, reading. Address: c/o BBC TV Elstree, Borehamwood. Birthsign: Gemini. **Favourite Place:** 'The view from my son's bedroom across to the church in apple blossom time.'

TROTTER, Robert
Actor, b. 7 March 1930 Dumbarton. Originally an English teacher and university lecturer in drama. Since 1971 has worked as an actor and director in Scotland, at Royal Court Upstairs and King's Head, London. Spent 19 years in radio and was with the BBC Drama Repertory Company. Numerous TV appearances incl STV's *Take The High Road*. Hobbies: reading, music. Address: c/o Young Casting Agency, Glasgow. Birthsign: Pisces. **Favourite Place:** 'Dumbarton Castle, overlooking the rivers—the setting for long childhood summers.'

TROUGHTON, Michael
Actor, b. 2 March 1955 Hampstead, London. Started career as acting assistant stage manager with the Unicorn Theatre. Then Watford, Young Vic and Leeds Playhouse. Theatre incl: *Hay Fever*. Numerous TV appearances incl: *Backs To The Land*; *Testament Of Youth*; *The Mill On The Floss*; *A Moment In Time*; *Nancy Astor*; *A Fatal Spring*; *Night Life*; *Grudge Fight*; *A Member For Chelsea*; *Take Three Women*; *Squadron*; *Strangers And Brothers*; *Tales Of The Unexpected*; *Sorrell & Son*; *A Crack In The Ice*; *Minder*; *CATS Eyes*. m. Caroline Rake; 1 s. Matthew. Hobbies: collecting old toys, model-making, golf, gardening. Address: c/o Joseph and Wagg, London. Birthsign: Pisces. **Favourite Place:** 'St Ives Bay, Cornwall, for childhood memories of summer holidays from school.'

TROUGHTON, Patrick

Actor, b. 25 March 1920 London. Trained at the Embassy School of Acting and won a scholarship to New York. After war service at sea joined the Old Vic. Best known on TV as Doctor Who, a part he played for three years. Films incl: *Frankenstein*; *The Protector*; *Doomwatch*; *Scars Of Dracula*; *Viking Queen*; *Sinbad And The Eye Of The Tiger*; *The Omen*. Numerous TV roles incl: *Coronation Street*; *Only When I Laugh*; *All Creatures Great And Small*; *Suez*; *Nanny*; *King's Royal*; *John Diamond*; *PQ17*; *Box Of Delights*. m. Shelagh; 2 d. Joanna, Jane, 1 step-d. Gill, 4 s. David, Michael, Peter, Mark, 1 step-s. Graham. Hobbies: sailing, golf, gardening, countryside. Address: c/o Film Rights, London. Birthsign: Aries. **Favourite Place:** 'Hickling Broad, Norfolk, for the sailing.'

TUMMINGS, Chris

Actor, b. 14 April 1961 Hackney, London. Trained with the Anna Scher Theatre in London and theatre incl: *Mama Dragon*; *Tooth Of Crime*. Film: *Water*. TV incl: *No Problem*; *Party At The Palace*; *Johnny Jarvis*; *Tales Of The Unexpected*; *Jangles*; *The Gentle Touch*. 2 d. Leanne, Christine. Hobbies: swimming, martial arts, music (playing the saxaphone). Address: c/o Anna Scher Theatre Management, London. Birthsign: Aries. **Favourite Place:** 'Amsterdam. I've got a lot of friends there—it's like a second home to me.'

TUSA, John

Reporter/presenter, b. 2 March 1936 Czechoslovakia. Joined BBC as trainee 1960–62. Presented *The World Tonight* on Radio 4 1970–78, then moved to TV as presenter of *Newsweek* on BBC 2 1978–79, when he became presenter of *Newsnight*. Also presented TV series *The Unsettled Peace*. From 1982–84 presented BBC's first history magazine *Timewatch*. Royal TV Society TV Journalist of the Year 1983; BAFTA Richard Dimbleby Award 1983. m. Ann Hilary; 2 s. John, Francis. Hobbies: playing squash, watching opera. Address: c/o BBC TV, London. Birthsign: Pisces. **Favourite Place:** 'Ballconneely Bay, Connemara: total silence except for the call of the curlew, the shriek of the heron.'

TWIGGY

Actress, b. 19 Sept 1949 London. Hairdresser's assistant turned top model, became an actress at 20. First film role in *The Boy Friend*. Stage debut in *Cinderella* 1974. Theatre incl: *Captain Beaky's Musical Christmas*; *My One And Only* (on Broadway). Films incl: *W*; *Shadow Of Evil*; *There Goes The Bridge*; *The Blues Brothers*; *The Doctors And The Devils*; *Club Paradise*. TV incl: *Twiggs*; *Twiggy*; *The Frontiers Of Science*; *Bring On The Girls*; *Roller Coaster*; *The Muppet Show*; *Pygmalion*; *Jukebox*. Records incl: *The Boy Friend*; *Twiggy*; *Here I Go Again*; *Please Get My Name Right*; *A Woman In Love*; *Tomorrow Is Another Day*; *My One And Only*. Books: *Twiggy* (autobiography); *Unlimited Twiggy*. 1 d. Carly. Address: c/o Neville Shulman, London. Birthsign: Virgo. **Favourite Place:** 'Sunset on a deserted beach.'

URE, Gudrun
Actress, b. 12 March 1926
Campsie, Scotland. Began in
broadcasting while still at school.
Joined the Children's Theatre,
before moving to Glasgow's
Citizens' Theatre for several
seasons, including tours. Has also
worked at the Bristol Old Vic,
London Old Vic, Perth
Repertory. Stage incl: *The Gentle
Shepherd*; *Othello*; *Comedy Of
Errors*; *The Kingfisher*; *Something
Unexpected*. Films incl: *Doctor In
The House*; *Million Pound Note*.
Considerable radio incl: Agatha
Christie's *Unexpected Guest*. TV
incl: *Dr Finlay's Casebook*;
Sutherland's Law; *Nanny*; *Super
Gran*. m. John. Hobbies: art,
music. Address: c/o John French,
London. Birthsign: Pisces.
Favourite Place: 'Walking
beside the sea, windy or not,
breathing that marvellous ozone
smell. Invigorating and reviving.'

URQUHART, Robert
Actor, b. 16 Oct 1922 Ullapool,
Scotland. Trained at RADA and
then rep. London debut in *The
Second Mrs Tanqueray* and was
Horatio to Alec Guinness's
Hamlet 1951. Films incl: *You're
Only Young Twice*; *Knights Of
The Round Table*; *The Dunkirk
Story*. TV incl: *Helen—A
Woman Of Today*; *The Awful Mr
Goodall*; *The Inheritors*; *The
Button Man*; *Happy Returns*; *The
Professionals*; *Man And Boy*;
Brideshead Revisited, *Bleak House*;
Sharma And Beyond. m. (1st)
actress Zena Walker (dis.), (2nd)
Jean; 2 d. Alison, Rebecca, 1 s.
Jonathan. Hobbies: boating,
reading. Address: c/o Boyack and
Conway, London. Birthsign:
Libra.

USTINOV, Peter, CBE
Actor/producer/director/
novelist/playwright, b. 16 April
1921 London. Trained at the
London Theatre Studio. Stage
debut 1938 in *The Wood Demon*;
rep in Aylesbury and Richmond.
Other stage incl: *Swinging The
Gate*; *Squaring The Circle*;
Frenzy; *Romanoff And Juliet*;
Beethoven's Tenth. Films incl:
Odette; *Quo Vadis*; *Logan's Run*;
Death On The Nile. TV incl:
Omnibus; *History Of Europe*;
Thirteen At Dinner. As a writer,
plays incl: *House Of Regrets*; *The
Love Of Four Colonels*; *Photo
Finish*. Films incl: *Vice Versa*;
School For Secrets; *Memed, My
Hawk*. Books incl: *Dear Me*; *My
Russia*. Awards include two
Academy Awards, a Grammy,
and three Emmys. m. (3rd) Helen
Du Lau D'Allemans; 3 d. Tamara
(from 1st m.), Pavla, Andrea, 1 s.
Igor (all from 2nd m.). Hobbies:
cars, music. Address: c/o William
Morris, London. Birthsign: Aries.

VALENTINE, Anthony
Actor, b. 17 Aug 1939
Blackburn, Lancs. Trained at the
Valery Glynne Stage School.
Debut at 10 in the film, *No Way
Back*. As child actor, stage incl:
two seasons at Sadler's Wells
Opera; *Anniversary Waltz*; *Two
Stars For Comfort*; *Sleuth*; *Half A
Sixpence*. TV incl: *Vice Versa*;
Children Of The New Forest; *Rex
Milligan*; *Billy Bunter*. As an
adult, films incl: *The Damned*; *To
The Devil A Daughter*; *Murder Is
Easy*; *Escape To Athens*; *Masada*.
TV incl: *An Age Of Kings*; *The
Donati Conspiracy*; *Colditz*;
Raffles; *The Dancing Years*; *Tales
Of The Unexpected*; *Minder*;
Robin Of Sherwood; *Dangerous
Corner*. m. Susan Skipper.
Hobbies: squash, boardsailing,
skiing, photography. Address: c/o
London Management, London.
Birthsign: Leo. **Favourite
Place:** 'The Borrowdale Valley
in the Lake District or at home in
front of the fire.'

VAUGHAN, Frankie, OBE
Entertainer, b. 3 Feb 1928 Liverpool. Started career at Kingston Empire in 1950 and his first TV appearance came two years later. Has since been topping the bill in theatres, cabaret and TV shows in Britain and America. Many films incl: *These Dangerous Years*; *The Lady Is A Square*; *Let's Make Love*; *It's All Over Town*. m. Stella; 1 d. Susan, 2 s. David, Andrew. Hobbies: charity work for boys' clubs, golf, fishing, painting. Address: c/o Peter Charlesworth, London. Birthsign: Aquarius. **Favourite Place:** 'Majorca at siesta time – a most civilised way to relax.'

VAUGHAN, Norman
Entertainer, b. 10 April 1927 Liverpool. Stage debut at the age of 14 with a boys' troupe. At 15 formed his own trio, The Dancing Aces, and toured until the war. Army shows with Harry Secombe, Spike Milligan and Ken Platt. Stage incl: *Boeing-Boeing*; *Play It Again Sam*; *The Happy Apple*; *The Tempest*; *No, No, Nanette*; *Once More Darling*; *There Goes The Bride*; *Wizard Of Oz*; *A Bedful Of Foreigners*; *Love At A Pinch*; plus pantomimes and summer seasons. TV incl: compère of *Sunday Night At The London Palladium*; *The Golden Shot*; and many guest appearances and quiz shows. m. ex-dancer Bernice; 1 s. David. Hobbies: driving, reading, golf. Address: c/o Richard Stone, London. Birthsign: Aries. **Favourite Place:** 'The view from the terrace of the Incasol Hotel, Marbella. The view of the sea is breathtakingly beautiful.'

VAUGHAN, Peter
Actor, b. 4 April 1924 Shropshire. Joined Wolverhampton Rep after school. Stage incl: *Entertaining Mr Sloane*; *Portrait Of A Queen*; *Season's Greetings*. Films incl: *Twist Of Sand*; *The Naked Runner*; *The Bofors Gun*; *Hammerhead*; *Alfred The Great*; *Straw Dogs*; *The Man Outside*; *Death In Rome*; *The Mackintosh Man*; *Valentine*; *Zulu Dawn*; *The French Lieutenant's Woman*; *The Razor's Edge*; *Forbidden*; *Brazil*. TV incl: *The Gold Robbers*; *Oliver Twist*; *Great Expectations*; *Citizen Smith*; *Winston Churchill—The Wilderness Years*; *Bleak House*. m. (1st) actress Billie Whitelaw (dis.), (2nd) actress Lillias Walker; 1 s. David (from 2nd m.). Address: c/o ICM, London. Birthsign: Aries. **Favourite Place:** 'Lords' Cricket Ground on a sunny summer's day.'

VENTURE, Richard
Actor, b. 12 Nov 1923 West New York, New Jersey. Trained for the stage at the Abbey Theater School, Arena Stage and regional theatre. Stage incl: *The Merchant Of Venice*; *You're Too Tall But Come Back Next Week* (also playwright). Films incl: *All The President's Men*; *Man, Woman And Child*; *Onion Field*; *Airport 77*; *Man On The Swing*; *Being There*. TV incl: *Benson*; *Family*; *Falcon Crest*; *Newhart*; *The Thorn Birds*; *Executioner's Song*; *Street Hawk*; and the TV films: *Cocaine*; *From Here To Eternity*; *Tenth Month*. m. actress Lorraine O'Donnell; 2 s. Tony, John, 2 d. Rebecca, Kathy (all from previous m.). Hobbies: Tai Ji and the martial arts, running. Address: c/o Century Artists, 9744 Wilshire Blvd, Beverly Hills, CA 90212. Birthsign: Scorpio. **Favourite Place:** 'I love London and catch all the plays when I'm there.'

VERNON, Richard
Actor, b. 7 March 1925 Reading, Berks. Trained at the Central School of Speech and Drama. Stage incl: *Peter Pan*; *Any Other Business?*; *Hay Fever*; *Saturday, Sunday, Monday*; *The Passion Of Dracula*; *Pack Of Lies*. Films incl: *The Human Factor*; *Gandhi*; *Evil Under The Sun*; *Lady Jane*. TV incl: *Man In Room 17*; *Sextet*; *Sarah*; *Upstairs, Downstairs*; *The Duchess Of Duke Street*; *The Sandbaggers*; *Ripping Yarns*; *Suez*; *The Hitch-Hiker's Guide To The Galaxy*; *Something In Disguise*; *Nanny*; *Waters Of The Moon*; *Roll Over Beethoven*; *Paradise Postponed*. m. actress Benedicta Leigh; 1 d. Sarah, 1 s. Tom. Hobby: sailing. Address: c/o Leading Artists, London. Birthsign: Pisces. **Favourite Place:** 'The Solent—for sailing.'

VEZEY, Pamela
Actress, b. 19 Sept Bath. Trained at the Bristol Old Vic Theatre School and subsequently with the company and at various reps incl: Watford, Guildford, Farnham, Edinburgh, Exeter, Richmond, Coventry, Birmingham, Windsor. Stage incl: *The Pyjama Game*; *The Ha-Ha*. TV incl: *The Common (Play Of The Month)*; *Billy Liar*; *Grange Hill*; *Sounding Brass*; *Crossroads*. Hobbies: reading, gardening. Address: c/o Leading Players Management, London. Birthsign: Virgo. **Favourite Place:** 'No particular favourite but any hill that's taken quite a climb.'

VILLIERS, James
Actor, b. 29 Sept 1933 London. After two years at RADA he spent a season at Stratford-on-Avon before his West End debut in *Toad Of Toad Hall* in 1954. He then spent two years with the Old Vic in England and America, and then a year with the English Stage Company. Stage incl: *Write Me A Murder*; *The Burglar*; *The Little Hut*; *The Doctor's Dilemma*; *The White Devil*; *The Last Of Mrs Cheyney*; *Henry IV*; *Saint Joan*; *The Ghost Train*; *Peter Pan*. His many films incl: *King And Country*; *Nothing But The Best*; *The Amazing Mr Blunden*; *For Your Eyes Only*; *Under The Volcano*. TV incl: *The First Churchills*; *Lady Windermere's Fan*; *Pygmalion*; *The Other 'Arf*. Hobbies: watching football and cricket. Address: c/o Peter Crouch, London. Birthsign: Libra. **Favourite Place:** 'Lords' Cricket Ground during a heat wave.'

VINCENT, Jan-Michael
Actor, b. 15 July Denver, Colorado. Films incl: *Hooper*; *Big Wednesday*; *Shadow Of The Hawk*; *Baby Blue Marine*; *Bite The Bullet*; *The World's Greatest Athlete*; *Going Home*; *The Undefeated*; *Los Bandidos*. TV incl: *Police Story*; *Tribes*; *Marcus Welby, MD*; *Dan August*; *Gunsmoke*; *Dragnet*; *Lassie*; *The Banana Splits' Adventure Hour*; *Toma*; *Men At Law*; *Air Wolf*. m. (dis.); 1 d. Amber. Hobbies: surfing, cycling, sailing, skydiving, composing country music. Address: c/o Jim Golden, Management III, Universal Studios, 100 Universal City Plaza, California. Birthsign: Cancer. **Favourite Place:** Malibu, it enables him to surf, cycle and sail.

VINE, David

Sports commentator/interviewer/presenter/consultant, b. 3 Jan 1936 Barnstaple, Devon. Started on local weekly newspaper; writer and news and sports interviewer for Westward TV 1962, BBC 1966. Specialises in equestrian sport, winter sports and bowls. TV incl: *The Superstars*; commentaries for the Olympic Games, Commonwealth Games, Horse Of The Year Show, World Ski Cup, Wimbledon Championships. Address: c/o BBC TV, London. Birthsign: Capricorn. **Favourite Place:** 'Home—visits are too rare!'

VINE, John

Actor, b. 20 Feb 1951 Banbury, Oxfordshire. Trained at the Rose Bruford College of Speech and Drama and has since worked in rep, fringe and revue theatres, as well as London's West End. Films incl: *Richard's Things*; *Gandhi*; *Eureka*; *The Keep*. TV incl: *Seven Dials Mystery*; *King's Royal*; *Kate The Good Neighbour*; *Death Of An Expert Witness*; *Shroud For A Nightingale*; *Cover Her Face*; *Murder Not Proven*; *QED*. m. Alex; 2 s. Tom, Oliver. Hobbies: comedy writing, all sports and games, especially snooker. Address: c/o Jeremy Conway, London. Birthsign: Pisces. **Favourite Place:** 'Bed—with two small sons it's a place I don't visit often enough!'

WADDINGTON, Bill

Comedian/character actor/after dinner speaker, b. 10 June 1914 Oldham, Lancs. Started in variety and concert party and has starred in every variety theatre in Britain. First radio broadcast 1940. First TV 1946 with Margaret Lockwood. Plays Percy Sugden in TV's *Coronation Street*. Other TV incl: *Talent*; *Family At War*; *Fallen Hero*; *Second Change*. m. (dec.); 2 d. Barbara, Denise. Hobby: breeding thoroughbred racehorses. Address: c/o Granada TV, Manchester. Birthsign: Gemini. **Favourite Place:** 'At my stud, seeing my new arrivals, foals, on the day of birth if possible.'

WALBERG, Garry

Actor, b. 6 Oct 1921 Buffalo, New York. Joined the Jane Keeler Studio Theater School in Buffalo, then the Erwin Piscator Dramatic Workshop and American Theater Wing. Spent seven years acting in summer stock, off and on Broadway and is now best known for his role as Lt Monahan in TV's *Quincy*. Other TV incl: *Peyton Place*; *The Odd Couple*. 2 s. Gerrit, Kevin. Hobbies: racehorses, carpentry, gardening. Birthsign: Gemini. **Favourite Place:** 'Morning workouts at the race track and training centers for thoroughbred horses, because I want to be involved and be a part of racing the thoroughbred.'

WALLER, David

Actor, b. 27 Nov 1920 Street, Somerset. Trained under Eileen Thorndike at the Embassy School of Acting. Rep before and after the war then Old Vic 1951–53 and 1957–58. Joined Royal Shakespeare Company 1964 and is an associate artist. Author of play *Happy Returns*. Films incl: *Work Is A Four Letter Word*; *Perfect Friday*. Numerous TV roles incl: *Edward And Mrs Simpson*; *Airport Chaplain*; *Waxwork*; *Enemy At The Door*; *The Tempest*; *Cribb*; *The Brack Report*; *PQ17*; *The Pickwick Papers*; *Shadowlands*. m. Elisabeth Vernon. Hobbies: cooking, gardening, painting. Address: c/o Fraser & Dunlop, London. Birthsign: Sagittarius. **Favourite Place**: 'The Hotel La Colombe D'Or, St Paul De Vence—a magical place.'

WALTER, David

Political correspondent, b. 1 Feb 1948 Newcastle-upon-Tyne. After Trinity College, Oxford, where he took a Classics degree, joined the BBC 1971 as a producer, first of *Nationwide* and then *Newsweek*. Joined ITN as political correspondent in 1980. m. Pamela May; 1 d. Natalie, 1 s. Peter. Hobbies: tennis, squash, gardening. Address: c/o ITN, London. Birthsign: Aquarius.

WALTERS, Julie

Actress, b. 22 Feb 1950 Birmingham. Stage debut in *The Taming Of The Shrew*, Liverpool. Came to London in *Funny Peculiar* 1976. In Royal Shakespeare Company's *Educating Rita*. Recent theatre incl: *Jumpers*; *Fool For Love*. Films: *Educating Rita*, for which she was nominated for an Oscar; won Golden Globe, BAFTA and Variety Club Best Actress awards; *She'll Be Wearing Pink Pyjamas*. TV incl: *Wood And Walters*; *Nearly A Happy Ending*; *Living Together*; *Happy Since I Met You*; *Say Something Happened*; *Intensive Care*; *The Boys From The Black Stuff*; *Family Man*; *Unfair Exchanges*; *Victoria Wood As Seen On TV*; *The Secret Diary Of Adrian Mole*. Hobbies: travel, friends, champagne, Patricia Highsmith's novels. Address: c/o Saraband Assocs, London. Birthsign: Pisces. **Favourite Place**: 'My bed.'

WALTERS, Thorley

Actor, b. 12 May 1913 Teingrace, Devonshire. Trained at the Old Vic. Many films incl: *Young Winston*; *The Aventures Of Sherlock Holmes' Smarter Brother*; *The Silver Blaze*; *The People That Time Forgot*; *Walking In The Sun*; *Wildcats Of St Trinians*; *The Little Drummer Girl*. TV incl: *The Duchess Of Duke Street*; *Jennie*; *Malice Aforethought*; *Henry V*; *Tinker, Tailor, Soldier, Spy*; *Strangers*; *Bulman*; *After The Party*; *In The Secret State*. Hobbies: recording music, playing music and listening to music. Address: c/o John Redway & Assocs, London. Birthsign: Taurus. **Favourite Place**: 'Deserted beaches.'

WANAMAKER, Zoë
Actress, b. 13 May 1949 New York. Trained at Central School of Speech and Drama in London and has worked extensively in the theatre, appearing at Leeds Playhouse; Edinburgh Lyceum; The Young Vic, London; Cambridge Theatre Company; Nottingham Playhouse. Joined the Royal Shakespeare Company 1976 and theatre incl: *Wild Oats*; *Once In A Lifetime*; *Piaf* (also New York). Also musicals incl: *Guys And Dolls*; *Cabaret*. Films incl: *The Hunger*; *The Last 10 Days of Hitler*; *Inside The 3rd Reich*. TV incl: *The Silver Mask*; *Village Hall*; *Beaux Strategem*; *The Devil's Crown*; *Baal*; *Strike*; *All The World's A Stage*; *Richard III*; *Magnox*; *Paradise Postponed*. Hobbies: travel, painting, reading, music, theatre, cinema. Address: c/o Jeremy Conway, London. Birthsign: Taurus. **Favourite Place:** 'Greece.'

WARING, Derek
Actor, b. 26 April 1930 London. Served in Indian and British armies before training at RADA, then rep. West End theatre incl: with the Royal Shakespeare Company; *Cards On The Table*; *My Fair Lady*; *The Boy Friend*. Films incl: *Last Days Of Hitler*; *Battle Of Britain*. TV incl: *Z Cars*; *The Avengers*; *Moody And Peg*; *Flaxborough Chronicles*; *Wings*; *George And Mildred*; *The Professionals*; *Partners*; *Don't Rock The Boat*; *The Happy Apple*; *The Funny Side*. Brother of writer Richard Waring. m. actress Dorothy Tutin; 1 d. Amanda, 1 s. Nicholas. Hobbies: natural history, music, boats, cooking. Address: c/o Barry Burnett, London. Birthsign: Taurus. **Favourite Place:** The churchyard of St-Just-in-Roseland, Cornwall, which is beautiful, botanically fascinating and a stunning view.'

WARING, George
Actor/director, b. 20 Feb 1927 Eccles, Lancs. Joined RAF at 18 and acted in RAF Rep Company. Then joined Century Theatre, also rep and West End. Film: *Squaring The Circle*. TV appearances incl: *Z Cars*; *Mrs Thursday*; *Doctor Who*; *Softly, Softly*; *Castle Haven*; *Crown Court*; *Armchair Thriller*; *Six Days Of Justice*; *Coronation Street*; *Emmerdale Farm*; *Mixed Blessings*; *The Prisoner Of Zenda*; *No Place Like Home*. m. (1st) (dis.), (2nd) actress Geraldine Gwyther; 1 d. Georgina, 1 s. Geoffrey. Hobbies: listening to good music, interior decorating, cooking, tennis. Address: c/o Bernard Gillman, Tolworth, Surrey. Birthsign: Pisces. **Favourite Place:** 'The Kremlin, for its extraordinary and quite unexpected beauty.'

WARREN, Michael
Actor, b. 5 March South Bend, Indiana. Won an athletics scholarship to UCLA where he studied film. Best known as Officer Hill in TV's *Hill Street Blues*. Made film debut in *Drive, He Said* as basketball adviser, then given a part in the film. Other films incl: *Norman, Is That You?*; *Fast Break*. Other TV incl: *Adam—12*; *Marcus Welby, MD*; *Mod Squad*; *Paris*; *Sierra*; *The White Shadow*. m. Susie; 1 d. Koa, 1 s. Cash. Hobbies: reading, music, basketball, tennis. Address: c/o Sandy Bressler and Assocs, 15760 Ventura Blvd, Encino, California 91436. Birthsign: Pisces. **Favourite Place:** 'Home—both in LA and Indiana.'

WARWICK, James

Actor, b. 17 Nov 1948 Broxbourne, Herts. Trained at Central School of Speech and Drama and made his TV debut as an ostrich in *Late Night Line-Up*. As well as seven years working in the theatre, TV incl: *The Onedin Line*; *Rock Follies*; *The Terracotta* House; *Edward VII*; *Turtle's Progress*; *Tales Of The Unexpected*; *Doctor Who*; *The Nightmare Man*; *The Bell*; *Why Didn't They Ask Evans?*; *The Seven Dials Mystery*; *Partners In Crime*; *Scarecrow And Mrs King*; *Dead Head*. Hobbies: swimming, gardening, music. Address: c/o ICM, London. Birthsign: Scorpio. **Favourite Place:** 'My study overlooking the garden: for reading, thinking, talking on the telephone and listening to music.'

WARWICK, Richard

Actor, b. 29 April 1945 Dartford, Kent. Trained at RADA. Films incl: *Romeo And Juliet*; *If . . .*; *The Bedsitting Room*; *First Love*; *Nicholas And Alexandra*; *The Breaking Of Bumbo*; *Alice In Wonderland*. TV incl: *The Vortex*; *Please Sir!*, *Last Of The Mohicans*; *Warship*; *School Play*; *A Fine Romance*. Hobbies: tennis, sailing, riding. Address: c/o ICM, London. Birthsign: Taurus. **Favourite Place:** Winnepeg.

WASHINGTON, Denzel

Actor, b. 28 Dec Mt Vernon, New York State. Trained with the American Conservatory Theater. Theatre incl: *Ceremonies In Dark Old Men*; *The Mighty Gents*; *Coriolanus*; *When Chickens Come Home To Roost*; *Othello, Malcolm X*; *A Soldier's Play*. Film: *Carbon Copy*. Best known as Dr Chandler in TV's *St Elsewhere*. Other TV incl: *Wilma*; *Flesh And Blood*. 1 s. John David. Hobbies: travel, skiing, chess, reading, stereo buff. Address: c/o William Morris Agency, 151 El Camino Drive, Beverly Hills, California 90212. Birthsign: Capricorn. **Favourite Place:** 'Back home in New York.'

WATERMAN, Dennis

Actor/singer, b. 24 Feb 1948 London. Acting debut aged 11 in *Night Train To Inverness*. Trained at Corona Stage School and by 16 had been in *The Music Man*, a season at Stratford-on-Avon, starred in the first TV *Just William* and been to Hollywood. Theatre incl: *Windy City*; *Cinderella*; *Same Time Next Year*. Films incl: *Up The Junction*; *Sweeney*; *Sweeney 2*. TV incl: *Sextet*; *The Sweeney*; *Give Us A Kiss*; *Christabel*; *Dennis Waterman—With A Little Help From His Friends*; *Minder* (five series); *The World Cup—A Captain's Tale*. Also writes, sings and records. m. (1st) Penny (dis.), (2nd) actress Patricia Maynard (dis.), now with Rula Lenska; 2 d. Hannah, Julia (both from 2nd m.). Hobbies: playing guitar, writing songs. Address: c/o ICM, London. Birthsign: Pisces. **Favourite Place:** home.

WATFORD, Gwen
Actress, b. 10 Sept 1927 London. Trained at the Embassy Theatre, London, then rep and Old Vic. Theatre incl: *Singles; Bodies; Present Laughter* (SWET Award 1981); *The Jeweller's Shop; Fall.* Films incl: *Never Take Sweets From A Stranger; The Very Edge; Cleopatra.* Many TV roles, incl: *Second Time Around; The Train Now Standing . . .; A Bit Of An Adventure; A Provincial Lady; A Suitable Case For Killing; Love Me To Death; Don't Forget To Write; Present Laughter; Sorrell And Son; The Body In The Library.* m. actor Richard Bebb; 2 s. Mark, Owen. Hobbies: piano, gardening. Address: c/o Miller Management, Teddington. Birthsign: Virgo. **Favourite Place:** 'Top of the Tor beside the Tide's Reach in Devon—the most beautiful spot I know.'

WATSON, Moray
Actor, b. 25 June 1930 Sunningdale, Berks. Trained at Webber Douglas Academy of Dramatic Art, then rep before London's West End and his first hit *The Grass Is Greener* (also film version with Cary Grant and Robert Mitchum). Other theatre incl: *The Incomparable Max* (his one-man show); *You Never Can Tell; The Rivals; Hay Fever.* Films incl: *Every Home Should Have One; The Sea Wolves.* TV incl: *Compact; Upstairs, Downstairs; The Pallisers; Murder Most English; Rumpole Of The Bailey; Pride And Prejudice; Doctor Who; Nobody's Perfect; Union Castle; Minder; Body In The Library; Seal Morning.* m. actress Pam Marmont; 1 d. Emma, 1 s. Robin. Hobby: gardening. Address: c/o Leading Artists, London. Birthsign: Cancer. **Favourite Place:** 'In a boat, on the Thames, under the sun—gazing at the London I love.'

WATT, Tom
Actor, b. 14 Feb 1956 London. Studied drama at Manchester University. Theatre incl: *Alberto Y Los Trios Paranoias;* in San Francisco with rep and improvisational companies; Europe tour with East West Co; UK and India tour with Graeae Theatre. TV incl: *The Old Firm; A Kind Of Loving; My Father's House; Never The Twain; Family Man; EastEnders.* Hobbies: swimming, Indian vegetarian cookery. Address: c/o Actorum Ltd, London. Birthsign: Aquarius. **Favourite Place:** 'Highbury Stadium—east stand, lower tier seat E177—on a Saturday afternoon when Arsenal have beaten Spurs.'

WAXMAN, Albert Samuel
Actor/director, b. 2 March 1935 Toronto, Canada. Studied film technique in London and New York. Much theatre experience in rep, off-Broadway and in London's West End. Films incl: *Wild Horse Hank; Double Negative; Atlantic City; Tulips; Deathbite; Class Of '84.* On TV has acted in *King Of Kensington* and *Cagney And Lacey.* Has directed on TV *The Crowd Inside; The Littlest Hobo; Cagney And Lacey.* m. Sara; 2 s. Tobaron, Adam. Hobbies: tennis, film and theatre going. Birthsign: Pisces. **Favourite Place:** 'My own home in Toronto, because I love my family and my home town.'

WEBB, Lizzie
Fitness teacher/choreographer, b. 12 Aug 1948 London. Trained as a teacher of English, drama and movement. Was with Dundee Repertory Theatre 1970, then taught at a boys' school, then a year teaching disturbed adolescents. From 1975, taught at London dance centres, Richmond Ice Rink, Guildford School of Acting and stage schools incl Italia Conti. Also worked as choreographer. Has been with TV-am since May 1983 as their 'keep fit lady'. Has made an exercise video and written a children's book, *Lizzie Webb's Exercise Zoo*. m. (dis.); 1 s. Ben. Hobbies: theatre, music, sport. Address: c/o TV-am, London. Birthsign: Leo. **Favourite Place:** 'The Forest of Dean—rough, unspoilt countryside with warm, friendly natives!'

WEEKS, Alan
Sports commentator, b. 8 Sept 1923 Bristol. First broadcast while in Royal Navy during the war, giving situation report over ship's radio. Public address announcer Brighton Sports Stadium 1946–65. First commentary for BBC TV on ice hockey 1951. Has presented *Summer Grandstand*; Olympic Games (1960, 64); World Cup (1962); *Pot Black* (1970–84); soccer commentator (1956–78). Also commentator World Cup; Winter Olympics; Olympic Games; Commonwealth Games; ice skating; gymnastics; swimming. m. Barbara Jane; 1 d. Beverly, 2 s. Nigel (dec.), Roderick. Hobbies: swimming, football. Address: c/o Bagenal Harvey, London. Birthsign: Virgo. **Favourite Place:** 'Brighton sea front and the Palace Pier—my father was piermaster for 27 years.'

WEIR, Helen
Actress, b. 9 April 1942 Oxfordshire. Trained at RADA and North West School of Speech and Drama, Southport. Now best known as Pat Sugden in TV's *Emmerdale Farm*. Theatre incl: Royal Shakespeare Company member; *Dark Lady Of The Sonnets*; *Murder In The Cathedral*; *The House Of Bernarda Alba*; *The Importance Of Being Earnest* (West End). Film: *The Boy Who Turned Yellow*. Other TV incl: *Rogue's Gallery*; *Armchair Theatre*. m. (dis.); 1 s. Daniel. Hobbies: preserving old properties, eating. Address: c/o MLR, London. Birthsign: Aries. **Favourite Place:** 'My home.'

WEITZ, Bruce
Actor, b. 27 May Norwalk, Connecticut. Trained with Long Wharf Rep Theater, Tyrone Guthrie Theater. After 11 years in theatres all over US, acted on Broadway in *Death Of A Salesman*; *The Basic Training Of Pavlo Hummel*; *Norman, Is That You?*; also with Joseph Papp's *Shakespeare In The Park*. In Los Angeles, he had guest roles on TV incl: *Quincy*; *Kojak*; *One Day At A Time*; *The White Shadow*; *Lou Grant* before being cast at Det Mick Belker in *Hill Street Blues*. Other TV appearances incl: *Happy Days*; *Mork And Mindy*; *Kaz*; *The Rockford Files*. m. (dis.). Hobbies: gourmet cooking, racquetball, scuba-diving, travel. Address: c/o Lippin & Grant, 8124 West Third St, Suite 204, Los Angeles, California 90048. Birthsign: Gemini.

WELLAND, Colin

Actor/writer, b. 4 July 1934 Liverpool. Was an art teacher before joining Manchester's Library Theatre. Briefly compère of BBC's *North At Six* and an appearance in *The Verdict* before becoming PC Graham in *Z Cars* for three years. Took to writing and his plays incl: *Leeds United*; *Kisses At Fifty*; *The Wild West Show*; *Your Man From Six Counties*. Acted in many of his own plays. Also presenter *How To Stay Alive*. Films incl: *Kes*; *Villain*; *Straw Dogs*; *Sweeney*; *Yanks* (wrote film script); *Chariots Of Fire* (won an Oscar for his film script). m. former teacher Pat; 3 d. Genevieve, Catherine, Caroline, 1 s. Christie. Hobbies: cricket, rugby, singing. Address: c/o Peter Charlesworth, London. Birthsign: Cancer. **Favourite Place:** 'Sty Head, Cumbria, for a glimpse of the earth as it was before we were here ruining it!'

WELLING, Albert

Actor, b. 29 Feb 1952 London. Trained with the National Youth Theatre and has since acted with the Royal Shakespeare Company; Royal Court Theatre, London; the Actors' Company; Nottingham Playhouse; Liverpool Playhouse; Young Vic; Royal Exchange, Manchester. TV incl: *Telford's Change*; *Cribb*; *Rumpole's Return*; *A Voyage Round My Father*; *Crown Court*; *Auf Wiedersehen Pet*; *Out Of Step*; *The Consultant*; *The Clarion Van*; *The Gathering Seed*; *Shine On Harvey Moon*; *Paradise Postponed*. m. Judy Riley; 1 s. Benedict. Hobbies: sub squa wreck diving, snooker, woodwork, music. Address: c/o David White Assocs, London. Birthsign: Pisces. **Favourite Place:** 'A monastery by a tributary of the Moselle river—tranquillity, scenery and wine.'

WENDT, George

Actor, b. 17 Oct Chicago, Illinois. Trained and acted with Chicago's Second City Comedy Workshop. Best known as Norm Peterson in TV's *Cheers*, but other TV incl: *Alice*; *Soap*; *Taxi*; *Hart To Hart*; *American Dream*. m. Bernadette; 2 step-s. Joshua, Andrew. Hobbies: writing, baseball, football, basketball. Address: c/o Writers and Artists, 11726 San Vincente Blvd, Los Angeles, CA 90049. Birthsign: Libra.

WEST, Timothy, CBE

Actor, b. 20 Oct 1934 Bradford, Yorks. Son of theatrical parents, started as assistant stage manager Wimbledon 1956 then rep until London debut 1959 in *Caught Napping*. Acted in West End, with Royal Shakespeare and Prospect Companies, UK and abroad. Films incl: *Nicholas And Alexandra*; *The Day Of The Jackal*; *Agatha*; *The Thirty-Nine Steps*; *Rough Cut*; *The Antagonists*; *Oliver Twist*. TV incl: *Hard Times*; *Henry VIII*; *Crime And Punishment*; *Churchill And The Generals*; *Brass*; *The Last Bastion*; *Tender Is The Night*. m. (1st) Jacqueline Boyer (dis.), (2nd) Prunella Scales; 1 d. Juliet (from 1st m.), 2 s. Sam, Joe. Hobbies: listening to music, exploring old railway lines, travel. Address: c/o James Sharkey, London. Birthsign: Libra. **Favourite Place:** 'The Randolph Hotel, Oxford, and I'm not saying why.'

WHICKER, Alan
Writer, b. 2 Aug 1925 Cairo,
Egypt. After service on Italian
warfront as Major commanding
battle cameramen, became Fleet
Street foreign correspondent, war
correspondent in Korea. Joined
BBC 1957 at start of *Tonight*
programme and has become TV's
most travelled man. *Whicker's
World* began in 1958. Joined ITV
1968 to become Yorkshire TV's
largest private shareholder.
Returned to BBC TV 1982 for
*Whicker's World—The First
Million Miles*; *South Pacific* series;
A Slow Boat to China; *Whicker's
New World*. Winner of numerous
awards incl Richard Dimbleby
Award and *TV Times* Special
Award. Wrote best-seller *Within
Whicker's World*; also *Whicker's
New World*. Address: c/o Jersey,
Channel Islands. Birthsign: Leo.
Favourite Place: 'My garden
on a wooded clifftop overlooking
France, for its profound
therapeutic qualities.'

WHITE, Frances
Actress, b. 1 Nov 1938 Leeds.
Trained at Central School of
Speech and Drama, London. First
West End play was *Fit To Print* in
1962. Other theatre incl: *A
Severed Head*. Films incl: *Mary
Queen Of Scots*; *Press For Time*.
Numerous TV appearances, the
most recent incl: *Raging Calm*;
Rooms; *The Secret Agent*; *The
Stick Insect*; *I, Claudius*; *Prince
Regent*; *Looking For Vicky*;
Crossroads; *Nobody's Perfect*; *I
Woke Up One Morning*. m.
Anthony Hone (dis.); 1 d. Kate.
Hobbies: gardening, reading.
Address: c/o Bryan Drew,
London. Birthsign: Scorpio.
Favourite Place: 'The patio of
my back garden surrounded by
favourite plants—wisteria,
honeysuckle, roses, clematis.'

WHITE, Sheila
Actress/singer/dancer, b. 18 Oct
Highgate, London. Started with
Terry's Juveniles at 12 then with
the Corona Stage School. Much
stage work incl: *The Sound Of
Music*; *Dames At Sea* (also in
France). Recent theatre incl:
Royal Variety Show (1984);
They're Playing Our Song; *Little
Me*. Films incl: *Oliver!*; *The
Spaceman And King Arthur*; *Silver
Dream Racer*. TV incl: *I,
Claudius*; *Poldark*; *Dear Mother,
Love Albert*; *Minder*; *Don't Rock
The Boat*. m. Richard Mills.
Hobbies: riding, golf, swimming,
cooking, country walks, singing,
listening to records, driving,
gardening. Address: c/o ICM,
London. Birthsign: Libra.
Favourite Place: 'Richmond
Hill, for the view.'

WHITEHEAD, Benjamin
Child actor, b. 14 Oct 1982
Otley, West Yorkshire. Since he
was two weeks old has played the
part of young Sam Skilbeck in
Yorkshire TV's *Emmerdale Farm*.
He got the part after a chance
meeting with the actress Jean
Rogers, who was expecting a
baby in the series. He was chosen
for his blonde hair, blue eyes and
'natural talent'. He is the third
child of Richard and Sue
Whitehead. Education: pending.
Hobby: playing with his toys.
Address: c/o Yorkshire TV,
Leeds. Birthsign: Libra.
Favourite Place: splashing
around in the bath.

WHITEHEAD, Geoffrey
Actor, b. 1 Oct 1939 Sheffield.
Trained at RADA then rep at
Canterbury, Coventry and
Sheffield. TV incl: *Bulldog Breed*;
Z Cars; *Last Of The Best Men*;
Robin's Nest; *The Foundation*;
Sherlock Holmes; *Inside The Third
Reich*; *Pinkerton's Progress*; *Alas
Smith And Jones*; *Who Dares
Wins*; *There Comes A Time*; *The
Cleopatras*; *Reilly Ace Of Spies*;
Peter The Great. m. Mary
Hanefey; 1 s. Jonty, 1 d. Clare.

Hobbies: football, cricket, piano,
organ. Address: c/o Bryan Drew,
London. Birthsign: Libra.
Favourite Place: 'South Stand,
Sheffield, row A, seat 116,
looking north. A place of infinite
excitement.'

WHITELEY, Richard
Presenter, b. 28 Dec 1943
Bradford, Yorks. After
Cambridge University, TV
trainee with ITN 1965, joined
Yorkshire TV 1968. Presenter of
Calendar and associated
programmes incl: *Calendar
Sunday*; *Calendar Tuesday*;
Calendar People; *Calendar Forum*;
Election Calendar; *Good Morning
Calendar*; *Goodnight Calendar*;
Calendar Profile; *Country
Calendar*; *Calendar Specials*;

Calendar Commentary. Other TV
incl: *Enterprize 82*; *Past Masters*;
Ferret Lovers' Weekly; presenter
Countdown on C4 since Nov
1982—the first face on C4.
Hobbies: country pubs, walking.
Address: c/o Yorkshire TV,
Leeds. Birthsign: Capricorn.
Favourite Place: 'Giggleswick
School Chapel seen from
Buckshaw Brow in Craven.
Breathtaking and impressive with
its giant green dome.'

WHITFIELD, June, OBE
Comedy actress, b. 11 Nov
London. Trained at RADA and
appeared on stage in shows such
as *Love From Judy*. Came to the
fore as Eth in radio series *Take It
From Here* (1953). Recent radio:
News Huddlines. On TV has been
the foil to the best funny men in
the business. Films incl: *Carry On
Abroad*; *Bless This House*; *The Spy
With The Cold Nose*. TV incl:
Beggar My Neighbour; *The Best
Things In Life*; *Hancock's Half*

Hour; *Scott on* . . . First worked
with Terry Scott 1969 and they
have made five series of *Happy
Ever After*; six series of *Terry And
June*. m. surveyor Tim Aitchison;
1 d. actress Susan. Hobby:
cooking. Address: c/o April
Young, London. Birthsign:
Scorpio. **Favourite Place:** 'West
Sussex—the view from a friend's
house—rolling fields and trees on
all sides!'

WHITLOCK, Lee
Actor, b. 17 April 1968 London.
Trained at the Corona Stage
School. Has appeared on TV in:
Spooner's Patch; *The Gentle
Touch*; *Cribb*; *Behind The Bike
Sheds*; *Hold Tight*; *Rowen's
Report*; *The Dick Emery Show*;
Merry Wives Of Windsor; *Shine
On Harvey Moon*; *Comrade Dad*;
Hold The Back Page. Hobbies:
football, snooker, swimming.
Address: c/o Jeremy Conway,
London. Birthsign: Aries.

Favourite Place: 'Mijas in
Spain—it's the Chelsea of
Spain.'

WHITMORE, Richard

TV news presenter/reporter, b. 22 Dec 1933 Hitchin, Herts. Became junior reporter 1951 on the *Hertford Express*; left to develop own freelance agency. Freelance reporter for BBC South-East radio and TV. Staff correspondent for BBC Radio and TV News 1964 and travelled extensively on news stories; also assignments to Northern Ireland 1969–72, when he became a newsreader on the *Nine O'Clock* News. 1981 presenter of BBC TV's *News After Noon*. Author of four books on Victorian life. m. Wendy; 4 d. Jane, Sarah, Kate, Lucy. Hobby: amateur dramatics. Member of Herts amateur dramatic society, The Bancroft Players, of which he is president. Co-founder of the Queen Mother Theatre. Address: c/o BBC TV, London. Birthsign: Capricorn. **Favourite Place:** 'Southwold, Suffolk—a tranquil and beautifully-preserved resort.'

WHITTAKER, Roger

Singer/entertainer/songwriter, b. 22 March 1936 Nairobi, Kenya. Called up at 18 into Kenya Regiment. Became a school master, singing in his spare time. Came to Britain, got a biochemistry degree but decided to try show business after his first record, *Steel Man*, made the charts. TV incl: own series Ulster TV 1963; *Whittaker's World Of Music*; *The Roger Whittaker Show*; *Night Music*. Prolific songwriter with hits incl: *Durham Town*; *New World In The Morning*; *Mammy Blue*. Since 1980 toured US and appeared on top US TV shows. TV musical 1982 *Roger Whittaker In Kenya*. m. Natalie; 3 d. Emily, Lauren, Jessica, 2 s. Guy, Alexander. Hobbies: photography, flying, collecting antiques. Address: c/o Tembo Entertainments, London. Birthsign: Aries. **Favourite Place:** 'Kenya, my homeland. God's own country.'

WILCOX, Paula

Actress, b. 13 Dec 1949 Manchester. Joined National Youth Theatre while still at school and started in TV after leaving school. Theatre incl: *The Cherry Orchard*; *Romeo And Juliet*; *Heartbreak House*; *Time And The Conways*; *Pygmalion*; *The Birthday Party*; *Hedda Gabler*; *Bedroom Farce*; *Blithe Spirit* (Australia, Middle and Far East); *See How They Run*. TV incl: *The Lovers* (also film); *Man About The House* (also film); *Miss Jones And Son*; *Remember The Lambeth Walk?*; *The Bright Side*. m. Derek Seaton (dec.). Hobbies: swimming, walking, watching football, theatre, concerts, cinema. Address: c/o Marmont Management, London. Birthsign: Sagittarius. **Favourite Place:** 'My small house in London. I seem to be away working such a lot, it's wonderful to get back!'

WILLCOX, Toyah

Actress/singer/songwriter, b. 18 May 1958 Birmingham. Theatre incl: *Vienna Woods*; *American Days*; *Sugar And Spice*; *Trafford Tanzi*. Films incl: *Jubilee*; *The Corn Is Green*; *Quadrophenia*; *The Tempest*. TV incl: *Quatermass*; *Dr Jekyll And Mr Hyde*; *Shoestring*; *Minder*; *Toyah* (documentary); *Tales Of The Unexpected*; *Little Girls Don't*; *Dear Heart*; *The Ebony Tower*. A successful pop star, with albums incl: *Toyah, Toyah, Toyah*; *Warrior Rock*; *Love Is The Law*. Many hit singles incl: *I Want To Be Free*. Hobbies: writing stories, poetry, songs. Address: c/o EG Management, London. Birthsign: Taurus. **Favourite Place:** 'The Bahamas—I can really get away from it all and the sun makes me feel wonderful!'

WILLIAMS, Billy Dee
Actor/singer, b. 6 April 1937
New York. Studied music and
art. Broadway acting debut aged
seven in *The Firebrand Of
Florence*. Other theatre incl: *The
Cool World*; *Blue Boy In Black*; *A
Taste Of Honey*; *Hallelujah, Baby*.
Films incl: *The Last Angry Man*;
Lady Sings The Blues; *Mahogany*;
The Empire Strikes Back; *Return
Of The Jedi*; *Nighthawks*. TV
films incl: *Brian's Song*; *The
Great Pretender*. Well known as
Brady Lloyd in TV's *Dynasty*, but
other TV incl: *The FBI*;
CHIEFS. m. (3rd) Teruko
Nakagami; 1 s. Corey (from 1st
m.), 1 step-d. Miyako, 1 d.
Hanako (from 3rd m.). Hobbies:
oil painting, racquetball, jogging,
swimming, cooking. Address: c/o
William Morris Agency, 151 El
Camino Drive, Beverly Hills,
California 90212. Birthsign:
Aries. **Favourite Place:** 'Just
returned from a trip to the Orient
and loved it.'

WILLIAMS, Kenneth
Actor, b. 22 Feb 1926 London.
Started as a lithographic
draughtsman but began acting
career at Newquay Repertory
Theatre 1948. Other rep
engagements before London
debut in *Peter Pan* 1952. Has since
appeared in plays, pantomimes
and revues and more than 25
Carry On . . . films. Other films
incl: *Raising The Wind*; *Twice
Round The Daffodils*; *The Hound
Of The Baskervilles*. Also regular
radio broadcasts incl: *Round The
Horne*; *Stop Messing About*; *Just
A Minute*. As well as chat shows
and panel games, TV incl:
Hancock's Half Hour; *What's My
Line?*; *Password*; *International
Cabaret*; *The Kenneth Williams
Show*; *Meanwhile*; *Let's Make A
Musical*; *Jackanory*. Book: *Acid
Drops*. Hobbies: reading,
walking, doodling, music.
Address: c/o ICM, London.
Birthsign: Pisces.

WILLIAMS, Michael
Actor, b. 9 July 1935 Manchester.
Trained at RADA, joined
Nottingham Playhouse 1959,
appeared in *Celebration* at the
Duchess Theatre, the revue *Twists*
at Arts Theatre, and some TV
work. Joined Royal Shakespeare
Company 1963, and appeared in
plays incl: *Comedy Of Errors*; *The
Merchant Of Venice*; *As You Like
It*; *King Lear*. Films incl: *Marat
Sade*; *Eagle In A Cage*; *Dead Cert*;
Enigma. Many TV credits incl:
Elizabeth R; *Comedy Of Errors*;
My Son, My Son; *Love In A Cold
Climate*; *Amnesty*; *Shakespeare
Master Class*; *A Fine Romance*
which he starred in with his wife,
actress Judi Dench. Hobby: his
family. Address: c/o Leading
Artists, London. Birthsign:
Cancer.

WILLIAMS, Nigel
Actor, b. 30 March 1949
Wallasey, Cheshire. Trained at
RADA and worked in rep all
over the country. In tours to
Canada, Singapore, Hong Kong,
Belgium, Germany. Also worked
with the Prospect Theatre and the
New Shakespeare Company.
London theatre incl: *The Wolf*;
Déjà Revue; *Very Good Eddie*. TV
incl: *The Long Chase*; *Great Big
Groovy Horse*; *Secret Army*;
Target; *Wainwright's Law*; *Fanny
By Gaslight*; *Play For Today*; *Hi-
De-Hi!*; *Crossroads*; *She'll Have
To Go*; *Cranford*. m. Angela.
Hobbies: tennis, badminton, golf,
electronics. Address: c/o Leading
Players, London. Birthsign: Aries.
Favourite Place: 'The Blue
Lake, top of the Horseshoe Pass,
North Wales. Go there and you'll
see why.'

WILLIAMS, Simon
Actor, b. 16 June 1946 Windsor, Berks. One of the tallest actors in the business (6 ft 4 in) he started in pantomime 1965 then rep. West End theatre incl: *A Friend In Need*; *Hay Fever*; *His, Hers And Theirs*; *The Collector*; *No Sex Please, We're British*; *Gigi*; *The Last Mrs Cheyney*; *See How They Run*. Films incl: *Jabberwocky*; *No Longer Alone*; *The Prisoner Of Zenda*; *The Fiendish Plot Of Dr Fu Manchu*. Well known on TV for role as Captain Bellamy in *Upstairs, Downstairs*. Other TV incl: *The Regiment*; *Man In A Suitcase*; *Romance*; *Wodehouse Playhouse*; *Mr Big*; *Liza*; *Agony*; *Company And Co*; *Strangers*; *Kinvig*; *Sharing Time*. m. Lucy Fleming; 1 d. Amy, 1 s. Tamlyn. Hobbies: riding, reading, writing. Address: c/o Barry Burnett, London. Birthsign: Gemini.

WILLIS, Wincey
Presenter, b. 8 Aug 1954 Gateshead. Formerly in the record business and a travel courier for five years. Entered TV through her hobby of animals. Presented weather reports for Tyne Tees TV 1981, also *Graham's Ark* and own series *Wincey's Pets*. Appears on TV-am and C4's *Treasure Hunt* as well as guest appearances on programmes incl: *Punchlines*; *On Safari*; *Saturday Starship*. m. Malcolm. Hobby: everything to do with animals. Address: c/o Peter Charlesworth, London. Birthsign: Leo. **Favourite Place:** 'The reptile house in Jersey Wildlife Preservation Trust, because I'd love to have one just like it.'

WILMOT, Gary
Entertainer, b. 8 May 1956 Kennington, London. Started in show business entertaining in a bar in Spain. Formed a double act, Gary Wilmot and Judy, when back in Britain and toured theatres and clubs, then won TV's *New Faces* three times. In 1979 he decided to go solo and has appeared on numerous TV shows incl. *The 6 O'Clock Show*, *Ebony*, *Children's Royal Variety Show*; *Royal Night Of 100 Stars*; many variety shows. m. Carol Clark; 1 d. Katie. Hobbies: football, running, rugby, DIY. Address: c/o Dee O'Reilly Management, London. Birthsign: Taurus. **Favourite Place:** 'After home, the top of Nelson's Column, which I climbed for tea.'

WILSON, Bob
Sports presenter, b. 30 Oct 1941 Chesterfield, Derbyshire. Former Arsenal and Scotland goalkeeper. Joined the club 1963 from Loughborough College where he was a teacher of physical education. Joined BBC TV in 1974 to present *Football Focus* in *Grandstand*. Other TV incl: presenting sport on *Breakfast Time*. m. Megs; 2 s. John, Robert, 1 d. Anna. Hobbies: golf, squash, tennis, running. Address: c/o Dennis Roach, St Albans. Birthsign: Scorpio. **Favourite Place:** 'Christchurch, Dorset. And the Algarve, Portugal.'

WILSON, Francis
Weather presenter, b. 27 Feb 1949 Irvine, Ayrshire. Took his BSc at Imperial College, London University. Associate, Royal College of Science and Fellow, Royal Meteorological Society. Trained at RAF Farnborough with the Met Research Flight for three years. Started career on TV with Thames and then joined BBC TV's *Breakfast Time* in 1983. m. Eva; 1 s. Joshua. Hobby: sitting in the sun. Address: c/o BBC TV, London. Birthsign: Pisces. **Favourite Place:** 'Dunoon Castle, Strathclyde— atmospheric.'

WILSON, Jennifer
Actress, b. 25 April London. After training at RADA, worked in rep, at the Regent's Park Open Air Theatre; the Old Vic and on tour to US, Canada, India. Theatre incl: *Spring And Port Wine*; *Pygmalion*; *The Grass Is Greener*. Recent theatre incl: *84 Charing Cross Road*; *Alfie* (tour). On TV played Jenny Hammond in *The Brothers* for six years. Other TV incl: *Nicholas Nickleby*; *Antigone*; *The Second Mrs Tanqueray*; *The Befrienders*; *Cavalcade*; *You And Me*. m. (1st) S Swain (dis.), (2nd) actor/ director Brian Peck; 1 d. Melanie (from 2nd m.). Hobbies: collecting pictures, cooking. Address: c/o Michael Ladkin, London. Birthsign: Taurus. **Favourite Place:** 'A little village behind St Tropez called Ramateuille. Lovely food, wine, very simple and unspoilt by time.'

WILSON, Jocky
Professional dart player, b. 22 March 1949 Kirkcaldy, Fife. Made his professional debut in 1979 and has since appeared on TV in *The Cannon And Ball Show*; *Bullseye*; *Christmas Bullseye*; *The 6 O'Clock Show*; *TV Times Family Challenge*; *A Question Of Sport*. m. Malvena; 1 d. Anne Marie, 2 s. John, Willie. Hobbies: fishing and breeding fish. Address: c/o Mel Coombes Management, Eastcote, Pinner. Birthsign: Aries. **Favourite Place:** 'On my fishing trawler out in a nice calm sea.'

WILSON, Richard
Actor/director, b. 9 July 1936 Greenock, Renfrewshire. Gave up career as research scientist for the stage at 27. Trained at RADA then in rep. Recent theatre incl: *An Honorable Trade*; *Some Of My Best Friends Are Husbands*. Also directed stage productions, being an associate director Oxford Playhouse and assistant director Stables Theatre, Manchester. Recent stage direction: *Other Worlds* at Royal Court Theatre, London. Film: *A Passage To India*. Recent TV incl: *Strangers*; *Poppyland*; *The Last Place On Earth*. Directed for TV incl: *The Remainder Man*; *Under The Hammer*. Hobby: squash. Address: c/o Jeremy Conway, London. Birthsign: Cancer. **Favourite Place:** 'View of Firth of Clyde from above Greenock.'

WINDING, Victor
Actor, b. 30 Jan 1929 London.
Trained as a draughtsman but
acted in amateur dramatics and
taught drama at night school. At
29 joined Farnham Rep and three
years later went to Old Vic,
London. West End theatre incl:
Next Time I'll Sing To You; *Poor
Bitos*; *The Merchant of Venice*.
Films incl: *The System*; *The
Medusa Touch*; *Sailor's Return*.

Numerous TV incl: *The Saint*;
Doctor Who; *The Expert*; *The
Flaxton Boys*; *Warship*;
Crossroads; *Bognor*; *It Takes A
Worried Man*; *Shelley*; *Gemima
Shore*; *Angels*; *Little And Large*.
m. Rosalind (dis.); 3 d. Celia, Kay,
Jane, 1 s. Julian. Hobbies: music,
travel, gardening. Address: c/o
Richard Stone, London.
Birthsign: Aquarius. **Favourite
Place:** 'Flying across the Alps as
dawn is breaking, heading for
pastures new.'

WING, Anna
Actress, b. 30 Oct 1914 Hackney,
London. Trained at Croydon
School of Acting. Rep and many
theatre credits incl: *The Birthday
Party*; *Heartbreak House*; *A Place
On Earth* (one-woman show).
Films incl: *Providence*; *Full Circle*;
Runners; *Darkest England*. Many
TV parts incl: *Sink Or Swim*;
Sorry!; *Father's Day*; *The Witches
And The Grinnygog*; *Give Us A
Break*; *The Invisible Man*;

Comrade Dad; as Lou Beale in
EastEnders. m. (1st) Peter Davey
(dis.), (2nd) Patrick O'Connor
(dis.); 2 s. actor Mark Wing-
Davey, Jon Wing-O'Connor.
Hobbies: trying to be orderly,
ballet and music concerts,
dreaming. Address: c/o Darryl
Brown Personal Management,
London. Birthsign: Scorpio.
Favourite Place: 'Anywhere
with friends near—preferably
sun, sea and a place for quiet
reflection.'

WINTERS, Bernie
Comedian, b. 6 Sept 1932
Islington, London. Went into
show business on leaving school
and later formed a double act
with his brother Mike. They
appeared in numerous variety,
musical and TV shows incl: *Six-
Five Special*; *Big Night Out*,

Blackpool Night Out. Went solo
1978 with own series *Bernie*. Host
of *Whose Baby?* and *Scribble*
series; guest in shows incl
Punchlines; *Bob Monkhouse Show*;
Super Troupers; *Give Us A Clue*;
Flanagan & Allen. Toured in stage
show *Bud And Ches* with Leslie
Crowther. m. ex-dancer Siggi
Heine; 1 s. Ray. Hobbies:
football, tennis. Birthsign: Virgo.
Favourite Place: 'Sydney
Harbour with the majestic
bridge.'

WISE, Ernie, OBE
Comedian, b. 27 Nov 1925
Leeds. Child entertainer with his
father in working men's clubs.
London debut in *Band Wagon*
1939. *Youth Takes A Bow* 1941,
met Eric Morecambe and formed
a double act. Radio incl: *Worker's
Playtime*; *You're Only Young
Once*. Films incl: *The Intelligence
Men*; *That Riviera Touch*; *The
Magnificent Two*. TV incl:
*Sunday Night At The London
Palladium*; *The Morecambe And*

Wise Show. Following sad death
of Eric Morecambe in 1984, he
has continued in a solo capacity.
TV incl: *Bring Me Sunshine* and
*The Morecambe And Wise
Classics*, both tributes to Eric;
What's My Line? m. Doreen.
Hobbies: cricket, writing,
boating, gardening, tennis,
swimming. Address: c/o London
Management, London. Birthsign:
Sagittarius. **Favourite Place:**
'Walking along the Thames
between Windsor and Bray.'

WITCHELL, Nicholas
TV news correspondent/
presenter, b. 23 Sept 1953
Cosford, Shropshire. Joined the
BBC on News Graduate Training
Scheme 1976–77. Various
assignments for BBC TV News,
including Northern Ireland,
Beirut, Falklands. BBC TV News
correspondent with Margaret
Thatcher for the General Election
1983. Became co-presenter of *The
Six O'Clock News* in 1984.
Hobbies: reading, travel.
Address: c/o BBC TV, London.
Birthsign: Libra. **Favourite
Place:** 'Drumnadrochit, on the
banks of Loch Ness, Inverness—
mystery and romance.'

WOGAN, Terry
Broadcaster, b. 3 Aug 1938
Limerick, Ireland. Many awards
incl: Radio Personality of the
Year; *TVTimes* Award Most
Popular TV Personality seven
years running; Variety Club
Showbusiness Personality Award
1984. Radio incl: *Terry Wogan
Show*; *Pop Score*; *Punchlines*;
Twenty Questions; *Quote,
Unquote*; *Year In Question*.
Numerous TV appearances incl:
Lunchtime With Wogan; *Come
Dancing*; *Miss World*; *Eurovision
Song Contest*; *A Song For Europe*;
Variety Club Awards; *Carl-Alan
Awards*; *Disco*; *Startown*;
Blankety Blank; *What's On
Wogan*; *You Must Be Joking*;
weekly and then thrice-weekly
chat show *Wogan*. m. former
model Helen Joyce; 1 d.
Katherine, 2 s. Alan, Mark.
Hobbies: family, reading, golf.
Address: c/o Jo Gurnett, London.
Birthsign: Leo.

WOLFE, Dave
Entertainer, b. 1 March 1953
Manchester. Started as a Bluecoat
at Pontins. Winner of LWT's
Search For A Star. Own TV
show: *Search For A Star Special*.
TV incl: *Punchlines*; *Starburst*;
Clubland; *Night Of 100 Stars*;
Blankety Blank. m. Barbara Lowe.
Hobby: golf. Address: c/o Kim
Newman, Manchester. Birthsign:
Pisces. **Favourite Place:** 'On the
golf course, or watching TV with
my wife.'

WOOD, Victoria
Comedienne/writer, b. 19 May
1953 Prestwich, Lancs. Studied
drama at Birmingham
University and appeared with her
husband in *Funny Turns* until
1982. One-woman show: *Lucky
Bag*. Started writing TV plays
1978 incl: *Talent*; *Nearly A
Happy Ending*; *Happy Since I Met
You*. Also wrote *Wood And
Walters* series in which she starred
with Julie Walters. She also
starred in *Victoria Wood As Seen
On TV*. Other TV incl: *New
Faces*; *Pebble Mill At One*; *Call
My Bluff*; *Insight*; *Take The Stage*;
Give Us A Clue; *Cabbages And
Kings*; *Live From Two*; *Friday
Night . . . Saturday Morning*. m.
magician Geoffrey Durham (The
Great Soprendo). Hobby:
swimming. Address: c/o Richard
Stone, London. Birthsign:
Taurus. **Favourite Place:** 'View
from the Windermere Ferry, it
looks wonderful and no one can
get at you.'

WOODYATT, Adam
Actor, b. 28 June 1968 Walthamstow, London. Trained at Sylvia Young drama classes. Has appeared on stage in *Oliver*; *On The Razzle*. TV incl: *Baker St Boys*; *The Witches And The Grinnygog*. Also plays Ian Beale in BBC TV's soap opera *EastEnders*. Hobbies: cricket, ice skating, going to the cinema, eating. Address: c/o Sylvia Young, London. Birthsign: Cancer. **Favourite Place:** 'Lee Valley Ice Rink. It's a great place and East London's biggest attraction, in my opinion.'

WOOLLARD, William
Presenter/producer, b. 20 Aug 1939 London. Joined RAF after Oxford, then worked for an oil company all over the world. Learnt Arabic at Foreign Office school in Beirut. Worked in social science before joining BBC producing, directing and then presenting films for *Tomorrow's World*. Other TV incl: *The Risk Business*; *The Secret War*; *The History Of The Fighter*; *Cross Channel*; *Top Gear*; *Connections*; *Policing The Eighties*; *2001 And All That*. Now runs own film company, Sky Films. m. Isobel; 1 d. Jessica, 2 s. Alexander, Julian. Hobbies: sailing, golf, skiing, windsurfing. Address: c/o Jon Roseman Assocs, London. Birthsign: Leo. **Favourite Place:** 'The Osthang ski run, St Anton, because it has moguls as big as barn doors, raising the hairs on the back of your neck.'

WRIGHT, Jenny Lee
Actress, b. 21 Feb London. Left school at 16 to train with Ballet Rambert and at 17 travelled the world with a French cabaret group. Returned to Britain and joined Lionel Blair's dancers. Worked on TV with most top comedians incl Morecambe and Wise, Jimmy Tarbuck, Benny Hill and Frankie Howerd. Films incl: *Husbands*; *The Triple Echo*; *The Revenge Of Dr Death*. TV incl: *The Protectors*; *The Golden Shot*; *Paul Temple*; *Public Eye*; *General Hospital*; *Beryl's Lot*; *The Generation Game*; *The Masterspy*; *Search For A Star*. Hobbies: water-skiing, snow-skiing, sailing, travel. Address: c/o International Artistes, London. Birthsign: Pisces. **Favourite Place:** 'The breathtaking beauty of Mont Blanc and the surrounding mountains at sunrise and sunset — with the brilliant blue sky it's stunning and so peaceful.'

WYATT, Tessa
Actress, b. 23 April 1948 Woking, Surrey. Studied at Elmhurst Ballet School, Camberley and went on to appear in rep. Theatre incl: *Minor Murder*; *The Philadelphia Story*; *The Crucible*; *Double Cut*; *Run For Your Wife*; several pantomimes. Films incl: *Wedding Night*; *I Think You'll Die Young Man*; *Spy Story*. Over 300 TV performances, incl: *The Tempest*; *The Black Tulip*; *Z Cars*; *Dixon Of Dock Green*; *Sanctuary*; *Out Of The Unknown*; *The Main Chance*; *Love Story*; *The Goodies*; *Within These Walls*; *Seaside Special*; *Celebrity Squares*; *Robin's Nest*. Hobbies: tennis, squash, interior design. Address: c/o John Miller, Teddington. Birthsign: Taurus. **Favourite Place:** Barbados.

WYMAN, Jane

Actress, b. 5 Jan St Joseph, Missouri. Was hired by Paramount Studio as a chorus dancer and bit player and went on to win an Oscar for *Johnny Belinda*. Other films incl: *My Man Godfrey*; *The Lost Weekend*; *The Yearling*; *The Blue Veil*; *Magnificent Obsession*; *Princess O'Rourke*; *Stage Fright*. Now best known for her role in the TV soap opera *Falcon Crest*. Other TV incl: *The Jane Wyman Theater*; *The Incredible Journey Of Dr Meg Laurel*. m. (1st) Myron Futterman (dis.), (2nd) Ronald Reagan (dis.), (3rd) bandleader Fred Karger (dis. twice); 1 d. Maureen, 1 s. Michael. Hobbies: painting, helping the Arthritis Foundation. Address: c/o Michael Mesnick, 500 South Sepulveda Blvd, Los Angeles, California 90049. Birthsign: Capricorn. **Favourite Place:** 'A religious retreat near Los Angeles.'

YARWOOD, Mike, OBE

Impressionist, b. 14 June 1941 Stockport, Cheshire. Started in show business by entering a pub talent contest. Appeared in pubs and clubs at night while working as a traveller. Warm-up for *Comedy Bandbox* led to engagements throughout the country, the London Palladium, *Royal Variety Performances* and TV incl: *Will The Real Mike Yarwood Stand Up?*; *Look—Mike Yarwood*; *The Best Of Mike Yarwood*; *Mike Yarwood In Persons*; also documentary, *Mike Yarwood—And This Is Him!* Autobiography: *And This Is Me*. m. ex-dancer Sandra Burville; 2 d. Charlotte, Clare. Hobbies: football, golf, tennis. Address: c/o International Artistes, London. Birthsign: Gemini.

YATES, Marjorie

Actress, b. 13 April 1941 Birmingham. Trained at Guildhall School of Music and Drama and then in rep at Liverpool. London theatre incl: Royal Court Theatre (*Sea Anchor*, *Small Change*, *Inadmissable Evidence*); National Theatre (*As You Like It*); *Night Mother*, Hampstead. Films incl: *Priest Of Love*; *Wetherby*. TV incl: *Kisses At Fifty*; *All Day On The Sands*; *Couples*; *Change In Time*; *Marks*; *Morgan's Boy* m. London University official and local councillor Michael Freeman; 1 d. Polly, 1 s. Carl. Hobbies: birdwatching, natural history. Address: c/o Jeremy Conway, London. Birthsign: Aries. **Favourite Place:** 'Sitting by my garden pond with waterfall and willow tree.'

YATES, Pauline

Actress, b. 16 June Liverpool. Went to Oldham rep straight from school. Also worked in rep at Liverpool but career mainly in TV incl: *Hancock*; *The Second Interview*; *Harriet's Back In Town*; *Nightingale's Boys*; *Going, Going, Gone Free*; *Rooms*; *My Honourable Mrs*; *Crown Court*; *The Fall And Rise Of Reginald Perrin*; *England's Green And Pleasant Land*; *Keep It In The Family*. Also films: *The Four Feathers*; *She'll Be Wearing Pink Pyjamas*. m. actor/writer Donald Churchill; 2 d. Jemma, Polly. Hobbies: theatre, tapestry. Address: c/o Kate Feast Management, London. Birthsign: Gemini.

YOUNG, Jimmy, OBE

Radio/TV broadcaster, b. 21 Sept Cinderford, Gloucs. First amateur performances with RAF concert parties as singer/pianist. First radio broadcast 1949. Singer/ pianist/bandleader in London's West End 1950–51. Broadcast with Radio Luxembourg, BBC Radio 1 and own show Radio 2 since 1973. Also many TV appearances incl: *Whose Baby?*; *Jimmy Young TV Programme.* Also made many records incl: *Too Young*; *Miss You.* Many awards incl Sony Award Radio Personality 1985. m. (1st) Wendy Wilkinson (dis.), (2nd) Sally Douglas (dis.); 1 d. Lesley. Address: c/o MAM Agency, London. Birthsign: Virgo. **Favourite Place:** 'Florida. The one place where I can switch off from work and relax.'

YOUNG, John

Actor, b. 18 June 1916 Edinburgh. Trained in rep at Edinburgh Lyceum, Theatre Royal Glasgow and Wolverhampton Grand Theatre. More recently appeared at Glasgow Citizens' Theatre and with the Scottish Theatre Company. Many films incl: *Ring Of Bright Water*; *The Life Of Brian*; *Chariots Of Fire*; *Time Bandits*; *The Dollar Bottom.* Many TV appearances incl: *McKenzie*; *Hamlet*; *Square Mile Of Murder*; *The Walls Of Jericho*; *Her Mother's House*; *Take The High Road*; *Brigadista.* m. Winifred (Freddie); 1 s. actor Paul. Hobby: making home movies. Address: c/o Young Casting Agency, Glasgow. Birthsign: Gemini. **Favourite Place:** 'The Old Mill Inn, Blyth Bridge in the Scottish Borders—delightful atmosphere, great cuisine.'

ZAVARONI, Lena

Singer, b. 4 Nov 1963 Greenock. Trained at the Italia Conti Stage School in London. Came to fame 1973 by winning *Opportunity Knocks*, singing *Ma, He's Making Eyes At Me.* Became the youngest ever artist to appear on TV's *Top Of The Pops.* Since toured the world, appeared in a *Royal Variety Show* and had TV show with her friend, Bonnie Langford, on TV. Topped the bill at London Palladium. First BBC TV series 1979 *Lena Zavaroni And Her Music*, then own series on BBC for three years. Other TV incl: *Des O'Connor Show*; *A Night Of 100 Stars*; *The Jimmy Cricket Show.* Hobbies: reading, tennis. Address: c/o Dorothy Solomon Associated Artistes, London. Birthsign: Scorpio. **Favourite Place:** 'View from a Swiss mountain, because it's so beautiful and peaceful.'

ZMED, Adrian

Actor, b. 14 March Chicago, Illinois. Films incl: *Bump In The Night*; *Grease II*; *Bachelor Party.* TV incl: *Love On The Run*; *Victim For Victims*; *Flatbush.* Plays Vince Romano in *TJ Hooker.* Guest appearances incl: *Starsky And Hutch*; *Good Time Girls*; *Riker*; *I'm A Big Girl Now*; *Bosom Buddies.* m. Barbara; 1 s. Zachary. Hobbies: singing rock, dancing. Address: c/o Studio City, California. Birthsign: Pisces. **Favourite Place:** 'Chicago. The softball capital of the country— softball always reminds me of home.'

Updating of Entries

We will be regularly updating our files for future editions of *Who's Who On Television* and welcome submissions at any time.

For names included in this edition we would particularly like to receive details of major new credits, or of any change of agent, changes in family, honours awarded, etc.

For names not included in this edition we would like to receive submissions set out in the style outlined below (or on our own special forms, obtainable free of charge from ***Who's Who On Television*, 247 Tottenham Court Road, London, W1P 0AU**).

The following scheme should always be followed: *name; any honours (e.g. OBE); preferred designation (actor, comedian, presenter, etc), date of birth; place of birth; education; training/background; credits; family details (marriage partner/s, children); hobbies; professional address (could be agent or TV company, etc); birthsign.*

In addition, a recent head-and-shoulders photograph should be included (with name and source clearly marked on the reverse), and a contact address or telephone number to be used only by our compilers when checking information. This contact address will be treated as strictly confidential by us and will **not** be recorded in any edition of *Who's Who On Television*.

Useful Addresses

BBC

Headquarters:
BBC, London W1A 1AA
Tel: 01 580 4468

Television:
Television Centre, Wood Lane, London W12 7RJ
Tel: 01 743 8000

Publications:
35 Marylebone High Street, London W1M 4AA
Tel: 01 580 5577

BBC Enterprises Ltd:
Woodlands, 80 Wood Lane, London W12 0TT
Tel: 01 743 5588 or 01 576 0202

Scotland:
Broadcasting House, Queen Margaret Drive, Glasgow G12 8DG
Tel: 041 339 8844

Broadcasting House, 5 Queen Street, Edinburgh EH2 1JF
Tel: 031 225 3131

Broadcasting House, Beechgrove Terrace, Aberdeen AB9 2ZT
Tel: 0224 635233

12/13 Dock Street, Dundee DD1 4BT
Tel: 0382 25025/25905

Wales:
Broadcasting House, Llantrisant Road, Llandaff, Cardiff CF5 2YQ
Tel: 0222 564888

Broadcasting House, Meirion Road, Bangor LL57 2BY
Tel: 0248 362214

32 Alexandra Road, Swansea SA1 5DZ
Tel: 0792 54986

Northern Ireland:
Broadcasting House, 25–27 Ormeau Avenue, Belfast BT2 8HQ
Tel: 0232 244400

IBA Offices

Headquarters:
70 Brompton Road, London SW3 1EY
Tel: 01 584 7011

Northern Ireland:
Royston House, 34 Upper Queen Street, Belfast BT1 6HG
Tel: 0232 248733

Scotland:
Fleming House, Renfrew Street, Glasgow G3 6SU
Tel: 041 332 8241/2 and 041 332 7260

Ground Floor Office, 9 Queen's Terrace, Aberdeen AB1 1XL
Tel: 0224 642041

Wales and West of England:
Elgin House, 106 St Mary Street, Cardiff CF1 1DX
Tel: 0222 384541/2/3

8th Floor, The Colston Centre, Colston Avenue, Bristol BS1 4UB
Tel: 0272 213672

East of England:
24 Castle Meadow, Norwich NR1 3DH
Tel: 0603 23533

Midlands:
Lyndon House, 62 Hagley Road, Birmingham B16 8PE
Tel: 021 454 1068

10–11 Poultry, Nottingham NG1 2HW
Tel: 0602 585105

North-East England, The Borders, Isle of Man:
3 Collingwood Street, Newcastle Upon Tyne NE1 1JS
Tel: 0632 610148/323710

49 Botchergate, Carlisle CA1 1RQ
Tel: 0228 25004

North-West England:
Television House, Mount Street, Manchester M2 5WT
Tel: 061 834 2707

South of England:
Castle Chambers, Lansdowne Hill, Southampton SO1 0EQ
Tel: 0703 331344/5

Ground Floor, Lyndean House, Albion Place, Maidstone ME14 5DZ
Tel: 0622 61176/7

South-West England, Channel Islands:
Royal London House, 153 Armada Way, Plymouth PL1 1HY
Tel: 0752 663031/662490

Yorkshire:
Dudley House, Albion Street, Leeds LS2 8PN
Tel: 0532 441091/2

Independent Television Companies

Anglia Television:
Anglia House, Norwich NR1 3JG
Tel: 0603 615151

Brook House, 113 Park Lane, London W1Y 4DX
Tel: 01 408 2288

Border Television:
Television Centre, Carlisle CA1 3NT
Tel: 0228 25101

33 Margaret Street, London W1N 7LA
Tel: 01 637 4363

Central Television:
(West Midlands) Central House, Broad Street, Birmingham B1 2JP
Tel: 021 643 9898

(East Midlands) Television Centre, Lenton Lane, Nottingham NG7 2NA
Tel: 0602 863322

46 Charlotte Street, London W1P 1LX
Tel: 01 637 4602

Channel Television:
The Television Centre, St Helier, Jersey, Channel Islands
Tel: 0534 73999

The Television Centre, St George's Place, St Peter Port,
Guernsey, Channel Islands
Tel: 0481 23451

Channel Four Television:
60 Charlotte Street, London W1P 2AX
Tel: 01 631 4444

Grampian Television:
Queen's Cross, Aberdeen AB9 2XJ
Tel: 0224 646464

Albany House, 68 Albany Road, West Ferry, Dundee DD5 1NW
Tel: 0382 739363

23/25 Huntly Street, Inverness IV3 5PR
Tel: 0463 242624

10 Manor Place, Edinburgh EH3 7DD
Tel: 031 226 3926

29 Glasshouse Street, London W1R 5RG
Tel: 01 439 3141

Granada Television:
Granada Television Centre, Manchester M60 9EA
Tel: 061 832 7211

Derby House, Exchange Flags, Liverpool L2 3UZ
Tel: 051 236 3741

36 Golden Square, London W1R 4AH
Tel: 01 734 8080

HTV Wales:
Television Centre, Culverhouse Cross, Cardiff CF5 6XJ
Tel: 0222 590590

HTV West:
Television Centre, Bath Road, Bristol BS4 3HG
Tel: 0272 778366

LWT:
South Bank Television Centre, Kent House,
Upper Ground, London SE1 9LT
Tel: 01 261 3434

Scottish Television:
Cowcaddens, Glasgow G2 3PR
Tel: 041 332 9999

The Gateway, Edinburgh EH7 4AH
Tel: 031 557 4554

7 Adelaide Street, London WC2N 4LZ
Tel: 01 836 1500

Thomson House, Withy Grove, Manchester M60 4BJ
Tel: 061 834 7621

Thames Television:
Thames Television House, 306–316 Euston Road, London NW1 3BB
Tel: 01 387 9494

149 Tottenham Court Road, London W1P 9LL
Tel: 01 388 5199

Teddington Lock, Teddington, Middlesex TW11 9NT
Tel: 01 977 3252

Television South West:
Derry's Cross, Plymouth, Devon PL1 2SP
Tel: 0752 663322

TSW House, 18–24 Westbourne Grove, London W2 5RH
Tel: 01 727 8080

The Colston Centre, Colston Street, Bristol BS1 4UX
Tel: 0272 21131

TV-am:
Breakfast Television Centre, Hawley Crescent, London NW1 8EF
Tel: 01 267 4300 and 01 267 4377

Television South:
Television Centre, Southampton SO9 5HZ
Tel: 0703 34211

Television Centre, Vinters Park, Maidstone ME14 5NZ
Tel: 0622 54945

Spenser House, 60–61 Buckingham Gate, London SW1E 6AJ
Tel: 01 828 9898

Tyne Tees Television:
The Television Centre, City Road, Newcastle Upon Tyne NE1 2AL
Tel: 0632 610181

15 Bloomsbury Square, London WC1A 2LJ
Tel: 01 405 8474

Ulster Television:
Havelock House, Ormeau Road, Belfast BT7 1EB
Tel: 0232 228122

6 York Street, London W1H 1FA
Tel: 01 486 5211

Yorkshire Television:
The Television Centre, Leeds LS3 1JS
Tel: 0532 438283

Television House, 32 Bedford Row, London WC1R 4HE
Tel: 01 242 1666

Independent Television News:
ITN House, 48 Wells Street, London W1P 4DE
Tel: 01 637 2424

Independent Television Companies Association:
Knighton House, 56 Mortimer Street, London W1N 8AN
Tel: 01 636 6866

Independent Television Publications:
247 Tottenham Court Road, London W1P 0AU
Tel: 01 323 3222

Agents & Agencies

Susan Angel Associates Ltd,
10 Greek Street, London W1V 5LE
Tel: 01 439 3086

Arlington Enterprises Ltd,
1–3 Charlotte Street, London W1P 1HD
Tel: 01 580 5642

The Bagenal Harvey Organisation Ltd,
1a Cavendish Square, London W1M 9HA
Tel: 01 637 5541

George Bartram Enterprises Ltd,
266 Broad Street, Birmingham B1 2DS
Tel: 021 643 9346

Brunskill Management
Suite 8, 169 Queen's Gate, London SW7 5EH
Tel: 01 584 8060

Peter Browne Management
Pebro House, 13 St Martin's Road, London SW9 0SP
Tel: 01 737 3444

Barry Burnett Organisation Ltd,
Suite 42–43, Grafton House, 2–3 Golden Square, London W1R 3AD
Tel: 01 437 7048/9 or 01 734 6118

CCA Personal Management Ltd,
4 Court Lodge, 48 Sloane Square, London SW1W 8AT
Tel: 01 730 8857

Peter Charlesworth Ltd,
2nd Floor, 68 Old Brompton Road, London SW7 3LQ
Tel: 01 581 2478

Chatto and Linnit Ltd,
Prince of Wales Theatre, Coventry Street, London W1WV 7FE
Tel: 01 930 6677

Jeremy Conway Ltd,
109 Jermyn Street, London SW1 6HB
Tel: 01 839 2121

Vernon Conway Ltd,
19 London Street, London W2 1HL
Tel: 01 262 5506/7

Crouch Associates
59 Frith Street, London W1N 5TA
Tel: 01 734 2167/8/9

Larry Dalzell Associates Ltd,
126 Kennington Park Road, London SE11 4DJ
Tel: 01 735 2294

Felix de Wolfe
1 Robert Street, Adelphi, London WC2N 6BH
Tel: 01 930 7514

Jean Drysdale Management
15 Pembroke Gardens, London W8 6HT
Tel: 01 603 8192

Clifford Elson (Publicity) Ltd,
Richmond House, 12–13 Richmond Buildings,
Dean Street, London W1V 5AF
Tel: 01 437 4822/3

Kate Feast Management
43 Princess Road, London NW1 8JS
Tel: 01 586 5502

Fraser & Dunlop Ltd,
91 Regent Street, London W1R 8RU
Tel: 01 734 7311–5

Green and Underwood
3 The Broadway, Gunnersbury Lane, London W3 8HR
Tel: 01 993 6183

Jo Gurnett Personal Management
45 Queen's Gate Mews, London SW7 5QN
Tel: 01 584 7642

Harbour & Coffey
9 Blenheim Street, New Bond Street, London W1Y 9LE
Tel: 01 499 5548

Hatton & Baker Ltd,
18 Jermyn Street, London SW1Y 68N
Tel: 01 439 2971

Duncan Heath Associates Ltd,
Paramount House, 162–170 Wardour Street, London W1V 3AT
Tel: 01 439 1471

Barry Hearn
1 Arcade Place, South Street, Romford, Essex
Tel: 01 702 4023

Hope & Lyne
5 Milner Place, London N1 1TN
Tel: 01 359 5407

Howes & Prior Ltd,
66 Berkeley House, Hay Hill, London W1X 7LH
Tel: 01 493 7570

ICM
388–396 Oxford Street, London W1N 9HE
Tel: 01 629 8080

International Artistes
4th Floor, 235 Regent Street, London W1R 8AX
Tel: 01 439 8401/2/3/4

Joy Jameson Ltd,
7 West Eaton Place Mews, London SW1X 8LY
Tel: 01 245 9551

Joseph & Wagg
2nd Floor, 78 New Bond Street, London W1Y 9DA
Tel: 01 629 1048/9

Rolf Kruger Management Ltd,
22–23 Morley House, 314–322 Regent Street, London W1R 5AB
Tel: 01 580 9432/3

Michael Ladkin Personal Management Ltd,
11 Garrick Street, London WC2E 9AR
Tel: 01 379 7688

Leading Artists
60 St James's Street, London SW1A 1LE
Tel: 01 491 4400

Leading Players Management Ltd,
31 Kings Road, London SW3 4RP
Tel: 01 730 9411/2

Tony Lewis Entertainments
235 Regent Street, London W1A 2JT
Tel: 01 734 2285

London Management
235–241 Regent Street, London W1A 2JT
Tel: 01 493 1610

Ken McReddie Ltd,
91 Regent Street, London W1R 7TB
Tel: 01 439 1456

John Mahoney Management
30 Chalfont Court, Baker Street, London NW1 5RS
Tel: 01 486 2847

MAM (Agency) Ltd,
MAM House, 24–25 New Bond Street, London W1Y 9HD
Tel: 01 629 9255

Marmont Management Ltd,
Langham House, 308 Regent Street, London W1R 5AL
Tel: 01 637 3183

Marina Martin Management
7 Windmill Street, London W1P 1HF
Tel: 01 323 1216

William Morris Agency Ltd,
147–149 Wardour Street, London W1V 3TB
Tel: 01 734 9361

Kim Newman Management
19 Reddish Lane, Gorton, Manchester M18 7JH
Tel: 061 231 3827

Performing Arts
1 Hinde Street, London W1M 5RH
Tel: 01 486 8029

Plant & Froggatt Ltd,
4 Windmill Street, London W1P 1HF
Tel: 01 636 4412

Plunkett Greene Ltd,
91 Regent Street, London W1R 8RU
Tel: 01 437 5191

Peter Pritchard
9 Risborough, Deacon Way, London SE17 1UP
Tel: 01 701 6414

Joan Reddin Ltd,
2 Taverners Close, Holland Park, London W11 4SA
Tel: 01 603 2261

John Redway & Associates
16 Berner Street, London W1P 3DD
Tel: 01 637 1612

Saraband Associates
153 Petherton Road, London N5 2RS
Tel: 01 359 5136

Anna Scher Theatre Management Ltd,
70–72 Barnsbury Road, London N1 0ES
Tel: 01 278 2101/2

Scott Marshall Personal Management
44 Perryn Road, London W3 7NA
Tel: 01 749 7692

James Sharkey Associates
3rd Floor Suite, 15 Golden Square, London W1R 3AG
Tel: 01 434 3802

Annette Stone Associates
66 Wellington Road, Hatch End, Middlesex HA5 4NH
Tel: 01 428 7791

Richard Stone
18–20 York Buildings, Adelphi, London WC2N 6JU
Tel: 01 839 6421/8

Roger Storey Ltd,
71 Westbury Road, London N12 7PB
Tel: 01 346 5727

Paul Vaughan Associates Ltd,
100 Park Street, Mayfair, London W1Y 3RJ
Tel: 01 408 0841

David White Associates
31 Kings Road, London SW3 4RP
Tel: 01 730 9488

April Young Ltd,
31 Kings Road, London SW3 4RP
Tel: 01 730 9922